LATIN AMERICAN LITERATURE IN TRANSITION
1930–1980

Latin American Literature in Transition 1930–1980 explores the literary landscape of the mid-twentieth century and the texts that were produced during that period. It takes four core areas of thematic and conceptual focus – war, revolution, and dictatorship, metropolis and ruins, solidarity, and aesthetics and innovation – and employs them to explore the complexity, heterogeneity, and hybridity of form, genre, subject matter, and discipline that characterized literature from the period. In doing so, it uncovers the points of transition, connection, contradiction, and tension that shaped the work of many canonical and non-canonical authors. It illuminates the conversations between genres, literary movements, disciplines, and modes of representation that underpin writing from this time. Lastly, by focusing on canon and beyond, the volume visibilizes the aesthetics, poetics, politics, and social projects of writing, incorporating established writers but also those whose work is yet to be examined in all its complexity.

AMANDA HOLMES, Associate Professor at McGill University, has written extensively on Latin American cultures. Her publications include *City Fictions: Language, Body and Spanish American Urban Space* (2007), *Politics of Architecture in Contemporary Argentine Cinema* (2017), and *Cultures of the City: Mediating Identities in Urban Latin/o America*, coedited with Richard Young (2010).

PAR KUMARASWAMI is Professor of Latin American Studies and Director of the Centre for Research on Cuba/Cuba Research Forum at the University of Nottingham. Her publications include *Literary Culture in Cuba: Revolution, Nation-Building and the Book* (with Antoni Kapcia, 2012) and *The Social Life of Literature in Revolutionary Cuba: Narrative, Identity and Well-Being* (2016).

LATIN AMERICAN LITERATURE IN TRANSITION

Editor

Mónica Szurmuk, National Scientific and Technical Research Council of Argentina and Universidad Nacional de San Martín

This series proposes a new organization of Latin American literature through a focus on moments of transformation, change, revitalization, and retreat. Latin American Literature in Transition explores the way in which the field has transitioned and how what is considered the rubric of Latin American Literature has evolved and changed. It moves beyond national, regional, and linguistic traditions and introduces a continental, multifaceted account of Latin American literature.

Books in the series

Latin American Literature in Transition Pre-1492–1800 edited by Rocío Quispe-Agnoli & Amber Brian

Latin American Literature in Transition 1800–1870 edited by Ana Peluffo & Ronald Briggs

Latin American Literature in Transition 1870–1930 edited by Fernando Degiovanni & Javier Uriarte

Latin American Literature in Transition 1930–1980 edited by Amanda Holmes & Par Kumaraswami

Latin American Literature in Transition 1980–2018 edited by Mónica Szurmuk & Debra A. Castillo

LATIN AMERICAN LITERATURE IN TRANSITION 1930–1980

EDITED BY

AMANDA HOLMES

McGill University

PAR KUMARASWAMI

University of Nottingham

CAMBRIDGE
UNIVERSITY PRESS

CAMBRIDGE
UNIVERSITY PRESS

University Printing House, Cambridge CB2 8BS, United Kingdom

One Liberty Plaza, 20th Floor, New York, NY 10006, USA

477 Williamstown Road, Port Melbourne, VIC 3207, Australia

314–321, 3rd Floor, Plot 3, Splendor Forum, Jasola District Centre,
New Delhi – 110025, India

103 Penang Road, #05–06/07, Visioncrest Commercial, Singapore 238467

Cambridge University Press is part of the University of Cambridge.

It furthers the University's mission by disseminating knowledge in the pursuit of
education, learning, and research at the highest international levels of excellence.

www.cambridge.org
Information on this title: www.cambridge.org/9781009177764
DOI: 10.1017/9781009177771

© Cambridge University Press 2023

This publication is in copyright. Subject to statutory exception
and to the provisions of relevant collective licensing agreements,
no reproduction of any part may take place without the written
permission of Cambridge University Press.

First published 2023

A catalogue record for this publication is available from the British Library.

Library of Congress Cataloging-in-Publication Data
NAMES: Holmes, Amanda, 1972– editor. | Kumaraswami, Par, editor.
TITLE: Latin American literature in transition, 1930–1980 / edited by Amanda Holmes, McGill
University, Montréal; Par Kumaraswami, University of Reading.
DESCRIPTION: Cambridge, United Kingdom ; New York , NY : Cambridge University Press,
2022. | Series: Latin American literature in transition ; volume 4 | Includes bibliographical
references and index.
IDENTIFIERS: LCCN 2022004210 (print) | LCCN 2022004211 (ebook) | ISBN 9781009177764
hardback | ISBN 9781009177771 ebook
SUBJECTS: LCSH: Latin American literature – 20th century – History and criticism. | Literature
and society – Latin America – History – 20th century. | LCGFT: Literary criticism. | Essays.
Classification: LCC PN849.L29 L378 2022 (print) | LCC PN849.L29 (ebook) | DDC 860.9/98–dc23/
eng/20220427
LC record available at https://lccn.loc.gov/2022004210
LC ebook record available at https://lccn.loc.gov/2022004211

ISBN 978-1-009-17776-4 Hardback

Cambridge University Press has no responsibility for the persistence or accuracy of
URLs for external or third-party internet websites referred to in this publication
and does not guarantee that any content on such websites is, or will remain,
accurate or appropriate.

Contents

List of Contributors	*page* viii
Introduction: Transitions in Mid-Century Latin American Literature *Amanda Holmes and Par Kumaraswami*	1

PART I WAR, REVOLUTION, DICTATORSHIP

1	Revolutions and Literary Transitions: The 1960s *Jorge Fornet*	17
2	Jorge Luis Borges: Probing the Limits of World War *Kate Jenckes*	32
3	Anti-Fascism and Literature in Brazil: The Many Wars of Antônio Callado *Daniel Mandur Thomaz*	46
4	Disaster Innovation in the Mid-century Spanish American Novel: Carpentier, Asturias, Donoso *Stephen Henighan*	65
5	Struggle at the Margins: Intersections of Gender, Race, and Sexuality in Brazil's Literature of Revolution *Rebecca J. Atencio*	81

PART II METROPOLIS AND RUINS

6	Economic, Political, and Ecological Disasters: The Metropolis and Its Ruins in Latin American Poetry in the 1960s and 1970s *Cecilia Enjuto Rangel*	99

v

vi **Contents**

7 Mexican Miracle Modernism 116
Ignacio M. Sánchez Prado

8 Crime and the City: A Critical Walk through Latin
American Crime Fiction and Urban Places 131
Emilio J. Gallardo-Saborido

PART III SOLIDARITY

9 "Dar Testimonio" as a Lens for Rethinking the Mexican
Literary Canon 149
Sarah E. L. Bowskill

10 Landscapes of Heterogeneity in a Mid-Twentieth-Century
Quechua Poem 164
Charles M. Pigott

11 Beyond the Nation Frame: Rethinking the Presence
of Indigenous Literatures in the Spanish American
Novel circa 1950 182
Estelle Tarica

12 Femininity in Flux: Gabriela Mistral's Madwomen 198
Amanda Holmes

13 The Representation of Afro-Cuban Orality by Fernando
Ortiz, Lydia Cabrera, and Nicolás Guillén 211
Miguel Arnedo-Gómez

PART IV AESTHETICS AND INNOVATION

14 Eros: After Surrealism and Before the Revolution (1945–1967) 229
Sarah Ann Wells

15 The Return of the Galleons: Transitions in the Work of Alejo
Carpentier 245
Graziella Pogolotti

16 "Un Híbrido de Halcón y Jicotea": *Testimonio* and Its
Challenge to the Latin American Literary Canon 260
Par Kumaraswami

17	Literature and Revolution in Transition: An Aesthetics of Singularity *Bruno Bosteels*	275
18	Divergence and Convergence: Avant-Garde Poetics in Twentieth-Century Spanish America and Brazil *Odile Cisneros*	290
19	Cortázar's Transitional Poetics: Experiments in Verse behind Experiments in Prose *Marcy Schwartz*	306
	Index	322

Contributors

Editors

AMANDA HOLMES is Associate Professor of Hispanic Studies in the Department of Languages, Literatures and Cultures at McGill University in Montreal.

PAR KUMARASWAMI is Professor of Latin American Studies and Director of the Centre for Research on Cuba/Cuba Research Forum at the University of Nottingham.

Chapter Authors

MIGUEL ARNEDO-GÓMEZ is Senior Lecturer in Spanish and Latin American Studies in the School of Languages and Cultures of Victoria University, Wellington, New Zealand.

REBECCA J. ATENCIO is Associate Professor of Portuguese and Gender & Sexuality Studies at Tulane University.

BRUNO BOSTEELS is Professor and Chair of the Department of Latin American and Iberian Cultures and Professor in the Institute for Comparative Literature and Society at Columbia University.

SARAH E. L. BOWSKILL is Senior Lecturer in Latin American Studies at Queen's University Belfast.

ODILE CISNEROS is Professor in the Department of Modern Languages and Cultural Studies at the University of Alberta.

CECILIA ENJUTO RANGEL is Associate Professor of Spanish at the University of Oregon.

JORGE FORNET is Director of the Centro de Investigaciones Literarias of Casa de las Américas (Havana, Cuba) and of the journal, *Casa de las Américas*.

List of Contributors

EMILIO J. GALLARDO-SABORIDO is Associate Researcher in the Escuela de Estudios Hispano-Americanos, Spanish National Research Council (CSIC).

STEPHEN HENIGHAN is Professor of Spanish and Hispanic Studies in the School of Languages and Literatures at the University of Guelph, Ontario, and a longlist finalist for international literary prizes.

KATE JENCKES is Professor of Spanish in the Department of Romance Languages and Literatures at the University of Michigan.

DANIEL MANDUR THOMAZ is Lecturer in Lusophone Studies at the Department of Spanish, Portuguese and Latin American Studies, King's College London, and Associate Fellow at King's Brazil Institute, School of Global Affairs, King's College London.

CHARLES M. PIGOTT is Lecturer in Hispanic Studies at the University of Strathclyde, Quondam Fellow of Hughes Hall (University of Cambridge), and Research Associate of Centre of Latin American Studies (University of Cambridge).

GRAZIELLA POGOLOTTI is a Cuban essayist and cultural critic, Professor Emeritus of the Universidad de La Habana, Premio Nacional de Literatura, and currently President of the Fundación Alejo Carpentier. In 2021 she received Cuba's Order of José Martí.

RAFAEL RODRÍGUEZ BELTRÁN is Professor of Francophone Language and Literature at the University of Havana and Vice-President of the Fundación Alejo Carpentier.

IGNACIO M. SÁNCHEZ PRADO is the Jarvis Thurston and Mona van Duyn Professor in the Humanities at Washington University in St. Louis.

MARCY SCHWARTZ is Professor of Latin American Literature and Culture in the Department of Spanish and Portuguese at Rutgers University-New Brunswick.

ESTELLE TARICA is Professor of Latin American Literatures and Cultures in the Department of Spanish and Portuguese at the University of California, Berkeley.

SARAH ANN WELLS is Associate Professor of Literary Studies at the University of Wisconsin–Madison.

Introduction
Transitions in Mid-Century Latin American Literature
Amanda Holmes and Par Kumaraswami

A series of wars and revolutions provide the fiery, unsettled bedrock for mid-twentieth-century Latin American literature: on a global scale, World War II and the Cold War mar political alliances; the Cuban Revolution, Peronist Argentina, and the 1968 student movements are some of the regional responses that develop from these international conflicts. Latching onto a transforming world, authors in this era appropriate the discomfort of transition to produce literary works of international acclaim. Mid-century Latin American literature has been framed as a market-driven phenomenon that opened the region up through an exoticization that captured international recognition. This volume takes a different approach, one that rests uncomfortably on a deep political instability – worldwide as well as regional – that is engaged aesthetically by literary authors. It argues that the literature of mid-century Latin America locates its strength within global and regional political conflicts, as well as from within the cultural and social tensions spurred on by economic disparities.

While political tensions spawned violent struggles, Latin American authors sought to reflect this through aesthetic and stylistic experimentation. By pushing the limits of representation to the edges, authors found ways to engage the instabilities of mid-century transitions. From the "marvelous real" of Alejo Carpentier's *El reino de este mundo* (*The Kingdom of This World*) and the "magical realism" of Gabriel García Márquez's *Cien años de soledad* (*One Hundred Years of Solitude*) to the surrealism and experimentation of the Vanguard poets, writers innovated with style and language to generate new ways of representing the era. Along with Carpentier and García Márquez, Jorge Luis Borges, Octavio Paz, Augusto Roa Bastos, Julio Cortázar, Juan Rulfo, Jorge Amado, Miguel Ángel Asturias, Carlos Fuentes, Mario Vargas Llosa, and Pablo Neruda emerged as canonical writers and international figures during this period. This volume embeds the literary giants in the context of the era; experiments in style and aesthetics reflect on and underscore revolutionary political, economic, and social transitions.

Although the voice of the male elite defines the cultural expression of the region during this literary "Boom" and poetic vanguard, authors of conventionally marginalized identities, whether through gender or ethnicity, increasingly become exposed during this era. Victoria Ocampo in Argentina gathers the (mostly) male Argentine intelligentsia and builds careers in salon-style meetings at her home, and through her pivotal journal, *Sur*, founded in 1931. Gabriela Mistral's receipt of the Nobel Prize in Literature in 1945 – the first Latin American author to receive one – projects women writers into the spotlight; only after accepting this prestigious award is Mistral fully appreciated as a poet in her native country of Chile. In Peru, César Vallejo and José María Arguedas make headway in the representation of Indigenous identities in ground-breaking works that record the syncretic lifestyles of the Andean region. *Négritude* serves as the philosophical backdrop for the work of the Cuban poet, Nicolás Guillén, who incorporates the pathos of the musical son into his poetry to capture the identity politics of the Afro-Cuban and, by extension, the African American.

While this era in Latin American literature represents some of the most internationally acclaimed authors in the region's history, this time period has been somewhat neglected by scholars over the past decade. Older textual anthologies or "readers" are available to aid and accompany undergraduate survey-of-literature and language courses (Garganigo; Méndez-Faith), and the Modern Language Association published a guide on *Teaching the Latin American Boom* (2015), edited by Lucille Kerr and Alejandro Herrero-Olaizola. During the past decade, excellent focused analyses of various aspects of the era have been produced. These works interpret one author (Cabello Hutt; García Liendo; Clayton; Henighan), one characteristic theme (Feinsod; Arellano; Kuhnheim), or the literary production from one Latin American country (Sánchez Prado, Nogar, and Serra; Albuquerque and Bishop-Sanchez). However, what is clearly needed for academic scholarship of the period is a contemporary overview of mid-century literature that builds on these new approaches.

To this end, this volume structures analysis of this era through four principal topics that capture key elements of the relationship between conflictual transitions and cultural output: "War, Revolution, Dictatorship"; "Metropolis and Ruins"; "Solidarity"; and "Aesthetics and Innovation."

Introduction 3

Part I: War, Revolution, Dictatorship

Part I presents analyses of the transitions in global and regional conflicts and their impact on Latin American literature. From the "cultural diplomacy" of the 1930s to the imperialism of the Cold War, culture has played a central role in the mid-century relationship between the United States and Latin America. During World War II, United States imperialist politics supported allies (Mexico, Brazil) and shunned enemies (Chile, Argentina), a stance that influenced the economic profits of the different regions that were intimately connected to their northern neighbor. The United States continued to redefine regional alliances during the Cold War as it policed the region to root out communist "infiltration," while it also sought to promote its own economic interests through land development and exploitation. Contemporaneously, the Spanish Civil War particularly disturbed Latin American authors who maintained a strong connection with Spain and their colleagues on the Spanish peninsula; César Vallejo, Pablo Neruda, and Nicolás Guillén all respond explicitly to this European-based conflict in poetic works.

Outcomes of these globally shaped ideologies emerged in three key transitional moments that were fundamental (in different ways) to mid-century Latin American culture: Peronist Argentina (1946–55); the Cuban Revolution (1959); and the student movement in Mexico that resulted in the Tlatelolco Massacre (1968). Juan Domingo Perón's first presidency, which favored nationalist and populist culture at the expense of erudite literature influenced by Europe and the United States (represented by the members of the Grupo Sur), deeply affects acclaimed authors such as Jorge Luis Borges, who was famously demoted from his position as national librarian during the Perón era, and Julio Cortázar, who in 1951 chose a self-imposed exile in Paris instead of life in Buenos Aires. During the Peronist era, Argentine authors questioned the role of freedom of expression in literature, a topic that became even more central in the intellectual debates among Latin American authors regarding censorship after the Cuban Revolution. For the left-leaning intelligentsia, the Cuban Revolution not only offered a transition toward a more egalitarian way of life on the Caribbean island but also professed the possibility for change in Latin America as a whole. While the Revolution was received with optimism by many, disillusionment with its approach to the intersections of culture and politics in the late 1960s and early 1970s (among other questions) led to important debates among authors. Especially for Mexico, 1968 stands as a transitional year for the representation of the country's identity. Authors expressed horror at the government's murderous response to the student protest demonstration at the Plaza de Tlatelolco. To mark their outrage, authors responded with literary works – a collection of testimonies of the massacre in Elena Poniatowska's *La noche de Tlatelolco* (*Massacre in Mexico*) or Octavio Paz's dark series of poems in "Ciudad de México."

The five chapters in this part identify transitions in the rapid political shifts that led also to cultural and literary responses, from both the overarching lens of Latin American literature as a continental phenomenon and from the perspectives of particular authors of the era. In Chapter 1, Jorge Fornet unpacks the intricate relationship between literature, culture, and politics throughout the 1960s. His historical analyses chart the literary congresses and journals that brought Latin American authors together from the vantage points of different political players at the heart of the Cold War: the United States, Europe, and the leftist movements. Important public and written debates among Latin American literary authors questioned the role of the author in propelling political ideologies. Fornet traces the transitions across this era's iterations of the complex intersections between culture and politics.

Jorge Luis Borges' philosophical contemplations on the "totalizing order" are the focus of Kate Jenckes' reading of two of his acclaimed stories about the two world wars. Jenckes identifies in these stories possibilities for transitions from this totalizing epistemological and political perception to other infinite multiple orders. This plays out in "Deutsches Requiem" in the contrast drawn between Nationalism Socialism and the multiplicity identified in the works of Jerusalem, Shakespeare, and Brahms. In "El jardín de los senderos que se bifurcan" ("The Garden of Forking Paths"), a story set during World War I, Jenckes argues that while the totalizing structure is represented by enmity, difference signals multiple orders creating a tension between the two and finally suggesting possibilities for the finality of the totalizing order.

In his chapter, Daniel Mandur Thomaz situates the Brazilian playwright Antônio Callado in the context of post–World War II currents of anti-fascism, socialism, and his response to military dictatorship. Mandur Thomaz identifies Callado's newly discovered BBC radio plays, which he wrote while working as a correspondent for the BBC Latin American Service in the 1940s, as significant contributions to knowledge about this playwright and the era. According to Mandur Thomaz, this employment led to Callado becoming a novelist in Brazil in the 1950s and 1960s and his transition to left-wing politics.

Novelists Alejo Carpentier, Miguel Ángel Asturias, and José Donoso are the subject of Stephen Henighan's study of the significance of transitions

Introduction

to define Latin American literary categories. Henighan argues against reading pre- and post-Boom novels as transitional literature into, and out of, the Boom era, while privileging personal and arbitrary transitions in the works he studies in his chapter. The novels Henighan analyzes respond to three contemporary political "disasters." In his analysis, Carpentier reacts to the Spanish Civil War with *El reino de este mundo*, a novel that underscores the Cuban author's questioning of the universality of European culture as a result of this conflict. Henighan then depicts Asturias' *Mulata de tal* (*Mulata*) as one of the most overlooked novels; he explains how the work reacts to the Guatemalan US-led military coup and resulting atrocities. Finally, on the other side of the Boom era, Donoso's *El jardín de al lado* (*The Garden Next Door*) serves as Henighan's final study as the piece represents the realities of Chilean exiles after the 1973 political overthrow. Henighan suggests that the readings of these works should be revised by privileging personal transitions over those defined by the categories of literary history.

In her analysis of survivors of the violent political oppression in Brazil between 1969 and 1973, Rebecca J. Atencio highlights an unconsidered aspect of Brazilian identity in the final chapter of this part. Most of these autobiographies are by white heterosexual men; Atencio emphasizes inter-sectional identities in this genre in her interpretation of writing by Herbert Daniel, a gay militant, and Mariluce Moura, a Black heterosexual woman. In Atencio's analysis, these writers experience connections between their sexual and political identities in that sexuality informs their politics, while politics also impacts their sexual identities, as they record a country transitioning into democracy.

Part II: Metropolis and Ruins

The city in transition serves as the focus for Part II of this volume. In this era, authors were confronted by the instability brought on by the rapid growth of cities, along with a growing respect for the centers' Indigenous histories. At the same time, the unique example of the 1950s planning and construction of Brasilia represented a cultural output of Brazilian modernism that took hold of the artistic sphere in alignment with global cultural movements. The Latin American metropolis assumed such a principal role that certain authors became associated with "their" cities: among others, Borges with Buenos Aires and Paz and Fuentes with Mexico City.

During this era, Latin American authors attempted to capture the contemporary experience of urban spaces in two principal ways: through works that focus on how the past resonates in cities and through texts that try to comprehend the urban whole within one fictional representation. While the bustling chaos of the metropolis countered the disaster evidenced in ruins, the line between thriving city and devastated ruin remained precarious. Central to literary expression, cities depicted society's political transformations for these authors who in their works recorded a sensitivity to Indigenous ruins – such as Tenochtitlán for Paz and Macchu Picchu for Neruda. Simultaneously, the ambitious "totalizing" novels of the period attempted to capture all of urban life in one text; Fuentes' *La región más transparente* (*Where the Air Is Clear*) and Cortázar's *Rayuela* (*Hopscotch*) exemplify this tendency.

The chapters in this part examine mid-century responses to urban spaces by authors across Latin America. In the first chapter, Cecilia Enjuto Rangel analyzes how a wide range of poets depict the city as ruins in this era, starting with the representation of Indigenous sites in Pablo Neruda and Octavio Paz's poetry and finishing with the depictions of Mexico in the 1970s in the works of the Mexican poets Rosario Castellanos and José Emilio Pacheco. Enjuto Rangel identifies political, ecological, and economic disasters as the context for these authors to undertake a critical view of the contemporary in their poetry.

Chapter 7 by Ignacio M. Sánchez Prado provides a snapshot of the Mexican cultural expression prominent between 1940 and 1968 during a time of economic growth and political transition between revolution and the modern era. Calling the literary production at this time "Mexican miracle modernism," Sánchez Prado identifies the centrality of a number of genres outside of the canonical works, including especially detective, speculative, and fantasy fiction, to end with a focus on the chronical genre in Salvador Novo's "Nueva grandeza mexicana" ("New Mexican Grandeur"). These works developed a cultural mediation for understanding the complexities of mid-century Mexico as it grappled with the opposing cosmopolitan and nationalist notions.

The final chapter in this part is a study of the representation of the city through detective fiction. Emilio J. Gallardo-Saborido analyzes how this genre mediates the city in his analyses of three novels that represent three Latin American urban spaces at three historical moments: Buenos Aires in *Seis problemas para don Isidro Parodi* (*Six Problems for Don Isidro Parodi*, 1942) by Jorge Luis Borges and Adolfo Bioy Casares; Havana in Armando Cristóbal Pérez's novel *La ronda de los rubíes* (*Ruby Patrol*, 1973); and Mexico City in *Días de combate* (*Days of Combat*, 1976) by Paco Ignacio Taibo II. Gallardo traces crime fiction from this era from the Argentine

Introduction

parody of Borges and Bioy to Cuban revolutionary detective fiction in Cristóbal Pérez and, finally, the Mexican interrogation of the nation in Taibo.

Part III: Solidarity

This third part studies literature that aimed to transform negative perceptions of marginalized peoples through a range of methods, all predicated on relationships of solidarity. In an effort to understand the unsettled identities of the multiethnic and economically unbalanced societies of the Americas, mainstream authors forged a cultural solidarity with the marginalized and oppressed in works from this era. Alejo Carpentier and Carlos Fuentes captured the syncretism and heterogeneity of Latin American society in their novels, while Miguel Ángel Asturias and José María Arguedas were pioneers in incorporating an understanding of the perceptions and belief systems of Indigenous populations in Guatemala and Peru, respectively.

As the women's rights movement increased in centrality during this period, certain women authors achieved recognition for their works, while they also reached out to women in society. In her poetry and writings, Gabriela Mistral affirmed the woman's identity as mother and teacher in Latin America; Clarice Lispector's "écriture feminine" ("women's writing") recorded human experience through the female voice; literature by Rosario Castellanos supported feminist causes; and Silvina Ocampo's surrealist short stories underscored disquieting and hierarchical realities for mid-century Argentine women.

In Cuba, the events of 1959 launched debates to reconfigure the relationship between literature, an elite cultural form, and a mass readership created by the 1961 Literacy Campaign. These events, while broadening access to the written text, also sparked intense discussion about how the activity of literature could itself promote solidarity through giving voice to new writing subjects, and the combined impact of the Cuban Revolution, the Tlatelolco Massacre, and the civil rights movement was felt across the Americas. In the United States, Luis Valdéz started "El teatro campesino" ("The Farmworker's Theater") in 1965 to give voice to Chicano farmworkers. Like Valdéz's project that served as the cultural arm for César Chávez's National Farmworkers Association, authors across Latin America sought to convey and propel through literature positive economic changes for workers. García Márquez and Guillén reported in their works on the horrific treatment of workers by the US owners of Central American plantations, while Ernesto Cardenal and Jorge Amado promoted communist ideals that supported the plight of workers during this era. Perhaps not as univocally optimistic regarding the medium of literature as were the directors of New Latin American Cinema in the 1960s, who regarded the camera as a revolutionary weapon to enact change, writers from the region also tried to promote the workers' cause through their literary works and, to this end, sought as wide a readership as possible. Neruda insisted that his 1950s "Odas" be published in the news section of the newspaper *El Nacional* in Caracas when he was offered a weekly spot for these poems. The Cuban and Sandinista revolutionary governments reconfigured public spaces and institutions in order to create an infrastructure for the population to participate in literature. For his part, in the 1980s García Márquez turned to the production of *telenovelas* alongside his fictional writing and journalism; the Colombian author explained that just one episode would reach a greater audience than all of the readers of *Cien años* since its publication in 1967. In this way, the radical political literary proposals of the 1960s set the stage for literary developments that brought to light, in an attempt to correct, the sociocultural fractures and economic inequalities that the complex legacies of colonialism, modernity, and the economic dependence imposed by US imperialism had inflicted on the continent. Writers and intellectuals responded through visibilizing "new" subjects, proposing "new," more ethical disciplines, and imagining the possibility of relationships with their subject matter – the *materia prima* that is the peoples, landscapes, and histories of Latin America – that were based more on moral and political responses rooted in solidarity than the hierarchical, anthropophagic, or extractive practices of the traditional literary environment.

In this context, all the chapters in this part engage with different ways of enacting solidarity through literature. Sarah E. L. Bowskill's chapter reconceptualizes processes of canon formation in Mexico by putting gender and feminist solidarity at the center of interpretation. In order to go beyond the hermeneutic circle of canonization that is so often based on narrow definitions of genre, she argues, a different lens is required: if we take on the concept of "dar testimonio" instead of the now exhausted concept of *testimonio*, a new group of women writers emerges. And, by placing established and lesser-known Mexican women writers together, grouped around the concept of giving testimony, we can provide new literary periodizations that can themselves inform new ways of doing literary history.

Introduction

Charles M. Pigott's chapter continues the focus on solidarity but in a darker mode: through analysis of a bilingual poem in Quechua and Spanish by the Peruvian writer Teodoro Meneses Morales, who formed part of an explosion of Quechua writing in the mid-twentieth century. By employing the concepts of heterogeneity (Cornejo Polar) and heterotopia (Westphal) to the poem "Pacha manchariptin," Pigott demonstrates how Andean poets represented the loss of solidarity between humans and their environment as they observed a world in transition that threatened to transform Andean worldviews irrevocably.

Estelle Tarica continues and develops the Indigenous focus through her chapter on two emblematic *indigenista* novels from the mid-twentieth century: Miguel Ángel Asturias' *Hombres de maíz* (*Men of Maize*) and José María Arguedas' *Los ríos profundos* (*Deep Rivers*). The chapter conceptualizes these novels as early, and thus inevitably flawed, attempts to incorporate and inscribe the figure of "the Indian" into the imagined communities of nation and continent; in these two novels, intertextuality and polyphony give voice to the Indigenous population. However, and in line with the other chapters in this part, it questions the grounds for claims of true commonality of interest (true solidarity) between traditional national authors and the Indigenous peoples, and proposes that decentering texts from their place in nation, and taking them as the centers of their own worldviews and aesthetic projects, can yield new readings.

Amanda Holmes' chapter takes us to Chile to perform a rereading of Gabriela Mistral's series of poems "Locas mujeres" in order to reveal Mistral's feminist solidarities. Through locating this series in the broader context of Mistral's poetry, the chapter undertakes close textual analysis of poems from the series in order to demonstrate Mistral's commitment to expressing the complexity, multiplicity, and invisibility of being a woman. The "locas mujeres" of her poetry are defined by a constant movement or transition between free self-expression and the comfort of social convention, an inescapable dual existence that is best understood as a form of insanity.

The last chapter in this part, by Miguel Arnedo-Gómez, picks up some of the core areas of focus in this part – the force of disciplines and their methods, the relationship between expert observer/recorder and their object of study (through the notion of salvage ethnography), and, crucially, the possibility of solidarity that is offered by subjective and creative representation – to explore the literary representation of Afro-Cuban orality by three major Cuban literary figures of the twentieth century: Fernando Ortiz, Lydia Cabrera, and Nicolás Guillén. It examines the first two of these emblematic figures in terms of their at times ambivalent relationship with the raw material of anthropological and ethnographic enquiry and reporting, and goes on to foreground the poetics of Nicolás Guillén as a way of tracing a more creative representational transition, centered around the Cuban rhythm of the *son*, that is not without its own problems.

Part IV: Aesthetics and Innovation

Part IV examines the stylistic innovations of Latin American authors in their efforts to grasp the unsettling transitions of the era in their writing during this period. In what has become the stylistic hallmark of the period, magical realism and its fantastical variants appealed to readers globally and drew them to Latin American literature. While the originality of these Boom-period novels attracted the world to experience the region through literature, the style also succeeded in capturing the instabilities in the region. Employing anachronisms, embracing hybridity, and representing syncretic belief systems that existed alongside phenomenal economic disparities, authors who challenged the limits of realism harnessed Latin America's sense of disquiet and political unrest.

The Vanguard poets of this era found the voice of the region best captured in profound experimentation. Guided by inspiration, and informed by surrealism, Octavio Paz, Gabriela Mistral, César Vallejo, Alejandra Pizarnik, Pablo Neruda, José Lezama Lima, Nicolás Guillén, Jorge Luis Borges, and Nicanor Parra developed unique poetic voices during this period that pushed boundaries through their use of neologisms, free verse, concrete poetry, and song forms.

In an attempt to inspire their audiences to think critically – also a key characteristic of New Latin American Cinema – authors of both fiction and poetry from this era sought to push their reading public to participate actively in the reading process, or to act as a *"lector cómplice,"* as Cortázar called it. Boom-period novels often challenge the reader to process an unwieldy number of characters or to follow plots that are formatted unconventionally. They experiment with chronology or incorporate incongruous elements. Vanguard poetry might offer images in hermetic forms or through automatic writing, both elements that require a patient and critically minded reader. Equally, testimonial writing might attempt to change the rules of the game completely by allowing the multiplicity of subaltern experiences to reach readerships primed to hear the small or silenced voices of history but also to unsettle the expectations of established

Introduction

reading audiences. Whatever the method, genre, or textual mode, authors sought to enlighten their public in order to help shape an informed and thoughtful population required to enact transformations in society, and to use innovative representational strategies in order to do so. Not least as a response to the hyperrealism and trauma of the Spanish Civil War and dictatorship in Spain, of World War II and the clear presence of fascism, of the dehumanization and commodification of culture in the postwar years, writers sought to uncover and recover the potential of art to condemn socioeconomic violence, inequality, and injustice in novel and aesthetically radical ways.

Sarah Ann Wells opens the part with a study of post–World War II women visual artists and writers from Brazil, Argentina, and Uruguay. Her chapter aims to provoke a questioning of the assumptions that much critical work applies to surrealism (as connected to modernism and, later, the Boom), and she does this by introducing multiple surrealisms through the work of women who foreground eros as the motor and representation of alternative economies for women. She argues that, since the promise of surrealism as a postcolonial project was ultimately unfulfilled, not least undone by its enduring misogyny, the exploration of these and other women writers and visual artists can lead to new histories and new typologies of surrealism.

Graziella Pogolotti's essay (with a brief bio-bibliographical note by Rafael Rodríguez-Beltrán) traces the developments and transitions in the oeuvre of Alejo Carpentier through underlining his evolution from a canonical reliance of European traditions and aesthetics to ways of writing that aimed to decolonize both content and form. Using the metaphor of Columbus' galleons, she argues that Carpentier's iconic novels and novellas all reflect an emancipatory drive to send the galleons back to their origins.

Par Kumaraswami presents a chapter that takes a different approach to *testimonio* in light of the critical cul-de-sacs that were reached in Latin American Studies by the end of the twentieth century. By examining the conceptualization of testimonial writing from within the decolonizing project of the Cuban Revolution, her chapter indicates that the aesthetic and narrative features of magical realism and *testimonio* were not dissimilar, but that the political events of the late 1960s represented a turning point in terms of the potential of Latin American literature in the world.

Bruno Bosteels takes two Mexican authors – Juan Rulfo and Nellie Campobello – and explores how the collective voices that are the basis of oral storytelling are configured in their writing to produce an aesthetics of singularity, based on specificity. Examining Campobello's *Cartucho* and Rulfo's *El llano en llamas* (*The Burning Plain*), Bosteels demonstrates how the epic, collective experience of the Mexican Revolution becomes singularized in these works, which rest on aesthetics of self-sufficiency and self-containment rather than assume their place in the pantheon of collectivist narratives of the Revolution.

Odile Cisneros' chapter takes us back to avant-garde poetics through tracing the early twentieth-century evolution of *Vanguardismo* in Spanish America and *Modernismo* in Brazil as radical local responses to nineteenth-century Europe's modernisms. With equal attention paid to contexts and the texts that emerged within them across the continent, Cisneros charts the influence of the aesthetics of the 1920s and 1930s on instances of divergence and convergence in subsequent poetry in Brazil and Spanish America.

The last chapter in the part, and in the volume, is Marcy Schwartz's study of the poetic work of Julio Cortázar. Through careful textual analysis and archival reconstruction of his textual production, the chapter demonstrates how his experiments in poetry underpinned and prefigured his later, more politically motivated prose writing. Crucially, the chapter and its insights demonstrate how our understanding of Latin American literature is always incomplete, always partial, and always in transition – that the interpretive act is always, and can only ever be, a bridge to another reading. The chapter thus serves as a fitting conclusion to the volume.

Works Cited

Albuquerque, Severino João and Kathryn Bishop-Sanchez, eds. *Performing Brazil: Essays on Culture, Identity, and the Performing Arts*. Madison, WI: University of Wisconsin Press, 2015.

Arellano, Jeronimo. *Magical Realism and the History of the Emotions in Latin America*. Lewisburg, PA: Bucknell University Press, 2015.

Cabello Hutt, Claudia. *Artesana de sí misma: Gabriela Mistral, una intelectual en cuerpo y palabra*. West Lafayette, IN: Purdue University Press, 2018.

Clayton, Michelle. *Poetry in Pieces: César Vallejo and Lyric Modernity*. Berkeley: University of California Press, 2011.

Feinsod, Harris. *The Poetry of the Americas: From Good Neighbors to Countercultures*. New York: Oxford University Press, 2017.

García Liendo, Javier. *El intelectual y la cultura de masas: Argumentos latinoamericanos en torno a Ángel Rama y José María Arguedas*. West Lafayette, IN: Purdue University Press, 2017.

Introduction

Garganigo, John F. *Huellas de las literaturas hispanoamericanas.* 2nd ed. Upper Saddle River, NJ: Prentice Hall, 2002.

Henighan, Stephen. *Sandino's Nation: Ernesto Cardenal and Sergio Ramírez – Writing Nicaragua, 1940–2012.* Montreal: McGill-Queen's University Press, 2014.

Kerr, Lucille and Alejandro Herrero-Olaizola, eds. *Teaching the Latin American Boom.* New York: The Modern Language Association of America, 2015.

Kuhnheim, Jill S. *Beyond the Page: Poetry and Performance in Spanish America.* Tucson: University of Arizona Press, 2014.

Méndez-Faith, Teresa. *Panoramas literarios: América Hispana.* Boston, MA: Houghton Mifflin, 1998.

Sánchez Prado, Ignacio M., Anna M. Nogar and José Ramón Ruisánchez Serra, eds. *A History of Mexican Literature.* Cambridge: Cambridge University Press, 2016.

PART I

War, Revolution, Dictatorship

CHAPTER I

Revolutions and Literary Transitions
The 1960s

Jorge Fornet

Translated by Amanda Holmes

Political Transitions

"El mundo era tan reciente" ("the world was so recent"), read the first lines of one of the most acclaimed Latin American novels, "que muchas cosas carecían de nombre, y para mencionarlas había que señalarlas con el dedo" ("that many things lacked names, and in order to indicate them it was necessary to point"). If we stretch the interpretation a little, we could say that in the 1960s, similar to the founders of Macondo in *Cien años de soledad* (*One Hundred Years of Solitude*), the whole continent found it necessary to rename things.

For Latin America, the decade of the 1960s actually began in 1959. On the first day of this year, a revolution in Cuba led by Fidel Castro – who worked closely with the Argentine *guerrillero*, Ernesto Guevara, better known as Che – defeated the dictator Fulgencio Batista. Thus began a profound process of economic, political, and social transformation, one that would soon confront those of the then privileged classes, as well as, of course, those with US interests on the island. Among these transformations, culture played an important part. Culture, in fact, assumed an unexpected position of prominence: it stimulated both the revision of Latin American history and, in a way, the reconfiguration of the literary canon.

Soon the events taking place in Cuba transcended the island's borders and evoked interest in other countries in the region and the world. Many of the most notable intellectuals of the era began traveling en masse to Havana and writing about the experience. Figures such as Jean-Paul Sartre, Simone de Beauvoir, Waldo Frank, and C. Wright Mills are only some of those who were fascinated by the Cuban experience. As for Latin American intellectuals, most sympathized from the beginning with the Cuban Revolution and, following the same course as the Revolution, these intellectuals also became radicalized. They changed from being simply "left-wing" to becoming, in many cases, "revolutionary" intellectuals. A good number of the era's discussions revolved around the role that this new figure should play: the intellectual in an era of transformations. A consequence of the intelligentsia's devotion to this process was that, from their left-wing positions, almost all the most notable writers of the moment participated in the debates of the time. At least during the 1960s, many also came to support armed takeover, as well as contemporary terms such as "revolution," "guerrilla," "political engagement" (*compromiso*), "decolonization," and "(anti-)imperialism." Paradoxically, the same era that celebrated the rise of a new historical cycle and entrance into the revolutionary era – that at that time seemed inevitable on a regional scale – was seen by its protagonists as a period of transition into a new, as yet undefined stage.

The continent's cultural production was promoted by Cuba in a previously unseen way. Both Tyrians and Trojans recognized it: both allies and sympathizers of the Cuban project along with figures who would soon oppose it. For example, Emir Rodríguez Monegal, the Uruguayan critic and editor of the celebrated journal *Mundo Nuevo* (which played a polemical role in the Latin American cultural field in the second half of the 1960s and tried to dispute the hegemony of Havana's Casa de las Américas), was emphatic when he recalled that "el triunfo de la Revolución Cubana es uno de los factores determinantes del *Boom*" ("the triumph of the Cuban Revolution is one of the determining factors of the *Boom*") (649) from Latin America and key to propelling a forgotten nation and continent to the center of the international political arena. What is certain is that Cuba successfully created institutions that spread its cultural politics and wove effective intellectual networks, especially through the aforementioned Casa de las Américas, its literary prizes, its journal, and its publications. For Rodríguez Monegal, without the political and cultural "Boom" generated by the Cuban Revolution, "el otro *Boom*, con mayúscula, que es el que todos comentan, tal vez no hubiera llegado a ocurrir, o no habría tenido la misma repercusión" ("the other *Boom*, with a capital letter, commented on by everyone, would perhaps not have happened or would not have had the same repercussions") (651). From the other side of the spectrum, Julio Cortázar insisted on underscoring the extraliterary reasons that help explain the success of the Latin American novel of the era, and he blamed José Donoso's book *Historia personal del "Boom"* (*Personal History of the "Boom"*) for avoiding "toda referencia al panorama político latinoamericano, al hecho esencial de que también el *Boom*, mírese como se mire, es un hecho histórico y político" ("all

Revolutions and Literary Transitions

references to the Latin American political landscape, to the essential fact that the *Boom*, however it may be viewed, is a historical and political event") (1520).

By the end of the 1960s, the political positions of many writers and their relation to the Cuban proposals had been modified. The invasion of Czechoslovakia by the Soviet Union and the countries from the Warsaw Pact in summer 1968, which put a dramatic end to the Prague Spring, was supported, despite many misgivings, by the Cuban government. That same year the Padilla affair, a disagreement within the Cuban cultural sphere, would become the first part of a prolonged crisis that would culminate in 1971. Especially outside Cuba, this controversy was understood as a symptom of more conservative forces gaining ground inside the island's cultural arena. And both events were perceived as part of a growing alignment between Cuba and the Soviet Union. Some notable representatives of the intelligentsia associated with the Cuban Revolution began to distance themselves from it. Probably the most well-known case of all was that of the Peruvian author Mario Vargas Llosa. In fact, a segment of the Latin American intelligentsia had begun to distance themselves beforehand, but events like those mentioned above became the catalyst for accelerating disagreements that were bound to have developed sooner or later.

The significant events that took place at the most disparate points of the planet in 1968 (from the massive mobilizations of students and workers in Paris to the Prague Spring; from the anti-war demonstrations in Washington to the Tlatelolco Massacre in Mexico) were preceded by one that would mark the end of an era. On October 8, 1967, the *guerrillero* Ernesto "Che" Guevara was captured by regular forces of the Bolivian army. He would be assassinated the next day in the village school of La Higuera. Even though at the time this seemed to intensify Latin America's revolutionary spirit, observed from a distance this small occurrence represented the decline of the positive attitude toward armed takeover. If the 1960s were dominated by left-wing thought and by the idea of an almost imminent continental revolution, the 1970s – preceded by the death of Che Guevara in 1967 and the Tlatelolco Massacre in 1968 – signified a withdrawal of the left and the steady ascent of the right.

The close of the decade in Latin America coincided with the triumph and assumption of power in Chile, by election, of the Unidad Popular government led by Salvador Allende. The so-called *vía chilena* (Chilean road) to socialism sparked the enthusiasm of the left-wing forces and, therefore, most of the intellectuals. At the time, this became an

20   JORGE FORNET

unparalleled experience that complicated the revolutionary theory sustaining the necessity of armed power. Nevertheless, the tragic conclusion of that experience, swept away by the cruel military coup three years later, had the consequence of consolidating the military dictators of the continent.[1]

Ideological Transitions

The passage of the Cold War to Latin America complicated the rules of the game by converting what had until then been an East–West conflict into one that was also North–South. From that moment on, it no longer only represented a confrontation between the "free world" and "communism," as so many saw it during the 1950s; now it also incorporated a conflict between developed and dependent countries, exactly at the same time that the process of the decolonization of the so-called Third World was accelerating.[2] This process was accompanied simultaneously by another more complex and profound decolonization of culture and minds. *The Wretched of the Earth* by Franz Fanon – which Che Guevara had published in Cuba with a prologue by Sartre – became one of the bibles of the era.

The 1960s brought a proliferation of centers and meetings that were designed to stimulate the creation of efficient intellectual networks. If, from the nineteenth century on, Spanish American intellectuals knew and read each other and would meet and even engage in passionate debates (one of the most notable was that between the Venezuelan Andrés Bello and the Argentine Domingo Faustino Sarmiento); if, in the first decades of the twentieth century, especially at the height of the Vanguard movements, intellectuals began meeting, reading, and publishing together and reciprocally in the various journals of the continent; in the 1960s, the idea of establishing and strengthening these networks became relevant once again. Even though these meetings did not represent a new development,[3] what is clear is that they did become a current tendency, this time inspired by a different project. Rather than the now-tired idea of Hispanism that had helped erase the ethnic and cultural plurality of "*nuestra* América" ("*our* America"), another sentiment spawned these meetings, one galvanized by more radical convictions that mixed major literary with major political transgressions.

Diverse institutions, groups, publishing houses (mostly Latin American but also Spanish), journals, and literary supplements contributed to these networks that once more gained particular relevance, as they had during the vanguard era. Publications such as *Casa de las Américas*, *Marcha*, *La*

Cultura en México, *Primera Plana*, and other journals with much more surprising and picturesque titles, such as *El Corno Emplumado*, *El Ornitorrinco*, *El Grillo de Papel*, *El Escarabajo de Oro*, *Asomante*, *Sin Nombre*, *Rayado sobre el Techo*, *Pájaro Cascabel*, *La Espiga Amotinada*, *Pucuna*, and many more, vouched for the transformations that were taking place while they also gathered the intelligentsia of the continent. They all had something new to say, or, at least, they were in tune with the pulse of the region. The legendary journal *Sur* – which brought together the crème de la crème of the Argentine intelligentsia (beginning with Jorge Luis Borges) and fostered the literary greats from inside the continent and beyond – scarcely survived this decade, only to disappear in 1971.

Well-known Latin American writers' conferences took place from Mexico in the north to Concepción, Chile, in the south (organized by the poet Gonzalo Rojas from the end of the 1950s), and they even moved to other continents. One of the most important and beneficial conferences, in which a significant number of intellectuals from Latin America participated, took place in Genoa, Italy, in 1965, organized by Miguel Ángel Asturias and Amos Segala for the founding of the journal *América Latina* by the Colombianum foundation. Segala recounted that even though they were unsuccessful in founding a Latin American journal in Europe, they did find a substitute, *Mundo Nuevo*, that "llenó esta laguna con una prestigiosa publicación de signo contrario" ("filled this gap with a prestigious publication of a different kind") (*Vida, obra y herencia*, 438). These kinds of meetings functioned as spaces for reunion and consensus among intellectuals, even though in a good many cases it was difficult to reconcile the tensions and discrepancies that surfaced. Perhaps the final great meeting of the era, which surpassed the geographic limits of the continent and the concept of the intellectual understood in the broadest sense, was the Cultural Congress of Havana, which took place in January 1968 and proposed to unite "por primera vez desde 1936, un congreso mundial de intelectuales, apelando a todas las formas posibles de lucha contra el imperialismo, el colonialismo y el neocolonialismo" ("for the first time since 1936, a world congress of intellectuals, appealing to all possible forms of struggle against imperialism, colonialism, and neocolonialism") (Gilman 118).

From within this context, the cultural Cold War, which had caused significant conflicts in Europe, needed to shift its attention rapidly to Latin America. The US organizations responsible for combating this were disconcerted. "La Revolución Cubana había sorprendido al Congreso [por la Libertad de la Cultura] desprevenido y desarmado editorialmente" ("The Cuban Revolution had surprised the Congress [for Cultural Freedom] which was editorially unprepared and defenseless"), María Eugenia Mudrovcic remembers. "La única revista en español que financiaba, *Cuadernos*, no tenía buena reputación en América Latina, donde era percibida como un espacio copado por el exilio anticomunista español que pocas veces se ocupaba de América Latina y, cuando lo hacía, no podía evitar la mirada condescendiente y distante" ("The only journal in Spanish that it financed, *Cuadernos*, did not have a good reputation in Latin America. It was perceived there as a space filled by anti-communist Spanish exiles who rarely thought about Latin America and, when they did, they could not hold back their condescending and distant perception") (Mudrovcic 86). They tried to remedy the problem by turning the journal over to the Colombian writer Germán Arciniegas and presenting it as a "Latin American journal," but at this point *Cuadernos* was incapable of winning over the continent's left-wing intelligentsia.

At the beginning of the 1960s – late, but not coincidentally so – a campaign was initiated to consecrate Borges at the global level. Although his name had been known in Latin American intellectual circles since the 1920s, he was still considered foreign in other languages. The *Premio Formentor* that was awarded him in 1961 (shared with Samuel Beckett) undoubtedly contributed to his recognition and international dissemination, also explicable for reasons outside of literature. The Congress for Cultural Freedom tried to consecrate him by contrasting him with notable left-wing figures such as Miguel Ángel Asturias and Pablo Neruda, renowned names on a career path to the Nobel Prize (the former received it in 1967, the latter in 1971; Borges, unjustly, never did). It was in this way that the most prestigious journal of the Congress, *Encounter*, initiated "la glorificación de Borges a nivel mundial" ("the glorification of Borges on a global level"). They did so "con un espaldarazo que puso en marcha el aluvión de traducciones que siguió a su viaje consagratorio por Europa a principios de 1963" ("with an endorsement that precipitated a flood of translations that continued during his emblematic tour of Europe at the beginning of 1963") (Mudrovcic 96). Years later, on April 26, 1966, the *New York Times* published a revealing article with news that was later reiterated in the London *Sunday Times* and *The Observer*: the Congress for Cultural Freedom was, in fact, a front for the CIA. Consequently, the journals it supported (the English *Encounter*, the French *Preuves*, and the aforementioned *Mundo Nuevo*) were placed in an uncomfortable position.

Revolutions and Literary Transitions

The fact is that the US onslaught to take the initiative in disseminating Latin American literature was intense. Deborah Cohn has signaled that institutions such as the Association of American University Presses (AAUP) (and its Latin American Translation Program, the Center for Inter-American Relations (CIAR)) and the Inter-American Foundation for the Arts (IAFA) were founded as part of that offensive that took place in the United States to counter the Cuban influence on Latin American writers. All these promoted the translation and edition of authors including José Martí and José Carlos Mariátegui, as well as Borges and Octavio Paz. They also passed through names closer to the Boom, such as Juan Rulfo, Juan Carlos Onetti, Julio Cortázar, José Donoso, Carlos Fuentes, and Guillermo Cabrera Infante, among others. Even the translation of *Cien años de soledad* (*One Hundred Years of Solitude*) into English, carried out in 1970, formed part of this program. From his personal perspective, the essayist and professor John Beverley observed the notable increase in the topic's relevance in the United States:

> Fue la Revolución Cubana la que dio origen al gran incremento de estudios latinoamericanos ... en la década de 1960 y principios de la de 1970. ... La literatura latinoamericana, que cuando yo era estudiante se consideraba la última de las literaturas en idioma extranjero, tiene hoy un prestigio y una influencia excepcionales (It was the Cuban Revolution that gave origin to the great increase in Latin American Studies ... in the 1960s and the beginning of the 1970s. ... Latin American literature, which when I was a student was considered the last of the literatures in a foreign language, possesses today exceptional levels of prestige and influence). (33–34)

In 1968, as part of this peak, the *Times Literary Supplement* dedicated its November 14 edition to Latin American literature. This edition included an announcement proclaiming: "There is no doubt that the most significant contribution to world literature today comes from Latin America." After this first piece, the edition presented a heterogeneous mix of authors including Borges and Neruda, as well as Fidel Castro and Che Guevara, along with Gabriel García Márquez and even the French intellectual Regis Debray, the ideologue of *guerrillero* warfare in Latin America.

In the midst of this atmosphere, inside the continent agitated debates were taking place that foregrounded the role of the intellectual in society; intense polemics occurred surrounding the limits of liberty of expression in socialism; incendiary disputes transpired regarding the status of literature in a revolutionary society, and so on. Parallel to the creation of unanimously celebrated great novels, new forms of speech and even "minor" genres forged a path, the most outstanding being the testimony genre, to which I will return. One of the great discussions of the era, which caused rivers of ink to flow, considered the role of the intellectual and the writer's predicament. Numerous texts, discussions, roundtables, and journal issues were dedicated to this topic. Most of the writers felt the need to participate, and they did so, in the majority of cases, from left-wing positions. This does not mean that they surrendered their work – as has been said – to their political convictions. From the midst of the clamorous polemics at the end of the decade, Julio Cortázar called for the need for revolutionaries of literature more than readers of the Revolution; "los Che Guevara del lenguaje" ("Che Guevaras of language"), he came to say (Collazos, Cortázar, and Vargas Llosa 76).

An inevitable question at that time was: how can an author be useful to the Revolution through language or, in other words, how are revolutions written? Far from being a minor problem, for its protagonists it caused sleepless nights: the creation of art in tune with historical circumstances. What is more, at a revolution's height, it is often feared that art and literature are incapable of expressing the profound transformations that every social earthquake triggers. We are talking about an obsession, of course, plagued by misunderstandings. In this way, Russian writers regretted that their own Revolution had not produced *their* poet, the Pushkin for whom they yearned, when they already had Mayakovsky. Parallel to this, in Mexico, writers got tangled up in agitated discussions and lamented the lack of a virile literature in the country that was worthy of the Revolution they had just had, when many years before the first signs of what would later be known as the Novel of the Mexican Revolution had emerged. The fact is, however, that the decade of the 1960s, which supposedly called on the *literatos* (men of letters) of the Revolution, was in practice the one that produced the most notable revolutionaries of literature.

The identification of the figure of the intellectual with the revolutionary (often understood as its incarnation par excellence, the *guerrillero*) reached a point where the authors of the era wove the fantasy of choosing between arms and letters. The title of Claudia Gilman's book (in other respects, very perceptive and timely) *Entre la pluma y el fusil: Debates y dilemas del escritor revolucionario en América Latina* (*Between the Pen and the Gun: Debates and Dilemmas of the Revolutionary Writer in Latin America*) (2003) confirms this disjunction. Many contemporary authors have read the era and have retrospectively simplified it. This approach distorts the perception of the era in a way that seems to suggest that the great novels of the 1960s and 1970s were written between revolutionary slogans and the heat of battle, when, in fact, they were written in the same way that all great novels are written.

At the same time, positions clashed regarding the configuration of the intellectual model. One of the greatest polemics took place at the end of the 1960s, and it resonated in diverse publications on the continent. I am referring to the polemic between Julio Cortázar and the Peruvian novelist José María Arguedas. In May 1967, the Argentinian sent a letter to Roberto Fernández Retamar, editor of the journal *Casa de las Américas*, as a contribution to the issue dedicated to the situation of the Latin American intellectual. In this issue 6 (April to June 1968), the Peruvian journal *Amaru* published the first chapter of the novel *El zorro de arriba y el zorro de abajo* (*The Fox from Above and the Fox from Down Below*), in which Arguedas responded to that text and attacked many of the most celebrated writers of the time. Its author traced there, without mentioning them explicitly, two literary currents: one represented by authors such as Juan Rulfo and João Guimarães Rosa, into which he also fits; and the other represented by that sort of "cosmopolitan" author against whom he addressed his response. The polemic was extended to new chapters and attested to how, even among left-wing writers, diametrically opposed postures existed about the place, role, and expectations of writers. The idyllic image of the Boom of authors and novels, in vogue at that time, did not satisfy everyone.

Literary Transitions

It is inevitable that our reference to Latin American literature of the 1960s will be associated with the so-called Boom in Latin American narrative, more specifically the novel. One of the main objections that tends to be made to the denomination of the Boom is that it suggests that, before it, there existed a vacuum through which, suddenly, the great literary movement flourished. Actually, at the time this explosion occurred, writers of the stature of Borges, Carpentier, Rulfo, Onetti, Arguedas, and Asturias had already been in full production for decades; that is, if we are only referring to those writers notable for narrative fiction. The fundamental difference between these and their successors is associated less with their literary quality than with the type of reception they received. If they had been read in their time, with luck, as isolated stars, the authors grouped in the Boom were made visible as a group involved in a common cause. In fact, the perspective of the 1960s was the element that united them and that allowed them to be read as part of a group that seemed predestined to change literary history. In the same way that revolutions channel and bring formerly invisible social conflicts to the political space, the idea of a Latin American revolution in the 1960s brought a complete literary movement – through some key names – to the fore.

The Uruguayan critic Ángel Rama, one of the sharpest and most profound scholars of the Boom phenomenon, chooses the initial date as the year 1964. "Consciente del especial avance que estaba llevando a cabo la narrativa latinoamericana" ("Conscious of the special progress that Latin American narrative was achieving"), which had been fertilized by the Vanguard poets and the North American novel, Rama proposed that the journal *Casa de las Américas* dedicate an issue to "la impetuosa producción narrativa que después habría de ser bautizada – desdichadamente – como el Boom" ("the impetuous narrative production that would be baptized afterwards – unfortunately – as the Boom") (18). This issue – number 26, from 1964 – included chapters from Alejo Carpentier, Ernesto Sábato, Juan Carlos Onetti, Julio Cortázar, Carlos Fuentes, and Mario Vargas Llosa, as well as critical texts about these and other authors, and was preceded by the essay "Diez problemas para el novelista latinoamericano" ("Ten Problems for the Latin American Author"), in which Rama tried to reason, as he would affirm years later, about the diverse routes that the Latin American art of the novel had taken in light of "las demandas del exaltado pueblo de los años sesenta" ("the demands of the enthusiastic population of the 1960s") (457). The fact is that in 1964 the new narrative "cobró reconocida carta de ciudadanía en toda América" ("earned a renowned citizenship card throughout América"), Rama would say, as much with the essay that appeared in *Casa de las Américas* as with his prologue to an anthology that he prepared for the weekly *Marcha*; both texts, in this case, initiated "una estimación global y panorámica del movimiento" ("a global assessment and panorama of the movement") (18).

It is worth adding that even if political and cultural circumstances are key to understanding the Boom, the phenomenon goes way beyond that initial spark. It was promoted also by the interests of editors, critics, and readers from diverse Latin American capitals, and, by establishing itself in Barcelona (the new home of some of the Boom's most prominent members), it grew even more extensively and garnered even more influence. In this regard, the work of the Seix Barral publishing house and its Biblioteca Breve prize was fundamental for decisively promoting a notable group of writers.[4] Even though it is difficult to define those who were integral to the Boom, in the many lists that proliferate – and that granted or denied favor – four names recurred that are usually accepted as the pillars of the

Revolutions and Literary Transitions

group: the Argentinian Julio Cortázar, the Colombian Gabriel García Márquez, the Mexican Carlos Fuentes, and the Peruvian Mario Vargas Llosa. Even if these four had begun publishing before, it was the almost simultaneous appearance of novels such as *La muerte de Artemio Cruz* (*The Death of Artemio Cruz*, 1962) by Fuentes, *Rayuela* (*Hopscotch*, 1963) by Cortázar, and *La ciudad y los perros* (*The Time of the Hero*, 1963) by Vargas Llosa that contributed to giving more visibility and international recognition to the new Latin American novel.

But if one book represents the Latin American literature of the 1960s, it is, without doubt, *Cien años de soledad* (*One Hundred Years of Solitude*, 1967). García Márquez's novel enjoyed a fulminating success and the Buendía saga was read as an authentic example of a Latin American epic. In passing, magical realism, the formula in which the novel was pigeonholed, became – in a way that was as erroneous as it was inevitable – the factory brand of Latin American literature. Mario Vargas Llosa was one of the first to proclaim that they were dealing with "una novela total, en la línea de esas creaciones demencialmente ambiciosas que compiten con la realidad real de igual a igual, enfrentándole una imagen de una vitalidad, vastedad y complejidad cualitativamente equivalentes" ("a total novel, in line with those insanely ambitious creations that compete on equal terms with reality by confronting it with a qualitatively equivalent image of vitality, vastness and complexity") (xxv). Soon Macondo embodied a whole continent. For Mario Benedetti, "ese pueblo mítico ... fue quizá una imagen de Colombia toda; pero ahora Macondo es aproximadamente América Latina; es tentativamente el mundo" ("that mythical people ... were perhaps an image of the whole of Colombia; but now Macondo is approximately Latin America; it is tentatively the world") (19). Gerald Martin spoke of "a man who writes about village, nation and the world using the discoveries of the great Western myths ... the great Western classics ... and the greatest precursors from his own continent ... to produce a work – a mirror – in which his own continent at last recognizes itself, and thus founds a tradition" (302).

The consensus shows that they were dealing with a foundational story in which Latin America could recognize itself. I wonder if to some degree the incomparable success of the novel (as well as some of the objections raised after its publication) was not part of a misunderstanding, offering a continental dimension to the specific zone represented by this literature, the Caribbean tradition – quite different, of course, from that of the Andes or the River Plate. It is not difficult to conjecture that behind that universalist perception were extraliterary reasons, a predisposition to read as continental a book that, under other circumstances, would have been

28   JORGE FORNET

highly celebrated without its recognition as the Latin American novel par
excellence.

Beyond those four extraordinary names, many others came and went
from the numerous lists of Boom members. As if this were not enough, at
the same time an admirable collection of works continued to be written
(not just narrative, of course, because the decade produced outstanding
books of poetry, essays and plays if we refer only to the traditional genres)
that delved into universes that were radically distinct from those of the
works most acclaimed by the critics and – it must be said – by the market.
It is evident that the Boom (as much as its antecedents, as one understands
them) was a distinctly masculine phenomenon. María Rosa Olivera-
Williams has emphasized, nevertheless, that if Borges, Asturias, Onetti,
and Rulfo were important for the Boom, also significant were the works
that were less advertised by female writers such as the Chilean María Luisa
Bombal (*La amortajada* [*The Shrouded Woman*] and *La última niebla*
[*House of Mist*]), Mexicans Rosario Castellanos (*Balún Canán* [*The Nine
Guardians*]) and Elena Garro (*Los recuerdos del porvenir* [*Recollections of
Things to Come*]), and the Uruguayan Armonía Somers (*La mujer desnuda*
[*The Naked Woman*]) (280). She cites, on the other hand, what Rosario
Ferré denominated the *Boomito*, in reference to the small Boom of female
authors that followed the more well-known Boom – works with which
they dialogued explicitly or implicitly and distanced themselves at the same
time thanks to the use of parody (287–288).

I have already said that during the 1960s, the Boom forced the powerful
production of poetry in Latin America to a less important position. Apart
from the inevitable influence of older greats such as César Vallejo and
Pablo Neruda, two figures exerted an influential role on the young poets of
the time: the Chilean Nicanor Parra and the Nicaraguan Ernesto
Cardenal – guardians of "*antipoesía*" ("anti-poetry") and conversational
poetry in Latin America – in whose footsteps it is possible to see an
outstanding group of authors who knew how to find their own voice.
Two of them, it is worth saying in passing, explicitly address their transitional condition. They do so not without a certain amount of irony. The
era that placed the idea of the Revolution at the center and involved a large
number of its intellectuals also established the idea of the transitional: from
an old to a new world, from an old man to a new man, from one literature
to another. But it is enough to consider a few texts to perceive that this
notion requires some nuancing. The Mexican José Emilio Pacheco
expresses in his poem "Manifiesto" ("Manifesto"): "Todos somos poetas
de transición: // la poesía jamás se queda inmóvil" ("We are all poets of

Revolutions and Literary Transitions

transition: // poetry never stays immobile"). For his part, the Cuban Roberto Fernández Retamar makes this more evident from the very title of his long poem "Usted tenía razón, Tallet: somos hombres de transición" ("You Are Right, Tallet: We Are All Men of Transition"), which concludes with the following verses: "después de todo, compañeros, quién sabe // Si solo los muertos no son hombres de transición" ("after everything, comrades, who knows // If only the dead are not men of transition"). Many of them recognize that transitional condition in themselves. With time, they warn that this is intrinsic to the human condition and its expressions.

I have left to the end the presence and development in the decade of the 1960s a genre that would take shape in these years, *testimonio*, even though it emerged earlier; in fact, before the North American nonfiction novel. In the face of the novel, traditionally understood as the "bourgeois genre," *testimonio* seemed to embody and give voice to a new subject. In any case, consensus affirms that the first great example of the genre (as understood in its modern variant because literatures that "give testimony" have existed since antiquity) is *Operación Masacre* (*Operation Massacre*, 1957) by the Argentinian writer and journalist Rodolfo Walsh. The circumstances of a particularly convulsive decade like the 1960s, filled with transformations and the readiness to displace traditional politics with revolutionary battle, stimulated the publication of new texts like *Biografía de un cimarrón* (*Autobiography of a Runaway Slave*, 1966) by the Cuban Miguel Barnet and *La noche de Tlatelolco* (*Massacre in Mexico*, 1971) by the Mexican Elena Poniatowska. Although unique among these titles, a volume such as *Diario de Bolivia* (*Bolivian Diary*, 1968) by Che Guevara, published in 1968, can also be read within this framework. Two years later, without doubt under significant pressure from a literary field with a growing presence of books with these characteristics, Casa de las Américas announced a new genre for the first time – which it coined as *testimonio* – as part of its literary prizes. Thanks to this, the genre was given the legitimacy and literary status it had lacked. The genre has generated, furthermore, discussions around the status of truth and authorship. Facing the dominance of the novel and its authors' visibility, protagonism, and prestige, *testimonio* would come to occupy its counterpart; both the forgotten character and the unknown author imply a reformulation both of the literary canon and of the way in which the continent regarded itself. These two poles embody the extremes in which Latin American literature moved in the 1960s, engaged as much in transforming itself as was the world from which its books emerged.

JORGE FORNET

Notes

1. Even though coup d'états and new dictatorships took place in the South Cone during these years (Chile and Uruguay in 1973, Argentina in 1976), it is obvious that this was a "*viejo mal*" ("old evil") on the continent, with frequent antecedents in Central and South America and in the Caribbean. However, the dictatorships of the 1970s were the national and international right-wing response to the convulsive situation of the 1960s. In 1964, another military coup deposed the constitutional president of Brazil João Goulart. Although Brazil is part of Latin America and for decades governments, institutions, and intellectual networks have made a sustained effort to strengthen the ties that connect it to continental Latin America, its historical and cultural singularities mean it is often seen as an independent universe. I regret that these pages do not include the particularities of the Brazilian process.
2. Roberto Fernández Retamar once proposed that the old dichotomy of "developed countries/underdeveloped countries" be replaced by another that would take into account the historical and political process: "underdeveloped countries/underdeveloping countries." See Roberto Fernández Retamar, "Responsabilidad de los intelectuales de los países subdesarrollantes." *Casa de las Américas* 47 (1968): 123. Even if his proposal did not succeed, it records the tendency, then in vogue, to signal and name forms of colonialism.
3. The idea to establish a Casa de las Américas in Havana precedes its definitive creation by a number of years. And other societies, such as the Sociedad Colombista Panamericana and the Asociación de Escritores y Artistas Americanos (Association of American Writers and Artists), operated beforehand in the building that the nascent institute would occupy. See Nadia Lie, *Transición y transacción: La revista cubana "Casa de las Americas" (1960–1976).* Gaithersburg, MD: Hispamérica, 1996 and Lorena Sánchez, "La casa antes de la Casa," *Casa de las Américas* 295 (2019): 8–16.
4. See the extensive and helpful study by Xavi Ayén, *Aquellos años del Boom: García Márquez, Vargas Llosa y el grupo de amigos que lo cambiaron todo.* Barcelona: RBA Libros, 2014.

Works Cited

Benedetti, Mario. "Prólogo." In Gabriel García Márquez, *Cien años de soledad*. La Habana: Casa de las Américas, 1968, vii–xviii.

Beverley, John. *Del Lazarillo al sandinismo: Estudios sobre la función ideológica de la literatura española e hispanoamericana.* Minneapolis, MN: Published by the Prisma Institute in cooperation with the Institute for the Study of Ideologies and Literature, 1987.

Collazos, Óscar, Julio Cortázar, and Mario Vargas Llosa. *Literatura en la revolución y revolución en la literatura (Polémica).* Mexico City: Siglo XXI Editores, 1970.

Cortázar, Julio. *Cartas 1969–1983.* Buenos Aires: Alfaguara, 2000.

Revolutions and Literary Transitions

Gilman, Claudia. *Entre la pluma y el fusil: Debates y dilemas del escritor revolucionario en América Latina*. Buenos Aires: Siglo Veintiuno Editores Argentina, 2003.

Lorena Sánchez, "La casa antes de la Casa," *Casa de las Américas* 295 (2019): 8–16.

Martin, Gerald. *Gabriel García Márquez: A Life*. New York: Vintage, 2010.

Mudrovcic, María Eugenia. "Borges y el Congreso por la Libertad de la Cultura," *Variaciones Borges* 36 (2013): 77–99.

Nadia Lie, *Transición y transacción: La revista cubana "Casa de las Americas" (1960–1976)*. Gaithersburg, MD: Hispamérica, 1996.

Olivera-Williams, María Rosa. "*Boom, Realismo Mágico – Boom* and *Boomito*." In *The Cambridge History of Latin American Women's Literature*, pp. 278–295. Eds. Ileana Rodríguez and Mónica Szurmuk. New York: Cambridge University Press, 2016.

Rama, Ángel. *La novela en América Latina: Panoramas 1920–1980*. Bogotá: Procultura/Instituto Colombiano de Cultura, 1982.

Roberto Fernández Retamar, "Responsabilidad de los intelectuales de los países subdesarrollantes." *Casa de las Américas* 47 (1968): 123.

Rodríguez Monegal, Emir. "La nueva novela vista desde Cuba," *Revista Iberoamericana* 92–93 (1975): 647–662.

Vargas Llosa, Mario. "*Cien años de soledad*: Realidad total, novela total." In *Gabriel García Márquez, Cien años de soledad: Edición conmemorativa*, pp. xxv–lviii. Madrid: Real Academia Española/Asociación de Academias de la Lengua Española, 2007.

Vida, obra y herencia de Miguel Ángel Asturias, 1899/1999. Catálogo de la exposición organizada por la UNESCO y la Colección Archivos en el marco de la XXX Conferencia General de la UNESCO (*Life, Works and Legacy of Miguel Ángel Asturias, 1899/1999*. Catalogue of the Exhibition Organized by UNESCO and the Archives Collection within the Framework of the XXX General Conference of UNESCO), 1999.

Xavi Ayén, *Aquellos años del Boom: García Márquez, Vargas Llosa y el grupo de amigos que lo cambiaron todo*. Barcelona: RBA Libros, 2014.

CHAPTER 2

Jorge Luis Borges
Probing the Limits of World War

Kate Jenckes

Borges wrote his best-known fictions during World War II, and many of them explore the limits of what he calls the bewitching allure of a totalizing order ("Tlön," OC 1.473).[1] In "Deutsches Requiem" and "El jardín de senderos que se bifurcan" ("The Garden of Forking Paths"), he focuses on the ideal of totality underlying twentieth-century modernity in the context of the two world wars. In these stories Borges demonstrates how the fight for sovereignty exemplified by war is supported by epistemological and technological forms that are used to subject the differential nature of time, existence, and the possibility of relation.[2] These forms include long-standing representational apparatuses such as historiography, philosophy, philology, and aesthetics, as well as technological innovations including new forms of telecommunication, warfare, and transportation. Although the two war stories seem to demonstrate the imminence of a global sovereignty at once epistemological and political, they also probe the limits of the drive to totality, stressing points of fissure and excess that constitute the condition of possibility for an experience of reality in which time and singularity are not subjected to a single order.

In an essay on the nature of fascism in the 1940s, Borges describes how the extreme ideas promoted by the Nazis are less exceptional than one might wish to think. In "Anotación al 23 de agosto de 1944," he puzzles over the unexpected enthusiasm of Argentine supporters of Hitler at the news of Paris' liberation. He conjectures that their celebration indicates a belief that the Allied victory perpetuated, rather than opposed, the ideal of totality imposed by the Nazis. He writes, "para los europeos y los americanos, hay un orden – un solo orden – posible: el que antes llevó el nombre de Roma y que ahora es la cultura del Occidente" (OC 2.112) ("for Europeans and Americans, one order and only one is possible: it used to be called Rome, and now it is called Western Culture" [SNF 211]). This single

32

order, he goes on to explain, forms the basis of a single understanding of reality, from which a differential understanding of singularity is excluded. Although this totalizing ideal is not new, its scale and pervasiveness have expanded during the twentieth century to include the "world" and everything in it. The Nazi supporters who celebrated the liberation of Paris, Borges surmises, perceived a transition from a continental, imperial horizon to a global one.[3]

"Deutsches Requiem" is a fictional exploration of the ideas presented in "Anotación al 23 de agosto de 1944." Although it is narrated by a Nazi and concerns the rise and fall of Nazism, it should be viewed not only as a cautionary tale about German fascism but also, especially in the light of "Anotación al 23 de agosto de 1944," as indicating a conceptual structure that exceeds any single manifestation. The story narrates the perspective of a Nazi man of letters, Otto Dietrich zur Linde, who becomes subdirector of a concentration camp. It is structured as his account of his participation in the rise and fall of National Socialism on the night before his execution.

Dietrich's declaration begins with a seemingly innocuous account of his family history, with an emphasis on ancestors who played a role – often merely by dying – in the establishment of modern Germany, leading up to his own anticipated execution. He mentions that it is natural, given the circumstances, for him to be thinking of his ancestors, "ya que tan cerca estoy de su sombra, ya que de algún modo soy ellos" (OC 1.617) ("since I am come so near their shadow – since, somehow, I am they" [SF 229]). This reflection introduces an ahistorical ideal that forms the basis of his ideological commitment to Nazism. He insists that the Nazi worldview constitutes our ineluctable future:

> Quienes sepan oírme, comprenderán la historia de Alemania y la futura historia del mundo. Yo sé que casos como el mío, excepcionales y asombrosos ahora, serán muy en breve triviales. Mañana moriré, pero soy un símbolo de las generaciones del porvenir. (OC 1.617) (Those who heed my words shall understand the history of Germany and the future history of the world. I know that cases such as mine, exceptional and astonishing now, will very soon be very unremarkable. Tomorrow I shall die, but I am a symbol of the generations to come. [SF 229])

Dietrich describes himself as a symbolic link to a world history that extends into the past and future without significant change: he is (*soy*) at once both past and future generations. His individuality may seem exceptional, but in reality he represents a timeless norm, a permanent state of exception.

The "trivial" (translated by Hurley as "unremarkable") nature of his individual case does not mean a lack of significance, nor does it *only* mean – since this is a central idea in the story – that particularity is superseded by the universal. The etymological sense of the word "trivial" conjures both the sense of crossroads (*tri-via*) and the medieval trivium of grammar, rhetoric, and logic; that is, the verbal mechanics for conveying truth. Both connotations relate to Dietrich's surname, *zur Linde*, which evokes the Spanish word *linde* or limit. He understands his individual being (*soy*) as being situated at the crossroads or on the limit between a present particularity and the universal, which encompasses both past and future. He thereby constitutes a symbolic manifestation of that universal, which his pre-execution declaration explains and justifies through language and logic.

The way that Dietrich describes himself and his words as a direct link to Germany's role in a new world history resembles the description that appears in the second footnote of the story. This footnote appears in relation to his explanation of the philosophical influences that led him to National Socialism, including the work of Friedrich Nietzsche and Oswald Spengler. The footnote elaborates his views on the latter's *The Decline of the West* in particular:

> Otras naciones viven con inocencia, en sí y para sí como los minerales o los meteoros; Alemania es el espejo que a todos recibe, la conciencia del mundo (*das Weltbewusstein*). Goethe es el prototipo de esa comprensión ecuménica. (OC 1.618) (Other nations live naively, in and for themselves, like minerals or meteors; Germany is the universal mirror that receives all others – the conscience of the world [*das Weltbewusstsein*]. Goethe is the prototype of that ecumenical mind. [SF 230])

In this simplified and slightly exaggerated account of Spengler's book (a reckoning or *Abrechnung* calculated to cancel any "debt" to his contemporary), Dietrich describes Germany as an ideal space that transforms the perception of material particularities – associated with other nations, which exist only in themselves and for themselves – into world consciousness. Johann Wolfgang von Goethe is hailed as having produced a foundational version of this transformative reflection through his literature, which produces a "comprensión ecuménica" in which the world is understood from an imperial perspective (ecumene, *oikouménē gē*). From a Nazi perspective, Goethe's conception of *Weltliteratur*, like Dietrich's declaration, constitutes a linguistic prototype in the sense of original version or first blow (Gr. *proto-typos*) of a world understanding, to which National Socialism will add the finishing touches.

Jorges Luis Borges

Whereas the above examples demonstrate Dietrich's understanding of how letters and literature are capable of creating and transmitting a totalizing image of history and the world, Dietrich also mentions several instances in which aesthetic production disturbs and disrupts such totalization. The first is his description of his love for the work of Johannes Brahms and William Shakespeare, who, he says, diverted him (*"me desvió"*) from the totalizing pretensions of theology with

> la infinita variedad de su mundo. Sepa quien se detiene maravillado, trémulo de ternura y de gratitud, ante cualquier lugar de la obra de esos felices, que yo también me detuve allí, yo el abominable. (OC 1.618) (the infinite variety of their world. I wish anyone who is held in awe and wonder, quivering with tenderness and gratitude, transfixed by some passage in the work of these blessèd men, to know that I too was once transfixed like them – I the abominable. [SF 230])

In contrast to the figure of the world as a static temporal and spatial totality, produced through the optics of Germany, Goethe, and Dietrich, here the world is described as infinitely differential. Likewise, in contrast to the act of militant comprehension said to be available to Goethe and the reader of Dietrich's declaration, the encounters with the worlds of Brahms and Shakespeare are described as leaving the recipient vulnerable and unsettled, "trémulo de ternura y de gratitud." It is not possible to internalize these worlds; one passes before them, stopping (*detenerse*) to allow their greatness to disturb the ostensible unity of the self, leaving it trembling tenderly.[4] Furthermore, in contrast to the *oiko*-menical mirror of hypernationalist Germany, produced by killing Jews and others perceived as threats to its limpidity, the works of Brahms and Shakespeare are open to anyone who chooses to pause before them, even someone as "abominable" (not quite human, L. *ab homine*) as Dietrich.

Dietrich's description of the works of Brahms and Shakespeare resonates with the account of the Jewish poet David Jerusalem, the only victim mentioned by name of the concentration camp in which Dietrich serves as subdirector. Dietrich begins his description of Jerusalem's work with a reference to Albert Soergel (a poetry critic who became a Nazi), who purportedly compared Jerusalem to Whitman, but he rejects the comparison, stating that "Whitman celebra el universo de un modo previo, general, casi indiferente; Jerusalem se alegra de cada cosa, con minucioso amor" (OC 1.620) ("Whitman celebrates the universe a priori, in a way that is general and virtually indifferent; Jerusalem takes delight in every smallest thing, with meticulous and painstaking love" [SF 232]). The poet who

36 KATE JENCKES

celebrates blades of grass and the air in his mouth appears "general, casi indiferente" in comparison to Jerusalem, whose poetry by implication must be even more radically singular that Whitman's, in its engagement with, as Dietrich says of Brahms and Shakespeare, the "variedad infinita" of the world.

Although Dietrich clearly admires Jerusalem, he says he is compelled to destroy him, not only because he is a Nazi and Jerusalem a Jew but also, he says, because Jerusalem awakens in him a "piedad" (OC 1.619; SF 231). Such "piedad" can be understood as compassion for another, which might open onto care for many others, even the "infinite variety" of the world, which runs counter to his philosophical justification of National Socialism. Whereas the aesthetic works of Jerusalem, Brahms, and Shakespeare appeal to an infinite and endlessly emerging multiplicity, Nazism is for Dietrich conceptually bound to a unifying and totalizing order.

In the end, this totalizing order prevails over Nazism and Dietrich himself. Echoing Borges' conjecture in "Anotación al 23 de agosto de 1944," Dietrich describes an odd sense of satisfaction when he realizes that the structure of totality requires the sacrifice of all particulars, even its most fanatical supporters: "Muchas cosas hay que destruir para edificar el nuevo orden; ahora sabemos que Alemania era una de esas cosas" (OC 1.622) ("There are many things that must be destroyed in order to build the new order; now we know that Germany was one of them" [SF 234]). Although his compatriots may resist, he says he is personally pleased with this destiny, which he describes as an "orbicular and perfect gift," a sacrificial entry to an *oikos-menical* world order. The final paragraph of the story displays this sacrifice in a split image, as it were. Dietrich looks at himself in the mirror and observes the difference between his physical body and the ideal of totality, which his individuality serves merely to reflect. His parting glance in the mirror "para saber quién soy" ("to know who I am") confirms his earlier assertion that his existence (*soy*) links past, present, and future in a single static order. Although the story concludes with Dietrich's simultaneously self-assured and self-annihilating confidence in the tri-umph of a single unifying order, the description of the relationship to singularity and difference in the works of Jerusalem, Brahms, and Shakespeare suggests a different possible ending, one that Borges' story – as indeed his work in general, far as it is from Goethe's ecumenical mirror – can be seen as trying to elicit.

In "El jardín de senderos que se bifurcan" there is a similar struggle between a differential experience of time and singularity, on the one hand, and the imposition of a single and atemporal form of order, on the other – in this case (ironically, since it concerns World War I), not the umbilical One of empire but the divided One of enmity. Like "Deutsches Requiem," the story is structured as a declaration of a man about to be executed who affirms his victory in spite of his impending death. Nonetheless, "El jardín de senderos que se bifurcan" emphasizes the struggle between order and excess more than the other. It is for this reason that I have chosen to reverse the chronological order of the stories, since in "Deutsches Requiem," written later about a subsequent war, the intensification of the dominant order makes it hard to discern any excess or remainder beyond the ghostly reverberations of Brahms, Shakespeare, and, especially, Jerusalem.

In "El jardín de senderos que se bifurcan" the tension between the One, or the split unity of enmity, is evident in the figures that represent the primary antagonism between the Central and the Allied powers of the war. The narrator, Yu Tsun, is a Chinese-born professor of English (from a town near British-occupied Hong Kong, who taught in a German school in German-occupied Qingdao), who is acting as a spy for Germany; his antagonist and pursuer is Richard Madden, an Irish agent working for Britain.[5] Both characters are colonized subjects fighting for their colonizers and both are described as reluctant and even cowardly participants in this war that is not of their own making. However, in spite of their reluctance, they both seem determined to overcome their perceived cowardice through their missions for the imperial powers, as though the divided totality of this "European war" were the only possible reality (OC 1.506).

The basic plotline is that as the Battle of the Somme, one of the bloodiest conflicts in recorded history, rages on a few hundred miles away in France, Yu Tsun, positioned in England, endeavors to send a message to his boss in Germany, who will then authorize an aerial attack on an artillery field in the middle of that ferocious battle. The story is therefore organized around the structure of telecommunication, which can be understood as collapsing distance into a common (in the sense of single or shared) space of understanding.[6] Yu Tsun spends the entire story trying to bridge difference and distance to deliver his message and thereby prove his worth as equal to his colonizer. The medium of his message is the name of a man he murders, Stephen Albert, which the boss deciphers as the name of the artillery field and promptly orders destroyed. Both the medium and the result of his message are destructive, and they constitute a response to the destructive instruments of the enemy. Such is communication in wartime.

In addition to its staggering number of casualties, the Battle of the Somme has the dubious distinction of being among the first battles in which both trench and aerial warfare were extensively employed. In trench warfare, armed conflict is simultaneously face to face and mediated by the distance and depth of the trenches; in aerial combat, the distance between combatants is increasingly widened and telecommunication plays a more important role. Indeed, Yu Tsun's "enfermo y odioso" ("sick and hateful") boss, who sits in his office in Berlin waiting for missives (*noticias*) about his subordinates in the field, exemplifies the kind of remote-control warfare that was initiated during this period (OC 1.507; SF 120). However, although the story can be seen as tracing the arc of this transformation, based on the success of telecommunication and subsequent aerial bombing at the end, it also stresses some of the ways that distance and proximity resist and disrupt any simple division of enmity or unification into a static commonality.

The story begins in a doubly disrupted fashion, *in medias res*, because of some missing pages of the transcript of Yu Tsun's declaration, and starting with the words, ". . . y colgué el tubo" (OC 1.506) (". . . and I hung up the receiver" [SF 119]). The story is therefore framed by the motif of telecommunication, although the introduction of the motif exhibits an important difference from its conclusion. The opening telephone call does not constitute a successful act of communication in the sense of establishing a common space of understanding, since it is intercepted by the enemy and subsequently cut off or suspended (hung, *colgado*). The rest of the story consists of Yu Tsun's circuitous efforts to contravene this interception with his own fatal form of communication.

From the intercepted telephone call, Yu Tsun rushes to take a train to the country village to find Albert, the medium of his message. Trains do not collapse distance, like telephones, but they traverse it in such a way that standardizes the experience of space and time. Thanks to the train schedule, Yu Tsun knows how far he has to go to find his victim and he knows how long he has until Madden can follow him. He describes a sensation of "felicidad cobarde" ("cowardly cheerfulness") as the train carries him away from his pursuer and toward his victim, entrusting what might in a previous form of war have relied entirely on face-to-face encounter and the will to kill to the mediation of modern technology, albeit still driven by sovereign intentionality, perhaps even in an intensified form (OC 1.508; SF 121).

Once on board the train, Yu Tsun reflects on the relationship between time and his deadly objective:

> Preveo que el hombre se resignará cada día a empresas más atroces; pronto no habrá sino guerreros y bandoleros; les doy este consejo: "El ejecutor de

Jorges Luis Borges 39

una empresa atroz debe imaginar que ya la ha cumplido, debe imponerse un porvenir que sea irrevocable como el pasado." Así procedí yo, mientras mis ojos de hombre ya muerto registraban la fluencia de aquel día que era tal vez el último, y la difusión de la noche. (OC 1.508) (I foresee that mankind will resign itself more and more fully every day to more and more horrendous undertakings; soon there will be nothing but warriors and brigands. I give them this piece of advice: "He who is to perform a horrendous act should imagine to himself that it is already done, should impose upon himself a future as irrevocable as the past." That is what I did, while my eyes – the eyes of a man already dead – registered the flow of that day perhaps to be my last, and the spreading of the night. [SF 121–122])

Yu Tsun's description transforms time into a linear train-track of intention, in which the future is considered as "irrevocable" as the past. Irrevocable here suggests resolution and immutability but also, with the root of *vox* resonating with the motif of communication, already spoken and received. In other words, the increasing commonality of atrocity constitutes a form of already-achieved communication in which distances and differences, as well as the "fluencia" and "difusión" of time, are contained and controlled. Such a description, furthermore, recalls "Deutsches Requiem" in that it links the individual to the general, in which the past and present are fixed in an atemporal state, and in which one's own mortal perspective ("mis ojos de un hombre ya muerto") reveals a general state of death ("la difusión de la noche").

When he gets off the train, Yu Tsun walks along a bifurcating path in semi-darkness, where he loses his sense of certainty and pre-established completion. He reflects that there is in fact much that escapes wartime action and the generalized structure of enmity:

Pensé que un hombre puede ser enemigo de otros hombres, de otros momentos de otros hombres, pero no de un país; no de luciérnagas, palabras, jardines, cursos de agua, ponientes. (OC 1.509) (I was struck by the thought that a man can be the enemy of other men, the enemy of other men's other moments, yet not be the enemy of a country – of fireflies, words, gardens, watercourses, zephyrs. [SF 122–123])

As he moves closer to committing his atrocious act, he perceives forms of singularity that flicker like fireflies in the currents of the night, beyond the militant limits of intention and the schema of enmity in which he is caught up.

With these thoughts he arrives at a tall iron gate, and through its bars he deciphers ("*descifré*") a line of poplar trees and a pavilion (OC 1.509). The word "decipher" reinforces the motif of communication around which the

40   KATE JENCKES

story is built, which reappears at the end of the story when the boss in
Berlin deciphers Yu Tsun's long-distance message ("el Jefe ha descifrado
ese enigma," OC 1.514). That definitive and deadly deciphering evokes
a play on the root of the word cipher, which comes from the Arabic word
for zero or void (*sifr*). The successful delivery of a (wartime) missive in this
sense can be seen as a double negative that negates the zero by turning it
into a positive integer, of which the standard is the One. However, after
describing the success of his telecommunicative act, Yu Tsun reflects
forlornly that, in spite of successfully deciphering his sinister message, his
German boss "No sabe (nadie puede saber) mi innumerable contrición
y cansancio" (OC 1.514) ("does not know [no one can know] my endless
contrition, and my weariness" [SF 128]). The word *innumerable* stands out,
since sadness and fatigue are uncountable nouns, and suggests that even
though Yu Tsun has carried out his obligation to the order to which he has
sworn allegiance, there is something that exceeds that order, something
that is not reducible to a single totality.

   Returning to Yu Tsun's arrival at Albert's enclosure, it is this tension
between totality and difference, or the "innumerable" excess of the One,
that he "deciphers" through the bars of the gate and throughout his visit
with Stephen Albert. The description of Yu Tsun's approach and first
encounter with Albert emphasizes the ways in which his host is not
reducible to a target (name, missive, or cipher). As he draws near, he
notices (or actively does not notice[7]) the sound of music that seems to
prefigure a different form of communication, since it is described as similar
to language and involves a play of distance and proximity distinctly
different from the organization of distance crucial to the structure of
enmity: "Una música aguda y como silábica se aproximaba y se alejaba
en el vaivén del viento, empañada de hojas y de distancia" (OC 1.509–510)
("A keen and vaguely syllabic song, blurred by leaves and distance, came
and went on the gentle gusts of breeze" [SF 122]). This description resembles the flow and diffusion of day and night that follows Yu Tsun's avowal
of determined action. Furthermore, his experience of hearing the music is
compared to a firefly-like dance of light in the dark – "el chisporroteo de
la música" (OC 1.510) ("the sputtering of the music" [SF 123]) – which is
visually echoed by Albert's approach, discernible at first only as the flicker-
ing light of a lantern, which the trunks of the trees "rayaban y a veces
anulaban, un farol de papel que tenía la forma de los tambores y el color de
la luna" (OC 1.510) ("[a lantern] cross-hatched and sometimes blotted out
altogether by the trees, a paper lantern the shape of a drum and the color of
the moon" [SF 123]). The sparks and glimmer of both the music and the

lantern's approach suggest a fragile uncertainty that does not reveal the approaching other in any solar fashion: "No vi su rostro; me cegaba la luz" (OC 1.510) ("I could not see his face because the light blinded me" [SF 123]). Furthermore, the description of the music as a *chisporroteo*, in addition to constituting a synesthetic trope that corresponds to the paper lantern's combustibility and evokes seeing not as visual capture but as auditory receptivity, also suggests the effect of electrical overload that occurs when electrical flow is not sufficiently isolated or insulated. The sound and sight of sparks thereby not only prefigure the perception and communication of the two characters but also indicate an involuntary effect of their proximity that overloads their individual systems, or "corrects" what may never really be individual or isolated in the first place. This latter sense is suggested by the first words that Albert utters as he welcomes Yu Tsun – even while mistaking him for someone else – as a "correction" to his solitude (OC 1.510).[8]

The misrecognition is overlooked because of a name that is of common interest for both men: Ts'ui Pên, a Chinese ruler and scholar who secluded himself for thirteen years to produce a book and a labyrinth, who was a forebear of Yu Tsun and is an object of study for Albert, who turns out to be an avid Sinologist. Yu Tsun resolves to put wartime on hold – "Mi determinación irrevocable podia esperar" (OC 1.510) ("My irrevocable decision could wait" [SF 123]) – in order to hear Albert's account of his intriguing ancestor. In a sense, Yu Tsun is seeking to shift the authoritative command of enmity, the atrocious imperative to kill the other, to the authority of his cultural and familial past; to recuperate a truer affiliation through bloodline – and ironically through the man he is determined to kill – than the one for which he feels compelled to shed blood. While his murderous intentions are on pause, he seeks to recover the light of his "ilustre antepasado" (OC 1.510) ("illustrious ancestor" [SF 123]), which might redeem or reorient his murky present.

In his conversation with Albert about Ts'ui Pên's enigmatic legacy, Yu Tsun expresses frustration that the writings left by Ts'ui Pên appear incomprehensible, an unsuitable vessel for the continuity of the bloodline: "Los de la sangre de Ts'ui Pên ... seguimos execrando a ese monje. Esa publicación fue insensata. El libro es un acervo indeciso de borradores contradictorios" (OC 1.511) ("We who are descended from Ts'ui Pên execrate that monk. It was senseless to publish those manuscripts. The book is a contradictory jumble of irresolute drafts" [SF 124]). The word *acervo* signifies a heap or pile of things and also, oddly, cultural heritage, or the effort to shape the jumble of history into tradition.[9] Ts'ui Pên's book, however, appears to be a jumble that refuses to be shaped into a useful vehicle for the present. It does not provide a mandate that might replace or at least provide ballast to the "irrevocable determination" that drives Yu Tsun's present. It is indecisive, contradictory, and incomplete; mere drafts that do not cohere into a single, authoritative work. It is therefore appropriate that the key to its interpretation is found in a fragmentary letter, which articulates a different mode of inheritance: "Dejo a los varios porvenires (no a todos) mi jardín de senderos que se bifurcan" (OC 1.512) ("I leave to several futures [not to all] my garden of forking paths" [SF 125]). This fragmentary letter traverses space and time but describes the very structure of both message and legacy as constitutively fragmented, plural and not self-identical. This structure of communication and inheritance reflects the differential nature of both space and time, which, as Albert explains, Ts'ui Pên understood not as uniform and absolute *a prioris* but rather as a vertiginous web of differences that conditions thought, representation, and relation as shifting sands of possibility (OC 1.513–514; SF 127). In this labyrinthine experience of space and time, relation is determined not by the One, whether as bloodline, political allegiance, or elective affinity, but as a fundamentally differential plurality in which communication is possible but never guaranteed, and inevitably incomplete and unresolved, like Ts'ui Pên's fragmentary missives.

This incompletion is, however, generative and even constitutive of life, understood not as an individual subject subsumed by a totalizing order, affiliated with a proprietary bloodline or subjected by a predetermined objective, but as an experience of finitude that exceeds and unsettles human autonomy. At various points in which the structure of enmity is recalled in the course of his conversation with Albert, Yu Tsun describes feeling a powerful "pullulation": "Sentí a mi alrededor y en mi oscuro cuerpo una invisible, intangible pululación" (OC 1.513) ("I felt all about me and within my obscure body an invisible, intangible pullulation" [SF 126]); "Volví a sentir esa pululación de que hablé. Me pareció que el húmedo jardín que rodeaba la casa estaba saturado hasta lo infinito de invisibles personas. Esas personas eran Albert y yo" (OC 1.514) ("I felt again that pullulation I have mentioned. I sensed that the dew-drenched garden that surrounded the house was saturated, infinitely, with invisible persons. Those persons were Albert and myself" [SF 127]). Jolted by the return to an awareness of the global antagonism in which he is a player, Yu Tsun perceives the vertiginous web of differences that underlies all relations, both synchronic (exemplified here by the face-to-face with Albert) and diachronic (exemplified by the texts bequeathed by Ts'ui Pên). The word pullulation suggests a kind of larval swarm that infests both his sense of self and his relation to the other with a plural, burgeoning, but also fundamentally fragile and ephemeral form of possibility, akin to the *chisporroteo* that marked Yu Tsun's approach to this site of encounter and recalling also the aesthetic engagement with radical difference and singularity in "Deutsches Requiem."

As in the latter story, Yu Tsun disavows this multiplicity and pulls the trigger, sending his message via detonation, ostensibly reaffirming the triumph of the single order of a "central" power and simultaneously closing himself into an irrevocable end. Nonetheless, the closing mention of Yu Tsun's "*innumerable*" contrition indicates the irrepressible multiplicity of the future, and the possibility of new drafts and rewritings – such as these stories – that explore the limits of totalizing structures.

Notes

1. My references to Borges' texts come from his *Obras completas*, which I abbreviate throughout the text as OC. Translations are taken from Andrew Hurley's *Jorge Luis Borges: Selected Fictions*, abbreviated as SF, and Eliot Weinberger's *Jorge Luis Borges: Selected Non-Fictions*, abbreviated as SNF.
2. Borges criticism mirrors familiar divisions and developments in literary and cultural criticism. Until the 1990s, the consensus seemed to favor a ludic and self-referential reading of his work (see Balderston 2–3), with several intriguing exceptions. Concomitant with the advent of cultural studies in the 1990s, his work started to be considered in relation to political and historical concerns, although through different lenses, including New Historicism (Beatriz Sarlo, Edna Aizenberg, and Daniel Balderston, with important variations among them), a continued interest in literary craft (Ricardo Piglia, Hernán Díaz, Balderston), and a more philosophically or political-philosophical bent (Alberto Moreiras, Patrick Dove, David Johnson, Brett Levinson, Carlos Pérez Villalobos, Bruno Bosteels, Luis Othoniel Rosa, and Erin Graff Zivin). My work, which falls into the latter camp, owes a great deal to all the above-named critics, among others.

   Although there is a virtual *acervo* of criticism on the two stories that are my focus in this essay, there are few studies that engage the philosophical elements of the stories in relation to the literary details and the political context of world war. The analyses that have been particularly influential for me here include Johnson's discussion of "The Garden of Forking Paths" (159–169), Balderston's chapter on the same story in *Out of Context*, Eva Horn's discussion of enmity in "Borges's Duels," María Díaz Pozueta's "From Philosophical Idealism to Political Ideology in 'Tlön, Uqbar, Orbis Tertius' and 'Deutsches Requiem'," Graff Zivin's analysis of "Deutsches Requiem" in *The Wandering*

44   KATE JENCKES

Signifier, and Paul North's brief mention of "The Garden of Forking Paths" in
The Yield: Kafka's Atheological Reformation (221). This essay also develops
several ideas that I explored in the final chapter of my book *Reading Borges
after Benjamin: Allegory, Afterlife, and the Writing of History* and an article titled
"Walls, Towers, Books: Borges, Kafka, and the Limits of the Proper," published in *The Yearbook of Comparative Literature* (vol. 63, 2017).

3. This coincides in an interesting way with Carl Schmitt's postwar ideas. On
   another note, it is a little perplexing that Borges refers to August 23, 1944, since
   the Germans did not surrender until the 25th.
4. My reading here is influenced by Giorgio Agamben's discussion of Spinoza's
   account of the reflexive form of the verb *pasearse*, which divides the ostensible
   unity of the subject ("Absolute Immanence," *Potentialities: Collected Essays
   in Philosophy*, trans. Daniel Heller-Roazen, p. 234. Stanford, CA: Stanford
   University Press, 1999).
5. See Balderston's discussion of colonialism in this story (43–47).
6. My understanding of telecommunication in this story has been influenced by
   Jacques Derrida's work, including "Ulysses Gramophone: Hear Say Yes in
   Joyce" (trans. François Raffoul. In *Derrida and Joyce: Texts and Contexts*. Eds.
   Andrew Mitchell and Sam Slote, pp. 41–86. Albany, NY: SUNY Press, 2013)
   and "Faith and Knowledge" (trans. Samuel Weber. *Acts of Religion*. Ed. Gil
   Anidjar, pp. 40–101. New York: Routledge, 2002).
7. The fact that Yu Tsun describes his awareness of the music through distraction
   ("sin prestarle atención," 108) recalls Paul North's discussion of distraction as
   a significant alternative to intentionality. North's association between distraction and the structure of the labyrinth (as opposed to the visibly solvable maze)
   is also especially useful for understanding Yu Tsun's approach to Albert in this
   passage (North, *The Problem of Distraction*, p. 102. Stanford, CA: Stanford
   University Press, 2012). In a different vein, but equally intriguing, Balderston
   connects the figure of the labyrinth to trench warfare (50).
8. The misrecognition and wrong name here marks an important contrast with
   Yu Tsun's appropriation of Albert's life and name as a tool of wartime
   communication. If indeed one reads the story as an illustration of the ominous
   nature of successful communication, understood as arrival at a totalizing
   commonality, the scene of Yu Tsun's arrival at Albert's pavilion performs
   a significantly different possibility, in which arrival and communication always
   involve misunderstanding and alterity.
9. See Johnson's discussion of this passage (168).

Works Cited

Balderston, Daniel. *Out of Context: Historical Reference and the Representation of
   Reality in Borges*. Durham, NC: Duke University Press, 1993.
Borges, Jorge Luis. *Obras completas*. Buenos Aires: Emecé, 2006. 4 vols.

Jorge Luis Borges: Selected Non-Fictions. Ed. Eliot Weinberger. Trans. Esther Allen, Suzanne Jill Levine, and Eliot Weinberger. New York: Penguin Books, 1999.

Jorge Luis Borges: Selected Fictions. Trans. Andrew Hurley. New York: Viking, 1998.

Díaz Pozueta, María. "From Philosophical Idealism to Political Ideology in 'Tlön, Uqbar, Orbis Tertius' and 'Deutsches Requiem'," *CR: The New Centennial Review* 9.3 (2010): 205–228.

Graff Zivin, Erin. *The Wandering Signifier: Rhetoric of Jewishness in the Latin American Imaginary.* Durham, NC: Duke University Press, 2008.

Horn, Eva. "Borges's Duels." In *Thinking with Borges.* Ed. William Eggington and David E. Johnson, pp. 161–182. Aurora, CO: The Davies Group Publishers, 2009.

Jenckes, Kate. *Reading Borges after Benjamin: Allegory, Afterlife, and the Writing of History,* Albany, NY: SUNY Press, 2007.

Johnson, David E. *Kant's Dog: On Borges, Philosophy, and the Time of Translation.* Albany, NY: SUNY Press, 2012.

North, Paul. *The Yield: Kafka's Atheological Reformation.* Palo Alto, CA: Stanford University Press, 2015.

CHAPTER 3

Anti-Fascism and Literature in Brazil
The Many Wars of Antônio Callado

Daniel Mandur Thomaz

The spread of fascism in Brazil in the 1920s and 1930s produced a wealth of different cultural and literary responses, from poetry to chronicles, from novels to radio dramas. The geopolitical crisis that culminated in World War II and the radical change in the world order that character-ized its aftermath – the Cold War – had a crucial impact on Brazilian domestic politics and triggered important transformations in Brazilian society. Cultural reactions to these transformations frequently looked to the interwar period for inspiration and a critical vocabulary. In this sense, analyzing Brazilian literature through the lens of transition is a strategy to explore the dynamic connections between Brazilian cultural productions from these different historical moments. In this chapter I will discuss the emergence of anti-fascist ideas in Brazil in the 1920s and 1930s and map cultural productions addressing the topic before, during and after World War II. My aim is to explore how the work of the journalist, novelist, and playwright Antônio Callado (1917–97) can elucidate the historical and cultural links between anti-fascist propa-ganda, the opposition to the populist leader Getúlio Vargas and his dictatorial New State (1937–45), and the resistance to the authoritarian military dictatorship that ruled the country between 1964 and 1985. While the themes, strategies, and political alliances of many writers active in the 1930s and 1940s went through fundamental changes after World War II, and particularly in the 1950s, the work of Antônio Callado dwelled on themes deeply connected with his historical anti-authoritarian stance. In this sense, Callado's experience of cultural and political engagement during World War II informed key aspects of his response to the Brazilian military dictatorship.[1]

Callado's aesthetic and political principles were forged by his experiences as a journalist during Vargas' New State, and particularly while he was working in the British war propaganda machine writing anti-fascist radio

Anti-Fascism and Literature in Brazil

dramas for the BBC Latin American Service in the 1940s. As an intellectual who was not associated with the Brazilian Communist Party in the 1930s and 1940s – in contrast to major contemporary writers such as Jorge Amado, Rachel de Queiroz, and Graciliano Ramos – Callado was as critical of far-right authoritarianism as he was of Stalinism. A progressive Catholic intellectual in the 1950s, Callado's socialist turn in the 1960s was triggered by his frustration at Brazil's social inequalities and by his first political arrest in 1965, for protesting against the military regime. The novel *Quarup* (1967), published two years later, was characterized by critics as a synthesis of literary ambition and political engagement, becoming an iconic instance of cultural resistance against the military dictatorship (Ridenti, "The Debate," 85).

As Brazil transitioned from the 1940s to the 1950s and 1960s, the country's elites bet on a process of conservative modernization – a formula that combined urbanization and industrialization implemented by populist and/ or authoritarian regimes. Callado found in his political and aesthetic experiences in the 1930s and 1940s the themes and strategies to engage with, and respond to, this process.

Fascism and Anti-Fascism in Brazil

The foundation of the fascist-inspired organization *Ação Integralista Brasileira* (AIB) (Brazilian Integralist Action) by Brazilian modernist author and ultranationalist intellectual Plínio Salgado in 1932 represented the amalgamation of different reactionary and authoritarian ideas circulating in Brazil in the 1920s and early 1930s.[2]

Despite his timid presence in the São Paulo Art Week of 1922, Plínio Salgado's participation in Brazil's modernist movement is important to understand his later role as a leader of AIB. His first novel *O Estrangeiro* (*The Foreigner*, 1926) is usually described as containing elements that are key to an understanding of his authoritarian thought, which later developed into *Integralismo*, comprising: Catholic mysticism and moralism (Moraes, *A Brasilidade Modernista*, 128); ultranationalism and anti-liberalism (Candido, *Prefácio*, 20); and radical conservativism and the desire to reinvent the meaning of Brazilianness (Prado 77; Gonçalves 69). In fact, as Salgado pointed out himself in 1935, this novel was his "first Integralist manifesto" (Oliveira, *A produção modernista*, 329). Salgado's *Integralismo* would incorporate key elements of Italian fascism: corporate doctrine, disbelief in democracy, a certain "mythology of the leader," choreography of mass demonstrations, and youth doctrinarism (Bertonha, "Between Sigma and Fascio," 95).

As João Luis Lafetá argues, the modernist debate underwent a dramatic shift from its focus on aesthetic issues in the 1920s to become thoroughly infiltrated by ideological disputes in the 1930s (51). In 1930, Plínio Salgado was exposed to fascism while in Italy, where he met Mussolini in person, and was enthused by fascism's radical nationalism and call for action (Trindade, *Integralismo*, 74–76). One year later, in 1931, Oswald de Andrade, the magnetic intellectual who championed modernist debates in Brazil in the 1920s, became a member of the Communist Party. When Plínio Salgado returned to Brazil in October 1930, the coup d'état that put an end to Brazil's First Republic (1889–1930) and inaugurated a new era of conservative modernization had already taken place, putting Southern oligarch and politician Getúlio Vargas in power.[3]

In Brazil, texts criticizing Mussolini and his *Fasci Italiani di Combattimento* (Italian Fasces of Combat) already appeared in 1919 in anarchist newspapers circulating in the Italian migrant community in São Paulo. In the 1920s, the anti-fascist struggle was considered by many from the Brazilian left as a problem limited to the Italian community and, thus, to be addressed by the Italians (Konder 34–35). From an "Italian issue" in the 1920s to an international, and in fact very Brazilian, issue in the 1930s, anti-fascist activism in Brazil gained momentum with the foundation of the *Frente Única Antifascista* (FUA) (Anti-Fascist United Front) in 1933, an organization led by the Italian socialist Franscesco Frola.

FUA, together with other syndicalist organizations, had a key role in the most emblematic, and violent, confrontation between anti-fascists and *integralistas* in São Paulo, the so-called Battle of São Paulo's Cathedral Square (Praça da Sé) in 1934. The conflict resulted from a left-wing counterdemonstration against the public celebration of the Integralist Manifesto (published two years earlier), which had been organized by AIB to happen on October 7, 1934. The hostilities resulted in seven deaths, including one anti-fascist student, three *integralistas*, and three policemen. The Battle of São Paulo's Cathedral Square was a crucial event in the trajectory of the anti-fascist movement in Brazil. After the violent confrontation in São Paulo, a new coalition of different sectors of Brazilian left and syndicalist organizations led to the formation of the *Aliança Nacional Libertadora* (ANL) (National Liberation Alliance), whose first public manifesto was published in January 1935 (Castro 379).

Brazilian artists, many of whom associated with the Communist Party and ANL, openly supported anti-fascist ideas. Already in 1933, intellectuals such as journalist and author Afonso Schmidt and Brazilian painter Tarsila do Amaral supported the creation of the Brazilian section of the World

Anti-Fascism and Literature in Brazil 49

Committee Against War and Fascism (Castro 359). In 1937, Brazilian modernist Oswald de Andrade included many derogatory references to fascism in dialogues of the avant-garde theatre play fragment *A Sátira na Literatura Brasileira* (*The Satire in Brazilian Literature*), which Andrade refers to as an "antifascist text" (Cunha 123). The dialogue represents a crowd ("the multitude") blindly supporting a leader ("the boss") who communicates only through absurd sentences and is followed by other characters named after animals, including a donkey ("burro," which in Portuguese also means "stupid") and a vulture.

After frustrated communist military uprisings in Natal, Recife, and Rio de Janeiro in 1935, led by Luis Carlos Prestes and supported by the Comintern, the Vargas government immediately launched a witch-hunt against all sectors of the Brazilian left. Many members of ANL and intellectuals who had been associated with the Communist Party, such as Rachel de Queiroz and Jorge Amado, were arrested. Even those who were not officially associated with ANL in 1935 but were engaged with progressive politics were affected by Vargas' brutal political persecution, including the Brazilian writer Graciliano Ramos whose imprisonment is described in his *Memórias do Cárcere* (*Memories of Prison*), published posthumously in 1953.[4] Politically engaged modernists had turned their attention to social issues in the 1930s, a decade marked by neorealist and regionalist novels denouncing Brazil's brutal social inequality, portraying the decadence of the rural world and the contradictions of the country's uneven and conservative modernization (Marques and Bueno 10). This is the case in iconic examples of the so-called *Romance de 30* (1930s novels) such as *O Quinze* (*The Fifteenth*) by Rachel de Queiroz (1930), *Cacau* (*Cocoa*) by Jorge Amado, and *Vidas Secas* (*Barren Lives*) by Graciliano Ramos (1938).

In 1937, Vargas used the communist revolt of 1935 as an excuse to enact another coup, thereby avoiding the election of 1938. After a series of rumors involving a communist plot to take over the country, which was supported by documents later proven to be forged (the so-called Cohen Plan), Vargas imposed a new constitution on the country in 1937 and dissolved parliament. He established himself as a dictator and named the regime the New State. One year later, Brazilian *integralistas* who had eagerly supported Vargas' authoritarian coup, but who were then marginalized by the New State, attempted a frustrated fascist uprising in May 1938. As a result, the integralist movement was dismantled, many of its members were arrested, and its national leader Plínio Salgado went into exile.

Anti-fascism subsequently became more diffuse and broadly associated with the defense of liberal democracy during the escalation of geopolitical tensions in Europe in 1938, and particularly after the beginning of World War II in 1939. It was promoted by pro-Allies groups in Brazil and by US and British propaganda circulating in the country. Taking an anti-fascist stance regarding the war in Europe became an indirect way of criticizing Vargas' authoritarian New State (Calabre 136–137). From modernist poetry to radio soap-operas, references to the war and criticism of Nazi-fascism became widespread in the 1940s. However, Brazilian mainstream anti-fascism – as seen in popular culture and the media – reached a pinnacle after Brazil's entry into the war in August 1942, and especially after Brazilian troops were sent to the Italian Front in 1944 (Bonalume Neto 119; Fortes 179).

On August 22, 1942, following the bombing of Brazilian ships by German submarines, Brazil declared war against the Axis powers. The declaration of war in 1942 came after three years of neutrality under Vargas' regime. The project of state-led industrialization conducted by Vargas in the 1930s and 1940s included a plan to consolidate Brazil's status as a regional military power, which demanded huge investments in heavy industry and infrastructure (McCann 46). Vargas saw the war, and the American alliance with Britain (even before the USA's official declaration of war in 1941), as an opportunity to take advantage of the international situation to promote his national project. In truth, Vargas' government was composed of officials and high-ranking staff members who held different ideological positions. If, in the beginning, the balance was tipped in favor of fascist influences inside Vargas' administration, the agreement sealed with the United States in 1940 to create Brazil's first steel plant, Companhia Siderúrgica Nacional, marked a key change in the regime's alliances. An authoritarian figure, Vargas was above all a great strategist and a cunning opportunist.[5]

The impact of the war, and particularly of the intensive coverage of war events in the press and on the radio, moved and inspired many Brazilian artists and intellectuals, not only in the heat of the moment but also in the aftermath of the conflict. A good example is the collection of poems written between 1943 and 1945 by Brazilian modernist Carlos Drummond de Andrade: *A Rosa do Povo* (*The People's Rose*, 1945). References to the war and to the participation of Brazilian soldiers in the conflict also appear in works of other iconic poets such as Oswald de Andrade, Cecília Meirelles, and Murilo Mendes (Moura 103–345). On the prose front, chronicles of war with an anti-fascist tone were abundant. The most remarkable case is Rubem Braga's *Com a FEB na Itália* (*With the Brazilian Expeditionary Forces in Italy*), published in 1945 when Braga returned to Brazil after following the

Brazilian troops to the Italian Front in 1944 as a correspondent of the newspaper *Diário Carioca* (*Rio de Janeiro's Diary*). A key collection of war chronicles by Brazilian journalists was also edited by the BBC correspondent and Anglo-Brazilian journalist Francis Hallowell in 1946, *Scattoletas da Itália* (*Scatolettas of Italy*), a reference to the food cans distributed by soldiers to the starving Italian population (*scatolettas*). The collection is illustrated with drawings by Brazilian artist Carlos Scliar who went to Italy as a soldier. Among the chronicles in the book are texts by Francis Hallowell, Rubem Braga, and Silvia de Bittencourt, correspondent for the United Press and the only Brazilian female journalist reporting from the Front. Bittencourt also published a collection of her chronicles in 1951, *Seguindo a Primavera* (*Following the Spring*).

Some Brazilian authors engaged in anti-fascist propaganda in the Brazilian press. Jorge Amado, for example, wrote a column, "A Hora da Guerra" ("War Time"), in the newspaper *O Imparcial* (*The Impartial*). He published more than 460 chronicles about the conflict between 1942 and 1944. Rachel de Queiroz also wrote systematically about the war in her column for the newspaper *Correio da Manhã* (*The Morning Mail*) between 1944 and 1945, always with an anti-fascist tone (Palharine 12–14).

The memoirs of Brazilian soldiers and high-rank military officials are relatively abundant, but very few first-hand experiences at the front were reworked through literary strategies to become well-composed novels about the war. Boris Schnaiderman's *Guerra em Surdina* (*Muted War*, 1964) and Roberto de Mello e Souza's *Mina R* (*Mine R*, 1973) are very good exceptions (Carvalho 85–96). The trilogy memoir *O Espelho Partido* (*The Broken Mirror*) describes the daily life of Marques Rabello (the pen name of Eddy Dias da Cruz) during the war period in Rio de Janeiro using sophisticated novelistic strategies. The two final volumes *A Mudança* (*The Change*) (published in 1962 but focused on the years 1939–41) and *A Guerra Está em Nós* (*The War Is Within Us*) (published in 1968 but focusing on the years 1942–4) include fascinating passages on the impact of the war and the circulation of news about the conflict in Brazil.

Inspired by the news about the war, Brazilian playwright Dias Gomes wrote the play *Amanhã Será Outro Dia* (*Tomorrow Will Be Another Day*) in 1941. The play, which has an anti-fascist tone, dramatized the political persecution of a French politician in Nazi-occupied France (Carvalho Silva 81). In terms of popular dramatic productions with a clearly anti-fascist perspective, one of the earliest cases was the radio drama *O Ragabofe dos Vândalos* (*The Vandals' Feast*), written by Renato Murce and broadcast by Rádio Club do Rio de Janeiro in 1942 (Esquenazi 36). This production was a parody of the play *A Ceia dos Cardeais* (*The Cardinal's Supper*, 1902) by the prominent Portuguese writer Júlio Dantas. Instead of depicting three cardinals from Spain, France, and Portugal reminiscing while they enjoy a luxurious feast, Murce's parody presents three ridiculous caricatures of Hitler, Mussolini, and the Japanese prime minister Tojo. It became an immediate success, with many other stations buying copies of the script and rebroadcasting it (Esquenazi 36). Among the soap operas broadcast by Brazil's Radio Nacional, the war became a common theme by 1944.[6] According to Calabre, "In these radio scripts, the supporters of Nazism and Fascism are characterized as villains against humanity, enemies that must be persecuted" (133). This is not surprising since these soap operas were broadcast after Brazil had entered the war. However, in many cases, the criticism of Nazi-fascist authoritarianism and the defense of democratic ideas in the plots could also be read as a veiled criticism of the New State dictatorship (Calabre 130).

In fact, radio dramas are a form of popular literature that encapsulate the relationship between politics, aesthetics, and mass communication in the 1940s. As a literary genre, radio dramas emerged in the 1920s in an environment marked, on the one hand, by intense literary (modernist) experimentation and, on the other, by technological developments that made radio devices more affordable (Whittington 6). In the 1930s, radio drama acquired most of its form and genre conventions, at the same time that radio was being captured by political propaganda (Seul and Ribeiro 367). During the war, radio drama "came of age" and became an established genre (Drakakis 12). When the young journalist and aspiring writer Antônio Callado arrived in Britain to work at the BBC Latin American Service in 1941, radio dramas were the new frontier for propaganda.

The Case of Antônio Callado

Brazilian novelist and playwright Antônio Callado (1917–97) started working as a journalist in 1937, writing articles for *Correio da Manhã*, one of the most important newspapers in Brazil at that time. As we have seen, the year 1937 was also marked by the beginning of Vargas' New State (1937–45), a dictatorship characterized by censorship of the press and political persecution of the opposition. *Correio da Manhã*'s editorial line was critical of Vargas but, because of the fierce censorship by the New State's Department of Press and Propaganda (DIP), journalists working for the newspaper had to use subtle strategies to criticize the government in indirect ways. From a bourgeois Catholic family in social decay, Callado

Anti-Fascism and Literature in Brazil

was not involved in politics in the 1930s but became very critical of Vargas, mainly because of the experience of being a journalist under his regime. In 1941, Callado, then twenty-four years old, applied for a job that not many Brazilian journalists seemed interested in or qualified for: a six-month contract with the recently founded BBC Latin American Service (LAS) to work in Britain broadcasting news and features in Brazilian Portuguese. Taking the job would include, of course, crossing the Atlantic under the threat of German torpedoes.

The BBC LAS was created in March 1938 as part of the new external services in foreign languages, which were designed to counter Nazi and fascist propaganda at a global level and to capture audiences' sympathies and support for Britain (Seul and Ribeiro 367). Latin America was a region of strategic economic and military interest and a source of concern because of its large German and Italian migrant communities (Bratzel and Leonard 8). Italian and German radio stations had been broadcasting content in Portuguese and Spanish to Latin American audiences since the mid-1930s, which led the British authorities to decide that action should be taken in defense of their geopolitical influence in the region (Seul and Ribeiro 369). The programs broadcast by the BBC LAS varied in duration, from only thirty minutes in 1938 to four hours of content in Portuguese and in Spanish every evening by 1943, usually from 8:00 pm (Leal Filho 28). In 1943, the duration of transmissions was considerably lengthened as a result of both technological improvements and the fact that Brazil joined the war on the Allied side in 1942, which drew more attention to the Brazilian section and allowed it to develop more programs.[7] Now, in addition to reports on the war – fifteen-minute-long bulletins broadcast every evening – musical interludes, book reviews, and radio dramas became part of the transmissions. In order to write, produce, and broadcast these entertainment programs in Portuguese and in Spanish, a plethora of Latin American and Iberian intellectuals were hired by the BBC, making them key elements in Britain's war propaganda and cultural diplomacy. LAS functioned as a cultural contact zone where peripheral intellectuals would creatively interact and exchange references in an environment marked by diversity but also by power asymmetries based on geopolitical and colonial imbalances, which was characteristic of the BBC's "corporate cosmopolitanism" (Gillespie and Nieto McAvoy 192).

The recent discovery of a series of radio drama scripts written by Callado to be broadcast by the LAS to Brazilian audiences during and immediately after World War II reveals the role he played in disseminating British anti-fascist propaganda in Latin America.[8] The scripts shed new light on

Callado's work, especially in terms of three important aspects: dating, themes, and style. First, the discovery of these scripts written in the 1940s debunks official chronologies, which usually present Callado's literary debut as taking place in the 1950s, with the staging of his first theater play in Brazil, *O Fígado de Prometeu* (*Prometheus' Liver*, 1951). Now we know that Callado was not only working at the BBC as a journalist but also experimenting as a radio playwright and translator. Second, analysis of this material reveals that many themes that appeared in Callado's works in the 1950s, 1960s, and 1970s were already present in his scripts from the 1940s. For instance, the drama scripts he wrote for the BBC were exploring the relationship between mysticism and politics, which he revisited through the characters and plots of novels such as *Assunção de Salviano* (*The Ascension of Salviano*, 1954) and *Quarup* (1967). Another example is the link between intellectual work and political engagement, which he returned to in *Bar Don Juan* (1971) and *Reflexos do Baile* (*The Ball's Aftermath*, 1976). This is crucial because it reveals the formative influence his experience at the BBC, and his work on LAS anti-fascist propaganda, had on his future literary and political engagement. Finally, the analysis of these scripts, and related documents, now makes it possible to consider the contributions of BBC radio language and style to Callado's writing.[9]

Between 1943 and 1947, Callado wrote and broadcast nineteen radio dramas for the LAS. Although varied in theme, all these dramas share an effort to mobilize Brazilian audiences against the Axis powers and to counter fascist propaganda in the region with good doses of humor and irony. The dramas also have some solemn dialogues about the indignity of living under tyranny and the importance of fostering democratic values. Another repeated theme is, of course, Brazil and its role in the war. Callado seemed keen to justify the country's involvement in the conflict and, more specifically, to resolve symbolically a difficult contradiction: How could a country domestically ruled by a dictator get involved in a geopolitical conflict presented (rather simplistically) in war propaganda as a "struggle for freedom" against Nazi-fascist tyranny? Many of Callado's dramas addressed this contradiction and used references to the war to indirectly criticize Vargas' dictatorship and, in fact, Brazil's authoritarian tradition.

In Callado's drama scripts, the third-person narrator was initially predominant. In 1943, his most prolific year, he wrote ten scripts, of which only two vary from this pattern. However, in the following years, this literature-inspired master narrator would become less prevalent and dialogical radiophonic narratives conducted by two or more characters would become more frequent. This is the case, for example, in: *Cavalcade Carioca*

Anti-Fascism and Literature in Brazil

(*Rio de Janeiro's Cavalcade*, 1944), the story of a British amateur poet interested in writing about Brazil, narrated by a dialogue between the characters Maria (a Brazilian) and Mr. Smith (a British man); *Charles Dickens* (1944), narrated by two unnamed Brazilians discussing the work of Dickens while walking through the streets of London; and *Rui, o professor de República* (*Rui, the Republican Tutor*, 1944), narrated by two Brazilian soldiers at the Italian front discussing the legacy of Rui Barbosa and his struggle against authoritarianism (and military rule) during Brazil's First Republic (1889–1930).

There are also some striking cases of metalanguage when the narrator's voice is openly challenged by a character who tries to undermine his authority in order to take over his role or defy his point of view. This is the case with *Revista do ano* (*Review of the Year*, 1943), where a character who presents himself as "the year 1943" disputes the narrative with a radio announcer, and *Tristeza do Barão de Munchausen* (*The Sadness of Baron Munchausen*, 1944), in which the fictional character Baron Munchausen appears in the BBC studios during a broadcast and steals the microphone to mock the fabrications of Nazi propaganda. These narratives are examples of how Callado developed a polyphonic approach in his dramas and even how the authority of the (master) narrator is undermined and contested in some of these scripts. Callado's growing experience as a radio playwright gradually led him to develop new techniques that were more radiogenic, paving the way for new forms of narrative (Mandur Thomaz, *A Brazilian at the BBC*, 89–132). This was due also to his observation of the radical experimentalism that characterized many BBC productions before and during the war (Bloom 3; Whittington 83–116).

Many of these scripts have anti-fascist themes or are critical of authoritarian forms of government. *Jean e Marie* (*Jean and Marie*), for example, portrays the story of a French couple involved with the resistance against the Nazi occupation of France. In *Lord Byron e a Grécia* (*Lord Byron and Greece*), Byron's death fighting for Greece's independence against the Ottoman Empire is dramatized. In *Correio Braziliense* (*The Brazilian Mail*), Brazilian journalist Hipólito da Costa (1774–1823) is portrayed as a political exile in London shipping his newspaper to Brazil clandestinely to circumvent Portuguese colonial censorship and defend Brazilian independence.

Callado's work was clearly influenced by propaganda guidelines developed in cooperation between the BBC, the British Ministry of Information, and the Foreign Office. These guidelines included suggestions that BBC LAS programs should appeal to the audiences' "fear and self-interest," thus portraying fascism as an international threat. Other "suggestions" included: mobilizing the audiences' "emotions" (e.g., associating whenever possible Christian values with Britain and the Allies), portraying anti-fascist resistance as heroic (e.g., in references to anti-Nazi French resistance), and stressing historical ties of mutual interest and "friendship" between Brazil and Britain (Mandur Thomaz, *Propaganda and Entertainment*, 3–8).

In Callado's dramas, anti-fascism is explored by mocking Nazi-fascist propaganda, associating fascism with tyranny and authoritarianism, and presenting Brazil's position in the war as a commitment to Western liberal democracy. In many of Callado's scripts from the 1940s, the protagonists suffer censorship, violence, and political persecution by authoritarian governments. These could be read as anti-fascist dramas that make indirect critical references to the censorship and political persecution in Brazil during Vargas' regime. These recently discovered dramas put Callado at the center of an international anti-fascist (and pro-Allied) war propaganda machine created by Britain to counter Nazi-fascist propaganda in Latin America, but also reveal how Callado used the platform given to him by LAS to push his own political agenda: criticizing Getúlio Vargas' dictatorship (Mandur Thomaz, *Propaganda and Entertainment*, 10–13).

In 1947, when Callado returned to Brazil, he found a country under a different political regime and a society undergoing rapid transformation. His transition from a radio playwright and anti-fascist propagandist into a theater playwright and novelist occurred as Brazil transitioned from a dictatorship into a period democracy in the 1950s. However, when the effects the Cold War in Latin America were felt most in Brazil, and the escalation of tension led to the military coup of 1964, Callado's anti-fascist stance during World War II informed his political and cultural activism against Brazil's new authoritarian regime.

The Cold War and the Coup of 1964

The end of the war in 1945 was followed in Brazil by the collapse of the political structures that had supported Vargas. Resigning from his post under the threat of a military intervention in 1945, Vargas would still be a powerful presence in Brazilian politics until his death in 1954. The end of the New State, and the realignment of Brazilian political forces, meant that the left, but also the far-right, would reorganize in the period that followed. From the 1940s to the 1960s, Brazilian society experienced a radical process of industrialization, urbanization, and demographic growth (Brito 221–236).

Anti-Fascism and Literature in Brazil 57

The numeric increase of educated urban middle-classes led to the expansion of Brazil's cultural industry, creating more space for the professionalization of intellectuals in fields such as journalism, publishing, and the arts. In the 1950s, together with the novel (a successful commercial genre since the 1930s), films and theater productions became increasingly commercially viable (Miceli 187).

Although forced into illegality in 1947, the Brazilian Communist Party, together with other organizations on the left, became hugely influential in cultural circles, with members and sympathizers in key positions (Rodrigues 411–412). Together with the progressive *Cinema Novo* (*New Cinema*) movement, which included directors such as Glauber Rocha, Leon Hirszman, and Eduardo Coutinho, left-wing politically committed theater groups proliferated in the 1950s and 1960s, such as TPE (São Paulo Students' Company), Teatro de Arena (Theatre in the Round), CPC (Popular Center of Culture), and Grupo Opinião (Opinion Company) (Ridenti, *Cultura e Política*, 138). At the opposite end of the political spectrum, Plínio Salgado – the fascist leader involved in the 1938 putsch against Vargas' regime – returned from exile in 1945 and founded the Party of Popular Representation (PRP) in the same year. The party brought together former *integralistas* in a process of ideological reformulation that focused on anti-communism and ultranationalist rhetoric, Catholic conservativism, and authoritarian ideas, but downplayed their fascist inheritance (Gonçalves and Caldeira Neto 78).

The brief, and dysfunctional, democratic regime in Brazil between 1946 and 1964 was marked by increasing political polarization and economic instability. The impact of the Cold War, particularly the Cuban Revolution (1959) and the North American interventionism in Brazilian internal politics, prepared the conditions for the military coup of 1964 (Pereira 7–17). The most conservative sectors of Brazilian society, which were resistant to the reforms announced by center-left President João Goulart (formerly a Vargas protégé), welcomed and wholeheartedly supported the coup. Although the military dictatorship was not a fascist regime, the links between former members of AIB and the military government were undeniable. In fact, many figures who participated in the coup of 1964 had historical connections with Brazilian integralism (Trindade, *O radicalismo militar*, 123–141; Bertonha, "Sobre Fascismos e Ditaduras," 211; Gonçalves and Caldeira Neto 106–107).

In 1947, Callado returned to Brazil after living in Britain for more than five years. The scripts Callado wrote for the LAS between 1943 and 1947 clearly paved the way for him to become an author of fiction in Brazil. This becomes evident when we observe how he reused these scripts in Brazil, for example broadcasting some of them at Rádio Globo from 1947 to 1949 (Mandur Thomaz, *A Brazilian at the BBC*, 224). Callado managed to build on his experience in radio to start a career as a theater playwright and novelist in Brazil in the 1950s. His first successful theater play was *A Cidade Assassinada* (*The Murdered City*), staged in 1954 by Companhia Dramática Nacional and broadcast by the BBC Brazilian Section the following year. He also published his first novel, *Assunção de Salviano*, in 1954. The impact of the professional connections Callado established after his return to Brazil, now as a cosmopolitan intellectual, and the opportunities he had to travel in Brazil as a journalist, also had an important impact on his literary career (Martinelli 47).

In *Assunção de Salviano*, the eponymous protagonist is a carpenter who is co-opted by the Brazilian Communist Party to lead a peasant revolution in Brazil's northeast disguised as a Catholic preacher. Salviano, nevertheless, succumbs to his disguise and is converted by the very ideas he pretended to hold, becoming a messianic leader. This novel was well received by the influential Brazilian critic and Catholic intellectual Alceu Amoroso Lima and was followed by the publication of *A Madona de Cedro* (*The Cedar Madonna*, 1957), a story about a man who is commissioned by a mysterious criminal organization to steal a statue from a Baroque church and is subsequently haunted by guilt. This first phase of Callado's career as a novelist is usually characterized by critics as deeply marked by his Catholic background (Leite; Martinelli), and reveals a specific combination of neorealism, elements of modernist formal experimentalism, and the psychological exploration of characters' existential anguish. However, it was *Quarup* (1967) that became a bestseller and his most acclaimed work of fiction. It was translated by Barbara Shelby and published in New York by Alfred Knopf in 1970. It centers on the protagonist Nando, a Catholic priest who dreams of founding a utopian Indigenous community in the Amazon rainforest. After losing his faith, the protagonist engages in guerrilla warfare against Brazil's military regime. The novel is said to mark Callado's political turn to socialism in the aftermath of the right-wing military coup of 1964.

The critics who discussed *Quarup*, taking Callado's personal experience and Brazil's political and historical trajectory into account, tend to agree that the narrative is an effort to make sense of the country's recent history. The novel begins in the 1950s and key events such as the death of Getúlio Vargas (1954), the resignation of President Jânio Quadros (1961), and the military coup of 1964 are all represented in the narrative. The journey of Nando is a process of political awakening that represents the

Anti-Fascism and Literature in Brazil

desire of urban middle-class progressive intellectuals such as Callado to confront what was perceived as the Brazilian people's alienation in relation to the social and political imperatives of that particular historical period. *Quarup* was then characterized as an "engaged" novel by most critics, and Callado's work was described as having a "pedagogical" dimension, which led it to be celebrated by the Brazilian left as exemplary (Leite; Ridenti; Martinelli). Marcelo Ridenti sees the novel as the epitome of the "romantic revolutionary sensibility" that emerged from the reorganization of the left in Brazil during the relatively democratic period between 1946 and 1964 (*Artistas e Intelectuais* 85). The imperative to reformulate Brazil's national identity via a narrative that could critically represent the country's social problems was perceived as part of a cultural war against underdevelopment and injustice. Callado's commitment to this project of narrating the nation led critics to associate his work with Romantic (Indigenist) foundational narratives (Leite 141); the stream of socially engaged neorealist and regionalist art that emerged in the 1930s and 1940s (Ridenti, *Artistas e Intelectuais*, 88–89); and the long, and international, tradition of intellectuals who emphasized the educational, and moralizing, dimension of art, including contemporaries such as Jean-Paul Sartre and Bernard Shaw (Martinelli 20).

Callado's turn to socialism was triggered by the military coup of 1964 and his first imprisonment for political reasons in November 1965, while protesting against the new regime in front of the luxurious Glória Hotel in Rio de Janeiro during the conference of the Organization of American States (OAS). He remained behind bars for about twenty days together with other left-wing intellectuals, such as the filmmaker Glauber Rocha and the theater-director Flávio Rangel (Martinelli). Two years later, *Quarup* was published. Briefly after the imposition of Institutional Act number 5 by the military regime in December 1968 – considerably worsening the censorship, repression, and persecution of political dissidents – Callado was once more arrested because of his political views and "subversive activities" as a journalist. However, the seeds of Callado's intellectual and political journey can be found in his radio dramas written for the BBC in the 1940s. In fact, as we have seen, the impulse to produce narratives that address Brazil's contradictions, criticize the country's authoritarian tradition, and represent a commitment to progressive political ideas is something that characterizes Callado's fictional productions in his BBC scripts from the 1940s.

Further investigation of the links between historical forms of anti-fascism and the struggle against far-right authoritarianism in the 1960s is a necessary addition to the existing historiography on the complex and ambiguous links between former members of the fascist-inspired AIB and the military dictatorship (Trindade, Bertonha, Calil, Gonçalves, and Caldeira Neto). In contrast to intellectuals such as Jorge Amado, who gradually drifted from political engagement in the second half of the 1950s – particularly after Khrushchev's denunciation of Stalin's crimes in 1956 – Callado took the opposite path, moving toward left-wing politics in the 1960s.[10] While Amado adopted a more discreet political position after 1964, marked by ambiguous connections with the regime (Calixto 41), Callado built on his anti-fascist propaganda activities in the 1940s to develop his literary themes and authorial voice. In this context, *Quarup* represents both a key turning point in the author's trajectory (from a progressive Catholic to a "subversive" socialist) and an important bridge between his experimentation with radio dramas in the 1940s and his political and literary activism during the military regime.

As the specter of authoritarianism continues to haunt Brazil in the twenty-first century, confirming a long-lasting authoritarian tradition, the study of the transition from anti-fascism in the 1930s and 1940s to anti-authoritarianism in the 1960s becomes a timely enterprise.[11] Understanding how aesthetics and politics dialogue in contexts of political polarization can not only inform our approach to cultural history but also shed light on the conflicts and imperatives of our own times.

Notes

1. For current debates on the terminology of the authoritarian regime here addressed as military dictatorship, see Ridenti, *The Debate over Military (or Civilian-Military?) Dictatorship*, 33–42.
2. For an overview on the bibliography about fascism and integralism in Brazil, from the key work of Helio Trindade in the 1970s to more recent reassessments, see Bertonha, *Bibliografia orientativa*; Oliveira, "A evolução dos estudos sobre o integralismo"; and Ramos 324–347.
3. Although conservative in his political project, Vargas' regime marked the beginning of a process of vertiginous state-led industrialization and modernization of Brazil (Castro Gomes 35–70).
4. Graciliano Ramos only became a member of the Brazilian Communist Party in the 1940s, see Moraes (*O Velho Graça*).
5. For an extensive review of the literature about Brazil in World War II, see Ferraz 207–232. Regarding the participation of Brazilian intellectuals in the conflict, and particularly at the BBC, see Leal Filho; Esquenazi; and Guerrini, Jr.

Anti-Fascism and Literature in Brazil

6. We are distinguishing here between "soap operas" – a genre of serialized daytime dramas that emerged in the 1930s targeting housewives in particular (Horten 149) – and other radio dramas (usually not serialized) that either constituted theater plays adapted for radio or pieces specifically commissioned for the medium (Drakakis 1–36).
7. See, for example, File E17/96/8, BBC Written Archives Centre.
8. The discovery of these scripts in the BBC Archives was reported and discussed elsewhere; see Mandur Thomaz (*Stepping onto an Unknown Island*, 293–321). The author also organized a volume that brings together Callado's drama scripts for the BBC. References to these scripts are taken from this collection; see Callado (*Roteiros de Radioteatro*).
9. Critics such as Paulo Hecher Filho and Carlos Heitor Cony have raised questions about how cinema and even comics might have had an impact on Callado's writing; see Martinelli (45–46). Now there is a very strong case in support of the view that his work at the BBC, and especially his encounters with the work of Anglo-Irish modernists such as James Joyce and Louis MacNeice, had a considerable influence on Callado's writing and aesthetic strategies; see Mandur Thomaz (*A Brazilian at the BBC War-Front*).
10. In the opposite direction is Rachel de Queiroz, who moved from her involvement with the Communist Party and with Trotskyist groups in the 1930s to an enthusiastic support of conservative politics in the 1960s (Guerellus 232).
11. In 2018, far-right populist Jair Bolsonaro was elected with 57.8 million votes. His inflammatory rhetoric includes the celebration of the coup of 1964 and his government motto is "Brazil above everything, God above everyone," which recalls the *integralista* motto "God, Fatherland and Family."

Works Cited

Bertonha, João Fábio. "Radical Right Ideologies and Movements in Brazil." *Oxford Research Encyclopedia of Latin American History*. November 2, 2020. https://oxfordre.com/latinamericanhistory/view/10.1093/acrefore/9780199366439.001.0001/acrefore-9780199366439-e-841.

"Sobre Fascismos e Ditaduras: A Herança Fascista na Formatação dos Regimes Militares do Brasil, Argentina e Chile," *Revista de História Comparada* 9.1 (2015): 203–231.

Bibliografia orientativa sobre o Integralismo (1932–2007). Jaboticabal: Funep, 2010.

"Between Sigma and Fascio: An Analysis of the Relationship between Italian Fascism and Brazilian Integralism," *Luso-Brazilian Review* 37.1 (2000): 93–105.

Bloom, Emily. *The Wireless Past: Anglo-Irish Writers and the BBC 1931–1968*. Oxford: Oxford University Press, 2017.

Bonalume Neto, Ricardo. *A Nossa Segunda Guerra: Os Brasileiros em Combate, 1942–1945*. Rio de Janeiro: Editora Expressão e Cultura, 1995.

Bosi, Alfredo. *História Concisa da Literatura Brasileira.* 52nd ed. São Paulo: Cultrix, [1970] 2017.

Bratzel, John F. and Thomas M. Leonard. *Latin America during World War II.* Lanham, MD: Rowman and Littlefield Publishers, 2007.

Brito, Fausto. "The Displacement of the Brazilian Population to the Metropolitan Areas." *Estudos Avançados* 20.57 (2006): 221–236.

Calabre, Lia. "Encontro entre o real e o ficcional: o conflito e o nazi-fascismo nas novelas da Rádio Nacional." In *Batalha Sonora: O Rádio e a Segunda Guerra Mundial.* Eds. Cida Golin and João Batista de Abreu, pp. 125–38. Porto Alegre: EdiPUCRS, 2006.

Calixto, Carolina Fernandes. "Jorge Amado e a Esquerda: entre a história e a memória (1964–1985)." *Perseu* 8.6 (2008): 36–58.

Candido, Antônio. Prefácio. *O integralismo de Plínio Salgado: Foma de Regressividade no Capitalism Hiper-tardio.* By José Chasin, pp. 11–20. São Paulo: Livraria Ciências Humanas, 1978.

Carvalho, Vinicius Mariano de. "O Brasil na Segunda Guerra sob o olhar de um pracinha. A 'Guerra em Surdina', de Boris Schnaiderman." *Memórias da Segunda Guerra Mundial na Literatura, Cinema e Artes.* Ed. Volker Jaeckel and Elcio Cornelsen, pp. 85–96. Rio de Janeiro: Jaguatirica, 2018.

Carvalho Silva, Aline Monteiro de. "Entre a ficcão e a memória? Dias gomes e a trajetória de um intelectual subversivo." Diss. Universidade Federal Fluminense, 2017.

Castro, Ricardo Figueiredo de. "A Frente Única Antifascista (FUA) e o antifascismo no Brasil (1933–1934)." *Topoi* 3.5 (2002): 354–388.

Castro Gomes, Angela de. "Estado Novo: Ambiguidades e heranças do autoritarismo no Brasil." *A Construção Social dos Regimes Autoritários.* Ed. Denise Rollemberg and Samantha Viz Quadrat, pp. 35–70. Rio de Janeiro: Civilização Brasileira, 2010.

Callado, Antônio. *Roteiros de Radioteatro Durante e Depois da Segunga Grande Guerra (1943–1947).* Ed. Daniel Mandur Thomaz. Belo Horizonte: Autêntica, 2018.

Cunha, Valdeci da Silva. "Oswald de Andrade: da 'Deglutição Antropofágica' à 'Revolução Comunista" (1923–1937)." Diss. Universidade de Minas Gerais, 2012.

Drakakis, John. *British Radio Drama.* Cambridge: Cambridge University Press, 1981.

Esquenazi, Rose. *O Rádio Na Segunda Guerra: No Ar, Francis Hallawell, o Chico Da BBC.* Florianópolis: Editora Insular, 2014.

Ferraz, Francisco Cézar Alves. "Considerações Historiográficas sobre a Participação Brasileira na Segunda Guerra Mundial: Balanço da Produção Bibliográfica e suas Tendências." *Esboços: Histórias em Contextos Globais* 22.34 (2015): 207–232.

Fortes, Alexandre. "World War II and Brazilian Workers: Populism at the Intersections between National and Global Histories." *International Review of Social History* 62.25 (2017): 165–190.

Anti-Fascism and Literature in Brazil

Gillespie, Marie and Nieto McAvoy, Eva. "The BBC's Corporate Cosmopolitanism: The Diasporic Voice Between Empire and Cold War." *Cosmopolitanism in Conflict: Imperial Encounters from the Seven Years' War to the Cold War.* Ed. Dina Gusejnova, pp. 179–209. London: Palgrave, 2018.

Gonçalves, Leandro Pereira. "The Integralism of Plínio Salgado: Luso-Brazilian Relations." *Portuguese Studies* 30.1 (2014): 67–93.

Gonçalves, Leandro Pereira and Caldeira Neto, Odilon. *O Fascismo em Camisas Verdes: do integralismo ao neointegralismo.* Rio de Janeiro: FGV Editora, 2020.

Guerellus, Natália de Santanna. "Rachel de Queiroz Política: uma escrita entre esquerdas e direitas no Brasil (1910–1964)." *Caderno Espaço Feminino* 29.1 (2016): 211–236.

Guerrini, Jr., Irineu. 2006. "Brazilian Section: As Transmissões em Português da BBC Durante a Segunda Guerra Mundial." *Batalha Sonora: O Rádio e a Segunda Guerra Mundial.* Eds. Cida Golin and João Batista de Abreu, pp. 17–35. Porto Alegre: EdiPUCRS.

Horten, Gerd. *Radio Goes to War.* Berkeley: University of California Press, 2002.

Konder, Leandro. Introdução ao Fascismo. Rio de Janeiro: Graal, 1977.

Lafetá, João Luiz. *1930: A Crítica e o Modernismo.* São Paulo: Livraria Duas Cidades, 2000.

Leal Filho, Laurindo. *Vozes de Londres: memórias brasileiras da BBC.* São Paulo: EdUSP, 2008.

Leite, Lígia Chiappini. "Quando a pátria viaja: Uma leitura dos romances de Antônio Callado." *O Nacional e o Popular na Cultura Brasileira: Artes Plásticas e Literatura.* Ed. Carlos Zilio, João Luiz Lafetá, and Lígia Chiappini Leite, pp. 129–235. São Paulo: Brasiliense, 1983.

Mandur Thomaz, Daniel. "Propaganda and Entertainment in the BBC Latin American Service During WW2." *Media History* (2021): 1–18.

"A Brazilian at the BBC War-Front: Entertainment, Propaganda and Modernism in Antônio Callado's Radio Dramas for the Latin American Service (1941–1947)." Diss. University of Oxford, 2019.

"Stepping onto an Unknown Island: The Forgotten Radio Scripts of Antônio Callado." *Portuguese Studies Review* 23.1 (2015): 293–321.

Marques, Ivan and Bueno, Luís. "Em torno do romance de 30." *Teresa, Revista de Literatura Brasileira* 16 (2015): 8–11.

Martinelli, Marcos. *Antonio Callado: Um Sermonário à Brasileira.* São Paulo: Annablume, 2007.

McCann, Frank D. "Brazil and World War II: The Forgotten Ally—What Did You Do in the War, Zé Carioca." Estudios Interdisciplinarios de América Latina y El Caribe 6 2 (1995): 35–70.

Miceli, Sérgio. *Intelectuais à Brasileira.* São Paulo: Companhia das Letras, 2001.

Moraes, Eduardo Jardim de. *A Brasilidade Modernista.* Rio de Janeiro: Graal, 1978.

Moura, Murilo Marcondes de. *O Mundo Sitiado: A poesia brasileira e a Segunda Guerra Mundial.* São Paulo: Editora 34, 2016.

Oliveira, Rodrigo Santos de. "A produção modernista de Plínio Salgado e suas influências no Integralismo." *Historiæ, Rio Grande* 6. 1 (2015): 323–346.

"A evolução dos estudos sobre o integralismo." *Estudos Ibero-Americanos* 36.1 (2010): 118–138.

Palharine, R. S. "A segunda guerra mundial nas crônicas de Raquel de Queiroz (1944–1945): Diálogos." Diss. University of São Paulo, 2016.

Pereira, Anthony W. "The US Role in the 1964 Coup in Brazil: A Reassessment." *Bulletin of Latin American Research* 37.1 (2018): 5–17.

Prado, Antônio Arnoni. *1922—Itinerário de uma Falsa Vanguarda: os Dissidentes, a Semana e o Integralismo.* São Paulo: Brasiliense, 1983.

Ramos, Alexandre Pinheiro. "O integralismo, de Hélio Trindade, quarenta anos depois: Uma crítica à sua recepção." *Antítese* 7.14 (2014): 324–347.

Ridenti, Marcelo. "The Debate over Military (or Civilian-Military?) Dictatorship in Brazil in Historiographical Context." *Bulletin of Latin American Research* 37.1 (2018): 33–42.

"Artistas e intelectuais no Brasil Pós-1960." *Tempo Social* 17.1 (2005): 81–110.

"Cultura e Política: os Anos 1960–1970 e sua Herança." *O Brasil Republicano: o Tempo da Ditadura.* Ed. Jorge Ferreira and Lucilia A. N. Delgado, pp. 133–166. Rio de Janeiro: Civilização Brasileira, 2003.

Rodrigues, Leôncio Martins. "O PCB, os Dirigentes e a Organização." *O Brasil Republicano: Sociedade e Politica (1930–1964).* Ed. Angela de Castro Gomes, pp. 411–412. Rio de Janeiro: Bertrand Brasil, 1995.

Seul, Stephanie and Ribeiro, Nelson. "Revisiting Transnational Broadcasting: The BBC's Foreign-Language Services during the Second World War." *Media History* 21.4 (2015): 365–377.

Trindade, Hélgio. "O radicalismo militar em 1964 e a Nova Tentação Fascista." *21 anos de regime militar: Balanços e perspectivas.* Ed. G. Soares and M. C. D'Araujo, pp. 123–141. Rio de Janeiro: Editora da Fundação Getúlio Vargas, 1994.

Integralismo: o Fascismo Brasileiro na Década de 30. São Paulo: Difusão Européia do Livro, 1974.

Whittington, Ian. *Writing the Radio War: Literature, Politics and the BBC, 1939–1945.* Edinburgh: Edinburgh University Press, 2018.

CHAPTER 4

Disaster Innovation in the Mid-century Spanish American Novel
Carpentier, Asturias, Donoso

Stephen Henighan

In histories of the Spanish American novel written in the aftermath of the Boom, such as Ángel Rama's *La novela en América Latina: Panoramas 1920–1980* (1982) and Gerald Martin's *Journeys through the Labyrinth: Latin American Fiction in the Twentieth Century* (1989), aesthetic transition takes the form of a series of ever-enlarging spirals that encompass increasing cultural inclusiveness, ever-bolder technical innovation, and greater commercial success. Rama and Martin, whose insights have been highly influential, develop the terms "*transculturación narrativa*" ("narrative transculturation") (Rama 203–229) and "the Joycean novel in Latin America" (Martin, *Journeys through the Labyrinth*, 121–195) to analyze mid-twentieth-century works such as Alejo Carpentier's *El reino de este mundo* (*The Kingdom of This World*, 1949), Miguel Ángel Asturias' *Hombres de maíz* (*Men of Maize*, 1949), Juan Rulfo's *Pedro Páramo* (1955), and José María Arguedas' *Los ríos profundos* (*Deep Rivers*, 1958). In this characterization, works such as these represent the first stage in converting a novelistic tradition perceived as having been primarily regionalist in the 1920s and 1930s into one that absorbed the literary techniques of the international avant-garde to lend literary expression to animist cultures, particularly those of Afro-Caribbean, Mayan, Náhuat, and Inca descent, in order to produce a "*novela total*" ("total novel") capable of dramatizing Spanish American societies and their multiple ways of imagining the world. The consolidation of this creative repertoire, in this reading, lays the groundwork for the literary Boom of the 1960s and 1970s, identified most strongly with the novels of Gabriel García Márquez, Mario Vargas Llosa, Carlos Fuentes, and Julio Cortázar, but also exemplified by the work of many other novelists, "though none reached the heights of fame of these four" (Williamson 549).

The Boom's influence was sustained by the continental consciousness that arose through networks of solidarity in support of the Cuban

Revolution, particularly prior to 1971 when the crisis caused by the imprisonment of the poet Heberto Padilla divided the Spanish American left on the subject of Cuba (Iber 222–223). These networks created conditions in which writers "acquired something the area's intellectuals had never possessed before: a mass base" (Castañeda 190). The assumption of perpetual motion toward bigger, more innovative, more comprehensive, more widely read novels occurred in tandem with an optimism inspired by the hope that, as Vargas Llosa said in his influential 1967 speech, "La literatura es fuego" ("Literature Is Fire"), within a few years, "habrá llegado a todos nuestros países, como ahora a Cuba, la hora de la justicia social" (Vargas Llosa, *Contra viento y marea*, 135) ("the hour of social justice will arrive in our countries, as it has in Cuba") (*Making Waves*, 73). These progressive assumptions cast Spanish American novels of the mid-twentieth century into the role of provisional works: imperfect building blocks on the way to the novel that the Cuban Revolution's international notoriety, assisted by the growth of the publishing industry in Spain (Santana 33–63) and the emergence of professional literary agents such as Carmen Balcells (Ayén 181–229), would promote in the 1960s and the 1970s. From the perspective of the 1980s, when many critical commonplaces concerning the Spanish American novel were consolidated, midcentury novels were a transitional literature.

The perspective of the present enables readers to liberate these novels from their confining role as forerunners of the works of later decades by interrogating the portrait of a teleological arc leading to the perceived aesthetic pinnacle of the four central novelists of the Boom. Such challenges may involve problematizing the Boom's sometimes rigid chronology by questioning the inclusion of older writers, such as Ernesto Sábato or Juan Carlos Onetti, whose careers began decades earlier but who are often claimed by the Boom, or cases such as those of Manuel Puig or Fernando del Paso, whose work shares some of the Boom's aesthetic concerns but whose careers do not fit well within the movement's standardized temporal, ideological, or geographical parameters (Lindstrom 197–200). It may take the form of questioning the marginalization of writers whose historical, and even aesthetic, development would seem to correspond to the Boom's tenets but who are habitually excluded because their themes are insufficiently politically engaged, as in the work of Alfredo Bryce Echenique, or because their political engagement was out of step with the Boom's initial Castroite enthusiasms, as was the case of Guillermo Cabrera Infante. It may involve questioning why the Boom is presented as an entirely male phenomenon, omitting even women writers such as Luisa

Valenzuela, Cristina Peri Rossi, Marta Traba, and Elena Poniatowska, who had professional and/or personal connections to one or more of the four central figures.

Contemporary readers, enmeshed in ever-more unpredictable, multiple, disaster-afflicted societies, may interrogate the nature of this transition. From a twenty-first-century perspective, in which ecological crisis, pandemic, and an increasing concentration of wealth make citizens question their societies' medium-term stability, while the proliferation of digital technology debilitates the traditional influence of literary culture, the teleological notion of transition as "transition towards greater artistic achievement and aesthetic complexity" becomes difficult to sustain. The breakdown of the progressive narrative amplifies the significance of discrete events in the past; contemporary readers' immersion in crisis enhances our ability to perceive past disasters as fecund. This context facilitates interpreting midcentury works such as Carpentier's *El reino de este mundo* and Miguel Ángel Asturias' *Mulata de tal* (*Mulata*, 1963), the two novels that will be discussed here, along with José Donoso's *El jardín de al lado* (*The Garden Next Door*, 1981), included as a late-Boom coda, as responses to the disasters of their respective historical eras. It frees readers from viewing these works primarily as steps along the path to an emerging dominant movement in the case of the first two novels, or as representative of that movement's summit of achievement in the case of the latter title.

Bringing the calamitous present to bear on the formation of canons entails recognizing the decisive nature of disaster in cultural innovation. A twenty-first-century view of the origins of Spanish American novels (or, potentially, of any fiction) is, almost necessarily, an anti-tradition posited on a perception that disaster can be a catalyst that wrenches narrative into new shapes. It perceives novels more as products of specific places, histories, and psychologies than as conscious contributions to a hemispheric tradition, even though, by the mid-1960s, it is irrefutable that, among numerous writers of Spanish American novels, a consciousness had emerged of a movement that was larger than any single author. Perceiving innovative fiction, also, as a vital response to disaster, generally at a few years' remove, may draw us closer to the kernels of emotion out of which these works sprang.

Thomas Homer-Dixon labels disaster-inspired innovation "catagenesis": "catastrophe is followed by creativity and eventually renewal" (289). Homer-Dixon's view is not blandly optimistic, yet it does allow for the possibility that large-scale death and destruction may lay the groundwork

68 STEPHEN HENIGHAN

for new formations in human experience and social organization: "all highly adaptive systems go through cycles of breakdown and regeneration. Breakdown is greatly disruptive to parts of the system, but it need not be catastrophic overall, and it can produce exactly the conditions required for a burst of creativity, reorganization and renewal" (289). In a more ominous vein, Naomi Klein, employing some Latin American examples, argues that disaster may be seized upon by sinister forces as a pretext for restructuring societies in ways that concentrate power among a wealthy minority and convert the state into a repressive apparatus. Klein sees civil society structures as becoming "lost in transition" (203) in the scramble to supply ever-greater profits to voracious corporations whose actions are justified by free-market economists such as Milton Friedman and Jeffrey Sachs (93–95, 170–174). In the wake of such disasters as brutal dictatorship, as in 1970s Chile and Argentina, or ecological calamities that are exploited for profit, such as Hurricane Katrina in New Orleans in 2005, Klein interprets attempts to rebuild as movements that do not repudiate the past, or attempt to start again from an ideological clean slate, but rather reorganize the vestiges of what remains, maintaining a consciousness of history, yet reconstructing it in an original form: "renewal movements begin from the premise that there is no escape from the substantial messes we have created and that there has already been enough erasure – of history, of culture, of memory" (561). This is an important contribution to any understanding of catagenesis, and one that is pertinent when interpreting literary creation through the prism of disaster innovation. In Klein's summary, renewal movements "do not seek to start from scratch but rather from scrap, from the rubble that is all around" (561).

In 1937, the Swiss-born Spanish-language writer Alejo Carpentier, who had lived in France and Belgium until the age of ten (Wahlström 71–92), then in Cuba until he was twenty-four, had been residing in Paris for nine years. He had established himself in Parisian literary circles. When the Surrealist movement ruptured in 1929, Carpentier was one of the signatories of "Un cadavre" ("A Corpse"), the Surrealist dissidents' manifesto denouncing the movement's founder and leader, André Breton (Nadeau 300–301). Carpentier did not publicize his political positions on issues such as the ongoing disaster of the civil war in Spain, which the right-wing nationalist forces under General Francisco Franco were winning. When the Chilean poet Pablo Neruda organized a conference of anti-fascist writers to be held in July 1937 in Valencia, where the Republican forces had established their capital in November 1936, he did not regard Carpentier

Disaster Innovation in the Spanish American Novel 69

as a natural participant (Feinstein 127–128, 328). Yet Carpentier's contribution, which included translating the Latin American writers' final communiqué, read by the Cuban poet Nicolás Guillén, from Spanish into French, was crucial to the formation of his later vision as a novelist. On his return to Paris, Carpentier told the Surrealist writer Georges Ribemont-Dessaignes: "Usted no sabe la conmoción que este viaje ha causado en mi vida" ("You don't know what an upheaval this trip has caused in my life") (Vásquez 114). These emotions are evident in his four articles on his visit, collectively entitled "España bajo las bombas" (Carpentier, *Crónicas*, 205–244; "Spain Beneath the Bombs"), which were published in Havana in October 1937. These articles create a vision of the obliteration of centuries of European culture: "Pero bien veremos en Madrid, en la Puerta del Sol, que una bomba de avión, cayendo sobre un edificio, lo reduce a cuatro paredes vacías de todo contenido" ("As we would see clearly in Madrid, in Puerta del Sol, a bomb dropped from a plane, falling on a building, reduces it to four walls vacant of all content") (Carpentier, *Crónicas*, 221). Unlike writers such as Neruda, or George Orwell, the politically neutral Carpentier did not go to Spain to fight for socialism but rather to defend "culture." In his preamble to the four articles, Carpentier writes of how the suffering he witnessed in Spain alienated him from the European rationalism that he had perceived as the source of a universal culture: "nuestra 'lógica del pensamiento' se ha roto ante nuestra 'lógica del corazón'" (*Crónicas*, 205; "our 'rational logic' has broken down before our 'logic of the heart'").

Confronting the disaster of the Spanish Civil War caused Carpentier, who had been aesthetically adrift since his break with André Breton, to question the universality of European culture, and to innovate a cultural aesthetic for the Americas. Two years later, in mid-1939, Carpentier fled Paris for Cuba as General Franco consolidated his grip on Spain and World War II became inevitable, introducing the possibility of a fascist regime in France, the country Carpentier saw as the point of origin of a universal culture, as well as the source of his own identity. In his journalism he announced that the purpose of returning to one's country was to "revisar valores, a rejuvenecer sus nociones" ("to renew values, to rejuvenate one's ideas") (Carpentier, *Conferencias*, 181). His first literary creation after his return to the Americas, an adaptation of Edgar Allan Poe's short story "The Fall of the House of Usher" as a radio play, rewrites Poe's tale of incest and horror as an allegory of the decline of European culture (Henighan, "El hundimiento de la Casa Europa," 85–95). The transition Carpentier undergoes after his return is both of profession and identity: the music critic whose first book after his return to Havana was called *La música en*

70 STEPHEN HENIGHAN

Cuba (1946) became a novelist who promoted a distinctively Latin America aesthetic. Two trips Carpentier made, to Haiti in 1943 and to Mexico in 1944, extended the Europeanized writer's sense of "overseas" cultural difference from the locally Cuban to the broadly Latin American. The trip to Haiti, which was both Caribbean and Francophone, as he was, had a decisive impact on his creativity and provided him with the "scraps" that nourished his literary catagenesis.

Interpretations that depict *El reino de este mundo* as a precursor to Boom novels of the 1960s and 1970s emphasize the novel's transculturating religious syncretism and proto-magic realist transformations of people into animals (González Echevarría 107–129; Martin, *Journeys through the Labyrinth*, 190–191). The present reading focuses on Carpentier's positioning of the novel's cultural elements. This begins with the notorious prologue, in which Carpentier posits "lo real maravilloso" (Carpentier, *El reino de este mundo*, 13) ("the marvelous in the real" [Carpentier, *The Kingdom of This World*, n.p.]) as *the* distinctively Latin American form of cultural expression. Carpentier presents his theory as a refutation of André Breton's Surrealism, asserting the superiority of the intrinsic marvels of the Americas to "Lo maravilloso obtenido con trucos de prestidigitación, reuniéndose objetos que para nada suelen encontrarse: la vieja y embustera historia del encuentro fortuito del paraguas y de la máquina de coser sobre una mesa de disección" (Carpentier, *El reino de este mundo*, 8) ("The marvelous produced by means of conjuring tricks, bringing together objects which would never normally meet: the old and fraudulent story of the chance encounter of the umbrella and the sewing machine on an operating table" [Carpentier, *The Kingdom of This World*, n.p.]). In making this explicit reference to the central image of Breton's *Manifeste du Surréalisme* (*The Surrealist Manifesto*, 1924), Carpentier develops a counter-theory, twenty years after his break with Breton, to refute the Surrealist quest for marvels. The flaw in Carpentier's argument was that the marvelous was itself a European category, a means of exteriorizing cultures regarded as alien to European "universalism" as redoubts of "romance, exotic beings, haunting memories and landscapes, remarkable experiences" (Said 1). In proclaiming, "¿Pero qué es la historia de América toda sino una crónica de lo real-maravilloso?" (*El reino de este mundo*, 17) ("But what is the history of America if not a chronicle of the marvelous in the real?" [*The Kingdom of This World*, n.p]), Carpentier remained within European conceptual categories even as he proclaimed his liberation from their strictures. This contradiction did not prevent his personal catagenesis from reviving his creativity, enabling him to publish his first novel in

Disaster Innovation in the Spanish American Novel

sixteen years, a work far superior to his naturalistic debut novel, *¡Écue-Yamba-Ó!* (1933), and one that opened a creative path to his future novels.

El reino de este mundo tells the story of the slave revolt that led to the creation of an independent Haiti, whose inspiration lay in the slogans of the French Revolution. The slaves employ magic to oppose the European rationalist dictatorship of colonialism and slavery; yet their revolution, in whose imitation of European forms of dress Carpentier perceives "the marvelous in the real," becomes corrupt and decadent. The parallels between the slaves' appropriation of French Enlightenment ideology and Carpentier's own appropriation of Surrealist concepts of marvel and wonder to express an "autonomous" Spanish American vision of history are striking. Yet it is the slaves' reconstruction of a European social order, complete with an invented nobility, elaborate uniforms, and grandiose castles, that provides Carpentier with both the reassurance that the European culture fascism is destroying in Spain, France, and Germany can be rebuilt in the Americas and the insistence that, in its essence, European culture reconstructed in the Americas, by people of African or Indigenous American heritage, will possess a distinctive allure. Carpentier sees the possibility not only of aesthetic renewal in such events but also of liberation from oppressive norms. The novel's two central figures are the French colonist Monsieur Lenormand de Mezy and the slave Ti-Noel. When Lenormand de Mezy flees the slave revolt with Ti-Noel locked in the hold of his ship, he finds in the colonists' refugee community in Santiago, Cuba, a liberating creativity exemplary of disaster innovation effected by the transition from a corrupt old order of which he himself was one of the principal beneficiaries:

> Pero lo raro era que, despojados de sus fortunas, arruinados, con media familia extraviada y las hijas convalecientes de violaciones de negros—que no era poco decir— los antiguos colonos, lejos de lamentarse, estaban como rejuvenecidos ... los que nada habían podido salvar se regodeaban en su desorden, en su vivir al día, en su ausencia de obligaciones, tratando por el momento de hallar el placer en todo ... Todas las jerarquías burguesas de la colonia habían caído. (*El reino de este mundo*, 94–95)

> But the strange thing was that with their fortunes gone, ruined, half their families unaccounted for, and their daughters convalescing from Negro rapings – which was no small thing – the old colonists,[1] far from bemoaning their situation, seemed to have taken a new lease on life ... those who had salvaged nothing reveled in their improvidence, in living from day to day, in freedom from obligations, seeking, for the moment, to suck from everything what pleasure they could find .... All the bourgeois norms had come tumbling down. (*The Kingdom of This World*, 61–62)

This passage's metatextual import is clear: the former colonists innovate a more open society in eastern Cuba from the ruins of their privileged lives in Haiti as Carpentier parlays his experience of the destruction of European high culture into a renewed Latin American literary aesthetic. Though internally incoherent, Carpentier's theory of the marvelous in the real produces a striking literary richness, characterized by incongruous imagery and an engagement with Latin American history. Carpentier's focus on the picturesque qualities of the Haitian revolution – pseudo-French uniforms, European-style castles – does not distract him from the reality that the Haitian poor remain as exploited under the republic as they were under the colony: "Ti-Noel había gastado su herencia y, a pesar de haber llegado a la última miseria, dejaba la misma herencia recibida. Era un cuerpo de carne transcurrida" (*El reino de este mundo*, 196–197) ("Ti-Noel had squandered his birthright and, despite the abject poverty to which he had sunk, he was leaving the same inheritance he had received: a body of flesh to which things had happened" [*The Kingdom of This World*, 148]).

Carpentier's response to the disaster that dented his faith in European culture is intensely personal, as are the later novels in which he develops and enlarges upon his battle between European concepts and Latin American realities: *Los pasos perdidos* (*The Lost Steps*, 1953), *El siglo de las luces* (*Explosion in a Cathedral*, 1962), and *El recurso del método* (*Reasons of State*, 1974). The Guatemalan novelist Miguel Ángel Asturias, who lived in Paris from 1924 until 1933, coinciding with Carpentier for the last four years of his stay, experienced a far more limited interaction with French Surrealism (Henighan, *Assuming the Light*, 181–191). The "progressive" narrative of midcentury novels as a transition toward the 1960s and 1970s brackets Carpentier and Asturias as leading parallel careers in ways that are unhelpful to the appreciation of the fiction of Asturias in particular. Asturias' return in 1933 to a Guatemala ruled by the dictator General Jorge Ubico stifled his creativity. He came into his own during the ten-year liberal, democratic Guatemalan Spring of presidents Juan José Arévalo and Jacobo Árbenz, who governed the country from 1944 to 1954. Asturias served these governments as a diplomat and completed two major novels he had been working on for years: *El Señor Presidente* (*The President*, 1946) and *Hombres de maíz* (*Men of Maize*, 1949). The latter work, characterized by highly imaginative literary adaptations of Mayan mythological motifs, drafted into service to build a national myth of Guatemala, is seen as Asturias' major work. Like *El reino de este mundo*, *Hombres de maíz* has been read as a precursor to 1960s magic realism. There is no denying the novel's mythological force, even though it is susceptible to the criticism

Disaster Innovation in the Spanish American Novel

that it appropriates Mayan belief systems to buttress an ideology of mixed-race liberal nationalism. By contrast, the present analysis maintains that Asturias' most original novel, and arguably one of the greatest and most overlooked novels of modern Spanish American literature, is *Mulata de tal.*

In order to appreciate *Mulata de tal,* it is necessary to uncouple the author from the pairing of "Asturias and Carpentier" as creators of late 1940s and early 1950s fiction conceived as a transition toward the Boom. The roots of Asturias' creativity reach back to his childhood in a Catholic bourgeoisie besieged by the positivist dictatorship of Manuel Estrada Cabrera. Two early experiences were crucial in shaping Asturias' creativity: his family's condemnation to internal exile for five years of his early childhood, between 1903 and 1908; and the 1917 earthquake, which for the rest of his life he would portray as having disrupted Guatemala's social order, and which provided the catalyst for his art. Asturias wrote his first, unpublished novella between December 1917 and March 1918 while living in a tent in which his family had taken refuge after their house became uninhabitable. As he would write in his posthumous artistic testament: "Lo que salvé de mi casa, destruída por el terremoto, fue mi sabiduría poética" (Asturias, *Tres de cuatro soles,* 29) ("What I salvaged from my house, destroyed by the earthquake, was my poetic knowledge").

Mulata de tal is the product of a later disaster: the propagandistic misrepresentation of Guatemala's liberal government as "communist" in the US press (Schlesinger and Kinzer 79–97), which the United Fruit Company concocted to persuade the Eisenhower administration to overthrow the democratic government in 1954 and replace it with a US-backed military dictatorship. This hemispheric disaster convinced even liberal Latin Americans that the democratic road to reform was closed, and only armed struggle could change oppressive social structures, setting the stage for forty-five years of violent Cold War conflict. As Vargas Llosa writes: "la intervención norteamericana en Guatemala retrasó decenas de años la democratización del continente y costó millares de muertos" (*Tiempos recios,* 351) ("the United States intervention in Guatemala retarded the democratization of the continent by decades and cost thousands of lives"). In Guatemala, the US-organized coup led to the internal armed conflict of 1961 to 1996, which killed more than 200,000 people. Asturias, whose books were burned during the coup, spent the rest of his life in exile. As early as 1955, he began work on *Mulata de tal,* which, while it makes no overt reference to political events, became the vessel for his rage at the thwarting of his country's attempt at social reform and the forging of

74 STEPHEN HENIGHAN

a military-oligarchical alliance that, in a pattern described by Klein, oppresses Guatemala to this day.

Mulata de tal, "the most innovative novel to come out of Central America during the 1960s" (Arias 26), has been overlooked because its appearance in 1963, in the same year as Cortázar's seminal *Rayuela* (*Hopscotch*) and four years prior to García Márquez's *Cien años de soledad* (*One Hundred Years of Solitude*, 1967), disrupts the teleological narrative of the Boom novel's rise. During the 1960s Carpentier deftly positioned himself as the Boom's benevolent father-figure, enjoying "the paternity rights that he was exercising then over younger novelists" (González Echeverría 222). Asturias, by contrast, became the embarrassing old uncle that the Boom yearned to repudiate. Vargas Llosa wrote him off as a simple-minded imitator of antiquated "*naturalismo europeo*" ("European naturalism") (*Contra viento y marea*, 388); García Márquez "had been provoking Asturias for years" (Martin, *Gabriel García Márquez*, 354). In 1966 Asturias was criticized from the right for accepting the Soviet Union's Lenin Prize and from the left for accepting an ambassadorship from an ideologically murky Guatemalan president. His Nobel Prize for Literature in 1967 – the first awarded to a Latin American novelist – prompted a jealous reaction from Emir Rodríguez Monegal, the Yale University professor who popularized the idea of the Boom (Iber 198–210). *Mulata de tal*, the target of much derision, has been ignored; yet, more than *Hombres de maíz*, which for all its brilliance articulates the ladino-integrationist official ideology of the 1944–54 governments with regards to Indigenous Mayan people, this novel is an eccentrically individualistic response to national disaster. Its setting, while resembling highland Guatemala, has no fixed historical referent. In the novel's gusts of playful orality, all identities are in flux.

In order to add to his landholdings, the peasant Celestino Yumí makes a pact with the devil, Tazol, that he will enter the market of the adjoining village with his genitals exposed. The chain of events precipitated by this act are shorn of logic or causality. In the market, Yumí meets a mulatta, with whom he develops an antagonistic, sexualized relationship. The mulatta shrinks Yumí's wife, Catalina or Catarina, to dwarf-like proportions, briefly adopting her as a pet. In spite of her sexual voraciousness, the mulatta's gender identity remains unclear: "Para hombre le falta tantito tantote y para mujer le sobra tantote tantito" (Asturias, *Mulata de tal*, 65) ("She doesn't have enough inky-dinky for a man and she has too much dinky-inky for a woman" [Asturias, *Mulata*, 53]). Yumí and Catalina conclude that "existe un género que no es ni gallo ni gallina, el género

Disaster Innovation in the Spanish American Novel 75

neutro" (*Mulata de tal*, 66) ("There's a gender that's neither rooster nor hen, the neuter gender" [*Mulata*, 54). The novel's portrayals of sexuality as an emptiness – "el más solitario de los barrancos" (*Mulata de tal*, 136) ("the most solitary of pits" [*Mulata*, 111]) – for which individuals compensate through unstable elaborations of personalized gender identities, like its carnivalesque narrative randomness and postmodern combinations of discordant elements, were decades ahead of the critical practices of 1963. *Mulata de tal* narrates a frenzy of power struggles and arid sexual encounters between people and animals of a variety of gender identities. The images of sterility that attend these non-fertile couplings, like the arbitrary ways in which bodies expand and contract, names and identities shift, and species merge – the Salvajos (Sauvages), for example, are part human and part wild boar – represent both an opportunity for hectic creativity and a deep anguish at the absence of defined cultural components capable of welding together a stable identity, as *Hombres de maíz* marries ladino and Mayan cultures to buttress a unified Guatemalan nation. The patterns according to which elements are mixed in *Mulata de tal* are aleatory. References to ancient Babylon (*Mulata de tal*, 64) or Jewish Kabbalah numerology (112, 91–92) rub shoulders with Mayan deities such as Cal-Cuj, the devourer of heads (213, 173). Every allusion is brutally torn from its traditional context, being reduced to one more ductile element in a dazzling but despairingly meaningless, linguistically driven riffling through potential cultural juxtapositions. In the novel's concluding scene, a calamitous earthquake, even the basic coordinates of Latin American geography are ripped from their moorings: "la luna tan próxima a la tierra este verano, con los picos más altos de la Sierra Madre, parte de la cordillera andina" (*Mulata de tal*, 394) ("the moon, so close to the earth that summer. The highest peaks of the Sierra Madre, part of the Andean chain" [*Mulata*, 305]).

Even the devil Tazol, who causes Yumí's downfall, shrivels to a docile personage whom the aggrieved couple capture and subdue after Catalina returns to her normal size. Yet a more daunting devil, Cashtoc, ensures that by the novel's conclusion all of the village of Tierrapaulita is ruled by the forces of evil. The *mulata* is rejuvenated, but most of the other characters die amid a quasi-atomic dust raised by the earthquake. Brian Davisson points out that Yumí trades his wife to get land only once his land is threatened: "a clear parallel to both the historical loss of land by the *mestizo* and indigenous population of Guatemala and the repetition of this loss following the fall of the Árbenz government and the repeal of the Ley de Reforma Agraria" (197). The earthquake evokes both the 1917 earthquake and the 1954 coup. Whether *Mulata de tal* represents catagenesis is debatable – it produces no new theorization and offers no renewal of the reformist structures destroyed by the coup – yet in its startling randomness and consistent linguistic inventiveness it stands as one of the most anguished, innovative Latin American expressions of cultural loss.

The crushing of the Guatemalan Spring, whose destruction Ernesto "Che" Guevara witnessed as a tourist (Schlesinger and Kinzer 184), fed the violence of the Cuban Revolution. During the 1960s, inspired by Guevara and Fidel Castro, leftists became guerrillas disdainful of bourgeois democracy. Not until 1970 was sweeping reform again attempted by an electoral coalition. On September 11, 1973 Salvador Allende's Unidad Popular (Popular Unity) government in Chile, like its ideologically milder Guatemalan predecessor, was overthrown by a US-organized coup. The regime of General Augusto Pinochet implemented murderous oppression of the opposition and the destruction of Chile's social programs; these policies had been planned, with specific reference to Chile, at the University of Chicago since the mid-1950s (Klein 66–115). José Donoso, the country's best-known novelist, experienced the disaster of the coup as a change in status: having moved to Spain in the 1960s to join the ferment of the Boom in Barcelona (Ayén 415–454), he was transformed by the coup from voluntary expatriate to political exile.

No writer was more obsessed with the Boom, and with his own membership in it, than Donoso. He described the Boom as having "cuatro sillas fijas" ("four fixed posts"), belonging to García Márquez, Vargas Llosa, Fuentes, and Cortázar, and "una silla más movible, ocupada alternativamente por Ernesto Sabato y por el que esto escribe" (Donoso, *Historia personal del "boom,"* 147) ("a more movable post occupied alternatively by Ernesto Sábato and by he who is writing these pages"). The anxieties evident in this claim of provisional membership, underscored by Donoso's falsely self-effacing phrasing, reveal what his adoptive daughter, Pilar Donoso, described as her father's "conciencia siempre presente y doloroso de no ser un novelista popular, como otros del Boom" (*Correr el tupido velo*, 254) ("ever-present and painful awareness of not being a popular novelist like others of the Boom"). *El jardin de al lado* epitomizes disaster innovation in its move away from the phantasmagoric, quasi-magic realist *El obsceno pájaro de la noche* (*The Obscene Bird of Night*, 1970), which had earned Donoso his fifth-wheel membership in the Boom. In a particularly acrid vein, Donoso returns to the literary influence he had discovered in the early 1950s as a student at Princeton University: Henry James. Jamesian themes of transatlantic experience, social class,

Disaster Innovation in the Spanish American Novel 77

sexual ambiguity, and unreliable narration permeate this novel of Chilean exiles in 1970s Spain. The narrator, Julio Méndez, a minor Chilean writer, is obsessed with trying to break into the Boom. Rejected by an all-powerful literary agent based on Carmen Balcells, Méndez and his wife Gloria borrow a friend's flat in Madrid where he can rewrite his novel. Defying expectations of a Donoso novel, *El jardín de al lado* surprises the reader with its contemporaneity and realism, depicting a post-Franco Spain of ubiquitous marijuana smoking and casual sex, awash with exiled Argentines and Chileans. Roberto Bolaño ranked this as one of Donoso's best novels – "su testamento literario" (Bolaño, *Entre paréntesis*, 99) ("his literary testament," *Between Parentheses*, 108) – and a dramatic innovation in his work because of its use of humor. In it, the freewheeling sense of cultural reinvention conveyed by the Santiago chapter of *El reino de este mundo* combines with *Mulata de tal*'s consciousness of cultural loss.

The apartment Julio Méndez and his wife borrow overlooks the garden of a mansion occupied by a Franquista family whose decadent youth act out orgiastic rituals in a luxurious setting. The sight stirs multiple feelings of exclusion in Julio's mind: exclusion from youth because of his advancing age, the exile's exclusion from his host society, his exclusion from the glories of the Boom, and, most insistently in the novel's imagery, his exclusion from his ailing mother's garden in Santiago, Chile, to which he does not dare return. When Julio's mother dies and his relatives sell her house, Julio becomes aware that exile is not a question of nation but rather of intimate associations: "Uno no vuelve a un país, a una idea, a un pueblo: uno–yo por lo pronto–vuelve a un lugar cerrado y limitado donde el corazón se siente seguro" (Donoso, *El jardín de al lado*, 169) ("You don't go back to a country, a city, an idea; you – I mean me – go back to a house, a limited space where your heart feels safe") (*The Garden Next Door*, 152).

El jardín de al lado, the last novel Donoso published before his return to Chile, where his later work declined in quality, is the culminating novel of the Boom, both because it is explicitly about the waning of the Boom's influence – Méndez states: " el *boom* … era ya sin duda alguna, cosa del pasado" (*El jardín de al lado*, 36) ("The Boom was definitely a thing of the past") (*The Garden Next Door*, 26) – and because it accords a central place to the erosion of the male authority that was crucial in promoting the Boom. Diana Sorensen, who refers to the Boom as "the anxious brotherhood," observes that the novel's concluding Jamesian twist, where the reliability of Julio's narrative is impugned when Gloria becomes the narrator, displays "a telling, inverted symmetry" (158) with the revised edition of Donoso's history of the Boom, published two years later, in which his wife, María del Pilar Serrano, wrote the final chapter. Pilar Donoso recalls that while their return to Chile in 1981 was a dispiriting experience for her father, "a mi madre, en cambio, se le abrió todo un mundo" (*Correr el tupido velo*, 253) ("for my mother, on the other hand, a whole world opened up"), as she became a feminist activist and wrote her memoirs. The posthumous revelation of José Donoso's homosexuality converts Julio's queasy heteronormativity, complicated by his attraction to a friend's bisexual teenage son, and his wife's judgment that he is "ni chica ni limonada en la cama" (*El jardín de al lado*, 174) ("I don't amount to much in bed"[2] (*The Garden Next Door*, 156), into a reminder that, in an artistic context, the selection and arrangement of the "scraps" with which responses to political disaster are innovated, often at a decade's remove from the events, is a personal choice whose ultimate definition lies beyond the scope of any aesthetic movement.

Such intimate associations unravel the attractive, often illuminating, yet ultimately limiting notion that literary transition entails an orderly progression from one literary movement to its inevitable successor. The ruptures and "shocks," in Klein's sense of the word, that mark twenty-first-century experience encourage readers to reassess works that have been viewed as "transitional" – for example, as foreshadowing the Boom's beginning or lamenting its decline – as intimately personal responses to disaster. Viewing novels such as *El reino de este mundo*, *Mulata de tal*, and *El jardín de al lado* as products of catagenesis, and as belonging to the author alone rather than to a movement, does not expel them from literary history but rather enriches their place within it.

Notes

1. A more accurate translation would be "former colonists."
2. This translation does not capture the insinuation of sexual ambiguity conveyed by the original.

Works Cited

Arias, Arturo. *Taking Their Word: Literature and the Signs of Central America*. Minneapolis: University of Minnesota Press, 2007.

Asturias, Miguel Ángel. *Tres de cuatro soles*. Paris: Éditions Klincksieck/Fondo de Cultura Económica, 1977.

    Mulata. Translated by Gregory Rabassa. New York: Delacorte Press, 1967.

    Mulata de tal. 1963. Rpt. Nanterre: Colección Archivos 48, 2000. Ed. Arturo Arias.

Disaster Innovation in the Spanish American Novel 79

Ayén, Xavi. *Aquellos años del Boom: García Márquez, Vargas Llosa y el grupo de amigos quelo cambiaron todo*. Barcelona: RBA Libros, 2014.

Bolaño, Roberto. *Between Parentheses. Essays, Articles and Speeches, 1998–2003*. Ed. Ignacio Echevarría. Trans. Natasha Wimmer. New York: New Directions, 2011.

Entre paréntesis. Ensayos, artículos y discursos (1998–2003). Edición de Ignacio Echevarría. Barcelona: Editorial Anagrama, 2004.

Breton, André. *Manifeste du Surréalisme*. Paris: Jean-Jacques Pauvert, 1962. "First Surrealist Manifesto." In *Manifestos and Declarations of the Twentieth Century*. Ed. Patricia Cormack, pp. 203–226. Toronto: Garamond Press, 1998.

Carpentier, Alejo. *Conferencias*. Havana: Editorial Letras Cubanas, 1987.

Crónicas. Tomo II. Havana: Editorial Arte y Literatura, 1976.

The Kingdom of This World. 1967. Trans. Harriet de Onís. Rpt. London: André Deutsch, 1990. Prologue trans. Heather Martin.

El reino de este mundo. 1949. Rpt. Mexico City: Compañía General de Ediciones, 1967.

Castañeda, Jorge G. *Utopia Unarmed: The Latin American Left After the Cold War*. New York: Alfred A. Knopf, 1993.

Davisson, Brian. "Exile, Allegory and the Totality of the Nation: Miguel Ángel Asturias After the Guatemalan Revolution," *Symposium: A Quarterly Journal in Modern Literatures* 65.3 (2011): 186–206.

Donoso, José. *The Garden Next Door*. Trans. Hardie St. Martin. New York: Grove Press, 1992.

Historia personal del "boom": Nueva edición con Apéndice del autor seguido del "El 'boom' doméstico" por María Pilar Serrano. Barcelona: Seix Barral, 1983.

El jardín de al lado. Barcelona: Seix Barral, 1981.

Donoso, Pilar. *Correr el tupido velo*. Madrid: Alfaguara, 2009.

Feinstein, Adam. *Pablo Neruda: A Passion for Life*. New York: Bloomsbury Publishing, 2004.

González Echevarría, Roberto. *Alejo Carpentier: The Pilgrim at Home*. Ithaca, NY: Cornell University Press, 1977.

Henighan, Stephen. "El hundimiento de la Casa Europa: una reescritura carpentieriana de Edgar Allan Poe." In *Foro Hispánico 25: En el centenario de Alejo Carpentier (1904–1980)*. Eds. Patrick Collard and Rita De Maesseneer, pp. 85–95. Amsterdam: Editions Rodopi, 2004.

Assuming the Light: The Parisian Literary Apprenticeship of Miguel Ángel Asturias. Oxford: Legenda, 1999.

Homer-Dixon, Thomas. *The Upside of Down: Catastrophe, Creativity and the Renewal of Civilization*. London: Island Press, 2006.

Iber, Patrick. *Neither Peace nor Freedom: The Cultural Cold War in Latin America*. Cambridge, MA: Harvard University Press, 2015.

Klein, Naomi. *The Shock Doctrine: The Rise of Disaster Capitalism*. Toronto: Alfred A. Knopf Canada, 2007.

Lindstrom, Naomi. *Twentieth-Century Spanish American Fiction*. Austin: University of Texas Press, 1994.

Martin, Gerald. *Gabriel García Márquez. A Life*. New York: Penguin, 2008.

Journeys through the Labyrinth: Latin American Fiction in the Twentieth Century. London: Verso, 1989.

Nadeau, Maurice. *Histoire du Surréalisme*. Paris: Éditions du Seuil, 1964.

Rama, Ángel. *La novela en América Latina: Panoramas 1920–1980*. Bogotá: Instituto Colombiano de Cultura, 1982.

Said, Edward W. *Orientalism*. New York: Random House, 1978.

Santana, Mario. *Foreigners in the Homeland: The Spanish American New Novel in Spain, 1962–1974*. Lewisburg, PA: Bucknell University Press, 2000.

Schlesinger, Stephen and Stephen Kinzer. *Bitter Fruit: The Untold Story of the American Coup in Guatemala*. Garden City, NY: Doubleday & Company, 1982.

Sorensen, Diana. *A Turbulent Decade Remembered: Scenes from the Latin American Sixties*. Stanford, CA: Stanford University Press, 2007.

Vargas Llosa, Mario. *Tiempos recios*. Madrid: Alfaguara 2019.

Making Waves: Essays, 1962–1983. Ed. and trans. John King. London: Faber & Faber, 1997.

Contra viento y marea (1962–1982). Barcelona: Seix Barral, 1983.

Vásquez, Carmen. "Alejo Carpentier en París (1928–1939)." *Coloquio 2006. Escritores de América Latina en París* (Paris, 2006), Centro Virtual Cervantes: 101–114.

Wahlström, Victor. *Los enigmas de Alejo Carpentier: La presencia oculta de un trauma familiar*. Lund, Sweden: Études Romanes de Lund 107. Lund University Centre for Languages and Literature, 2018.

Williamson, Edwin. *The Penguin History of Latin America*. London: Penguin, 1992.

CHAPTER 5

Struggle at the Margins
Intersections of Gender, Race, and Sexuality in Brazil's Literature of Revolution

Rebecca J. Atencio

Of the many developments in Brazilian literature during the military-civilian dictatorship (1964–85), the boom in works about the revolutionary struggle waged by the clandestine left and its brutal repression by state security forces stands out as one of the most remarkable. The vast majority of works that make up the initial wave of this Brazilian literature of revolution are autobiographical accounts by actual survivors who began drafting their recollections while still imprisoned or exiled in the 1970s. Most only managed to publish their manuscripts after the regime enacted the 1979 Amnesty Law as the first step in a protracted, controlled process of political transition culminating in the inauguration of a civilian president in 1985 and the promulgation of a new constitution three years later.

Albeit the fruit of Brazil's democratic transition, this robust corpus of revolutionary literature has its roots in the 1960s. As that decade dawned, winds of political change seemed to be sweeping Brazil. The 1959 Cuban Revolution galvanized sectors of the left there as elsewhere in the region. The unexpected resignation of President Jânio Quadros in 1961 thrust left-leaning vice president João Goulart into executive office, whence the latter set out to accomplish an ambitious raft of reforms – land, education, and economic. The conservative Congress soon moved to curtail the presidential powers, but some sectors of society demanded a more forceful intervention. Over the night of March 31 to April 1, 1964, the Brazilian armed forces, backed by powerful civilian allies, deposed Goulart and forced him into exile in Uruguay. The generals quickly constituted a military government, branding it the March 31st Revolution.

Meanwhile, parts of the Left in Brazil were in the midst of planning a revolution of their own. Although the Brazilian Communist Party officially opposed armed struggle, the issue provoked a schism and dissidents left to form new groups, including the Communist Party of Brazil (known by its Portuguese acronym, PCdoB, created in 1962), the Popular Revolutionary Vanguard (VPR, 1966), and the National Liberation Alliance (ALN, 1967). Meanwhile, general unrest continued to build through late 1968, and the government responded by declaring its Fifth Institutional Act, suspending civil rights, and temporarily closing Congress. Known as AI-5, the measure unleashed widespread repression and drove most opposition underground. Hundreds of students, workers, peasants, and even some military officers joined clandestine organizations. Most groups advocated urban guerrilla warfare along the lines proposed by ALN leader Carlos Marighella, although the PCdoB also established an ill-fated base in the remote Araguaia region. The ALN and Movimento Revolucionário 8 de outubro (MR-8) (October 8 Revolutionary Movement) pulled off the most spectacular guerrilla operation, kidnapping US ambassador Charles Elbrick in September 1969. Despite such early successes, by 1973 security forces had all but decimated the armed opposition. Those survivors who managed to elude capture went into hiding or exile.

Support for the regime waned by the mid-1970s in no small part because censorship could not entirely suppress news of widespread torture, murder, and disappearances. Public disapproval of ongoing political incarceration and banishment of regime opponents spurred a broad-based social movement demanding amnesty for the persecuted, encapsulated in its rallying cry for "anistia ampla, geral, irrestrita" ("broad, general, unconditional amnesty"). By 1978 the odious AI-5 had expired, and in the face of increasing domestic and international pressure the government passed an amnesty law the following year – one that excluded some ex-revolutionaries and included language protecting torturers from prosecution.

Days after the Amnesty Law went into effect, a former MR-8 member by the name of Fernando Gabeira arrived in Brazil after having been banished for his role in the Elbrick kidnapping. In his suitcase he carried a manuscript with his insider's account of the operation, immediately published under the title *O que é isso, companheiro? depoimento* (a loose translation of the title of the book – which never came out in English – would be *What Happened, Comrade? A Testimony*; it was later adapted as a film: *Four Days in September* [1997]). Dozens of similar works by ex-revolutionaries soon followed, many containing riveting details about the armed struggle as well as shocking disclosures about the state's atrocities. Such revelations tested the limits of free expression with impunity. Back in 1977, authorities had tried to ban the novel *Em câmara lenta* (*In Slow Motion*) and charge the author, ex-revolutionary Renato Tapajós, with

Struggle at the Margins

fomenting subversion under the National Security Law, citing the book's detailed descriptions of guerrilla activities (the only time censors banned a work of Brazilian literature for explicitly political reasons). A military court acquitted Tapajós and lifted the ban, a ruling upheld upon government appeal. This humiliating legal precedent explains why the government tolerated the subsequent flood of revolutionary literature in relative silence (Atencio 54–55).

Most works of Brazilian revolutionary literature published during this period share in common the marked influence of socialist self-criticism in their treatment of the armed struggle. Self-criticism was a ritualized practice internal to organizations within the clandestine left that entailed the explicit admission – collective or individual, but invariably before an audience of one's fellow comrades – of mistakes requiring correction to ensure the success of the revolution. After 1979, militant-authors who published accounts often did so in the spirit of public self-criticism, acknowledging that the clandestine left had erred in persevering in the armed struggle after the writing was on the wall, or that the entire enterprise had been a tragic miscalculation (such admissions were tricky, however, because in making them ex-revolutionaries risked being misinterpreted as absolving state agents of responsibility for their crimes against humanity). Many also framed their past mistakes as a reservoir of experience that could help the left or even civil society navigate the uncharted waters of democratic transition.

Of the many works of revolutionary literature published in the final years of the dictatorship, three became instant classics: *Companheiro* (1979) by Gabeira; *Os carbonários: memórias da guerrilha perdida* (1980; *The Carbonari: Memoirs of a Lost Guerrilla Struggle*) by former VPR member Alfredo Sirkis, which tells of the author's participation in two kidnapping operations targeting foreign diplomats; and *Batismo do sangue: os dominicanos e a morte de Carlos Marighella* (1982; *Blood Baptism: The Dominicans and the Death of Carlos Marighella*) by Frei Betto (Carlos Alberto Libânio Christo), a first-person account of the role that a group of Dominican friars played in assisting Marighella prior to his assassination by security forces. All three books achieved the pinnacle of success, becoming instant bestsellers, winning the prestigious Jabuti literary prize in the memoir/biography category, and yielding successful film and TV adaptations. Together they have helped reinforce the notion that Brazilian revolutionaries were invariably straight, white, middle-class men (although Marighella was of African descent, this fact was rarely acknowledged in the 1970s and 1980s). Most works of revolutionary literature convey a similarly narrow range of experience.

There are at least two notable exceptions, however. One is ex-guerrilla Herbert Daniel's *Passagem para o próximo sonho: possível romance autocrítico* (*Ticket to the Next Dream: A Possible Self-Critical Novel*), which reflects upon the author's sense of exclusion as a gay participant in the armed struggle. The other is Mariluce Moura's *Revolta das vísceras* (*Revolt of the Viscera*), a *roman à clef* that fictionalizes the novelist's experiences as an Afro-descendant, heterosexual woman from Bahia who struggles with the revolution's hostility toward female eroticism. The two books illustrate that its ostensibly egalitarian ethos notwithstanding, the clandestine left marginalized, if not outright excluded, participants on the basis of sexuality, gender, and race (Daniel does not develop the theme of race to the extent that Moura does, although he does mention in passing his own Afro-Brazilian heritage). More specifically, both books explore how the Brazilian revolution shaped each militant-author's understanding of him or herself as sexual beings, and how sexual desire informed her or his revolutionary experiences and subsequent political trajectory. These shared preoccupations help account for each book's blending of memory and fiction to produce hybrid forms strikingly different from the straightforward testimonial mode favored by Gabeira, Sirkis, Frei Betto, and others who, as straight, white men, were writing from positions of relative privilege. More so than any other works published during the twilight of the dictatorship, *Passagem* and *Revolta* lend themselves to an intersectional analysis of the Brazilian revolution and subsequent democratic transition (Crenshaw; Akotirene).

Herbert Daniel's *Passagem Para o Próximo Sonho*

Within Brazil's literature of revolution, Herbert Daniel's *Passagem para o próximo sonho* is a *sui generis* work, as the subtitle *possível romance autocrítico* proclaims from the book's cover. Unlike the classics of this literary tradition, *Passagem* is neither a testimony nor a memoir; it is a novel. Whereas most militant-authors engage in self-criticism, few if any proclaim this intention so openly. And then there is the ambiguous qualifier *possível*, which gestures as much at the work's hybrid form (possibly not a novel at all) as the specific circumstances under which it was written (circumstances such as exile and censorship, imposed as much by the left – a central accusation in the book – as by the military government). Daniel continues this play with language in his preface, in which he turns the Portuguese term *prescrito* (amnestied) into a pun with *pr/escrito* (pre-written) as part of a reflection upon his state of limbo as one of the few

Struggle at the Margins 85

guerrillas who had yet to be amnestied by the government at the time he was writing in 1981:

> Esperei ser prescrito no retardíssimo maio de 1981. Como esperei! . . .
> Mero caso de funcionamento judicial, virei pré-escrito. Gosto do nome; como que: anterior ao escrito. Um que se escreve?
> Se estou, passo a me escrever. (12)

> I hoped to be amnestied in the extremely belated May of 1981. How I hoped! . . .
> On a mere technicality, the decision was postponed, and I became pre-written instead. But I liked the term: as if to say, prior to [one] being written. Or one who writes himself, perhaps?
> If that's my status, what I am, then I guess I'll write myself.

Behind all the punning is the postmodern insight that there is no stable self, nor is there a unitary truth. There is only always fiction; autobiography is impossible and therefore all autobiographies are actually novels, whether they are acknowledged as such or not. Moreover, Daniel employs a number of other techniques to destabilize himself as a testimonial subject, foremost being intermittent shifts to third-person narration of a character he dubs "nosso personagem-autor" ("our character author"), a device that serves as a reminder that the testimonial subject of revolutionary literature is more an avatar than a transparent representation. Although limited to a few chapters, this technique nudges readers to regard *Passagem* (and presumably all revolutionary literature) as something akin to autofiction, in which the first-person narrator-character shares a name and identity with the author but is understood to be a textual construct.

Daniel introduces his "personagem-autor" ("character-author") and begins the process of writing himself in earnest in one of the early chapters of *Passagem*, which begins: "Vamos brincar de faz de conta: imaginemos a possibilidade da existência de um personagem-autor de um romance imperfeito – este –, com as características que invento abaixo" (22) ("Let's play pretend: let's imagine the possible existence of a character-author of an imperfect novel – the one you are reading – with the traits that I've invented below"). Parodying a passport application or other document one fills out with personal information for some bureaucratic purpose, Daniel elaborates on a total of twelve categories pertaining to aspects of his identity, including name, age, sex, nationality, home state, parentage/race, color, religion, education, profession, and marital status. Beyond introducing himself to the reader, Daniel uses this laundry list of biographical data to critique the conventional ways human beings are classified into groups,

86 REBECCA J. ATENCIO

exposing how their tendency to erase intra-group differences leads to gross oversimplifications. The entry for the category of sex is illustrative in this regard:

> *Sexo – masculino*
> (sem nenhuma dúvida, nem vascilação. Embora entre os outros masculinos seja peculiar, minoritário: homosexual.) (22)

> *Sex – male*
> (without a doubt or vacillation, although among males he represents a peculiar minority: the homosexual.)

The descriptor "male" requires not only extra emphasis but also further elaboration insofar as gay men are relegated to the unenviable status of "peculiar minority," revealing it is far from a monolithic category. Daniel also presents his "character-author" as a vivid example of how, within the seemingly homogenous category of Brazilian nationality, a distinction exists between the majority of citizens who are by definition entitled to reside in their homeland and political exiles like him who are denied the right to repatriate. Similarly, his entry for the category of race underscores how factors such as military service and ethnicity complicate the apparent monoliths of "black" and "white." By deconstructing each of the twelve categories in this way, the author articulates a proto-intersectional understanding of how privilege and oppression work in Brazil.

Daniel's retrospection in *Passagem* has less in common with the kind of self-criticism that was de rigueur with Brazil's erstwhile revolutionaries during the democratic transition and more to do with Christian confession, in the Foucauldian sense that the focus of critique is sex as manifested in his thoughts and actions during his militancy (Foucault 19–21). As Daniel explains, like all guerrillas, he adhered rigidly to revolutionary ideology, a key tenet of which was to eschew anything considered "petty-bourgeois," including erotic pleasure. Because revolutionary ideology held that sex was a trivial and personal concern, as a budding militant Daniel decided that he must therefore suppress his homosexuality:

> Desde que comecei a militar, senti que tinha uma opção a fazer: ou eu levaria uma vida sexual regular ... ou então faria a revolução. Eu queria fazer a revolução. Conclusão: deveria 'esquecer' minha sexualidade. (96)

> From the moment I became a militant, I knew I had a choice to make: either I would lead a regular sexual life ... or else I would be a revolutionary. I wanted to be a revolutionary. Conclusion: I must "forget" my sexuality.

Struggle at the Margins   87

He explains that his solution was to remain celibate for the duration of his militancy: "Nenhuma relação homossexual obscureceu meus dias de militância" (97) ("No homosexual relationships tainted my days of militancy").

Daniel observes that if his homosexuality was never a problem for his heterosexual comrades in the organization, that was because either they did not know (because he hid it well) or they did know but preferred to follow his lead and pretend the "problem" did not exist. But this tacit accord with his straight comrades came at a significant personal cost: "*Para* mim, problema. Secreto. . . . Mantinha um comportamento purificado, o sexo na gaveta" (96–97, italics in original) ("*For* me, it was a problem. A secret problem. . . . I kept my conduct pure, and tucked sex away in a drawer"). It is this decision to sacrifice his sexuality for the sake of the revolution – or, more precisely, for the sake of the heteronormative culture of the clandestine organizations to which he belonged – that lies at the heart of the criticism that Daniel directs at both himself and his straight comrades, many of whom "refused ... even to countenance the idea of sexual revolution" (Cowan 64). Above all, his self-criticism focuses on his need to conform: "Se (pensava) nunca chegaria a ser um revolucionário perfeito (meus problemas me marcariam sempre) deveria fazer mais esforço que os outros, os *normais*" (97, italics in original) ("If, I reasoned, I would never be a perfect revolutionary – because my problems would always mark me – I must try harder than the others, the *normal* ones").

Most works of revolutionary literature published in the final years of the dictatorship exude excitement over the new political landscape that was opening up with the democratic transition but have little to say (and none of it critical) about the Amnesty Law, with Gabeira's *Companheiro?* being a prime example (Atencio 5). By contrast, *Passagem para o próximo sonho* represents an important critical intervention into the political debates of the time by arguing that the amnesty was a tool less for dismantling dictatorship than for allowing the military to control the terms of the transition to democracy. As he writes in his preface, "[a] anistia governmental foi decretada como restrição a um sonho geral. Porque o que tantos queriam ... no amplo e no irrestrito era um ato desinstitucional" (11) ("the government's amnesty was decreed to restrict a shared dream, because what we all really wanted when we demanded a broad unconditional amnesty was an act that would de-institutionalize the dictatorship"). The popular amnesty campaign was animated by a dream (of freedom, equality, democracy) that the Amnesty Law denied in various ways, especially by shielding torturers from criminal prosecution. Whereas much of the population acritically celebrated the amnesty, and some fellow militant-authors refrained from critiquing the law's trade-offs, Daniel used the platform his book provided to point out a number of inconvenient truths about the impunity the amnesty engendered, its exclusion of revolutionaries like him, and – through his revelations about homophobia in the sectarian left jockeying for political position in the transition to civilian democracy – its limitations as a vehicle for liberation.

Mariluce Moura's *Revolta das Vísceras*

Like Daniel, Mariluce Moura deviates from the norm of the political testimony/memoir by opting for a hybrid form that melds autobiography and fiction. But whereas Daniel invents a new form proximate to autofiction, what she writes is closer to a *roman à clef*, as she herself has classified the book (Barbosa de Lira 288). *Revolta das vísceras* centers around a woman named Clara and her grief over losing her husband and comrade Roberto, a *desaparecido* (no key is necessary to decode that these two characters are based on Moura and her disappeared first husband Gildo Macedo Lacerda). *Revolta* traces how Clara became active in an illegal revolutionary organization after 1968 and eventually met and married her comrade Roberto. The couple is abducted by the security forces in late 1973 and tortured, all while she was pregnant. The 1979 Amnesty Law functions in the novel as a key temporal reference (the main story is set in its aftermath), a major plot point (its passage extinguishes Clara's fantasy that Roberto might still be alive and forces her to confront her grief), and a target for political critique (specifically, of the popular interpretation of it as a harbinger of peace, harmony, and freedom – three buzzwords from the period that obscure the law's antidemocratic underside). The storyline set in the present of the democratic transition narrates, in the third person, how Clara decides to purge her grief and trauma by recording her memories of the revolution and her political imprisonment in an impassioned letter of farewell addressed to her disappeared husband in what she thinks of as his metaphysical exile. The letter, written in the first person, appears as fragments embedded throughout the novel and traces a process of self-reinvention through writing not unlike what Daniel proposes in his preface.

Clara's social location as an Afro-Brazilian woman, alluded to multiple times throughout the novel, profoundly shapes the way that she tells her story of revolution and differentiates it from most other works of revolutionary literature published in the late 1970s and early 80s. Perhaps the narrative's most unusual characteristic is its framing as a story of female friendship between Clara and Maria, a classmate whose older brother João is a revolutionary. In pondering where to begin in telling the story of her

Struggle at the Margins 89

militancy, Clara settles on this friendship: "Maria fora o primeiro meio e fascinara Clara porque sabia de coisas misteriosas e clandestinas, de partidos e nomes frios e vidas forjadas" (40) ("Maria was the initial contact and her knowledge of mysterious and clandestine things like illegal parties, code-names, and forged lives fascinated Clara"). As highschoolers – aged seventeen – the pair starts attending political assemblies and marches together; after these become illegal under the AI-5, they join an underground revolutionary group. In contrast to *Companheiro* and *Passagem*, *Revolta* focuses on the more mundane side of the clandestine left: Clara and Maria's activities consist mainly of trying to recruit other youth to the opposition cause, believing socialist revolution to be imminent and inevitable in Brazil despite obvious setbacks such as the AI-5, which persists for ten years despite the protagonist's certainty that "passaria logo" (46) ("it would soon be over").

The young women's friendship comes to represent the entanglement of – and tensions between – the sexual (embodied by Clara) and the political (personified by Maria), such that "Há Maria em Clara, há Clara em Maria" (38–39) ("There's some of Maria in Clara, and vice versa"). Unlike Daniel, Clara (and Maria) initially believes that their newfound politics are their path to sexual liberation. Their initiation into revolutionary life imbues them with a sense of empowerment in relation to conventional gender roles and sexual scripts as they experiment with new behaviors such as asking men out on dates. Indeed, whereas for Daniel the revolutionary code of conduct is only ever a heteronormative strait-jacket, for Maria it is a tool for questioning and rethinking the patriarchal institution most oppressive to women, marriage, a lesson she passes on to Clara when introducing her friend to the notion of premarital sex.

At the same time, there are early signs that joining the revolution might not be the path to true liberation. In the description of Clara's initiation into her clandestine organization, a sudden shift from third to second person signals the magnitude of the rupture in her life: "Clara não sabia, nem pressentia, aqui o corte, a mudança enorme .... Agora cada gesto será regido por uma doutrina, porque você será iniciada na doutrina, cada comportamento será cobrado em breve, por você mesma, pelos princípios da ideologia" (41) ("Little did Clara know just how much her life would change. . . . Now each gesture would be dictated by a doctrine because you've been indoctrinated, every little behavior will be scrutinized by you yourself as to whether it aligns with your new ideological principles"). Like Daniel, Moura depicts revolutionary ideology as a potent disciplinary tool that coerces militants into self-surveillance and self-disciplining.

Revolta portrays the clandestine left as a masculinist culture that demands conformity from female militants in particular. For Clara and Maria, making themselves legible as revolutionaries requires above all renouncing their femininity, symbolized by the organization's strict dress code, which the protagonist regards with profound ambivalence: "Clara se imaginava vestindo um vestido desbotado, o rosto lavado sem nenhuma pintura . . . uma ponta de tristeza se insinuava e ela a afastava com vigor, entregue ao seu destino" (44) "(Clara imagined wearing a shapeless dress, her faced scrubbed of all make-up . . .. She felt a prick of sadness, which she vigorously dismissed, resigned to her destiny"). Earning recognition as revolutionaries likewise requires the two women to retrain their bodies to perform their male comrades' revolutionary masculinity: "Imitar o andar, o falar, os gestos dos líderes que lhes pareciam mais atraentes e eram homens, sempre homens" (41) ("Imitating the strut, the speech, the gestures of the most attractive leaders and these were men, always men").

Revolutionary life imposes additional burdens on Clara as a Black woman, which come across most clearly in the novel's only direct description of the work she carries out for her revolutionary organization. On this occasion, the protagonist is walking to a remote Salvador neighborhood to discharge a vaguely defined revolutionary assignment, "de saia e blusa de manga cumprida numa manhã cheia de sol de domingo" (43) ("clothed in a skirt and long-sleeved blouse on a bright Sunday morning"):

> À sua frente passavam duas pretas novinhas, num caminhar provocante, ancas ondulando sensualmente. Sob a malha fina do vestido, a marca do biquíni, lá se iam para as praias distantes que escolhiam em dia de domingo todas as pessoas do bairro. Os rapazes que conhecia desde menina, . . . assoviavam à passagem das moças, deixe eu ir com você minha filha? Sacanas. Ela – Clara ou Maria? – segurava mais seu corpo duro, vencia o chão batendo com força os calcanhares e seguia. (43–44)
>
> Along the way, she noticed two young Black girls walking just ahead of her with their sensual gait, their hips asway. They were both clad in sundresses layered over bikinis, the outlines of which were just visible beneath the thin cloth. Some young guys she had known since she was little . . . whistled at the pair, catcalling them as they passed by – hey baby, can I come too? Creeps. She – Clara or Maria? – felt her rigid body clench more tightly, her heels pounding on the pavement as she hurried along.

Moura constructs the narrative of the incident as a series of contrasts, the main one being a leisurely walk on a sunny day that turns into an ugly scene of street harassment and misogynoir. Clara and the young girls are all made acutely aware of the oppressive male gaze, she in the prim outfit expected of

Struggle at the Margins 91

a female revolutionary (climatological conditions notwithstanding) and they in their sundresses layered over bikinis. Moreover, the casual and graceful gait of the two girls prior to being accosted by the young men contrasts sharply with the rigidity of Clara's body as she senses danger, as do Mao's commandment to love the people and the protagonist's own silent cursing of the harassers as "*sacanas*" ("creeps"). The ostensible confusion in names – "Clara or Maria?" – suggests a raging internal struggle between her ideological programming as a revolutionary (her inner "Maria") and her impulse to listen to her own body, with the former ultimately overriding the latter. In other words, Clara's indoctrinated belief that class is the root of all injustice wavers momentarily in the face of this unexpected reminder of how Black women and girls face oppression compounded by the intersection of gender and race. Much like Daniel, she quickly dismisses such personally relevant concerns as "rasteiras que a ideologia pequeno-burguesa, da qual ainda não conseguira se desvencilhar, lhe passava" (43–44) ("mind tricks played by the petty-bourgeois ideology she had yet to fully shed").

The full import of the catcalling episode only becomes apparent toward the end of the novel when Clara recalls the sense of powerlessness she felt at age twelve when a man molested her on a bus: "Gostaria de se virar para trás, dar uma bronca terrível, . . . ah, mas isso não tinha coragem de fazer, era um comportamento muito vulgar, assim lhe ensinaram" (102) ("She had wanted to confront him and chew him out . . . yeah, but she didn't have the courage to do it because it would be vulgar to make a scene, at least that's what she'd been taught growing up"). The seventeen-year-old budding revolutionary Clara is as disempowered as she was as a twelve-year-old schoolgirl on the bus, the only difference being that whereas before she remained silent in the face of sexual assault because of patriarchal norms, this time she refrains from reacting to the street harassers because of the very revolutionary ideology that she thought would bring her sexual liberation.

Clara comes to increasingly question revolutionary politics, primarily because of her group's oppressiveness toward women and its hostility toward female sexuality. The male leaders of the organization police the behavior of women, at one point interrogating and humiliating a female comrade who is romantically involved with a man unaffiliated with the cause, demanding she terminate the relationship. Within the hypermasculinist and heteronormative clandestine left portrayed in the novel, women militants are subjected to intense pressure to partner only with male comrades and disregard questions of attraction and compatibility, a state of affairs whose sole beneficiaries, she realizes, are the men within the organization. The clearest example of the patriarchal oppressiveness of the left comes from Maria. The only female character in the novel who restricts her pool of potential romantic partners to men in her organization as a matter of ideological conviction, she is left stricken and humiliated by a male comrade and romantic interest who repudiates her as a "puta descarada" ("shameless whore") after she does not bleed during sexual intercourse, a situation that he interprets as an affront to his masculinity (56). Recounting the ordeal to Clara, Maria expresses shock at her partner's machismo, a quality she views as unfitting of a revolutionary, venting to her friend: "Um companheiro, Clara, como pode? um militante?" (57) ("A comrade, Clara! How could a militant act that way?"). The episode, which is the only time Maria's revolutionary conviction appears shaken, dramatizes historians' contention that some men on the Brazilian left were just as fixated on their female comrades' virginity as was the dictatorship, which regarded opposition activity as a producer of fallen women (Langland 140).

Recalling all these scenes almost a decade later, and in light of the loving and erotically satisfying relationship she forged with Roberto, Clara is struck by the negative impact her militancy in the clandestine left had on her process of sexual awakening as a young woman just coming of age, associating the revolution with "o massacre de uma expressão afetiva livre, da sensualidade no seu sentido mais vasto" (47) ("the annihilation of a free expression of love, of sensuality in its broadest sense, of each person's human fragility"). Whereas Daniel sacrifices his sexuality in the name of revolution, suppressing his desire for the duration of his involvement in the armed struggle, Clara ultimately makes the opposite choice, abandoning her organization. Ultimately Clara does return to militancy, albeit on her own terms, and meets Roberto, a comrade whose politics and philosophy of pleasure aligns with her own. The novel ends with Clara dispatching her letter, indulging in one last erotic fantasy farewell to Roberto, and returning home to the open arms of her second husband.

Like *Passagem*, *Revolta* breaks with most literature of revolution by offering a sustained critique of the Amnesty Law. For Clara, the festive reunions with returning exiles are but painful reminders of the metaphysical exile from which Roberto will never return. She rejects the conflation of amnesty with peace, reconciliation, and freedom. These three buzzwords of the society-wide amnesty campaign appear like repeating motifs throughout the novel, but always treated as "palavras mortas" ("dead words") or "linguagem quase sempre postiça" (36) ("a language that was

Struggle at the Margins 93

almost always fake"). It is the letter she writes Roberto, not amnesty, that finally brings Clara a true sense of peace, reconciliation, and freedom. While the early parts of the novel repeatedly emphasize amnesty as a source of profound injustice for the families of the disappeared, the ending shifts the focus to Clara's ambivalence toward the promise it represents for the future. Hopeful for the possibility of building a new life with her second husband, she remains skeptical that the Amnesty Law heralds meaningful change for her as a Black woman. Fully cognizant of the "limite[s] da liberdade que havia agora" ("the limits of the freedom that existed now") she wonders at "as possibilidades verdadeiras de alargá-los" (122) ("the actual possibilities for expanding those limits").

As previously mentioned, both *Passagem para o próximo sonho* and *Revolta das vísceras* not only came out the same year, they were also published by the same small press, Codecri (the book publishing arm of *O Pasquim*, a satirical publication popular in leftist circles at the time). These similarities were almost certainly no coincidence. Herbert Daniel returned to Brazil in October 1981, the last political exile to receive amnesty. Soon after Codecri published *Passagem*, in March 1982, the press hired him as an internal editor specializing in literature and politics for a period of several months, tasking him with "sift[ing] through a closet full of manuscripts . . . and writ[ing] two-page summaries, either recommending publication or rejection"; he also served on the committee that gave final approval of all acquisitions (Green 198). Daniel's stint at Codecri coincided with the period during which *Revolta* would have been under consideration there.[1] Mariluce Moura had sent her manuscript to the Rio-based press after it was rejected by José Olímpio Press, which had awarded the work a literary prize. In an interview with literary scholar Cristiane Barbosa de Lira, Moura revealed that the editor of a different press turned her down flat on the pretext that he was not interested in publishing "poetry," while another patronizingly told her there was no market for a book by an unknown author without connections in Rio or São Paulo, rationales that exude sexism and racism. In any event, considering the circumstances as well as the affinities between *Passagem* and *Revolta*, it is almost certain that the latter's publication was championed by Daniel, who would have readily appreciated Moura's contribution to the literature of revolution even as other editors dismissed the manuscript.

Herbert Daniel and Mariluce Moura recount stories of marginalization within Brazil's revolutionary struggle of the late 1960s and early 1970s, and thus it is hardly surprising that their published accounts were similarly marginalized in relation to contemporary works – like Fernando Gabeira's *O que é isso, companheiro?* – considered critical and commercial successes. Nevertheless, *Passagem para o próximo sonho* and *Revolta das vísceras* are proof that the literature of revolution is less uniform than a look at the "classics" would suggest. The struggle waged by the clandestine left during the dictatorship – with spectacular kidnappings, daring bank robberies, and other exploits – might seem "sexy" to readers far removed from such events, but that revolution was also sexually oppressive toward women and homosexuals. The most exciting works to come out of this tradition are arguably those that critique the heteropatriarchal nature of the revolution while celebrating sexual pleasure – particularly non-normative varieties – as a legitimate path to liberation. It is a message that is just as relevant now as it was then: more than forty years after the 1979 Amnesty Law, the homophobia and misogynoir that Daniel and Moura boldly denounced is again on the rise in Brazil under President Jair Bolsonaro. All the more reason, then, to revisit these two authors' works.

Notes

1. I'm grateful to historian James Green for suggesting this possible connection to me.

Works Cited

Akotirene, Carla. *O que é interseccionalidade*. Belo Horizonte: Letramento, 2018.

Atencio, Rebecca. *Memory's Turn: Reckoning with Dictatorship in Brazil*. Madison: University of Wisconsin Press, 2014.

Barbosa de Lira, Cristiane. "Mulheres guerrilheiras: a representação de personagens femininas em narrativas brasileiras e argentinas relacionadas às ditaduras ocorridas entre 1964 e 1985." PhD Dissertation, Athens, GA: University of Georgia, 2016.

Cowan, Benjamin. *Securing Sex: Morality and Repression in the Making of Cold War Brazil*. Chapel Hill: University of North Carolina Press, 2016.

Crenshaw, Kimberlé. "Mapping the Margins: Intersectionality, Identity Politics, and Violence against Women of Color," *Stanford Law Review* 43.6 (July 1991): 1241–1299.

Daniel, Herbert. *Passagem para o próximo sonho: um possível romance autocrítico*. Rio de Janeiro: Codecri, 1982.

Foucault, Michel. *The History of Sexuality: An Introduction*. Vol. I. Trans. Robert Hurley. New York: Vintage Books, 1990.

Green, James. *Exile within Exiles: Herbert Daniel, Gay Brazilian Revolutionary.* Durham, NC: Duke University Press, 2018.

Langland, Victoria. *Speaking of Flowers: Student Movements and the Making and Remembering of 1968 in Military Brazil.* Durham, NC: Duke University Press, 2013.

Moura, Mariluce. *Revolta Das Vísceras.* Rio de Janeiro: Codecri, 1982.

PART II

Metropolis and Ruins

CHAPTER 6

Economic, Political, and Ecological Disasters
The Metropolis and Its Ruins in Latin American Poetry in the 1960s and 1970s

Cecilia Enjuto Rangel

Latin American poems about the modern city in ruins in the 1960s and 1970s reveal an urban space in a constant transitional phase; economic, social, and political injustices are normalized, transcribed as part of the dystopic landscape. Pablo Neruda's "Macchu Picchu" and Octavio Paz's "Tenochtitlán" became pivotal, symbolic spaces of the Indigenous heritage, a legacy that these authors sought to preserve amidst the threatening Eurocentric visions of the "thriving," modern urban space and its definitions of "progress." Modern poems on ruins in mid-twentieth-century Latin American poetics tend to avoid nationalist revisions of the past, criticizing rather the effects of present problems such as war or capitalist "progress." As I have argued in *Cities in Ruins*, "modern poems *historicize* ruins . . . and avoid a narcissistic, melancholic reading of destruction" (4). Ruins are often represented as "the witnesses and the victims of time, history, nature, war, pollution, oblivion, and melancholic fascination" (Enjuto Rangel 140).

Ruins are both a reminder of the past and a warning about the future. Diverse literary movements portray ruins as allegorical spaces that trace how the natural overpowers the historical. The modern city in ruins is often a result of modern warfare or the constant change imposed by the capitalist cult of the "new." Svetlana Boym synthesizes eloquently the development of the topos of ruins through history:

> the value of the ruin itself changes through history. In the baroque age, the ruins of antiquity were often used didactically . . . .. Romantic ruins radiated melancholy, mirroring the shattered soul of the poet and longing for harmonic wholeness. As for modern ruins, they are reminders of the war and the cities' recent violent past, pointing at coexistence of different dimensions and historical times in the city. The ruin is not merely

something that reminds us of the past; it is also a reminder of the future, when our present becomes history. (79)

The "slow violence" of modernization and the repressive violence of the state merge in José Emilio Pacheco's and Rosario Castellanos's portrayals of ruins. Like Neruda and Paz, their poems aim to *historicize* ruins by reading contemporary practices of political violence as a continuum, attached to the historical legacies of colonial and pre-Columbian eras.

Although their poetic tones and modes are clearly distinct, Neruda, Paz, Pacheco, and Castellanos all react to the discomfort of a constant state of transition. They reflect on how the many layers of the past support the edifices of the Metropolis, and how the legacies of the Indigenous peoples of Latin America are clearly alive, present, and not merely buried in layers of ruined spaces. These poems echo Walter Benjamin's vision of the angel of history and his critique of progress. Benjamin interprets the angel from Paul Klee's painting as a witness, whose face "is turned towards the past" (Benjamin 249). History is envisioned as "wreckage upon wreckage"; unable to fly, the "angel of history" is propelled by the storm of progress (249). For example, poems such as Castellanos' "Silencio cerca de una piedra antigua" ("Silence near an Ancient Stone," 1952) and Pacheco's "Manuscrito de Tlatelolco" ("Manuscript of Tlatelolco," 1968) reflect on a common history of political and cultural oppression as a product of Mexico's neocolonial state. Just as Neruda revisits the Inca ruins in *Canto general* and Paz evokes the Aztec ruins in "Piedra de sol" ("Sunstone," 1957), Pacheco and Castellanos connect the violence of the Conquest, and Aztec and Mayan legacies, with the contemporary ruins of modernity. Pacheco's and Castellanos' poems about the Tlatelolco massacre aimed to become historical testimonies of what happened in 1968 in the face of the government's cover-up. They intend to provoke in the reader a political awakening that reiterates Benjamin's critique of progress.

Slow Death in Neruda's Poetics of Ruins

Neruda's *Canto general* (1950) was inspired by various journeys across the Americas. The poet's trip to Macchu Picchu in 1943 allows him to redefine his sense of self. Neruda explains that he wrote "Alturas de Macchu Picchu" in 1945, stressing how the ruins made him realize his connection to "el antiguo hombre americano. Vi sus antiguas luchas enlazadas con las luchas actuales" ("the old American man. I saw their old struggles tied to today's struggles") (*Canto general* 235).[1] Neruda aims to reveal in his

Economic, Political, and Ecological Disasters

ambitious poetic project the connections between the contemporary plights for sociopolitical justice and the history of "slow" violence against the Indigenous peasantry by both the Inca empire and the Spanish colonial system. Rob Nixon defines slow violence as "occur[ring] gradually and out of sight, a violence of delayed destruction that is dispersed across time and space, an attritional violence that is typically not viewed as violence at all. Violence is customarily conceived as an event or action that is immediate in time, explosive and spectacular in space, and as erupting into instant sensational visibility" (2). He explains that slow violence can be the product of climate change and environmental catastrophes. The history of political oppression and environmental degradation and exploitation in colonial and postcolonial Latin America can be understood through the lens of slow violence as well. Lauren Berlant's "slow death" is tied to Nixon's "slow violence," as death is not always portrayed as a sudden, traumatic event but as an ordinary, "natural" part of the historical process. Facing that form of "slow death" for Neruda's speaker leads to a moment of revelation, to the Dante-esque journey of the self that leads to a form of "communion" with the buried "other."

The ruins of Macchu Picchu stage Neruda's poetic explorations with the notion of slow violence and the multiple forms of slow death. His critique of how Latin America has been plagued by social, racial, political, and economic exploitation, and slow environmental degradation, stems from the speaker's existential questions in the first section of the text. Different notions of death separate Neruda's "Alturas de Macchu Picchu" from *Canto general*, and the use of apostrophe personifies the concept, paradoxically giving the ruins a sense of living death: "La ponderosa muerte me invitó muchas veces" ("Mighty death invited me many times") (Canto IV) and "No eres tú, muerte grave, ave de plumas férreas" ("It was not you, solemn death, iron-plumed bird") (Canto V). Neruda's speaker encounters death in its existential ascension, which is also often characterized by metaphors of descending, or archeological comparisons: "hundí las manos / en los pobres dolores que mataban la muerte, / y no encontré en la herida sino una racha fría / que entraba por los vagos intersticios del alma" ("I sank my / hands / into the pitiful sorrows killed by death, and in the wound I found nothing but a chilling / gust / that entered through the vague interstices of the / soul") (Canto V). Here, the paradoxical image of an ancestral pain that kills death leads the speaker to an existential, spiritual anagnorisis.

Berlant's notion of "slow death" might come to mind when the neo-romantic poetics of the ordinary meets the extraordinary in *Canto general*.

Neruda's notions of death in the Inca ruins allude to the violence of the conquest, but also to the ordinary, slow violence of the construction of the city itself through the exploitation of the workers: "Devuélveme el esclavo que enterraste!" ("Bring me back the slave that you buried!") (Canto X). Berlant considers that "slow death prospers not in traumatic events, as discrete time-framed phenomena like military encounters and genocide can appear to do, but in temporal environments whose qualities and whose contours in time and space are often identified with the presentness of ordinariness itself" (759). Obviously, the traumatic events of the genocide produced by the Spanish conquest and colonialization are present in *Canto general*, but Neruda's notion of death in this poem responds as well to how death is defined as a slow, historical, ordinary process. Slow dying is a result of what Nixon considers "slow violence," and with those gestures Neruda is trying to make visible the slow violence that permeates throughout Latin American history. Natural metaphors of rebirth abound in "Alturas," where the slaves re-emerge, to be connected to contemporary workers. Far from idealizing Incan society as a petrified past, the speaker claims a position of political solidarity: "Macchu Picchu, pusiste piedras en la piedra, y en la base, harapo?" ("did you put / stone upon stone and, at the base, tatters?") (Canto X). The poem becomes an indictment against a present built on an unjust past. Neruda's accusation of an ancestral hunger that permeates in the present is intensified by the list of imperative verbs, and his prosopopeic act: "Sube a nacer conmigo, hermano . . . Yo vengo a hablar por vuestra boca muerta" ("Rise up to be born with me, my brother . . . I've come to speak through your dead mouths") (Canto XII). Neruda's allusions to the Whitmanian prophetic voice, to Dante's journey, and to Rodrigo Caro's "Itálica" have been amply studied (Santí; Goic; Rodríguez Monegal; Camayd-Freixas; Enjuto Rangel). Still, "Alturas" does not seek religious rebirth, but rather a political encounter with the "buried" voices of the Inca workers. As Harris Feinsod argues, Neruda and Paz reject "the appropriation of the pre-Columbian ruin as a reliquary of romantic nationalism" (1–3). Their poems on ruins reconfigure a poetic indigeneity as a hemispheric project. Both Neruda and Paz use the market-driven tendencies of exoticizing Latin America's historical ruins and the distress at political transitions and instability to revolutionize the poetic form.

Octavio Paz's Dystopian Landscapes

Already in his early works, such as *Puerta condenada* (*Condemned Door*, 1938–46), Octavio Paz explored ruins as a historical and poetic palimpsest.

Economic, Political, and Ecological Disasters 103

The five sonnets of "Crepúsculos de la ciudad" ("The City's Twilights") from this volume criticize the modern urban landscape to explore how modernity eerily defines progress as a constant process of self-destruction and reinvention. These early poems on ruins often embrace the elegiac tone, establishing a homage to the victims of war or "progress." During the same era, Paz's poems on the Spanish Civil War, such as "Elegía a un compañero muerto en el frente de Aragón" ("Elegy for a Friend Dead at the Front in Aragón," 1937), aim to give voice to the "voiceless," in a similar way to Neruda's speaker in *Canto general*. Fundamental texts to understand how to place Paz's work in the transition that leads to the poetics of the 1960s in Latin American poetry are "Himno entre ruinas" ("Hymn Among the Ruins," 1948), *Piedras sueltas* (*Loose Stones*, 1955), and "Piedra de sol" (1957), as they mark a political and historical moment for the Mexican poet. These texts respond both to the Cold War and to the way Indigenous legacies are redefined by contemporary poets.

The structure in "Himno entre ruinas" emphasizes a neo-Baroque chiaroscuro, where oppositional forces and landscapes are clearly differentiated (Fein; Wilson; Enjuto Rangel). Odd-numbered stanzas describe the Classical ruins of Europe, the mythical, natural Mediterranean landscape, and the metaphors of light, symbolized by Galatea. The apostrophe to the broken statue, devoured by time and light, evokes the traditional Baroque paradox: "¡Estatua rota, / columnas comidas por las luz, ruinas vivas en un mundo de muertos en vida!" (*Obra Poética* 233) ("A broken statue, / columns gnawed by the light, / ruins alive in a world of death in life!" ["Hymn Among the Ruins," 22]). In contrast, the even stanzas, written in italics, portray the Mexican ruins, the Cold War shadows, and the darkness of the historical, modern urban landscapes, symbolized by Polifemo, as a bored witness of history. The paradoxical imagery links the mythical with cyclical visions of time and condemns both in an anti-nationalist critique of the violent history of Aztec and European legacies. In this war-apocalyptic imagery, exemplified by "a trechos tirita un sol anémico" (234) ("Now and then an anemic sun shivers," 23), even the personified sun is left shivering, a victim of our dystopian world. However, in "Himno entre ruinas," Paz still clings to a reconciliatory, hopeful tone: "¡Día, Redondo día, / luminosa naranja de veinticuatro gajos ... / se reconcilian las dos mitades enemigas ... / Hombre, árbol de imágenes, / palabras que son flores que son frutos que son actos" (235) ("Day, round day, / shining orange with four-and-twenty bars ... the two hostile become one ... man, tree of images, / words which are flowers become fruits which are deeds," 23–24). "Himno entre ruinas" concludes when, through the apostrophe to

104 CECILIA ENJUTO RANGEL

the day, the sun becomes a juicy orange to reinstate the centrality of nature, cyclical time, and the fruitfulness of poetic acts. Michael Lazzara and Vicky Unruh introduce their collection of essays, *Telling Ruins in Latin America*, as one that "forcefully argue[s] that ruins are dynamic sites . . . palimpsests on which memories and histories are fashioned and refashioned" (Lazzara and Unruh 3). "Himno entre ruinas," *Piedras sueltas*, "Piedra de sol," and *Homenaje y profanaciones* (1960) provoke an ethical response to the ruins, in which literary palimpsests serve as a dynamic critique of a type of progress that ultimately still clings to political, poetic, and even spiritual awakening as a way out of the dystopian era.

The ruins of Mesoamerican cities permeate Paz's works. Echoes of Dante, Petrarch, Góngora, Quevedo, and Baudelaire resonate throughout "Piedra de sol," a poem in which Agamenón, Casandra, Moctezuma, and Robespierre all meet in the same stanza. It constructs its literary palimpsest as a dialogue between the self and the gendered other: "Melusina, / Laura, Isabel, Perséfona, María" (263). While paradoxically remembering this collage of poetic muses, the speaker sends them to oblivion, although toward the end the speaker calls again to "Eloísa, Perséfona, María" to show him "mi cara verdadera, la del otro / mi cara de nosotros siempre todos / cara de árbol y de panadero, / de chofer y de nube y de marino" (276) ("my turn and central face, that of the other, / my face of us all . . . face of the living tree and the breadman, / the driver and the thunderhead, the sailor" ["Sunstone," 44]). Similarly to Neruda in "Alturas de Macchu Picchu," Paz in 1957 also ends with a reference to Juan, an epitome of the common man (276). "Piedra de sol" is conceptualized as a dawn, a door to a new form of poetic conscience. In *City Fictions*, Amanda Holmes explains that:

> With its interlacing of the old and the new cities, "Piedra de sol" exemplifies the poet's perception of the empowering potential of pre-Hispanic Mesoamerican culture for the definition of contemporary identity. The permanence of stone and the circularity of time in this Aztec calendar point to the vitality of this past in the present environment, while the formal elements of the poem also resuscitate precolonial Mexico. (40)

The poetics of the instant, cyclical time, spiritual awakening, and rebirth are all symbolized by the 584-day cycle in the Aztec calendar and its structure, with its 584 hendecasyllables, as Holmes notes. In 1969, revisiting the prevalence of cyclical time, Paz conceptualizes the Tlatelolco massacre as a product of a history of violence, dating back to the Aztecs. Although the poems on the Tlatelolco massacre denounce a mainly "spectacular"

Economic, Political, and Ecological Disasters 105

event, in the sense that it had great visual impact, these poems also allude to a colonial form of slow violence, not limited to environmental catastrophes but extending to gradual forms of ethnic cleansing and genocide.

Paz's, Castellanos', and Pacheco's poetic responses to the Tlatelolco massacre voice a powerful cry for the victims, who were treated as debris in the name of the storm of "progress." The Tlatelolco massacre took place on October 2, 1968, under the government of President Gustavo Díaz Ordaz, just days before the opening ceremony of the Olympics in Mexico City. In *Posdata* (1969), Octavio Paz clearly condemns the Tlatelolco massacre. Although Paz immediately denounced the massacre and resigned from his diplomatic position in India in protest, some of his statements remain controversial. As "Piedra de sol" shows, the Mesoamerican legacy inspires his work, but in *Posdata*, his vision of cyclical time is easily understood as a form of blaming the government of President Díaz Ordaz and the Partido Revolucionario Institucional (PRI): "La matanza de Tlatelolco nos revela que un pasado que creíamos enterrado está vivo e irrumpe entre nosotros. Cada vez que aparece en público, se presenta enmascarado y armado; no sabemos quién es, excepto que es destrucción y venganza" ("The Tlatelolco massacre reveals that a past we believed buried is alive and it is bursting among us. Every time it appears in public, it appears masked and armed; we don't know who it is, except it's destruction and revenge") (*Posdata* 282). Wrath in the form of vengeance and destruction is a recurring motif in the poems that denounce the Tlatelolco massacre. The metaphor of the mask evokes not only Mesoamerican rituals of sacrifice but also the fact that there were a group of government agents, identified by a white glove, who were literally the *agents provocateurs* of the massacre. As Holmes surmises: "The right wing found *Posdata* 'anti-Mexican,' while the left were outraged by Paz's historical and mythological explanations of contemporary political decisions and practices. Mexican poet Antonio Deltoro accused Paz in 1978 of 'blaming the Aztec gods for the massacre' rather than the then president Gustavo Díaz Ordaz (Brewster 2005; 60–61)" ("Pen and Brush," 375). Paz explains in detail how this history is tied by "el hilo de la dominación" ("the thread of domination"), in which "los virreyes españoles y los presidentes mexicanos son los sucesores de los tlatoanis aztecas" ("the Spanish viceroys and Mexican presidents are the successors of the Aztec Tlatoanis") (*Posdata* 332).

Paz argues that the PRI government has betrayed the values of the Mexican Revolution, but he conceptualizes it as another phase in the unsettling logic and legacy of pre-Hispanic Mexico. Paz ends his essay

106   CECILIA ENJUTO RANGEL

asking: "¿Por qué hemos buscado entre las ruinas pre-hispánicas el arquetipo de México? ¿Y por qué ese arquetipo tiene que ser precisamente azteca y no maya o zapoteca o tarasco u otomí?" ("Why have we searched among the pre-Hispanic ruins for the archetype of Mexico? And why does that archetype have to be precisely Aztec and not Mayan or Zapotec or Tarasco or Otomi?") (354). Far from idealizing the Aztecs, Paz responds to this question by suggesting that contemporary Mexicans, from all races and social classes, are the heirs of that history, "los verdaderos herederos de los asesinos del mundo pre-hispánico" ("the true heirs of the murderers of the pre-Hispanic world") (354).

"Petrificada petrificante" ("The Petrifying Petrified") is Paz's poetic *Posdata*; his poetic response to the Tlatelolco massacre, and the cultural climate of Mexico. Holmes situates it in this context: "Paz's 'Petrificada petrificante,' originally published as the third of a series of three poems . . . records Paz's disillusionment with the Distrito Federal after the government's brutal massacre of students at the Tlatelolco demonstration in 1968" ("Pen and Brush," 371). "Petrificada petrificante" is Paz's ultimate critique of the dystopian landscapes he encounters in Mexico City. Full of neologisms and mythological references, the poem is also, as I and others have argued elsewhere, his personal homage to T. S. Eliot's *The Waste Land* (Nandorfy; González Acosta; Enjuto Rangel). Wrath, taking the form of Medusa, or the Virgin, portrays a feminized version of Mexico, both petrified and petrifying. The personified rage becomes a recurrent motif in the poems that denounce Tlatelolco: "Valle de México . . . / desmoronado trono de la Ira . . . / petrificada / petrificante / Ira / torre hendida" (608) ("Valley of Mexico . . . Rage's rotten throne . . . / petrified / petrifying / Rage / broken tower" ["The Petrifying Petrified," 108]). Anger as a recurring trope reveals what Paz argues in *Posdata* – that the current political violence of the PRI can be traced to Mexico's past, and how the state remembers and celebrates both the Aztec empire and the Spanish colonial period, legitimizing a history of political repression. However, fury here is not a pyramid, but a broken, cleft tower, a phallic symbol, feminized. The Valley of Mexico is the "desmoronado trono de la Ira." Wrath's throne is falling apart, revealing a city made out of the ruins of the past.

As Diana Sorensen argues in her analysis of Paz's *Posdata*, the Tlatelolco massacre reveals a foundational violence: "By underscoring the relationship between space and identity . . . Paz territorializes the events of October 2 and lends them the character of the bloody sacrifices of pre-Columbian times" (309). As Rubén Gallo explains, "city officials promoted this strange

Economic, Political, and Ecological Disasters   107

amalgam of Aztec pyramid, Spanish convent, and modernist planned city as the Plaza of the Three Cultures" (59). Linking Tlatelolco to the symbol of Mexico's three ethnicities (Indigenous, European, and Mestizo), Mario Pani's modernist housing complex intended it to represent current Mexican culture. Gallo explains how the housing complex became a reverse panopticon, a mousetrap, and thus the utopian architectural project became a symbol of modern dystopia: "As a *lieu de mémoire*, Tlatelolco points to two of the most traumatic events in recent Mexican history: the 1968 student massacre and the 1985 earthquake. As a modernist ruin, it represents the catastrophic failure of Pani's utopian plans for transforming Mexico City into an orderly, planned city" (69).

Castellanos' and Pacheco's Memory Sites

Castellanos' and Pacheco's poems also aim to become poetic *lieux de mémoire*. Castellanos' "Silencio cerca de una piedra antigua" ("Silence Near an Ancient Stone"), published in the 1952 collection *El rescate del mundo* (*The Rescue of the World*), questions the possibility of rescuing the buried Indigenous legacy and the dilemma of the Latin American poet as the "voice of the voiceless." Here, the speaker's "words" are the actual ruins, a silence provoked by the presence of the ancient stones. In contrast to "Silencio," in her "Memorial de Tlatelolco," the speaker lashes out; silence is not an option in her poetic protest against the 1968 student massacre. In both texts, antique and modern ruins shape the porosity and malleability of historical memory, and there is a political urgency to remember, especially in "Memorial." Castellanos' approach to the politics of instability is exemplified in these two poems, and they pose a transitional phase in her poetics. "Memorial" marks a shift in Castellanos' representation of ruins; in her text from the early 1950s the speaker feels inadequate to remember, and identifies herself as "el olvido," while by the beginning of the 1970s her poetic speaker feels compelled to remember, and her memory is an open wound, painful and bleeding.

Castellanos' "Silencio" ("Silence") emerges from silence, from words that lie there, unripe and untouched: "Estoy aquí, sentada, con todas mis palabras / como con una cesta de fruta verde, intactas" ("I'm sitting here, sitting, with all my words / as with a basket of green fruit, intact") (61, verses 1–2).[2] Words are like fruits, not ready to eat, not ready to communicate. Words are also compared to the fragments of the ancient ruins, of a thousand broken gods, who want to speak through her. Like Ozymandias' statue in Shelley's poem, the Mayan lost gods lie broken and forgotten, but here they want to be reconfigured into the statues they once were. Through metonymy and synesthesia, the speaker tastes the song of those "antepasados." Castellanos underlines the oral nature of the text with the mouths of the dead just as Neruda does in "Alturas de Macchu Picchu" to legitimize the poem as a song that speaks for the eroded and erased past. Yet the speaker in Castellanos' poem realizes that she cannot pretend to be the voice of the past. The speaker identifies with la Malinche: "Pero soy el olvido, la traición" ("But I am the oblivion, the betrayal") (61, verse 11). The poem reinforces the frustrating incapacity to communicate with the past, the slow invisible violence that ruins make visible in a metaphorical way. In contrast with earlier conventions of the topos of ruins, where the speaker is a historical witness, here Castellanos' speaker identifies as an empty casket of memories.

The speaker here is not a witness of history: "Yo no miro los templos sumergidos / sólo miro los árboles que encima de las ruinas / mueven su vasta sombra" ("I don't look at the submerged temples / I just look how the trees above the ruins / move their vast shadow") (61, verses 14–16). As conventionally stated, nature survives history's destruction, but here the speaker is not the traditional poet archeologist, and instead of excavating she decides to look ahead, to the trees. The presence of the voices of the dead is ambiguously accessible: "Pero yo no conozco más que ciertas palabras / en el idioma o lápida / bajo el que sepultaron vivo a mi antepasado" ("But I know nothing but certain words / in the language or tombstone / under which my ancestor was buried alive") (61, verses 30–32). The ancestors, who are buried alive, remind the speaker of the massacres of the colonization of the Americas. Castellanos' final verses reiterate the irony of a poem that sings to and for the ancestors using the language that was used to silence them.

Castellanos' "Silencio," a poem on the ruins of the Indigenous past, seems to have little in common with "Memorial de Tlatelolco" ("Memorial of Tlatelolco"), but both texts reflect upon how cultural memory is constructed. While "Silencio" is even ambiguous about which "antepasados" we are talking about, "Memorial de Tlatelolco" responds to the very specific 1968 massacre. Placing the poem within the context of other historical testimonies, such as Pacheco's texts in Elena Poniatowska's *La noche de Tlatelolco* (*Massacre in Mexico*), adds to the complexities and malleability of the testimonial genre.

"Memorial de Tlatelolco" begins with the moral darkness of the crime and the image of gunshots felt only through lighting, "su efecto de relámpago" ("its lightning effect") (287, verse 6). Benjamin's metaphor of the past that "can be seized only as image which flashes up at the instant"

Economic, Political, and Ecological Disasters

(255) is captured in "esa luz, breve y lívida" ("that light, brief and livid") (287, verse 7). The first stanzas introduce the night as an accomplice to the violence exerted by the state, so preoccupied with the image of Mexico as host of the Olympic Games that it tried to cover up how the massacre was orchestrated: "La oscuridad engendra la violencia ... / ¿quién es el que mata? / ¿quiénes ... los que mueren? / ¿Los que huyen sin zapatos?" ("Darkness begets violence ... / who kills? / ... who is dying? / Those who run away without shoes?") (287, verses 1, 7–9). The rhetorical, haunting questions point to the government's cover-up. These questions resemble the ones asked in José Emilio Pacheco's "Las voces de Tlatelolco" (October 2, 1978) in "Manuscrito de Tlatelolco," which also incorporates phrases from different testimonies taken from *La noche de Tlatelolco*.[3] Pacheco stresses: "¿Quién, quién ordenó todo eso?" ("Who ordered all of this?") (67, verse 28), pointing to the *agents provocateurs, el batallón Olimpia*. As Pacheco's poem underscores, these snipers killed people mercilessly in the peaceful crowd: "Vestidos de civil, los elementos / del batallón Olimpia / mano cubierta por un guante blanco / iniciaron fuego" ("Dressed as civilians, the elements / of the Battalion Olympia / hand covered by a white glove / started fire") (67, verses 7–10).

The speaker of Castellanos' "Memorial" responds with anger and sarcasm at the censorship of the media, complicit with the government that swept away the massacre's bloody traces: "La plaza amaneció barrida; los periódicos / dieron como noticia principal / el estado del tiempo" ("By dawn, the square was swept; newspapers / gave as main news / the weather") (verses 14–16). The weather is the only source of news as the government wants to continue pretending that life goes on as usual – the banquet of the Olympic Games, the feast of its neoliberal projects, embraced the façade of normalcy. Castellanos' critique of the government's erasure of the historical memory of the event alludes to Mexico's Indigenous legacy: "No busques lo que no hay: huellas, cadáveres, / que todo se le ha dado como ofrenda a una diosa; / a la Devoradora de Excrementos. / No hurgues en los archivos pues nada consta en actas" ("Do not look for what is not: footprints, corpses, / everything has been given as an offering to a goddess; / to the Devourer of Excrement. / Don't dig in the archives as nothing remains") (verses 22–25). However, reading the present through the pre-Hispanic past implies that, like Paz, she is blaming the forces of repressed indigeneity for the abuses of a repressive state.

Pacheco's "Lectura de los cantares mexicanos" (October 2, 1968) in "Manuscrito de Tlatelolco" reveals a similar anxiety with historical amnesia, yet he links the student massacre with a Nahuatl poem on the destruction of Tenochtitlán and the Spanish Conquest, "La visión de los vencidos," to suggest that the Mexican government was reproducing the same tactics of violence and betrayal that led to the demise of the Aztec empire (Carpenter; León-Portilla). Pacheco's poem explicitly alludes to the *icnocuícatl* to emphasize that history repeats itself, and that it is therefore crucial not to let "nuestra herencia" ("our heritage") become "una red de agujeros" ("a net of holes") (verse 24). Castellanos' "Memorial" also denounces government plans to erase the event from collective memory, but instead of echoing the Nahuatl poem, she connects the government's actions to the Aztec practices of human sacrifice. Here, she parodies the mythological past, and the goddess is just another modern machine. The remnants of the massacre, the dead bodies, are treated as waste. For Castellanos, remembrance is her way of shedding some light on the darkness of broken consciousness. The poem is also a condemnation against the impunity of President Díaz Ordaz. Castellanos cannot help but remember; memory is an ethical imperative; justice can only be attained through collective memory: "Recuerdo, recordemos / hasta que la justicia se siente entre nosotros" ("I remember, let's remember / until justice sits among us") (verses 37–38).

Pacheco's "Manuscrito de Tlatelolco," composed of both "Lectura" (1968) and "Voces" (1978), also concludes with a tone of indignation, but even though it is a plea to remember the massacre, it also seems to condemn how collective memory can swallow the event, petrifying it in its commemorative projects: "Algún día / habrá una lámpara votiva /en memoria de todos ellos. / Brotarán flores / entre las ruinas y entre los sepulcros" ("Someday / there will be a votive lamp / in memory of all of them. / Flowers will sprout / among the ruins and the tombstones") (verses 101–105). Flowers seem to take over the dead and its remnants, both homage to nature and a sad reminder of how the light is merely a symbol of remembrance. In a similar way, Pacheco's "Ciudad maya comida por la selva" ("Mayan City Taken Over by the Jungle," 1976) incorporates the conventions of the Baroque topos of ruins, as nature has taken over the ruins of the Mayan empire and there is no possibility of communicating with the past: "De la gran ciudad maya sobreviven / arcos, desmanteladas construcciones / vencidas por la ferocidad de la maleza" ("From the great Mayan city survive / arches, dismantled buildings / defeated by the ferocity of weeds") (verses 1–3). The paradoxical image of gods drowning in the heights of the sky is also contrasted with the image of the ruins as swallowed by the caves of the mountains. The conventional didactic message concludes

Economic, Political, and Ecological Disasters   III

the poem: "De tanta vida que hubo aquí de tanta / grandeza derrumbada / sólo perduran / las pasajeras flores que no cambian" ("From so much life / from all the / collapsed greatness / only the unchanging, passing flowers endure") (verses 8–10). Once again, ruins are governed by the paradox of the eternal, the constant presence of ephemeral flowers, emblems of nature's surviving the broken imperial symbols of power.

Rob Nixon's critique of environmental degradation and slow violence is particularly tangible in Pacheco's "The Dream Is Over," where there are no fish, no plants, and the dead Erie "como el lago de México (*Todo ante mí se vuelve alegoría*)" ("as Mexico's lake [*Everything in front of me turns into an allegory*]") (verses 3–4). Alluding to Baudelaire's "Le cygne," allegory predominates in *Irás y no volverás*, where the dead fish of "Marea baja," among many other poems, depict an ecological dystopia. Here, Pacheco is linking Baudelaire's critique of urban modern progress to the dead lake, one of the ultimate casualties of our environmental war against nature. Nixon signals that one of the problems with slow violence and its effects is that "both the causes and the memory of catastrophe readily fade from view as the casualties incurred typically passed untallied and unremembered" (9). In "Tacubaya 1949," Pacheco ends with a pessimistic tone: "Nada quedó. / También en la memoria / las ruinas dejan sitio a nuevas ruinas" ("Of this nothing stayed on / In the memory too / ruins make room / for newer ruins" [trans. George McWhirter]) (verses 7–9). As Stanton suggests, Pacheco's work oscillates between the prophetic and the ironic modes (114). Layers of ruins compose Mexico's history; its slow violence ends with collective memory as another net of holes.

Pacheco evokes the Aztec and Mayan ruins as emblems of the lost past in "Ruinas del Templo Mayor" and "Ciudad maya comida por la selva," and responds to the student massacre in "Manuscrito de Tlatelolco," alluding to Nahuatl poetry. "A las puertas del Metro" criticizes a devouring modernity and how the modern city-dwellers treat the homeless as waste. The poem depicts a man, a body in ruins in the doors of the metro: "Quisieran borrarlo como se barren latas de cerveza y envolturas de plástico, desechos deshechos de una sociedad capaz de producir estas imágenes" ("They would like to erase him, just as beer cans and plastic wraps are swept, waste from a society capable of producing these images") (*Tarde o temprano*, 222). Modern society produces this situation of living in the margins, poor, ageless, and abandoned. His body in ruins, "desechos deshechos," is the ethical and political reminder of an unequal society. The homeless man, chanting rock songs with a broken voice, dressed in torn jeans and a run-down t-shirt that epitomizes commercial culture, saying *Have a Pepsi*, is looked at as if *he* were a used can. But: "Si lo viera Ernesto Cardenal le diría que se levante, que en él están los frutos de cuatro siglos de hambre, violencia y opresión; pero también el genio que construyó las pirámides e hizo posible Machu Picchu, el calendario maya, los códices nahuas, la escultura azteca y la obra de Nezahualcóyotl" ("If Ernesto Cardinal saw him, he would tell him to rise up, because in him there are the fruits of four centuries of hunger, violence, and oppression; but also the genius who built the pyramids and made possible Machu Picchu, the Mayan calendar, the Nahuas codexes, the Aztec sculpture and the work of Nezahualcóyotl") (222). This anonymous man standing there in the margins, unable to get into the train of progress, also symbolizes the priceless cultural legacy of the Aztec, Inca, and Mayan pasts. Pacheco establishes continuity between the modern ruins of an urban Mexico City, and the traces and treasures of pre-Columbian history.

The man in the metro symbolizes the many gradual effects of different forms of slow violence and slow death in our urban landscape. Although their ironic tone distances Pacheco and Castellanos from certain poems on ruins by Neruda and Paz, these texts all aim to provoke a political anagnorisis in the reader. Castellanos' problematic representation of the Indigenous legacy as an impenetrable silence is contested years later in "Memorial" as a symbol of violence that continues to haunt and fuel the modern machine. However, for Pacheco, the Aztec and the Mayan legacies always have something to say to modern Mexico. Pacheco's political and ethical critique of modernity ranges from allusions to a Nahuatl *icnocuícatl* lamenting the loss of Tenochtitlán and the menace of historical amnesia, key in his testimonial poem of Tlatelolco, to the figure of the young Indigenous man, singing out of tune, literally at the doors of the metro, the symbol of a failed modern state. Midcentury Latin American poets such as Neruda, Paz, Castellanos, and Pacheco depict a modern city in ruins, in a permanent state of transition, where the invisible, gradual effects of slow violence, of environmental degradation, merge with the results of political injustice and instability. Their poetic works often offer a testimonial account of the multiple forms of violence they witness and aim to preserve the voices, the memories of those often forgotten.

Notes

1. All translations from the Spanish are mine except when noted.
2. All translations from poems by Castellanos and Pacheco, and from narrative texts such as Paz's *Postdata*, are mine except when noted.

Economic, Political, and Ecological Disasters 113

3. Pacheco wrote two different poems: "Lectura de los cantares mexicanos" (October 2, 1968) and "Las voces de Tlatelolco" (October 2, 1978) in "Manuscrito de Tlatelolco" as it appears in *Tarde o temprano* (1958–2009). Victoria Carpenter has thoroughly studied the four versions of "Lectura de los cantares mexicanos" written and published between 1968 and 2000.

Works Cited

Benjamin, Walter. *Illuminations.* Ed. Hannah Arendt. Trans. Harry Zohn. New York: Schocken, 1968.

Berlant, Lauren. "Slow Death (Sovereignty, Obesity, Lateral Agency)," *Critical Inquiry* 33.4 (Summer 2007): 754–780.

Boym, Svetlana. *The Future of Nostalgia.* New York: Basic Books, 2001.

Camayd-Freixas, Erik. "'Alturas de Macchu Picchu': Forma y sentido en su retórica elegíaca." *Romance Languages Annual* 7 (1995): 405–412.

Carpenter, Victoria. "'Y el olor de la sangre manchaba el aire': Tlatelolco 1521 and 1968 in José Emilio Pacheco's 'Lectura de los Cantares Mexicanos." *Bulletin of Hispanic Studies* 95.4 (2018): 451–474.

Castellanos, Rosario. *Poesía no eres tú (1948–1971).* Mexico City: Fondo de Cultura Económica, 1995.

Enjuto Rangel, Cecilia. *Cities in Ruins: The Politics of Modern Poetics.* West Lafayette, IN: Purdue University Press, 2010.

Fein, John. "Himno entre ruinas." *Aproximaciones a Octavio Paz.* Ed. Angel Flores, pp. 165–170. Mexico City: Mortiz, 1974.

"La estructura de *Piedra de sol.*" *Revista Iberoamericana* 38 (1972): 73–93.

Feinsod, Harris. *The Poetry of the Americas: From Good Neighbors to Countercultures.* Oxford: Oxford University Press, 2017.

Gallo, Rubén. "Tlatelolco: Mexico City's urban dystopia." In *Noir Urbanisms: Dystopic Images of the Modern City.* Ed. Gyan Prakash, pp. 52–68. Princeton, NJ: Princeton University Press, 2011.

Goic, Cedomil. "*Alturas de Macchu Picchu:* La torre y el abismo." *Pablo Neruda, el escritor y la crítica.* Ed. Emir Rodz, pp. 219–244. Madrid: Taurus, 1980.

González Acosta, Alejandro. "En la raíz mexicana: *Petrificada petrificante* de Octavio Paz." *Revista Iberoamericana* 57 (1991): 519–520.

Holmes, Amanda. "Pen and Brush in Dialogue: Octavio Paz and Antoni Tàpies in Their Trans-Atlantic *Livre d'Artiste*," *Bulletin of Hispanic Studies* 88.3 (2011): 369–383.

City Fictions: Language, Body and Spanish American Urban Space. Lewisburg, PA: Bucknell University Press, 2007.

Lazzara, Michael and Unruh, Vicky. "Introduction: Telling Ruins." *Telling Ruins in Latin America.* Ed. Michael Lazzara and Vicky Unruh, pp. 1–9. New York: Palgrave Macmillan, 2009.

León-Portilla, Miguel. *Visión de los vencidos: relaciones indígenas de la conquista.* 29th ed. Mexico City: UNAM, Coordinación de Humanidades, Programa Editorial, 2007.

114 CECILIA ENJUTO RANGEL

"Pensamiento de Nezahualcóyotl," *Humanistas de Mesoamérica*, vol. 1. [Online – Fondo 2000.] Available at: http://bibliotecadigital.ilce.edu.mx/sites/fond 02000/vol1/mesoamerica-i/html/4.html.

Nezahualcóyotl: poesía y pensamiento, 1402–1472. Mexico City: Biblioteca Enciclopédica del Estado de México, 1979.

Trece poetas del mundo azteca. Mexico City: UNAM, Instituto de Investigaciones Históricas, 1975.

Nandorfy, Martha J. "Petrificada petrificante." *Revista Canadiense de Estudios Hispánicos* 16 (1992): 567–586.

Neruda, Pablo. *Canto general.* Prólogo de Fernando Alegría. Caracas: Biblioteca Ayacucho, 1981.

Canto general. Trans. Jack Schmitt. Los Angeles: University of California Press, 1991.

Nixon, Rob. *Slow Violence and the Environmentalism of the Poor.* Cambridge, MA: Harvard University Press, 2013.

Pacheco, José Emilio. *Tarde o temprano (Poemas 1958–2000).* Mexico City: Fondo de Cultura Económica, 2000.

Selected Poems. Ed. George McWhirter. Trans. Thomas Hoeksema, George McWhirter, Alastair Reid, and Linda Scheer. New York: A New Directions Book, 1987.

Paz, Octavio. *Obra Poética (1935–1988).* Barcelona: Seix Barral, 1998.

"Himno entre ruinas/Hymn among the Ruins." In *Octavio Paz: Selected Poems.* Ed. Eliot Weinberger. Trans. William Carlos Williams, pp. 22–24. New York: New Directions, 1984.

"Petrificada petrificante/The Petrifying Petrified." In *Octavio Paz: Selected Poems.* Ed. and trans. Eliot Weinberger, pp. 107–111. New York: New Directions, 1984.

"Piedra de Sol/Sunstone." In *Octavio Paz: Selected Poems.* Ed. Eliot Weinberger. Trans. Muriel Rukeyser, pp. 29–45. New York: New Directions, 1984.

Posdata. Mexico City: Editorial Siglo XXI, 1969.

Rodríguez Monegal, Emir. *El acto de las palabras: Estudios y diálogos con Octavio Paz.* Mexico City: Fondo de Cultura Económica, 1997.

"El sistema del poeta." *Pablo Neruda, el escritor y la crítica.* Ed. Emir Rodz, pp. 633–691. Madrid: Taurus, 1980.

Neruda: El viajero inmóvil. Caracas: Monte Avila, 1977.

"Relectura de El Arco y la Lira." *Revista Iberoamericana* 37 (1971): 35–46.

Santí, Enrico Mario. "The Accidental Tourist: Walt Whitman in Latin America." *Do the Americas Have a Common Literature?* Ed. Gustavo Pérez Firmat, pp. 156–176. Durham, NC: Duke University Press, 1990.

Pablo Neruda: The Poetics of Prophecy. Ithaca, NY: Cornell University Press, 1981.

ed. *Luz espejeante: Octavio Paz ante la crítica.* Mexico City: Ediciones Era y la Universidad Nacional Autónoma de México, 2009.

Economic, Political, and Ecological Disasters 115

Stanton, Anthony. "José Emilio Pacheco, poeta elegíaco." *José Emilio Pacheco, reescritura en movimiento.* Ed. Yvette Jiménez de Báez. Mexico City: Colegio de México, 2014.

Sorensen, Diana. "Tlatelolco 1968: Paz and Poniatowska on law and violence," *Mexican Studies/ Estudios Mexicanos* 18 (2002): 297–321.

Wilson, Jason. *Octavio Paz.* Boston, MA: Twayne, 1986.

CHAPTER 7

Mexican Miracle Modernism

Ignacio M. Sánchez Prado

The opening sequence of *Distinto amanecer* (*Another Dawn*, Julio Bracho, 1943) features one of the most striking views of Mexico City in the history of cinema. The film takes us into a space defined by the images and sound of technology and contemporary life: the sorting machine of the post office, young men selling the newspaper, mannequins arranged to look at the trolleys and buses in the street, the nocturnal landscape defined by advertising marquees. The film, shot in the wake of Lázaro Cárdenas' socialist reforms and in the early days of the presidency of Manuel Ávila Camacho, sought to present a country experiencing the social accelerations of midcentury capitalism, and to understand this sensorium as the representation of Mexico's post-revolutionary project.[1] The film is evidently different from the rural imaginary of Mexico's so-called cinema of the Golden Age, typically identified – at least in reductive accounts of it – with an iconography of nationalism centered on the aestheticization of rural nostalgia and the cultural stereotyping of urban and countryside popular subjects.

Distinto amanecer provides a different understanding of the culture of the period. Bracho and his famous cinematographer, Gabriel Figueroa, capture the textures of a city deeply altered by the infrastructural transformations in Mexico's urban economy – technological advances in electricity and transportation, the consolidation of industry and labor movements, new networks of commerce and bourgeois social performance, a rapidly evolving mediascape led by newspapers and cinema, the emergence of features of middle-class life, the massification of social identities, and so on. To recall the work of Jesús Martín-Barbero, the film is representative of an emerging "espacio cultural" ("cultural space"), a term that the Colombian theorist used to describe the focalization on "*el lugar en el que se articula* el sentido que los procesos económicos y políticos tienen para una sociedad" ("the *site in which the articulation* of the sense that political and economic processes have for a society takes place") (224;

Mexican Miracle Modernism 117

emphasis in the original).[2] I coin here the term "Mexican miracle modernism" to describe the cultural space and the aesthetic regimes that formed the sensorium that mediated and imagined the socioeconomic processes of integration to the capitalist and cultural regimes of the late interwar period, for the consumption of emerging reading and viewing classes. Extrapolating Arjun Appardurai's insights on modernization to an earlier period of the twentieth century, I also understand Mexican miracle modernism to be a "mediascape"; that is, "image-centered, narrative-based accounts of strips of reality … out of which scripts can be formed of imagined lives, their own as well as those of others living in other spaces" (35). In this essay, I will use literary prose writing as the primary space in which I will develop this concept, understanding it as deeply connected to larger infrastructures of media, including film, radio, newsprint, magazines, and even advertising.

In speaking of the "Mexican miracle," I appropriate a term used – both academically and colloquially – to describe a period of vertiginous economic growth and stability, roughly between 1940 and 1968, although accounts of its exact dates differ (Aguilar Camín and Meyer 162). In practical terms, it refers to economic growth fueled by mixed economy policies modeled after the idea of Import-Substitution Industrialization, which would later become nationalized under the idea of "stabilizing development" (Morton 64). This economic model deepened ties to the United States and allowed for the generation of an Americanized cultural imaginary, even as Mexico was pushing forward in parallel the idea of revolutionary nationalism. In any case, the term was coined early on, and continues to be used as periodization in the field of economics and other social sciences (Gómez-Galvarriato). It is important to note that "Mexican miracle modernism" as a category is not meant to suggest a totalization of the idea of Mexican culture, or even to function as an all-encompassing periodization. It rather recognizes that, in the context of Mexico's deeply uneven development, this particular cultural space operated primarily in those urban sites in which the effects of capitalist economic growth were more palpable. The idea of the "Mexican miracle" has also been related by cultural historians and sociologists (for instance, Girola) to the conditions necessary for the formation of both social imaginaries of modernizations and intellectual elites with modernizing projects. It is not my claim that Mexican miracle modernism appeared solely in Mexico City. However, I focus here mostly (though not solely) on Mexico City-centered productions because the phenomena I relate here have a more available archive in the capital city. I also build on previous work about literature and the city, particularly centered on *modernismo* and the avant-garde (most importantly Gallo; Tenorio-Trillo), as well as on histories of Mexico City literature in general and of the chronicle-genre in particular (Quirarte; Gelpí). Therefore, Mexican miracle modernism is a term concerned not so much with the field of cultural production as such, or the imagination of modernity, but rather a series of formal, stylistic, and generic traits tied to the material infrastructures of writing and the arts brought about by capitalist modernization.

In claiming that these cultural spaces and their aesthetics comprise a "modernism," I am well aware of the fact that I use the term to describe a late period: after Spanish American *modernismo* and right after the historiographical end of Anglophone-centered ideas of modernism. Indeed, using the term is always perilous if one considers its somewhat vague utilization, as well as the complex ways in which traditions of critique have used the concept (Eysteinsson). To do so, I understand "modernism" to describe not only concrete cultural periods in different locations – including the processes of capitalist modernization between the nineteenth and twentieth centuries (Rama) – or the large-scale aggregate of broad cultural and artistic transformations taking place roughly between 1840 and 1945 (Gay). I embrace Susan Stanford Friedman's call to decentralize the term across space and time and understand modernism as "not a single aesthetic period, a movement or a style. Instead, the creative expressivities in all media constitute the modernisms of given modernities – on a planetary scale, across time" (4). A historically situated modernism names concrete aesthetic and institutional articulations between historically located fields of cultural production and the styles and artistic forms that these articulations generate. Methodologically, I concur with Friedman's procedure of turning first "to the specificities of a given modernity and then ask what creative forms it produced" (4). Mexican miracle modernism refers then to the creative forms that emerged in social spaces clearly defined by a form of capitalist modernity that only materialized, at least at the level of cultural production, in fragments and sections of national culture bound by new forms of media, labor, and consumption.

As mentioned before, Mexican miracle modernism is to be understood as a cultural paradigm that cuts across aesthetic disciplines, and it is worth remembering that the terms "modern," "modernist," and "modernism" frequently appear in discussions regarding the Mexican artworlds. Beyond works of cinema like *Distinto amanecer*, one could recall here Alejandro L. Madrid's (2008) work on classical composers like Julián Carrillo and Carlos Chávez, engaged in forms of modernist music critically negotiating the local and the cosmopolitan. Another generative approach is that of Sarah Beckhart (2013), who departs from the construction of the Torre Latinoamericana in Mexico City between 1948 and 1956 to describe the modernist sensibility of the Mexican miracle as shown in the material and media cultures – from the actual materials used in the construction of the tower to the imaginary set forth in texts like tourism pamphlets and engineering journals. The literature most illustrative of Mexican miracle modernism, to which I devote the rest of this piece, is defined at its core by the intermedial engagements with a network of creative forms primarily operating in the mediation between the cultural imagination of urban subjects and the processes of capitalist development, Americanization, and cosmopolitization. They are not the most canonical, but they are key to understanding the cultural and social transition in the 1940s toward the most well-known cultural works that came to the fore after 1950.

The core enterprises of the Mexican literary field in the 1940s rested roughly upon the intertwining of three processes: the re-narration of the rural and the past to the parameters of modernity, the mediation of Mexico's increasing cultural awareness of global forms of capital and geopolitics, and the search for the specificity of the national as an instrument of governance. Sergio González Rodríguez (2008) provides a very useful taxonomy of the decade's literature based on four intellectual enterprises: the setting of the city, the twilight of the countryside, the search for a national self, and the poetics of loss. This is accompanied by the construction of an autonomous literary field that constructs what I call elsewhere (*Naciones intelectuales*, 2009) "intellectual nations"; that is, alternative symbolic cartographies to the dominant process of revolutionary nationalism. It is almost a commonplace to note the significant role that the opposition between nationalism and cosmopolitanism has in this (and nearly any) period. Rather than defining Mexican miracle modernism as a cosmopolitan endeavor or style, its most significant work is performed in the mediation of frictions and contradictions between global flows and local sites of capitalist modernity as crystallized in cultural form.

The forms and styles of Mexican miracle modernism are rendered possible both by the cultural form of the urban and by the social forms of capitalism. I use "form" here following Caroline Levine's work, defining it on the basis of its "affordances" or the "potential uses or actions latent in materials and designs" (6). Key to this idea is that literary and social forms afford each other. A good example of this is the works articulated around the *noir* as genre, including larger definitions of detective and crime fiction. *Distinto amanecer* belongs, as I have argued elsewhere ("Peripheral Noir"), to a larger constellation of the *noir* as affective mediation of capitalist modernity. Yet, at a more practical level the detective novel proves a clear example of the mutual affordance between literary genre and social form. The novelty of the genre in the 1940s was not only obvious but also discussed. Alfonso Reyes enthusiastically endorsed detective fiction, calling it "el género clásico de nuestro tiempo" ("the classical genre of our times") and even defending it from accusations of it being too popular and too formulaic (460–461). This claim did not necessarily stem directly from Mexican fiction: the text was published just a year before the first major novel in the genre, Rodolfo Usigli's *Ensayo de un crimen* (1944), and it was more informed by Reyes' dialogue with José Luis Borges and his admiration for Dorothy Sayers.

Reyes had to defend crime fiction from being too popular, because its very form resulted from seismic changes in reading practices. Benjamin T. Smith (2018) has studied the Mexican press and civil society between 1940 and 1976. He notes the growth in the number of readers as a result of post-revolutionary alphabetization campaigns and the availability of subsidized paper, not only due to urban concentration but also because of a better communication network. At the same time, as Pablo Piccato (2017) studies in depth, the development of the crime press and, later on, crime fiction was tied to a greater social perception of violence, immunity, and the broken nexus between crime and justice. This resulted, according to Piccato, in crime fiction becoming "the most popular literary genre in the mid-twentieth century" (200). Putting together Reyes' perception of novelty and Smith and Piccato's accounts of the press and crime, it becomes palpably clear that the formal and structural novelty introduced by crime fiction was afforded both by social structures tied to modernization (crime as a factor of capitalist urban societies) and by the rapidly developing press mediascape. In turn, crime fiction, along with films like *Distinto amanecer*, generated a mediation that allowed Mexicans to engage with a subset of anxieties derived from social processes of the Mexican miracle. Crime was certainly one, but the bourgeoning nightlife (itself traumatic in a country that remained socially conservative), the growing sense of political corruption in the ruling class (a theme in many works), and the material spaces and sensations from urban life (cafés, advertisements, automobiles, etc.) are all formalized in crime fiction works.[3]

Crime fiction was often sidelined as a central form of writing in Mexican literary history, until critics like Vicente Francisco Torres (2003), among many others, began devoting attention to the works. It is hard to perceive today how major the genre was, since some of the foundational works have been out of print for years. Yet, when looking at them, it is notable not only how unusual some of them were within genre conventions but also the ways in which they were bound to cultural structures representative of the Mexican miracle. Usigli's *Ensayo de un crimen*, the most well-known entry in the genre, was told from the perspective of the criminal, Roberto de la Cruz, and the novel shows him dwelling across the city, reading the newspapers, visiting cafés and bars, and spending time in hotels. *Ensayo de un crimen* was an anomaly, since Usigli's success came from his writings as a playwright and this would be his only entry in the genre. Nevertheless, *Ensayo de un crimen* plays a significant role in understanding the ways in which crime fiction, as Fernando Fabio Sánchez (43–63) studies, is bound not only to the general interest of "murder as art" but also in crime as a mechanism of critical engagement with the failures of the post-revolutionary project.

Other lesser-known, but equally important, works provide even more of a window regarding the connections between crime fiction and Mexican miracle infrastructures. Antonio Helú, a second-generation Lebanese Mexican, published his novel *La obligación de asesinar* in 1946, the same year in which he founded *Selecciones policiacas y de misterio*, the publishing house Albatros, and the Club de la Calle Morgue, which would gather other writers in the genre (Piccato 200). Helú's founding editorial work is a materialization of the mediascape and cultural infra-structures afforded by the Mexican miracle. *Selecciones policiacas y de misterio* was inspired by a new transnational mediascape of popular readership, including *Ellery Queen's Mystery Magazine*, a publication founded in the United States in 1941 and still running, and *Selecciones*, the Cuba-based, Spanish-language edition of *Reader's Digest*, a mass-circulated miscellan-eous publication that came to Mexico in 1940. Editorial Albatros published the Colección Media Noche, which was a forum not only for Mexican and Mexico-based writers like Enrique F. Gual, a Barcelona-born writer exiled in the country, but also translations of major figures like Raymond Chandler and Georges Simenon. Helú is often neglected in literary criti-cism. However, as a recent study by Mike Strayer (2015) notes, he was not only recognized by major figures like Xavier Villaurrutia and Carlos Monsiváis but also developed a style in the intersection between popular culture and the avant-garde. In a way, this is a good encapsulation of Mexican miracle procedures: a moment in the popularization of reading, in the intersection between the reading affordances of the popular press and the internalization of avant-garde styles and aesthetics in a new urban sensorium.

Through the lens of Mexican miracle modernism, we can see that genres usually understudied by criticism, when not altogether ignored in favor of more canonical works, are perhaps more meaningful when one sees them as part of a cultural imagination that afforded different mediations of the modern social space. In some cases, it gives us a perspective to account for the interventions of women writers working in these forms and often marginalized from literary history and even from the literary field of their time. This is the case of María Elvira Bermúdez, who, in her novel *Diferentes razones tiene la muerte* (1953) and in other works, uses literature as clues in her mysteries, and ties into her narratives critiques of both the elite and the role of women in society. And, furthering the infrastructure of the genre, she was the editor of one of the landmark anthologies of police short fictions, published in 1955. In her work on realism, Anna Kornbluh (2019) suggests a reading of nineteenth-century fiction in terms of accounting for the ways in which literary form builds structures of the social. Under Mexican miracle modernism, genre fiction can be read in similar ways, focusing not on the deconstruction of their aporias but the ways in which literary imagination afforded socially shaping understandings of a dynamic social space. Canonical works of the 1940s focused on the rural – like José Revueltas' masterpiece *El luto humano* (1943) or Agustín Yáñez's paradigm-changing *Al filo del agua* (1947) – deployed other forms of high modernist technique but were fundamentally focused on a social space undergoing crisis and economic *impasse*. Conversely, writers like Usigli, Helú, and Bermúdez, while representing the crisis of the national-revolutionary project, also create affirmative formal architectures (also visible in the opening of *Distinto amanecer*) in which modernization and cosmopolitanism were already pushing toward social spaces not defined by the rigid constraints of official culture.

Crime fiction is by no means the only genre in which these processes are visible. Various modes of speculative fiction and fantasy captured the political and economic imagination of the Mexican miracle. A peculiar case was that of Diego Cañedo, the *nom de plume* of Guillermo Zárraga. His novels mediated domestic concerns about Mexico's present as well as its articulation into the geopolitics of World War II. These were captured in speculative plots and in the use of tropes of time travel, among other devices. In *El réferi cuenta nueve* (1943), Cañedo designs his novel as a manuscript written in 1961 but discovered in 1938. The novel, intended to persuade readers to side with the United States against Hitler, imagines an occupation of Mexico, and strongly advocates for overcoming past resentments with the neighboring country. Another book is *Palamás,*

Mexican Miracle Modernism

Echevete y yo o el lago asfaltado (1945), in which a professor from a future university travels across various periods of Mexican history, until landing in the novel's present. As Ross Larson notes, Cañedo's novels create worlds in which "time has no reality: there is only good and evil existing in an eternal present" (54). There is little trace of Cañedo in contemporary literary criticism, but as Juan Carlos Ramírez Pimienta (209) notes, the reception of his work at the time was very positive – in fact, Alfonso Reyes recommended reading *El réferi cuenta nueve* for its political message and balance, even if that meant sidestepping its technical flaws (338–339).

Another practitioner of speculative fiction, a surprising one, was Rafael Bernal, who would much later write his most canonical work, *El complot mongol* (1969), perhaps the most widely read entry in Mexican crime fiction. Bernal did write an earlier, less heralded, crime novel, *Un muerto en la tumba* (1946). But his most remarkable work in the 1940s is a peculiar climate novel: *Su nombre era muerte* (1947). Its protagonist is a man facing his own decline in the Lacandón jungle in Chiapas. In the jungle, he begins to develop a relationship with mosquitoes, until he begins working on a plot to ally with the insects for the destruction of humankind. As Francisco Serratos documents, Bernal wrote this book way before his literary fame, after his time working in Chiapas' banana industry (9). Just like Cañedo's advocacy against the Nazis, Serratos recalls that the book was very critical of a Mexican movement of the Catholic ultra-right, *sinarquismo* (9). The novel was a significant departure from most books interested in questions of the environment in Latin America. As Scott M. DeVries notes, "there is no rhetoric of development nor terror like in *La vorágine*, only an expression of respect for nature in which human rights are secondary to the magnificence of the *selva*" (150).

The proliferation of genre fiction is a fundamental characteristic of Mexican miracle modernism. Fictional forms allow for textual concretizations of anxieties exceeding the nationalist cultural project as such. The environmental undertones of both *Su nombre era muerte* and *Palamás*, in which a key element is the further covering of the lake of Texcoco under Mexico City's asphalt, are not so much a matter of critique of the state or disappointment in the revolution as they are reflections on the radical transformations that the process of modernization brought to a country that was moving from a primarily rural to an urban-centered model of capitalism. This is indeed also visible in a film as canonical as *Los olvidados*, in which Luis Buñuel, working with Gabriel Figueroa, represents the slums where rural migrants live with the unfinished constructions of the city in the background. *El réferi*'s concern with Nazism or Gual's Europe-set novels pointed to the growing awareness of Mexico's own position in the vicinity of a transnational superpower and in a world in which citizens, due to more widely available media, became increasingly concerned with geopolitics. These books foreground more canonical texts like *El complot mongol* which, in the 1960s, imagined Mexico at the center of a geopolitical conspiracy involving China, the United States, and the Soviet Union.

This internationalist bent would fuel the works of wildly popular writers often neglected in our current accounts of Mexican and Latin American literature. Mexican miracle modernism was the site of new cultures of the bestseller as a consequence not only of the same structures of alphabetization and income mentioned earlier but also because of the influx of mass media, mostly from the United States, in direct challenge to nationalist culture. Cosmopolitanism was a feature of elite culture for decades, but the 1940s are a moment in which cosmopolitan culture achieves a level of unprecedented democratization. I have studied elsewhere ("The golden age otherwise") that even a cursory look into the film showings in any given week of the period usually understood to be the heyday of Mexican cinema shows an array of international films that include noirs, thrillers, literary adaptations, and many other works in genre. But print culture was also expanding. In one of the most useful accounts of the history of reading between 1940 and 1960, Valentina Torres Septién (2010) documents a variety of phenomena, including new publishing houses founded, among others, by Spanish intellectuals and local entrepreneurs, the well-established newspaper industry in Mexico City and the growing sophistication of regional newspapers, and even the increase in popularity in graphic fiction of adults, much of which dabbled in genres like the Western and romance.

Unfortunately, Torres Septién's account does not consider how the bestseller evolved, but it is worth remembering the emergence of a key figure, Luis Spota. Spota would become the icon of commercially oriented fiction in midcentury Mexico and his career ran parallel to that of Carlos Fuentes. As Sara Sefchovich notes, both Fuentes and Spota were defined by Miguel Aleman's economic reforms in the 1940s. Sefchovich characterizes Spota as a writer aligned with mass culture "al que no le interesan las nuevas técnicas, las explicaciones o los pasados sino únicamente el hoy" ("who was uninterested in new techniques, explanations of pasts, but only the here and now") (151). There is an evident judgment here, contrasting Spota's schematic and superficial writing with the experimental and intellectual project of a writer like Fuentes. Yet, like the genre fiction discussed before, Spota's popularity and resonance is tied not so much to his intellectual

Mexican Miracle Modernism

project as to his successful capture of a mediascape that permeated the times. His 1947 novel *El coronel fue echado al mar* is a case in point. The book narrates the drama unfolding on the vessel *Anne Louise*, in which the only Mexican character is the narrator. Instead, as a reviewer of the day, Antonio Acevedo Escobedo (1947), noted, the text was defined by evasion, interested in universality rather than the "brutal crudeza" ("brutal rawness") of Mexico's revolutionary novel. This, continues the reviewer, is because, "influido indudablemente por el estilo nervioso, cortante y preciso de autores norteamericanos buenos y malos, nuestro autor escribe a ráfagas" ("undoubtedly influenced by the nervous, intermittent, and precise style of good and bad North American writers, our author writes in bursts") (25). The key here is that Spota, whose work would become widely read and translated in the 1950s and 1960s, finds his success in bringing into form the flows and aesthetics of the Mexican miracle, which are captured in the type of formulaic and entertaining prose that often accompanies capitalist modernization.

Beyond the realm of the commercial, Mexican miracle modernism was also the site of emergence of marginal and subversive aesthetics developed by authors who would for decades be considered "cult writers," until their recent recovery in publishing and criticism. One of them is Francisco Tario, a highly imaginative writer who delved into unprecedented forms of experimentation, and of engagement with Gothic and fantastic forms. He came to the scene in force in the 1940s with quite unique works like the short-story collection *La noche* (1943), the novel *Aquí abajo* (1943), and particularly original works of unclassifiable fiction, such as *Equinoccio* (1946) and *La puerta en el muro* (1946). As Alejandro Toledo (2014), editor of his complete works and his most dedicated critic, painstakingly documents, Tario's life and work was thoroughly marked by different vectors of modernity, from his foray into professional soccer in the 1930s to his life in Acapulco as the city was becoming an international tourist destination to his participation in urban intellectual culture. Tario has no real precursors in Mexico and he may be more comparable to writers elsewhere in Latin America, from the Uruguayan Felisberto Hernández to the Ecuadorian Pablo Palacio. In any case, Tario is thoroughly a Mexican miracle modernist, a writer that, from his stylistics to his life, became defined by the new cultural scene, its economies, and its mediascapes.

It should be clear by this point that, even as I have focused on work tied to crime fiction, speculative fiction, and the Gothic, I do not claim that Mexican miracle modernism is a single style, but rather an array for forms that capture and afford the cultural infrastructures that accompanied urbanization, development, and transnationalization in the 1950s. Writers such as Helú, Cañedo, and Tario are iconic in this regard because their work is thoroughly inscribed in this process. But it is also significant that most works of literary criticism often sidetrack them. José María Espinasa's account of the 1940s (131–182), while idiosyncratic, is telling: his account rests on Alfonso Reyes, Ramón Rubín, and Gilberto Owen, more representative of the way in which the legacies of the avant-garde and the pressures of cultural nationalism unfolded. Even in the history of literature I coedited (Sánchez Prado, Nogar, and Ruisánchez), this paradigm barely registers, something I am just noticing in retrospect. I would speculate that this marginalization has to do with the perception of many of these writers to simply be lesser in terms of literary talent, which is both palpable and subjective, and the undeniable fact that many of these works are simply too odd to fit into a cultural canon. But as a matter of cultural and literary history, Mexican miracle modernist works represent processes of modernization often erased by accounts centered on the problem of national culture, which also erase writers and cultural phenomena that, according to the historiographical evidence we have, were quite popular and known by large swaths of the reading public at the time, sometimes – as is the case of Spota – above and beyond more consecrated writers.

In any case, I will conclude this essay with a text that is very different from the ones I have examined up to this point, but that I consider to be one of the pinnacles and clearest illustrations of what I mean by Mexican miracle modernism: Salvador Novo's "Nueva grandeza mexicana" (1946). Novo's outside role in the reconfiguration of the Mexican *crónica* genre, and in the visibilization of dissident sexualities, has been discussed in great detail by various critics (see among many others Gollnick; Mahieux 93–125), so I will just note those conversations here. Rather, I want to highlight Novo's celebrated text. "Nueva grandeza mexicana" is a snapshot of Mexico City in the mid-1940s, written in a first-person voice that describes the ways in which he would guide a friend through town. This rich work exists at the crossroads of literary tradition, from colonial writers like Bernardo de Balbuena, whose *Grandeza mexicana* inspires Novo, to the well-established tradition of the newspaper chronicle, which included *modernistas* like Manuel Gutiérrez Nájera. Novo's writing captures the rhythms of the city through a Baroque prose that mimetizes both the accumulation of sites and the demographic explosion by filling pages with details, gossip, and a narrative that at points borders on polyphony. The tour is shaped by sites for various social practices that became prevalent in the Mexican miracle: a highly developed dining scene, coffee houses,

Mexican Miracle Modernism

theaters, cinemas, and so on. Novo also contrasts the public life of the streets with new architectures and logics of private life, which, in his opinion, indicated that the city had reached "una mayoría de edad urbana" ("urban adulthood") (235).

Novo talks about a city now centered on the automobile and its related social ordering. But in general, the "grandeza mexicana" that Novo is invested in relating is the crossroads between the country's long history and its quick modernization. Mexican miracle modernism, short-lived but decisive, was the aesthetic regime of transition and transformation between revolutionary turmoil and an irreversible modern age. Genres like the detective novel, science fiction, and others, often outside the purview of canonical histories of literature, occupied a central place in this process. This is the core of a transition that would unfold in decades to come, as Josefina Vicens, Carlos Fuentes, Elena Garro, Carlos Monsiváis, Ámparo Dávila, Elena Poniatowska, Fernando del Paso, and many others would develop the literature of Mexico's midcentury modernity.

Notes

1. For a recent reading of the film, its politics, and its aesthetics, see Castro Ricalde.
2. Even though there is a published English translation, I opted to do my own because this particular passage is erroneously translated. All other translations are my own except where otherwise noted.
3. A good study of the social conditions in the 1940s, centered on corruption, is Niblo.

Works Cited

Acevedo Escobedo, Antonio. "Luis Spota: El coronel fue echado al mar," *Revistas de la Universidad de México* 8 (1947): 25.

Aguilar Camín, Héctor and Lorenzo Meyer. *In the Shadow of the Mexican Revolution: Contemporary Mexican History 1910–1989.* Austin: University of Texas Press, 1993.

Appadurai, Arjun. *Modernity at Large: The Cultural Dimensions of Globalization.* Minneapolis: University of Minnesota Press, 1996.

Beckhart, Sarah E. "Modernist Sensibility: The Transformation of Space in Mexico City through the Torre Latinoamericana," *The Latin Americanist* 57.1 (2013): 21–41.

Bermúdez, María Elvira. *Diferentes razones tiene la muerte.* Mexico City: Talleres Gráficos de la Nación, 1953.

   ed. *Los mejores cuentos policiacos mexicanos.* Mexico City: Libro-Mex, 1955.

Bernal, Rafael. *El complot mongol*. Mexico City: Joaquín Mortiz, 1969.

Un muerto en la tumba: Novela policiaca. Mexico City: Jus, 1946.

Su nombre era muerte. Mexico City: Jus, 1947.

Cañedo, Diego. *Palamás, Echevete y yo: O el lago asfaltado*. Mexico City: Stylo, 1945.

El réferi cuenta nueve. Mexico City: Cvltvra, 1943.

Castro Ricalde, Maricruz. "*Un distinto amanecer* (Julio Bracho 1943), para la nación Mexicana," *Revista de Estudios Hispánicos* 51.3 (2017): 543–569.

DeVries, Scott M. *A History of Ecology and Environmentalism in Spanish American Literature*. Lewisburg, PA: Bucknell University Press, 2013.

Distinto amanecer. Dir. Julio Bracho. Films Mundiales, 1943.

Espinasa, José María. *Historia mínima de la literatura mexicana del siglo XX*. Mexico City: El Colegio de México, 2015.

Eysteinsson, Astradur. *The Concept of Modernism*. Ithaca, NY: Cornell University Press, 1990.

Friedman, Susan Stanford. *Planetary Modernisms. Provocations on Modernity Across Time*. New York: Columbia University Press, 2018.

Gallo, Rubén. *Mexican Modernity: The Avant-Garde and Technological Revolution*. Cambridge, MA: MIT Press, 2010.

Gay, Peter. *Modernism: The Lure of Heresy – From Baudelaire to Beckett and Beyond*. New York: W. W. Norton, 2008.

Gelpí, Juan. *Ejercer la ciudad en el México moderno*. Buenos Aires: Corregidor, 2017.

Girola, Lidia. "Elites intelectuales e imaginarios contrapuestos en la era del 'milagro mexicano' y su expresión en la revista *Cuadernos Americanos*," *Sociologías* 47 (2018): 170–208.

Gollnick, Brian. "Silent Idylls, Double Lives: Sex and the City in Salvador Novo's *La estatua de sal*," *Mexican Studies/Estudios Mexicanos* 21.1 (2005): 231–250.

Gómez-Galvarriato, Aurora. "La construcción del milagro mexicano: El Instituto Mexicano de Investigaciones Tecnológicas, el Banco de México y la Armour Research Foundation," *Historia mexicana* 69.3 (2020): 1247–1309.

González Rodríguez, Sergio. "La literatura mexicana en los años cuarenta." *La literautra mexicana del siglo XX*. Coord. Manuel Fernández Perera, pp. 203–259. Mexico City: Fondo de Cultura Económica/Conaculta/ Universidad Veracruzana, 2008.

Helú, Antonio. *La obligación de asesinar*. Mexico City: Albatros, 1946.

Kornbluh, Anna. *The Order of Forms: Realism, Formalism and Social Space*. Chicago, IL: University of Chicago Press, 2019.

Larson, Ross. *Fantasy and Imagination in the Mexican Narrative*. Tempe: Center for Latin American Studies/Arizona State University Press, 1977.

Levine, Caroline. *Forms. Whole, Rhythm, Hierarchy, Network*. Princeton, NJ: Princeton University Press, 2015.

Los olvidados. Dir. Luis Buñuel. Estudios Tepeyac, 1950.

Madrid, Alejandro L. *Sounds of the Modern Nation: Music, Culture and Ideas in Post-Revolutionary Mexico*. Philadelphia, PA: Temple University Press, 2008.

Mexican Miracle Modernism

Mahieux, Viviane. *Urban Chroniclers in Modern Latin America: The Shared Intimacy of Everyday Life*. Austin: University of Texas Press, 2011.

Martín-Barbero, Jesús. *De los medios a las mediaciones: Comunicación, cultura y hegemonía*. Bogotá: Convenio Andrés Bello, 2003.

Morton, Adam David. *Revolution and the State in Modern Mexico: The Political Economy of Uneven Development*. Lanham, MD: Rowman & Littlefield, 2013.

Niblo, Stephen R. *Mexico in the 1940s: Modernity, Politics and Corruption*. Wilmington, DE: SR Books, 1999.

Novo, Salvador. *Viajes y ensayos I*. Mexico City: Fondo de Cultura Económica, 1996.

Piccato, Pablo. *A History of Infamy: Crime, Truth and Justice in Mexico*. Berkeley: University of California Press, 2017.

Quirarte, Vicente. *Elogio de la calle: Biografía literaria de la Ciudad de México 1850–1992*. Mexico City: Cal y Arena, 2004.

Rama, Ángel. *Las máscaras democráticas del modernismo*. Montevideo: Arca, 1985.

Ramírez Pimienta, Juan Carlos. "Ciencia ficción y crítica social en tres novelas mexicanas de los años cuarenta," *Revista de Crítica Literaria Latinoamericana* 55 (2002): 207–220.

Reyes, Alfonso. *Obras completas IX. Norte y Sur: Los trabajos y los días. História natural das laranjeiras*. Mexico City: Fondo de Cultura Económica, 1996.

Sánchez, Fernando Fabio. *Artful Assassins: Murder as Art in Modern Mexico*. Nashville, TN: Vanderbilt University Press, 2007.

Sánchez Prado, Ignacio M. "Peripheral Noir, Mediation and Capitalism: Noir Form, Noir Mediascape, Sociological Noir." In *Noir Affect*. Eds. Christopher Breu and Elizabeth Hatmaker, pp. 137–155. New York: Fordham University Press, 2020.

"The Golden Age Otherwise: Mexican Cinema and the Mediations of Capitalist Modernity in the 1940s and 1950s." In *Cosmopolitan Film Cultures in Latin America*. Eds. Rielle Navitski and Nicolas Poppe, pp. 241–264. Bloomington: Indiana University Press, 2017.

Naciones intelectuales: Las fundaciones de la modernidad literaria mexicana 1917–1959. West Lafayette, IN: Purdue University Press, 2009.

Sánchez Prado, Ignacio M., Anna M. Nogar and José Ramón Ruisánchez Serra. *A History of Mexican Literature*. Cambridge: Cambridge University Press, 2016.

Sefchovich, Sara. *México: País de ideas, país de novelas. Una sociología de la literatura mexicana*. Mexico City: Grijalbo, 1987.

Serratos, Francisco. "¿Cómo rescatar a un escritor? El caso de Rafael Bernal." *Cuadernos fronterizos* 39 (2017): 7–10.

Smith, Benjamin T. *The Mexican Press and Civil Society 1940–1976: Stories from the Newsroom, Stories from the Street*. Chapel Hill: University of North Carolina Press, 2018.

Spota, Luis. *El coronel fue echado al mar*. Mexico City: Talleres Gráficos de la Nación, 1947.

Strayer, Mike. "The Avant-Garde Detective Fiction of Antonio Helú," *Romance Notes* 55.2 (2015): 273–283.

Tario, Francisco. *Obras completas*. 2 vols. Ed. Alejandro Toledo. Mexico City: Fondo de Cultura Económica, 2015–16.

Tenorio-Trillo, Mauricio. *I Speak of the City: Mexico City at the Turn of the Twentieth Century*. Chicago, IL: University of Chicago Press, 2012.

Toledo, Alejandro. *Universo Francisco Tario*. Mexico City: La Cabra/Conaculta, 2014.

Torres, Vicente Francisco. *Muertos de papel: Un paseo por la narrativa policial mexicana*. Mexico City: Conaculta, 2003.

Torres Septién, Valentina. "La lectura, 1940–1960." In *Historia de la lectura en México*, pp. 295–337. Mexico City: el Colegio de México, 2010.

Usigli, Rodolfo. *Ensayo de un crimen*. Mexico City: América, 1944.

CHAPTER 8

Crime and the City
A Critical Walk through Latin American Crime Fiction and Urban Places

Emilio J. Gallardo-Saborido
Translated by Rocío Adzo

Transitions in Cartographic Literature from Parody to Monstrosity (1930–1980): An Introduction

This chapter examines the evolution of Latin American crime fiction, focusing on the use of urban space as a key element of the genre's configuration, a topic that emerged as Latin America's cities steadily became more important. Broadly, crime investigation in a specific geographical space and that space's link with crime have become key markers of identity in present-day crime fiction, in both literature and film. More specifically in the case of Latin American crime fiction, a process that we can term "vernacularization" emerged in considering those specific spaces as worthy enough to accommodate such narratives (overcoming the preference for foreign settings), but also in making the spaces themselves into inanimate protagonists. That has become crucial to our understanding of the changing terrain upon which many different fictional characters have trodden, in a genre that, over time, has become more obscure but also simultaneously illuminating of the reality of the continent itself.

Whereas, in 1964, Professor Donald A. Yates was able to say that crime fiction is "essentially a type of literature that avoids direct contact with reality" (6), in the last version of his essay *El género negro (The Noir Genre)* (1984), Mempo Giardinelli argued that almost all Latin American crime novels address issues such as racism, violence, and desperation, either directly or indirectly (221). Between 1930 and 1980, Latin American crime fiction followed a path similar to that followed by its international counterparts: starting with adaptions of the detective games created by the English version (including notable parodies), it then looked to the darkness of the North

131

American noir genre, but finally established the basis of a more autochthonous genre that would allow "el reencuentro entre el esquema de la novela negra y los autores, y de éstos con paisajes e historias nacionales" ("the reencounter between the schemata of the noir novel and its authors, and these in turn with national landscapes and histories") (Taibo, "Herejías," 38).[1] The Mexican writer Paco Ignacio Taibo II identified 1976 as an important year in the development of a new Spanish-language crime narrative (Taibo, "Herejías," 38). On the question of terminology, in 1990 he referred to the "neopoliciaco mexicano" (Argüelles 14) and in 1996 Leonardo Padura Fuentes gave us a sweeping analytical survey of the "neopolicial iberoamericano" (Padura 136–149).

Similarly, starting with Yates' seminal anthology of Latin American crime fiction, we can see that the detective genre spread its tentacles across the whole of Latin America, moving beyond the "three main centres" (Buenos Aires, Mexico City, and Santiago de Chile), which he mentioned in his introduction (Yates 6–7). In the process, the Latin American city gradually found a literary genre that was able to narrate it from a new perspective, developing and losing its innocence by examining the city intensively.

This chapter therefore examines the evolution of the Latin American crime fiction genre through the relationship between three of the continent's major cities and three historical moments. The following case studies have been chosen: the Buenos Aires of the stories of *Seis problemas para Don Isidro Parodi* (*Six Problems for Don Isidro Parodi*, 1942) by Jorge Luis Borges and Adolfo Bioy Casares; the Havana of Armando Cristóbal Pérez's novel *La ronda de los rubíes* (*Patrol of the Rubies*, 1973), and the Mexico City of *Días de combate* (*Days of Combat*, 1976) by Paco Ignacio Taibo II. What is presented here is a textual journey taking us from the use of parody by Borges and Bioy Casares, who play with the English models of the mystery novel, to the scathing national questioning of the Mexican *neopolicial* by Taibo, passing through Cristóbal Pérez's political commitment and Cuban revolutionary crime literature.

The Parodic City: Buenos Aires and *Seis Problemas para Don Isidro Parodi* (1942)

The first stop in the tour of crime fiction is the collection of stories where Borges and Bioy Casares' parodies adapted different elements from foreign crime fiction to the context of Argentina. In their perspective, Buenos Aires is read and codified as a mythical center where a certain notion of Argentina was established, albeit without losing any of the sharpness of their vision of the present.

Crime and the City 133

In the 1940s and the first half of the 1950s, Borges and Bioy Casares campaigned vigorously to defend crime fiction and the best ways to understand it (Fernández Vega; Gramuglio; Hernández Moreno 64–114). The latter took the form of a range of resources: the 1943 anthology *Los mejores cuentos policiales* (*The Best Detective Stories*); the Emecé-published collection *El séptimo círculo* (*The Seventh Circle*) in 1945; critical texts in magazines such as *Sur*; and both authors' participation in the jury for a 1950 literary competition (held by *Vea y Lea*) for crime stories. Because of their common interest in crime fiction, Borges and Bioy Casares coauthored a collection of short stories titled *Seis problemas para Don Isidro Parodi* (1942) under the pseudonym of Honorio Bustos Domecq. They used the same pseudonym for their collaboration on *Dos fantasías memorables* (*Two Memorable Fantasies*, 1946), but used another alias, B. Suárez Lynch, for *Un modelo para la muerte* (*A Model for Death*, 1946). Decades later, they jointly published *Crónicas de Bustos Domecq* (*Chronicles of Bustos Domecq*, 1967) and *Nuevos cuentos de Bustos Domecq* (*New Short Stories by Bustos Domecq*, 1977).

Although *Seis problemas para Don Isidro Parodi* is intimately linked to the models of the mystery novel genre (Poe, Collins, and Chesterton, etc.), it is a very singular example of the application of a foreign model to a new and strange local context, given that the dialogue between Buenos Aires and the crime narrative takes place in an evidently ludic way, employing parody. Scheines writes of a "doble parodia: del mundillo intelectual de la época … y del género policial" ("double parody: of the intellectual scene … and of the detective genre") (527). On many occasions Borges himself referred to these texts' playful and satirical intention (Lafforgue and Rivera 55–58; Borges and di Giovanni 117). Similarly, Vizcarra makes clear that "los autores, aunque llevan a cabo una parodia cuyo *ethos* es claramente reverencial y lúdico, no subvierten la obra referencial" ("the authors, although they undertake a parody whose ethos is clearly reverential and ludic, do not subvert the referential work") (26), while Borges himself proposed a series of "critiques" of crime fiction, based on *The Scandal of Father Brown* (1935) by Chesterton ("Los laberintos policiales," 129).

Buenos Aires became a crucial city as the site for the task undertaken by Borges and Bioy Casares to implant and develop the crime genre in Argentinian literature. It was seen as a privileged enclave, offering multiple referents (cultural, historical, sociological, urban) and enabling a rereading of the English school of crime fiction (Marengo 2002 offers a full list of bibliographical references in different stories).

In this way, the semiotic power of the city's street map becomes a key element for understanding the book, taking us on a journey through the city where, with precise references to specific streets, the book's events take place between 1933 and 1942 (Margery Peña 87). Although Parodi, a prisoner in cell 273 of the National Penitentiary, becomes a reverse parody of Benjamin's *flaneur* detective (495), the narratives of the visitors who search for Parodi for answers to the different cases map out for us a detailed journey through Buenos Aires and its surrounding areas, from El Pilar (Borges and Bioy Casares 56) to Avellaneda (Borges and Bioy Casares 83), through the city's most characteristic barrios and areas (Barrio Norte, Palermo, Montserrat, Balvanera, etc.).

One of these remarkables places in the city's topography and in the vision that Borges offers of Buenos Aires is the Plaza del Once (Plaza Miserere) and its surrounding areas in Balvanera, repeatedly mentioned in the last story of the collection: "La prolongada busca de Tai An" ("The Prolonged Search of Tai An"). There, as on other occasions, we can see how Borges and Bioy Casares merged their sentimental cartography of the city into the specific places where the characters act. Every week Borges would go to that very Plaza to meet Macedonio Fernández, later recalling it all passionately (Borges and di Giovanni 70; Borges and Carrizo 132; Vázquez 76). In the story, the theme of false appearances is central and recurrent in the narrative, ranging from humorous allusions before the puzzle is solved to key elements in the end of the story; the confusion of identities of the hunter and the hunted, or the intertextual echo of Poe's *Purloined Letter* when discovering the location of the sought-after object (in this case, the talisman of the Goddess). Plaza del Once acts as a faithful recreation of *The Purloined Letter* because Borges and Bioy Casares, in Borges' own words, purposely chose "uno de los lugares más feos de la ciudad" ("one of the ugliest places in the city"), the most ordinary place, as the site for the investigation of a unique jewel endowed with great power.

By considering the semiotic power of urban networks, we can better understand the city's role in crime fiction. With that in mind, we should consider one further example: a review of the spaces that are central to Parodi's biography. Discussing the aforementioned vernacularization of the genre in a foreword, "Palabra liminar" ("An Introductory Word"), the author celebrates the fact that "en el abigarrado Musée Grevin de las bellas letras . . . criminológicas, haga su aparición un héroe argentino, en escenarios netamente argentinos" ("in the over-elaborate Musée Grevin, a museum of criminological fine arts, there should make an appearance an Argentine hero, in scenarios that are clearly Argentine"), and also that Bustos has deliberately chosen "para sus típicas aguafuertes el marco natural: Buenos Aires" ("for his typical etchings the natural frame: Buenos Aires") (Borges

Crime and the City 135

and Bioy Casares 14). He also argues that in the book we will find a "fresco de lo que no vacilo en llamar la *Argentina contemporánea*" ("a fresco in what I do not hesitate to term *Contemporary Argentina*") (16). Within that context, the *detective sedentario* (sedentary), Isidro Parodi, stands out: a barber, a *criollo viejo* (established native), based in the Sur barrio, specifically in "Calle México" (Borges and Bioy Casares 35), Parodi, as we soon learn, is locked up in the National Penitentiary in Palermo, having been falsely accused of murder in 1919.

To fully understand the nature of the vernacularization and how the representation of the city plays a role in it, we must look more deeply into the figure of the protagonist. Cristina Parodi (127–142) undertook an in-depth character analysis of Isidro Parodi by looking at the definition of *criollo viejo* and summarizing its features; at the same time, we know that such a status implied a degree of "ascenso" ("promotion") (Borges and Bioy Casares 93). Cristina Parodi therefore concluded that the paradox within the *criollo viejo* notion for someone with an Italian surname meant that "en la Argentina virtual de Bustos Domecq, lo genuino puede ser adquirido" ("In the virtual Argentina of Bustos Domecq, what is genuine can be acquired") (131). She also points out that the character is "un hombre de otra ciudad y de otra época, de los viejos tiempos anteriores al Centenario. En su celda, don Isidro vive fuera del tiempo" ("a man from another city and another era, from the old times before the Argentina Centennial. In his cell, don Isidro lives outside time") (136). Parodi is a photograph – or better still, a daguerreotype – of a Buenos Aires that is vanishing but one that will live on, thanks to its quality of locked myth, evoking Buenos Aires' transition from a mythical past to a questionable modernity. The urban map becomes particularly important for this reading, as Parodi is someone who has experienced a highly significant displacement, from the Sur barrio (on Calle México) to living in the penitentiary located in Avenida Las Heras in Palermo.

Meanwhile, it is productive to add to this reading the historical and political keys Aguilar suggests: "La cárcel – como máquina simbólica – da la medida de un Estado que Borges y Bioy piensan como *fuerza local* de sujeción y autoritarismo" ("Prison – like a symbolic machine – gives us the measure of a state that Borges and Bioy consider to be a *local force* for subjection and authoritarianism") (74). Gervasio Montenegro, in the aforementioned "Palabra liminar," specifies the historical moment when Parodi appears, identifying it as "una proeza argentina, realizada, conviene proclamarlo, bajo la presidencia del Doctor Castillo" ("an Argentinean feat, carried out, it must be declared, under the presidency of Dr Castillo") (17), a reference to Ramón S. Castillo's presidency (1942–3).

We know that Parodi's creation was determined by "razones literarias" ("literary reasons"), in the words of Bioy Casares (Zito 124). In this respect, in the 1951 prologue of Attilio Rosi's *Buenos Aires en tinta china* (*Buenos Aires in Chinese Ink*), Borges defended the choice of the Sur barrio: "la substancia original de que está hecha Buenos Aires, la forma universal o idea platónica de Buenos Aires" ("the original substance from which Buenos Aires, in its universal form or platonic idea, is formed") (Borges, "Prólogo," 8); at the same time, he recognized that the Sur barrio area was the embodiment of the nation. Furthermore, we particularly know that, from 1901, 564 Calle México was the site of the Biblioteca Nacional (National Library), of which Borges himself was director from 1955 to 1973 (Zito 222, 226). Parodi, as the lettered symbol that he is, could not have chosen a better neighborhood for his humble barbershop.

However, in the 1942 stories Parodi, beyond everything that might come to pass in future narratives, finds himself locked up in the National Penitentiary. Once again, sentimental cartography intersects with the literary scene, since both authors were very familiar with the area around the prison: Bioy and Silvina Ocampo's address was Avenida Coronel Díaz 2730. This number is connected to the Parodi's cell, 273 (Hernández 330). Borges lived at Bulnes 2216 for several months at the beginning of the 1920s (Vázquez 71; Zito 123). In fact, when *Seis problemas para don Isidro Parodi* was published, Borges resided in Anchorena, quite close to the prison (Zito 142).

To summarize, Don Isidro, the detective created by Borges and Bioy Casares as the hero of their vernacular crime fiction, embodies, as parody and paradox, both the city's consciously constructed literary myth and the certainty of its disappearance, instability, and limits. The city will thereafter go through visions that are more corrosive, placing it at the center of new crime fictions where metropolis, violence, and decay will all go hand in hand.

The Revolutionized City: Havana and Cuban Revolutionary Crime

The second stage of our journey through crime fiction and Latin American cities takes us to Cuba in the 1970s, when the genre experienced a new twist, creating revolutionary Cuban crime fiction. Although Cuba had seen forerunners of this type of fiction in earlier decades, it was the 1959 revolution that generated a real explosion in its development, allowing it to grow into the genre we see today.

After the 1971 publication of Ignacio Cárdenas Acuña's novel *Enigma para un domingo* (*Enigma for a Sunday*), the number of such books being published

Crime and the City

in Cuba multiplied, in great part thanks to the MININT (Interior Ministry) Concurso Aniversario del Triunfo de la Revolución (Anniversary of the Revolution Contest), which was launched in 1971 with a call for books with "un carácter didáctico" ("a didactic character"), which would provide "un estímulo a la prevención y vigilancia de todas las actividades antisociales o contra el poder del pueblo" ("a stimulus for the prevention and vigilance of all activities that are anti-social or against the power of the *pueblo*") (Comisión de Arte y Cultura 58).

A whole body of critical work was soon created that defined the ideal dimensions of the new crime fiction, arguing that the genre had the capacity to adapt to a socialist context and, as Portuondo put it, to "expresar una visión revolucionaria, socialista, de la realidad" ("express a revolutionary, socialist, vision of reality") (7). In 1972, Armando Cristóbal Pérez published in the magazine *Bohemia* "El género policial y la lucha de clases: un reto para los escritores revolucionarios" ("The Crime Genre and the Class Struggle: A Challenge for Revolutionary Writers"), where he outlined how revolutionary writers could face the "reto (de) transformar el género, sin que deje de serlo totalmente en cuanto a la forma, pero con un contenido diametralmente opuesto" ("the challenge of transforming a genre, without it ceasing to be that genre completely as regards form, but with a content that is diametrically opposed") (Cristóbal Pérez, "El género," 301). He specifically identified several fundamental elements: in opposition to the traditional pattern of the lone private detective, the need to prioritize cooperation between the *pueblo* and the various specialist state organizations responsible for solving crimes; a critique of gratuitous violence or sex; the search for new forms of expression; and the need to connect common crime and political crime (302–305).

All those premises would gradually build the architecture for this new direction in crime fiction, as seen in the novels of Cristóbal Pérez himself. Ideological motivation and a necessary and activist political commitment were explicit from the outset, and ultimately (from the 1990s) contributed to both the decline and the reshaping of the Cuban genre. The same political vocation permeated the cartographies in these books, reconfiguring the relationship between crime fiction and the city. That can be seen most clearly in Cristóbal Pérez's own novel, *La ronda de los rubíes*, which won the first competition in 1973.

Those novels generally draw a clear line between the guilty and the law enforcement officials, allowing us to see clearly which are the "positive" characters and which the "negative" ones. In *La ronda de los rubíes*, Lieutenant Julio explores Havana in search of the perpetrator of a jewel robbery in the Vedado neighborhood. Although we see different urban areas characterized by their former association with the pre-revolutionary past (the Vedado's decadent image, the Colón area's strong connection with common criminality, and, in the Tropicana, the presence of counter-revolutionary elements), in all of them we also see the overwhelming presence of characters linked to the Revolution, such as the police, the military, and members of the militia and of the Committees for the Defence of the Revolution (CDR). This all creates a sense of security under a government authority that, despite being challenged by both the remnants of the past and new enemies, seems to be in control.

The "negative" characters constitute a catalogue of monsters, a teratology of all that is counterrevolutionary, telling us much about the Revolution's past and present fears. In *La ronda de los rubíes*, we are given a CIA agent (Ñico), a *lumpen* character (Pepe, a pimp and numbers-runner), a possible prostitute (Teté), two politically disaffected people with a bourgeois past (Joaquina and Rosario), and a homosexual (Luisito). This bestiary not only captured perfectly what other literary genres (such as the theater) of the time also portrayed but also aligned itself with the main ideological principles underpinning revolutionary discourse in the early 1970s.

For example, it is clear that a supreme work ethic as a proof of one's ideological correctness leads to the fact that those male characters who seem excessively well groomed arouse suspicion, and their criminal tendencies are finally exposed. That is the case of Pepe in *La ronda de los rubíes* and Toño in José Lamadrid's 1973 *La justicia por su mano* (*Justice by His Own Hand*). Let us not forget that fashion (alongside "costumbres y extravagancies" ["customs and extravagancy"]) merited mention in the Declaration of the First National Congress of Education and Culture of 1971, identified as yet another ideological battleground ("Declaración," 10–11).

As for the "positive" characters, they all fulfill the new genre's fundamental principle of avoiding the conventional model of an individual law enforcement officer solving the cases on his own. Instead, they emphatically reflect the cooperation between law enforcement and the mass organizations, which develops methodically and with a scrupulous inclusivity: each step taken by MININT's Lieutenant Julio through Havana in his investigations includes interviews with individuals willing to cooperate with his enquiries, thereby underlining the aforementioned idea of control over the city. Thus, characters who assist the lieutenant include a female president of a local CDR, a military officer, a militiaman, and a Party member, all ultimately sharing the glory of solving the case, and thus also of defending the revolutionary cause in accordance with the "principio

Crime and the City

leninista de la elaboración colectiva y la responsabilidad individual" ("the Leninist principle of collective design and individual responsibility"), identified by Portuondo (11) as one of the defining features of the revolutionary Cuban crime novel.

This activity of a shared and systematic vigilance translates into a sense of security in the preservation of the established authority and in its control of the city. In that way, it demonstrates a generally benevolent topography, with only scattered sites of disaffection that are inevitably weakened by collective action.

The City of Disenchantment: Paco Ignacio Taibo II's Mexico City

Following this evolution of crime fiction's relationship with Latin American cities, we see that, from the mid-1960s and the 1970s, a new way of understanding the genre began to break into the Latin American scene, eventually christened "neopolicial iberoamericano" ("new Ibero-American detective novel"). One of its leading exponents was the Mexican author Paco Ignacio Taibo II, who, besides creating many of the genre's most significant works, also theorized the genre. In a 1990 interview, he outlined the characteristics of the new Mexican crime genre as being: "La obsesión por las ciudades; una incidencia recurrente temática de los problemas del Estado como generador del crimen, la corrupción, la arbitrariedad policiaca y el abuso de poder; un sentido del humor negro a la mexicana y un poco de realismo kafkiano" ("an obsession with cities; a recurrence of the theme that the state is responsible for generating crime, corruption, police arbitrariness, and abuses of power; black humor, Mexican style, and a little Kafkaesque realism") (Argüelles 14). In this context, Mexico City emerges as a crucial element, giving meaning to Taibo's *neopolicial* work, as he himself admitted when asked about the origin of the Héctor Belascoarán Shayne detective series (Nichols 223–224).

As an author, Paco Ignacio Taibo II developed his own link to the *neopolicial* genre, particularly in the Belascoarán series of ten books, nine of which were written by Taibo alone (published between 1976 and 1993). The tenth and final book, *Muertos incómodos* (*The Uncomfortable Dead*, 2005), was authored in collaboration with the Zapatista leader Subcomandante Marcos.

The first of that series, the 1976 *Días de combate*, is the focus of the third and final case study here. In it, we see the person of the detective Héctor Belascoarán Shayne who, in "una posición antiheroica" ("an anti-heroic position") (Varas), is central to our understanding of the postmodern skepticism underpinning Taibo's *neopolicial* aims. This is especially visible in Taibo's break, early on in the novel, with the genre's canonical stereotypes, such as the conscientious and skillful partner in the mold of Sherlock's Watson. Instead, Taibo gives us the plumber who shares Belascoarán's office. Similarly, the reader is invited to question the very existence of a detective such as Belascoarán in the Mexican context, who "suena muy neoyorquino, muy cosmopolita, poco mexicano. Sospecho que no es demasiado serio" ("sounds very New York, very cosmopolitan, not very Mexican. I suspect that he can't be too serious") (Taibo II, *No habrá*, 7).

The story takes place in 1975, when Belascoarán is confronted with a string of female murders by a criminal who calls himself "Cerevro" (a corruption of "cerebro," or "brain"). In *Días de combate*, the city is portrayed as a "monstruo urbano" ("urban monster") (Taibo II, *No habrá*, 93), which the strangler aims to reduce to universal terror, declaring "La ciudad es mía" ("The city is mine") (108). This tormented and chaotic image of the city dominates the text, reflecting the mental state of the protagonist, who has decided to abandon his comfortable job as an engineer at General Electric, to break up his marriage, and to embark on a search for something he does not quite know about yet in his new occupation as a detective, for which he has trained himself via correspondence courses.

This all leads to his ambivalence when he finds himself sitting in his friends' comfortable living room listening to bossa nova. He realizes that he will never be able to share their perspective of the city: "La ciudad diminuta y suave, blandengue y sonrosada. La ciudad lenta, de clase media afable. La ciudad inventada, por los que viven en un séptimo piso" ("The diminutive, soft city, soft and rosy. The slow city, of the affable middle class. The city invented by those who live on the seventh floor") (6). Taibo discovers that behind that sugary vision hides the side Belascoarán has to face, seeing it as "un monstruo, como el vientre fétido de una ballena, o el interior de una lata de conservas estropeada" ("a monster, like the fetid belly of a whale, or in the insides of a misshapen tin of preserves") (13).

The murderer's view of the city is heavily mediated by ideological and symbolic meanings. In fact, the conflict between criminal and detective can be understood as two different ways of conceptualizing the city. The women's bodies become the trophies for the exercise of both class and male violence, symbolizing the desire of the city's powerful to possess and oppress the exploited. At the beginning of the novel, and after six crimes have been committed, Belascoarán racks his brain to find a common pattern that is not based on geography ("cualquier parte de la ciudad fue

Crime and the City 141

escenario" ["any part of the city was the scene of the crime"]), age, profession ("estudiante, prostituta, secretaria, maestra de primaria, dentista, estudiante" ["student, prostitute, secretary, primary schoolteacher, dentist, student"]), or social background ("clase media y baja" ["middle class and low class"]) (Taibo II, *No habrá*, 10). However, the latter aspect will prove to be the most important when the killer admits: "No tocaré a las mujeres de mi clase. En ellas sólo quiero el reflejo de mis actos, de ellas sólo quiero el temor que la sombra de la imagen de un hombre les devuelva. A ellas sólo quiero reducirlas a su condición original" ("I won't touch women of my own class. They are only there to be the reflection of my acts, to feel the fear that the shadow of a man's image gives them. They are only there to be reduced by me to their original condition") (100). In the person of Cerevro, we can see a synecdoche that encompasses all the condemnations of capitalism, patriarchy, and violence against women.

That elitist and contemptuous attitude toward the lower classes is contextualized by other factors. The first is the intellectual references that build the profile of the murderer, who is presented to us as some sort of Nietzschean disciple (149) from Thomas de Quincey's *On Murder Considered as One of the Fine Arts*. The second is our need to take into account the binary opposition between the city areas linked to the hunter and the hunted. The murderer's decadent semi-palace contrasts sharply with Belascoarán's office: against the aristocratic magnificence of the former is set the harshness of the latter. The location of the murderer's residence in such a privileged area of Mexico City as Las Lomas de Chapultepec reinforces the credibility of a gloomy class-based refinement that will be seen as a characteristic of the businessman-murderer.

On the other hand, the fact that Belascoarán shares his office with a plumber not only says something of his working-class connections but also serves to parody the typical office of the hero of the North American noir crime novel. From the outset, the novel's text portrays his unusual circumstances. In fact, the novel begins in this way: "Abusado, güey, que me los pisa – le dijo al plomero, con el que compartía el despacho" ("'Watch your step, mate,' he said to the plumber, with whom he shared the office") (3); and we soon after learn that the sign at the entrance to their office is deeply tragic-comic: "BELASCOARÁN SHAYNE: detective / GÓMEZ LETRAS: plomero" ("BELASCOARÁN SHAYNE: detective / GÓMEZ LETRAS: plumber") (5). Taibo shows us that the carnivalization of the North American model can also be augmented: at the end of the novel, we discover that the plumber has sublet half of his office space to a certain Javier Villarreal who is "haciendo una investigación sobre la red de cloacas de la ciudad de México" ("investigating the network of sewers of Mexico City"), and Taibo continues: "Siempre me interesó mucho esa idea de que un día en esta ciudad nos íbamos a morir ahogados en mierda" ("I was always fascinated by the idea that one day we would all drown in shit in this city") (125). However, as Pardo has noted, these characters act as assistants for Belascoarán in his investigations, through bonds of friendship and solidarity that are established between them. Thus they contribute to a particular notion of the nation (Pardo 59), and (let us add further) they draw the working class into the challenges posed by the protagonist.

Another city space linked to Belascoarán is the Coyoacán area where his mother lives. From the start, we know that the protagonist is the fruit of the union of a Basque sea captain and an Irish folk singer. The Spanish connection also reinforces Belascoarán's ideological profile: when he is given his father's pistol, we see a case of political genetics, his father having used it in some of the most relevant revolutionary endeavors and acts of war in the first half of the twentieth century. Belascoarán is not particularly marked politically by a resounding ideological commitment (which is, however, very much his brother's case) but rather by being a progressive leftist, something that is made clear in passages where he expresses his support for the Palestinian cause, the US civil rights struggle, and the Cuban Revolution.

Throughout the novel, the detective journeys through a Mexico City that becomes an immense jigsaw puzzle whose pieces have to be fitted together to reveal the killer. But in this case the city should be read from deep within a geographical space, which is projected both above and below what is seen at first sight. In that way, the metro should be seen as a privileged area, not only allowing him to move quickly through different crime scenes and investigations but also allowing Belascoarán to reflect from the depths of the city, a place where he can become "un aparato pensante" ("a thinking device") (68). There is, additionally, an even higher plane superimposed on the puzzle, which is key to solving the case: television. Pardo (82), considering more broadly the role of the means of communication (especially press, radio, and television) in the Belascoarán series, has identified a triple function: as a nexus between the character and the environmental context, as a key tool for his inquiries, and as a resource to enable details about the protagonist's emotional life. In *Días de combate* specifically, Belascoarán decides to compete in a quiz program, his participation being based on the theme of "Great Stranglers in the History of Crime"; with that as bait, he hopes that communication with the murderer will be established.

Crime and the City 143

Indeed, by doing away with the criminal, Belascoarán knows that he is also destroying one part of the system previously called "El Gran Estrangulador" ("The Great Strangler") (149), which throughout the period of the different murders has been responsible for the state having "masacrado a cientos de campesinos" ("massacred hundreds of peasants") or having left "muerto de hambre o frío decenas más, de enfermedades curables otros centenares" ("dying of hunger or cold dozens more, with hundreds dying of curable illnesses") (149). Thus, the moral debate is substantially based on political confrontation, where we see a Marxist echo in one of the final dialogues: the detective, facing the murderer, seeks to establish himself as the champion of an admittedly limited, but revolutionary, justice:

> Le debo la venganza a doce muchachas muertas por un juego de salón en manos de un monstruo. Cierto, no es el único. Desde las alturas otros juegan al ajedrez con nosotros. No tengo al alcance esas alturas. Algún día será tomado el cielo por asalto, y al destruirlo se liberará lo que el cielo ha contagiado. (My debt is to avenge twelve girls killed in a parlor game at the hands of a monster. Of course, he's not the only one. From their lofty heights, others play chess with us. I can't reach those heights. One day the heavens will be taken by force, and their destruction will liberate all that they have contaminated). (150)

In conclusion, then, we see that the three cases studied here synthesize the different transitions through which the crime fiction genre has evolved, not only in a textual taxonomy but also, very particularly, in its relationship with the Latin American city from 1930 to 1980. A shared obsession with the city, however, develops here in very different ways. Hence, the vernacularization of the genre is expressed at the start in the parody realized by Borges and Bioy Casares, who place it in a space and time the Argentine reader will easily recognize. Their text uncovers different layers of Buenos Aires that combine to recreate a mythical past set against a biting reading of the present. The Cuban case takes us through the genre by placing at its core the affirmation of grand political narratives and by prioritizing a close link between literature and its propagandistic functions. In this case, the city becomes a board game where control and order lie unquestionably in the hands of the revolutionary authorities. Finally, Tabio announces, and inserts himself into, a postmodern version that Padura (137–138) has argued belongs to the genre's next transitional phase: *neopolicial* literature. Tabio's Mexico City is mapped out as a monster, an accumulation of iniquity and violence, where, even so, there remains a space for ideological struggle and hope.

144 EMILIO J. GALLARDO-SABORIDO

Notes

1. All English translations in this chapter are by Rocío Adzo.

Works Cited

Aguilar, Gonzalo Moisés. "Una historia local de la infamia (Sobre *Seis problemas para don Isidro Parodi* de H. Bustos Domecq)." *Tramas para leer la literatura argentina* 5 (1996): 69–80.

Argüelles, Juan Domingo. "Entrevista con Paco Ignacio Taibo II. El policiaco mexicano: un género hecho con un autor y terquedad." *Tierra adentro* 49 (1990): 13–15.

Benjamin, Walter. *Libro de los pasajes*. Madrid: Akal, 2005.

Borges, Jorge Luis. "Prólogo." In *Buenos Aires en tinta china* by Attilio Rossi (con poema de Rafael Alberti), pp. 7–9. Losada, 2010.

"Los laberintos policiales y Chesterton." In *Borges en Sur 1931–1980*, edición al cuidado de Sara Luisa del Carril y Mercedes Rubio de Socchi, pp. 126–129. Emecé, 1999.

"La presencia de Buenos Aires en la poesía." In *Textos recobrados, 1919–1929*, edición al cuidado de Sara Luisa del Carril. Emecé, 1997.

Borges, Jorge Luis and Adolfo Bioy Casares. *Obras completas en colaboración. 1. Con Adolfo Bioy Casares*. Madrid: Alianza Editorial, 1981.

Borges, Jorge Luis and Antonio Carrizo. *Borges el memorioso: Conversaciones de Jorge Luis Borges con Antonio Carrizo*. Mexico City/Buenos Aires: Fondo de Cultura Económica, 1982.

Borges, Jorge Luis and Norman Thomas di Giovanni. *Autobiografía 1899–1970*. Buenos Aires: El Ateneo, 1999.

Comisión de Arte y Cultura. Dirección Política. MININT. "Sobre género policiaco. Concurso XIII Aniversario del Triunfo de la Revolución." *Moncada* 6.2 (July 1971): 58.

Cristóbal Pérez, Armando. "El género policial y la lucha de clases: un reto para los escritores revolucionarios." *Por la novela policial*. Ed. Luis Rogelio Nogueras, pp. 298–305. Havana: Editorial Arte y Literatura, 1982.

La ronda de los rubíes. Havana: Letras Cubanas, 1979 (1st ed., 1973).

"Declaración del Primer Congreso Nacional de Educación y Cultura." *Casa de las Américas* 65–66 (1971): 4–19.

Fernández Vega, José. "Una campaña estética: Borges y la narrativa policial." *Variaciones Borges* 1 (1996): 27–66.

Giardinelli, Mempo. *El género negro: Orígenes y evolución de la literatura policial y su influencia en Latinoamérica*. Buenos Aires: Capital Intelectual, 2013.

Gramuglio, María Teresa. "Bioy, Borges y *Sur*: diálogos y duelos." Alicante: Biblioteca Virtual Miguel de Cervantes, 2012.

Hernández Moreno, Alberto. *Las tramas esquivas: Jorge Luis Borges, Adolfo Bioy Casares y la literatura policial*. Murcia: Tres Fronteras Ediciones, 2015.

Lafforgue, Jorge and Jorge B. Rivera. *Asesinos de papel*. Buenos Aires: Calicanto Editorial, 1977.

Crime and the City 145

Marengo, María del Carmen. *La obra de Bustos Domecq y B. Suárez Lynch: problematización estética y campo cultural.* 2002. University of Maryland, PhD dissertation. www.borges.pitt.edu/bsol/documents/LibroTesis.pdf.

Margery Peña, Enrique. "*Seis problemas para don Isidro Parodi.* Notas para su interpretación con alcances sobre el género policial." *Filología y Lingüística* 13.2 (1987): 61–91.

Nichols, William J. "A quemarropa con Manuel Vázquez Montalbán y Paco Ignacio Taibo II." *Arizona Journal of Hispanic Cultural Studies* 2 (1998): 197–232.

Padura, Leonardo. *Modernidad, posmodernidad y novela policial.* Havana: Ediciones Unión, 2000.

Pardo, Carlos. *El detective y la ciudad: El espacio urbano en las novelas de detectives de Paco Ignacio Taibo II y Leonardo Padura Fuentes.* Medellín: Editorial Universidad de Antioquía, 2017.

Parodi, Cristina. "Una Argentina virtual: El universo intelectual de Honorio Bustos Domecq." *Variaciones Borges* 6 (1998): 53–143.

Portuondo, José Antonio. "La novela policial revolucionaria." *La justicia por su mano*, by José Lamadrid Vega, pp. 7–15. Editorial Arte y Literatura, 1973.

Scheines, Graciela. "Las parodias de Jorge Luis Borges y Adolfo Bioy Casares." *Cuadernos Hispanoamericanos* 505–507 (1992): 525–533.

Taibo II, Paco Ignacio. *No habrá final feliz: La serie completa de Héctor Belascoarán Shayne.* New York: Harper Collins Publishers, 2009.

"Herejías en español: la 'otra' novela policíaca," *Cuadernos del Norte* 8.41 (1987): 38–43.

Varas, Patricia. "Belascoarán y Heredia: detectives postcoloniales." *CiberLetras: revista de crítica literaria y de cultura* 15 (2006).

Vázquez, María Esther. *Borges: Esplendor y derrota.* Barcelona: Tusquets, 1999.

Vizcarra, Héctor Fernando. "El ciclo de Isidro Parodi: reinterpretación paródica del relato de detección clásico." *Literatura: teoría, historia, crítica* 14.2 (2012): 13–29.

Yates, Donald A., ed. *El cuento policial latinoamericano.* Ediciones de Andrea, 1964.

Zito, Carlos Alberto. *El Buenos Aires de Borges.* Buenos Aires: Aguilar, 1998.

PART III

Solidarity

CHAPTER 9

"Dar Testimonio" as a Lens for Rethinking the Mexican Literary Canon

Sarah E. L. Bowskill

On the occasion of the first Feria del Libro y Festival de la Cultura (Book Fair and Festival of Culture) held in 1964 in Ciudad Juárez, Mexico, Rosario Castellanos gave a speech entitled "La novela mexicana contemporánea y su valor testimonial" ("The Contemporary Mexican Novel and Its Value as Testimony").[1] In this speech Castellanos declared that, since its inception, the Mexican novel "ha sido, no un pasatiempo de ociosos ni un alarde de imaginativos ni un ejercicio de retóricos, sino algo más: un instrumento útil para captar nuestra realidad y para expresarla, para conferirle sentido y perdurabilidad" ("has not been an idle hobby, a show of the imagination or an exercise in rhetoric, but something more: a useful tool to capture and express our reality, to give it meaning and durability"[2]) (Castellanos 223). In his 1967 acceptance speech for the Nobel Prize for Literature, Miguel Angel Asturias picked up on this idea of the testimonial value of the novel when he said that the role of the novelist was not to entertain but to bear witness ("dar testimonio"). The capacity for bearing witness, in his view, was not limited to any particular genre. For both Castellanos and Asturias, the pressing issue of the moment was to bear witness to the Indigenous populations of the Americas but, as Castellanos indicated, the testimonial role of the novel had a much longer history. This history has, to some extent, been obscured by narrower and more recent debates about the *testimonio* genre. Refocusing our attention on how, in a broad sense, Mexican letters bear witness enables us to rethink the twentieth-century literary canon and its continued domination by male authors and by what Castellanos succinctly referred to as the "novela nacional" ("national novel").[3]

As Jaume Peris Blanes reports, the idea of *testimonio* as a genre came to the fore when the Casa de las Américas prize for *testimonio* was established in 1970 because, in the preceding year, the jury had wanted to recognize changes occurring in Latin American literature, but some of the texts they

149

wished to reward did not fit the established categories of novel, short story, poetry, and essay (193). The creation of the Casa de las Américas prize thus represents a significant moment when there was a narrowing of understanding around the concept of *testimonio* compared to the way "dar testimonio" had been used only a few years earlier by Castellanos and Asturias. It is this earlier understanding of "dar testimonio" as an act of solidarity with the marginalized that this chapter seeks to reprise.

In returning to this prior understanding, I suggest that we take a step back from the debates over the definition of *testimonio* as a separate genre. These discussions, many of which connect to the decision to include *Me llamo Rigoberta Menchú* (*I, Rigoberta Menchú*) on the "Western Civilization" course of the Stanford curriculum, led to competing definitions of *testimonio* that were then problematized almost to the point of exhaustion.[4] *Testimonio* in these debates became a literary problem about generic boundaries and definitions. Instead, I propose, the concept of "dar testimonio" may prove more useful as a guiding concept for understanding a tradition of writing in Mexico that is based on an engagement with the "other" in a relationship of solidarity. In so doing, a different history of Mexican literature emerges to the one that has been told to date.

Solidarity is typically seen as being at the heart of the *testimonio* genre as the text tends to be based on an alliance between someone in a position of relative privilege and a subaltern or marginalized subject. As Asturias' Nobel speech makes clear, solidarity is also fundamental to his understanding of "dar testimonio" (bearing witness). Tracing the origins of witnessing back to pre-conquest accounts of heroic legends, Asturias argued that contemporary authors were writing "dentro de la tradición constante de compromiso con nuestros pueblos" ("from within the constant tradition of commitment to our communities") in solidarity with groups including those whose land has been dispossessed and plantation workers as "[n] uestras novelas buscan movilizar en el mundo las fuerzas morales que han de servirnos para defender a esos hombres" ("our novels seek to move the moral forces in the world that have to serve us in defending these men"). This use of "hombres" ("men") and the absence of women in Asturias' list of marginalized groups is, sadly, not surprising.

For Asturias and Castellanos, bearing witness to the experiences of marginalized groups as an act of solidarity is at the heart of an origins myth for Latin American and Mexican literature, respectively. It is therefore telling that Asturias' account excludes women as either the subject or the authors of such texts. Yet, as will be seen, women authors writing in different genres were bearing witness to the experiences of marginalized

Rethinking the Mexican Literary Canon

groups. By bearing witness to the experiences of other marginalized groups at a time when they were also marginalized, Mexican women authors in particular can be said to build coalitions at the margins that challenge official conceptualizations of who belongs to the *we* of the nation.

In Latin American literature, the period covered by the present volume (1930–80) is often seen as a time before which women authors emerged onto the literary scene.[5] While women were undoubtedly writing in this earlier period, this era is perhaps most commonly associated with the emergence of the male-dominated "boom" and magical realism.[6] In Mexico, following the search for a virile literature in the aftermath of the Mexican Revolution, the novel of the Revolution emerged as the driving force behind the nation's fiction.[7] In a very real sense, this literature, especially in its early years, gave testimony or bore witness to the events during the conflict, and some of the preeminent authors, including, for example, Mariano Azuela and Martín Luis Guzmán, had firsthand experience of it. However, with the exception of Nellie Campobello's 1931 novel *Cartucho: Relatos de la lucha en el norte de México* (*Cartucho: Tales of the Struggle in Northern Mexico*, 1988), women authors seldom feature in the literary history of the immediate post-revolutionary period.

Subsequently, women authors struggled to fit into the categories used in histories of Mexican literature. The prevailing periodization of twentieth-century Mexican literature can be ascertained by looking at histories of Mexican literature. Emmanuel Carballo, Julio Jiménez Rueda, José Luis Martínez, and Christopher Domínguez Michael, as I have argued elsewhere, are among those who had a defining influence on the formation of the twentieth-century Mexican literary canon.[8] In the first edition of his *Diecinueve protagonistas de la literatura mexicana del siglo XX* (*Nineteen Protagonists of 20th Century Mexican Literature*), for example, Emmanuel Carballo divides his authors into the following five groups: "Ateneo de la Juventud" ("Athenaeum of Youth"), "El colonialismo" (those interested in the colonial period as a source of national spirit), "Los contemporáneos" ("The Contemporaries Group"), "Narradores de la Revolución y Posrevolucionarios" ("Narrators of the Revolution and Post-Revolution"), and "Escritores Jóvenes" ("Young Writers"). Two women, Nellie Campobello and Rosario Castellanos, are included. A later edition from 1986 also included Elena Garro. No further women were added to the 1994 edition despite there being by that time a body of scholarship on Mexican women authors. Many of the same categories are found in histories of literature such as *La literatura mexicana del siglo XX* (*Mexican Literature in the 20th Century*), which was a collaboration between

Martínez and Domínguez Michael updating Martínez's earlier *Literatura mexicana del siglo XX (20th Century Mexican Literature)*, which was first published in 1949 and then frequently revised. In the contents pages only one woman, Asunción Izquierdo Albiñana (Ana Mairena), is included in the section "Escritores Independientes" ("Independent Writers"). Although more women are mentioned in the text itself, they are not singled out as deserving special attention.

When Mexican women authors in the period 1930–80 have been recovered and recognized by feminist scholarship, little seems to connect their work other than gender and nationality. The diversity of women's contributions and the fact that they cannot be accommodated into a coherent overarching narrative could be considered a hindrance when it comes to securing them a place in the Mexican literary canon. Where connections between mid-century Mexican women authors have emerged, the focus has been on the Revolution and on better-known authors such as Campobello, Poniatowska, and Garro.[9] This chapter suggests that more connections are yet to be recognized.

In her study of women writers associated with the so-called "boom femenino" of women's writing post-1980, Emily Hind suggests: "With a telescope, Mexican women's work in the twentieth and twenty-first centuries appears as a grouping of unrelated planets . . . . By switching the telescope for a microscope, however, the critic discovers that beneath the obvious atmospheric disparities among the 'boom femenino' texts there lies a common molecular core of shared thematics" (51). Could "dar testimonio" be one of the core thematics connecting women writers before the "boom femenino" in the period 1930–80?

The following analysis proposes to build on more established links connecting Campobello, Poniatowska, and Garro to explore the ways in which we might start to further connect these three Mexican women, and others writing in the period who are less widely known, by viewing their work as giving testimony, as an act of solidarity with the "Other." I do not intend to suggest that these women influenced one another. Rather, I suggest that, taken together, these texts spanning half a century and viewed through the lens of "dar testimonio" come together to foreground an alternative history of watershed moments of transition in twentieth-century Mexico as marginalized groups struggled to be heard; and, I propose, the existence of these texts may have been pivotal in shifting from a male-dominated canon and society to increased opportunities for women and the advent of women writers into the mainstream in the late twentieth century.

Rethinking the Mexican Literary Canon 153

"Dar Testimonio" and the Mexican Revolution

As has been noted, perhaps the best-established connection between mid-century Mexican women authors is a shared interest in the Revolution, but viewing this interest in the broader context of bearing witness leads us to uncover other links. Writing about the Mexican Revolution is the cornerstone of the twentieth-century Mexican literary canon, and Elena Poniatowska is perhaps Mexico's best-known author of *testimonio*. In 1969, a year before the Casa de las Américas prize for *testimonio* was established, Poniatowska published *Hasta no verte Jesús mío* (*Here's to You, Jesusa!*, 2001). The text is about Josefina Bórquez's experience as a *soldadera* (female soldier) during the Revolution and her life afterward. The following year, Poniatowska became the first woman to win the Premio Mazatlán de Literatura (Mazatlán Prize for Literature) for what one contemporary critic described as a "testimonio y novela" ("testimony and novel").[10] While Doris Sommer suggests that the concept of a "testimonial novel" is a "contradiction in terms between immediacy and manipulation" (914) and Deborah Shaw suggests that critics have been caught up in debates as to "whether the text is a novel, a testimonial, an autobiography or a hybrid containing elements of all these" (119), it seems that these distinctions were less important for Mexico's critical establishment and reading public at the time, possibly owing to the currency of the concept of "dar testimonio," which provides a way of reconciling these supposed contradictions.

Selling over 20,000 copies in its first year, *Hasta no verte* was very well received. In contrast, Campobello's earlier text *Cartucho*, which bears witness to experiences of the Revolution in the north of Mexico through the eyes of a child narrator, took longer to be recognized. As Poniatowska herself wrote, Campobello was long overlooked and "of all the novelists of the Revolution she is the one who gets the least notice" (n.p.). *Cartucho* was probably overlooked because of its glorification of Pancho Villa who, as Ilene O'Malley notes, took longer to be accepted into official narratives of the unified Revolution.[11] Confronted with Villa's omission from the institutionalized Revolution and the accompanying erasure of the suffering endured by populations such as those featured in her stories, Campobello's text provided an alternative to the official history of the Revolution. This desire to correct established narratives and bear witness on behalf of the marginalized is perhaps most evident when the narrator reveals that, contrary to what was believed, revolutionary Colonel Nacha Ceniceros was not dead and the accepted version of events was untrue: "Ahora digo, y lo digo con la voz del que ha podido destejer una mentira: ¡Viva Nacha

Ceniceros, coronela de la revolución!" ("Now I say, and I say it with the voice of someone who has been able to unravel a lie, long live Nacha Ceniceros, Colonel in the Revolution!") (Campobello 107).

In her "Introduction" to the English translation of *Cartucho*, Poniatowska's description further draws attention to the text as being born out of a desire to "dar testimonio" to lived experience. She writes: "Nellie doesn't invent anything she tells; she saw, she lived, she recorded it all" (n.p.). Yet to suggest that *Cartucho* is an autobiography is to do a disservice to the way in which Campobello so clearly constructs the perspective from which she wishes to tell "her" story. It also ignores the way in which the narrator frequently draws attention to the sources who are people with whom she identifies from her community and whose memory she wishes to honor. For example, in "La muleta de Pablo López" ("Pablo López's Crutch"), the narrator begins: "Todos comentaban aquel fusilamiento, dijo Mamá ... ella no lo vio porque estaba en Parral. Martín se lo contó todo" ("Everyone talked about that execution, said Mother ... she did not see it because she was in Parral. Martín told her everything") (Campobello 125). Similarly, at the start of "Tomás Urbina," the narrator states: "Mi tío abuelo lo conoció muy bien .... Y narra, como si fuera un cuento, que el general Tomás Urbina nació en Nieves, Durango, un día 18 de agosto del año de 1877" ("My great uncle knew him very well. And he tells it as if it were a story that General Tomás Urbina was born in Nieves, Durango on the 18th August in the year 1877") (Campobello 127). And in "Los hombres de Urbina" ("Urbina's Men") she begins by underscoring the reliability of her sources: "Le contaron a Mamá todo lo que había pasado. Ella no olvidaba. Aquellos hombres habían sido sus paisanos" ("They told Mother everything that had happened. She did not forget. Those men had been her countrymen) (Campobello 119). By drawing in these other voices, as Meyer suggests, the narrator "collectivizes her testimony" (52) and *Cartucho* "crosses the boundaries between autobiography and testimony" (47). The account is both Campobello's and that of the people in her community with whom she feels solidarity as she and they suffered so much only to be written out of official history.

Cartucho is the best known of Campobello's works, but in *Apuntes sobre la vida militar de Pancho Villa* (*Notes on the Military Career of Pancho Villa*, 1940) she also bore witness and drew on the testimonies of others to do so.[12] But her impulse to bear witness through writing went beyond the Revolution. Campobello also wrote *Ritmos indígenas de México* (*Indigenous Rhythms of Mexico*, 1940). However, this text was omitted from her complete works as published by the Fondo de Cultura Económica in which Juan

Rethinking the Mexican Literary Canon 155

Bautista Aguilar described it as "una veta inacabada por descubrir en su interpretación literaria" ("an untapped vein whose literary interpretation is yet to be discovered") (26). In *Ritmos* she turned her attention to recording aspects of Indigenous life, and particularly traditional dance, in Mexico. Rather than being seen as an aside from Nellie Campobello's main body of work, viewing it through the lens of "dar testimonio" gives it a more central position in her oeuvre; it gives Campobello relevance beyond the novel of the Revolution and connects her to other women authors who also wrote about Indigenous populations.

"Dar Testimonio" and Mexico's Indigenous Populations

As one of Mexico's best-known women authors, Rosario Castellanos is recognized for her writings that bear witness to the experiences of Indigenous communities and reflect on her own marginalized position as a woman in a patriarchal society. *Balún Canán* (*The Nine Guardians*, 1957), *Ciudad Real* (*City of Kings*, 1960), and *Oficio de tinieblas* (*The Book of Lamentations*, 1962) are all examples of a new kind of *indigenista* literature that challenged official discourses and showcased "the authors' more intimate knowledge of indigenous cultures and their incorporation of myth and literary tradition (both written and oral) into their narratives along with the observations they made by living or working in indigenous communities, often as anthropologists" (O'Connell 61). *Indigenista* literature is an established category in histories of Mexican literature but, with the exception of Castellanos, women's contributions are often overlooked. Like many of Castellanos' works, María Lombardo de Caso's novel, *La culebra tapó el río* (*The Snake Blocked the River*, 1962), was also set in Chiapas and belongs to the same tradition of witnessing and *indigenista* literature, but it is less well known.

Other women authors who used their writings to "dar testimonio" regarding the experiences of Indigenous populations include Graciela Santana Fuentes de Szymanski, who drew on oral accounts of family and friends in Jalisco and from her work in Indigenous communities to write *Voces de Tepozpizaloya* (*Voices from Tepozpizaloya*, 1974), and Elvira Vargas.[13] Vargas was part of a generation of women journalists who, through their work in the national press, contributed to current debates.[14] Vargas wrote *Por las rutas del sureste* (*Along the Roads of the South East*, 1939) while reporting on President Lázaro Cárdenas' tour of Chiapas, Campeche, Tabasco, Yucatán, and Quintana Roo. While Castellanos connects the marginalization of women and that of Indigenous communities, Thea Pitman observes that Vargas elects not to write about women's position in society. Nevertheless, Pitman notes that it is significant that Vargas, as a woman, chose to speak out in solidarity with other marginalized groups because:

> al defender la causa de los indígenas y las comunidades campesinas sin derechos de los alejados rincones de la República, Vargas está dando implícitamente a las mujeres – otro grupo despojado de sus derechos – una voz: estas son las voces heterogéneas y alternativas que pueden desafiar las versiones oficiales de la identidad nacional. (Pitman 140–141)

> By defending the cause of the Indigenous peoples and rural communities deprived of their rights in the far-flung corners of the Republic, Vargas is implicitly giving women – another group deprived of their rights – a voice: these are the heterogeneous voices that can challenge official versions of national identity.

The same is true of the other women authors discussed in this chapter. By bearing witness to the marginalization of others, they can be said to be working to overcome their own marginalization.

"Dar Testimonio": Life in Exile and the Spanish Civil War

The arrival of Spanish exiles as a result of the Spanish Civil War (1936–9) had a significant impact on the Mexican cultural scene and on Mexican literature, yet the resulting body of literature rarely features in histories of Mexican literature. The influence of these exiles and their texts, which often bear witness to their experiences in Spain and in Mexico, is brought to the fore by a focus on "dar testimonio." In *España desde México: Vida y testimonio de transterrados* (*Spain from Mexico: Lives and Testimonies of Expatriates*, 1978), Ascensión Hernández de León-Portilla, herself a Spaniard who took Mexican nationality as a result of marriage to a Mexican historian rather than due to enforced exile, gathered together the testimonies of a group of exiles including authors, artists, and intellectuals.[15] In her selection of interviewees, Hernández explains that she spoke to academics from different disciplines who came from different regions of Spain and held different political positions on the left. Only one interviewee, Elvira Gascón, was a woman. While Hernández connects her work to the emerging discipline of oral history, and her subjects are from privileged backgrounds and so are able to participate in the editorial process, there are clear parallels with the approach adopted in the *testimonio* genre and her introduction speaks to her being motivated by a desire to "dar testimonio" and, like Campobello, to correct misconceptions and

Rethinking the Mexican Literary Canon   157

misunderstandings. In her case, she explains that she hopes to correct an overwhelmingly negative perception of Spain, to recover the memory of forgotten Republican exiles, and to contribute to a new atmosphere of hope that she sees as emerging in Spain since the end of 1974.

Hernández's text repeatedly reminds us that the accounts she has gathered are part of Mexican history as much as they are part of Spanish history, just as her text should be considered as part of both the Mexican and Spanish testimonial tradition. The sixteen testimonies are preceded by a lengthy introductory study by Hernández divided into three parts. Two of the three essays deal with the exiles' experiences in Mexico and Mexican-Spanish relations, further emphasizing the relevance of these exiles for Mexico and Mexican readers.

Carlota O'Neill's memoir, which was popular among Mexican readers, also bears witness to her experiences during the Spanish Civil War.[16] In exile, O'Neill acquired Mexican nationality and published her multivolume memoir *Una mujer en la Guerra de España* (*A Woman in the Spanish Civil War*, 1964), *Romanzas de las rejas* (*Music from Behind Bars*, 1964), and *Los muertos también hablan* (*The Dead Also Speak*, 1971).[17] Like other Spanish exiles who wrote about their experiences in Europe from their newly adopted country, O'Neill's work could be seen more as part of a Spanish literary tradition than a Mexican one. Yet, as Catherine O'Leary points out, "Carlota's account of her experiences survives because it was written and published when she was in exile" (160). For O'Neill and others, being in Mexico was fundamental to enabling their testimony and many now identified as Mexican.

Hernández notes that "[c]on particular intensidad, de 1940 a 1960, libros, folletos, revistas y periódicos sobre temas españoles inundaron el ámbito editorial mexicano" (15) ("with particular intensity between 1940 and 1960 books, pamphlets, magazines, and newspapers on Spanish topics flooded the Mexican publishing scene"). She also refers to the hundreds of accounts that exist "debidos a transterrados que en México han tomado la pluma para recoger y comunicar sus propios puntos de vista" (15) ("due to expatriates who have picked up their pens in Mexico to gather together and communicate their point of view"). This rich vein of literature born out of solidarity with the Republican cause perhaps contributed to the popularity of the concept of "dar testimonio" and ultimately to the emergence of the *testimonio* genre. Reconsidering Mexican literature through the lens of "dar testimonio," and writing in solidarity with others, brings texts about the Spanish Civil War and experiences of the resulting exile into sharper focus in relation to the broader Mexican canon, and reveals how literature

158 SARAH E. L. BOWSKILL

reflected a moment of transition within the Mexican cultural scene and the history of immigration in Mexico.

"Dar Testimonio": Workers' and Student Movements

Women authors also used their texts to bear witness to other moments of struggle, transition, and transformation in Mexico's history. Famously, Elena Poniatowska's *La noche de Tlatelolco* (1971; *Massacre in Mexico*, 1991) bore witness to the student protests of 1968. Combining images, eyewitness accounts, and creative responses, Poniatowska's multivocal text, subtitled "Testimonios de historia oral," (Oral history testimonies) is "by far the most widely read and most frequently studied text in a corpus of works that are normally categorised as 'Tlatelolco literature'" (Harris 483–484). Less well known, but in a similar vein to her earlier work, is Poniatowska's *El tren pasa primero* (*The Train Passes First*, 2006) about the trade union movement and railway strikes of the late 1950s, which can be seen as antecedents of the student movement. Interestingly, another better-known Mexican author, Elena Garro, also wrote about these strikes and the government repression of the period in *Y Matarazo no llamó* (*And Matarazo Did Not Call*).[18] Indeed, while Garro is not usually associated with politically engaged writing, the concept of "dar testimonio" nevertheless provides an interesting angle from which to review works including *Y Matarazo* and the play, *Felipe Ángeles* (1967), about the revolutionary general, which tend to be eclipsed by her novel, *Los recuerdos del porvenir* (*Recollections of Things to Come*, 1963).

Earlier women authors also bore witness to workers' struggles, although their texts may be less well known. As well as writing about the plight of the Indigenous population, Elvira Vargas documented the experiences of the oil workers in *Lo que vi en la tierra del petróleo* (*What I Saw in the Land of Oil*, 1938). In this text, Vargas gathers newspaper articles chronicling her "impresiones personales acerca de la vida de los trabajadores en los campos petroleros" (3) ("personal impressions of the lives of the oilfield workers"). Her first-person account is interspersed with the voices of those she met including the American bosses and the women living in the poor-quality housing provided for workers. Vargas' account is clearly partisan and written in solidarity with both Cárdenas' government policy of renationalizing the oil industry and the workers whose lives she describes. Thus, in a report on the Poza Rica region, she says she will focus not on statistical data but on "cómo lucha cómo vive la gente, qué quiere y qué exige con todo derecho. Y con esta descripción, será possible, tal vez, formarse un juicio sobre la necesidad imperativa de que la justicia llegue a los hombres

Rethinking the Mexican Literary Canon 159

olvidados que aunan sus esfuerzos en este rincón de la Patria enfrentándose al imperialismo extranjero" (20) ("how the people live and struggle, what they rightly want and demand. And with this description it will be possible, perhaps, to form a judgment about the imperative for justice for these forgotten men who combine their efforts in this corner of the Fatherland standing up to foreign imperialism").

Another woman who documented the still earlier struggles of Mexican workers was Benita Galeana. In *Benita*, published in 1994 but written in 1940, she describes her life, focusing on her childhood and experiences in the Mexican Communist Party spanning a period from 1907 to 1938/9.[19] Interestingly, Galeana connects the campaign for workers' rights with what we might consider her nascent feminist consciousness and writes in solidarity with the Communist Party. For those, like her, who had experienced the violent repression of the PCM under Presidents Emilio Portes Gil (1928–30) and Pascual Ortiz Rubio (1930–2), Galeana also writes to bear witness to the plight of women and out of solidarity with other women whose suffering she observes.

Writing in 2000, Beth Jörgensen noted with surprise that "*Benita* is still relatively little known and little studied in spite of new editions in Mexico in 1974, 1979 and 1990, and an English translation appeared in the U.S. in 1994" (47). Reviewing the limited existing literature on *Benita*, Jörgensen concludes: "All three critics refer to *Benita* rather loosely as *testimonio* and/or autobiography, but they do not situate the terms in the current critical debate" (48). The critics, it seems, sense that *Benita* is bearing witness, but when the text is scrutinized with reference to the narrow parameters of the *testimonio* genre, it is found wanting. In Jörgensen's words, "For today's reader the text appears to participate in the conventions of traditional autobiography and contemporary testimony while simultaneously challenging generic expectations in both directions" (48). By focusing on literatures that bear witness (*dar testimonio*) as an act of solidarity, texts such as *Benita* could come to occupy a clearer place in Mexican literary history.

Conclusion

Taking as its point of departure statements by two prominent authors writing in the period 1930–80, this chapter has taken the idea of "dar testimonio," giving testimony, as an act of solidarity with the "Other" and used it as a lens to examine how it might lead to new ways of viewing the existing categorization and periodization of Mexican literature, how it might

160   SARAH E. L. BOWSKILL

reveal connections between Mexican women authors in the period, and how it might bring to the fore less well-known texts by women authors. The scope of this chapter dictates that the examples given are only a selection of the many that could be mentioned. It may also be possible to present a different selection of texts by male authors also bearing witness, or to fall back on an emphasis on the "novela nacional" ("national novel") to argue that testimony was not central to the Mexican canon.[20] Be that as it may, I do not seek here to argue that we *ought* to reorganize the Mexican canon around the concepts of testimony and solidarity with the sense that doing so would allow the "correct" canon to emerge. Rather, the aim has been to show that in this period the idea that literature should bear witness had a currency that may have had a more profound influence than has been recognized, that it is possible to reimagine the canon around this axis, and that the results are of interest. The new canon casts light on established texts and gives new prominence to others. It foregrounds moments of transition in which marginalized groups that had been forgotten and misrepresented by hegemonic narratives and discourses tried to negotiate their entry into the nation, and shows that women authors felt solidarity with their marginalized subjects even as they were only too aware of women's own challenges. At the start of the period in question, women authors struggled to find their voice. By the end of it, often by lending their voice to the voiceless, women authors had claimed their own voice and were increasingly being heard.

Notes

1. The speech was subsequently published as Rosario Castellanos, "La novela mexicana contemporánea y su valor testimonial," *Hispania* 47.2 (May 1964): 223–230. Quotations are taken from this published version.
2. All translations are by the chapter author.
3. By "novela nacional," Castellanos was referring to those works that aimed to present a totalizing view of Mexico. Examples she discusses include the novels of Agustín Yáñez, Juan Rulfo, and Carlos Fuentes.
4. On the difficulties of defining *testimonio* and its relationship to other genres, see Nora Strejilevich, "Genres of the real: Testimonio, autobiography, and the subjective turn." In *Cambridge History of Latin American Women's Literature*, pp. 433–447. Cambridge: Cambridge University Press, 2016 and Emil Volek, "Testimonial Writing." In *Encyclopedia of Latin American Literature*. Ed. Verity Smith, pp. 783–785. Chicago, IL: Fitzroy Dearborn, 1997.
5. On the emergence of the so-called *boom femenino* after this period in Mexico, see Jane Lavery and Nuala Finnegan, eds., *The Boom Femenino Mexicano: Reading Mexican Women's Writing*. Newcastle: Cambridge Scholars Publishing, 2010.

Rethinking the Mexican Literary Canon   161

6. On Mexican women's writing before 1980, see, for example, Elena Urrutia, ed., *Nueve escritoras mexicanas nacidas en la primera mitad del siglo XX, y una revista.* Instituto Nacional de las Mujeres: El Colegio de México, 2006, http://cedoc .inmujeres.gob.mx/documentos_download/100798.pdf and Fabienne Bradu, *Señas particulares, escritora: Ensayos sobre escritoras mexicanas del siglo XX* (Mexico City: FCE, 1987). The work of the Taller de Teoría y Crítica Literaria Diana Morán and the series "Desbordar el canon: Escritoras mexicanas del siglo XX" have also been instrumental in bringing to light a tradition of Mexican women's writing.

7. On the debates around "virile" literature, see John E. Englekirk, "The 'Discovery' of Los de abajo," *Hispania*, 18.1 (1935): 53–62; Robert McKee Irwin, *Mexican Masculinities*, Minneapolis: University of Minnesota, 2003; Víctor Díaz Arciniega, *Querella por la cultura "revolucionaria" (1925)*. Mexico City: Fondo de Cultura Económica, 1989; Max Parra, *Writing Pancho Villa's Revolution: Rebels in the Literary Imagination of Mexico*. Austin: University of Texas Press, 2005.

8. See Bowskill 9.

9. On these connections, see Doris Meyer, "The dialogics of testimony: Autobiography as shared experience in Nellie Campobello's *Cartucho*." In *Latin American Women's Writing: Feminist Readings in Theory and Crisis.* Ed. Anny Brooksbank Jones and Catherine Davies, pp. 46–65. Oxford: Clarendon Press, 1996; Elena Poniatowska , "Introduction." In *Cartucho and My Mother's Hands*, transl. by Doris Meyer. Ed. Nellie Campobello, pp. vii–xiv. Austin: University of Texas Press, 2013; Norma Klahn, "Campobello, Nellie." In *Concise Encyclopedia of Mexico.* Ed. Michael Werner, pp. 60–6. London: Routledge, 2015; and Ela Molina Sevilla de Morelock, *Relecturas y narraciones femeninas de la Revolución Mexicana: Campobello, Garro, Esquivel y Mastretta.* Woodbridge: Boydell and Brewer, 2013.

10. "El Premio Literario Mazatlán, otorgado a Elena Poniatowska," *Novedades*, 17 de febrero 1971 CNL Archive Expediente. Elena Poniatowska.

11. On the positive reception of *Hasta no verte*, see "El Premio Literario Mazatlán."

12. On the use of the widow's testimony, see Poniatowska's introduction to the English edition, and on the possible use of Villa's own memoirs, see Juan Bautista Aguilar, pp. 22–23.

13. For a biography of Santana Fuentes de Szymanski, see "Graciela Szymanski," www.elem.mx/autor/datos/125753.

14. Other women in this group included Esperanza Velázquez Bringas, Adelina Zendejas, Magdalena Mondragón, Rosa Castro, and María Luisa Ocampo, many of whom also had literary careers beyond their journalism. Thea Pitman, "Identidad nacional y feminismo en el periodismo de mujeres: el caso de Elvira Vargas," *Literatura Mexicana* 18.1 (2007): 131–143, www .redalyc.org/pdf/3582/358242106006.pdf.

15. *Transterrado* is a neologism coined by Spaniard José Gass in exile in Mexico to refer to those able to make their home in a new country; see Hernández de León-Portilla 212–213.

16. See O'Leary (162) on the reception of O'Neill's work.
17. For a biography of Carlota O'Neill, see O'Leary.
18. Although not published until 1989, the manuscript is dated 1960. See Melgar.
19. On the circumstances surrounding the publication of *Benita*, see Jörgensen 49–50.
20. The concept of "dar testimonio" is clearly relevant, for example, to the works of Carlos Monsiváis and Carlos Montemayor, as well as to the male *indigenista* authors writing about Chiapas in the same timeframe as Castellanos, such as Ricardo Pozas, Eraclio Zepeda, and Carlo Antonio Castro.

Works Cited

Asturias, Miguel Angel. Nobel Lecture. NobelPrize.org. 2019. www.nobelprize.org/prizes/literature/1967/asturias/25600-miguel-angel-asturias-nobel-lecture-1967.

Bautista Aguilar, Juan. "Prólogo." In *Obra reunida*. Ed. Nellie Campobello, pp. 11–26.Mexico City: FCE, 2007.

Bowskill, Sarah E. L. *Gender, Nation and the Formation of the Twentieth Century Mexican Literary Canon*. Oxford: Legenda, 2011.

Campobello, Nellie. *Obra reunida*. Mexico City: FCE, 2007.

Carballo, Emmanuel. *Diecinueve protagonistas de la literatura mexicana del siglo XX*. 3rd ed. Mexico City: Empresas Editoriales, 1986.

    Diecinueve protagonistas de la literatura mexicana del siglo XX. 1st ed. Mexico City: Empresas Editoriales, 1965.

Castellanos, Rosario. "La novela mexicana contemporánea y su valor testimonial," *Hispania* 47.2 (1964): 223–230.

Galeana, Benita. *Benita*. Mexico City: Editorial Extemporaneos, 1994.

Harris, Christopher. "Remembering 1968 in Mexico: Elena Poniatowska's 'La Noche De Tlatelolco' as Documentary Narrative," *Bulletin of Latin American Research* 24.4 (2005): 481–495.

Hernández de León-Portilla, Ascensión. *España desde México: Vida y testimonio de transterrados*. Mexico City: UNAM, 1978.

Hind, Emily. "Six Authors on the Conservative Side of the Boom Femenino, 1985–2003: Boullosa, Esquivel, Loaeza, Mastretta, Nissán, Sefchovich." *The Boom Femenino Mexicano: Reading Mexican Women's Writing*. Ed. Jane Lavery and Nuala Finnegan, pp. 48–72. Newcastle: Cambridge Scholars Publishing, 2010.

Jörgensen, Beth. "Speaking from the Soapbox: Benita Galeana's Benita," *Latin American Literary Review* 28.55 (2000): 46–66.

Martínez, José Luis and Christopher Domínguez Michael. *La literatura mexicana del siglo XX*. Mexico City: CONACULTA, 1995.

Melgar, Lucía. "Silencio y Represión En 'Y Matarazo No Llamó …'" *Letras Femeninas* 29.1 (2003): 139–159.

Meyer, Doris. "The Dialogics of Testimony: Autobiography as Shared Experience in Nellie Campobello's *Cartucho*." *Latin American Women's Writing: Feminist Readings in Theory and Crisis*. Ed. Anny Brooksbank Jones and Catherine Davies, pp. 46–65. Oxford: Clarendon Press, 1996.

Rethinking the Mexican Literary Canon 163

O'Connell, Joanna. *Prospero's Daughter: The Prose of Rosario Castellanos*. Austin: University of Texas Press, 1995.

O'Leary, Catherine. "Bearing Witness: Carlota O'Neill's *Una mujer en la Guerra de España*," *Bulletin of Spanish Studies* 89.7–8 (2012): 155–168.

Peris Blanes, Jaume, ed. "El premio Testimonio de Casa de las Américas: Conversación cruzada con Jorge Fornet, Luisa Campuzano y Victoria García," *Kamchatka*, December 6, 2015, pp. 191–249.

Pitman, Thea. "Identidad nacional y feminismo en el periodismo de mujeres: el caso de Elvira Vargas," *Literatura Mexicana* 18.1 (2007): 131–143.

Poniatowska, Elena. "Introduction." *Cartucho and My Mother's Hands*. Nellie Campobello. Trans. Doris Meyer. Austin: University of Texas Press, 2013.

Shaw, Deborah. "Jesusa Palancares as Individual Subject in Elena Poniatowska's *Hasta no verte Jesús mío*," *Bulletin of Hispanic Studies*. 73.2 (1996): 119–204.

Sommer, Doris. "Taking a Life: Hot Pursuit and Cold Rewards in a Mexican Testimonial Novel," *Signs: Journal of Women in Culture and Society* 20.4 (Summer 1995): 913–940.

Vargas, Elvira. *Lo que vi en la tierra del petróleo*. Mexico City: México Nuevo, 1938.

CHAPTER 10

Landscapes of Heterogeneity in a Mid-Twentieth-Century Quechua Poem

*Charles M. Pigott**

Introduction: Quechua Languages and Literatures

This chapter discusses a poem by the twentieth-century Peruvian writer, Teodoro Meneses Morales (1915–87). The poem, which is detailed as being written in January 1941,[1] was composed in the Ayacucho variety of the Indigenous Southern Quechua language and has a version in Spanish, almost certainly by the same writer.[2] Its title in Quechua is "Pacha manchariptin" ("When the World Is Fearful"), and in Spanish, "Cuando cesan las lluvias coincidiendo con calamidades sociales" ("When the Rains Cease, Coinciding with Social Calamities"). My argument is that the poem evinces a loss of solidarity between humanity and the wider cosmos and that this perceived loss is the result of social, cultural, and environmental transitions occurring at the time.

The Quechua languages, which extend from southern Colombia to northern Argentina, are spoken by over 7.5 million people and comprise one of the largest Indigenous language-families in Latin America in terms of area and number of speakers (Eberhard, Simons, and Fennig). Linguistically, they have an agglutinative and polysynthetic structure. This means that words are formed by adding a chain of suffixes to a lexical root, and that most of the grammar occurs within the morphology of single words rather than at the syntactical level as in Spanish. The very different grammatical and semantic organization of the two languages means that many nuances of Quechua poetry are lost in translation, hence the close-reading approach adopted in this chapter.

While Southern Quechua served for centuries as the state language of the Incan empire, it was never written down until the sixteenth century,

---

* The author would like to thank Alan Durston and Julio Noriega Bernuy for their wonderful cooperation during the preparation of this chapter, and Carmen Lora, Director of Centro de Estudios y Publicaciones, for granting permission to reproduce "Pacha manchariptin."

Landscapes of Heterogeneity 165

when missionaries began transcribing it into the roman alphabet for the purpose of religious conversion (Noriega Bernuy, *Escritura quechua*, 32). By the eighteenth century, the Indigenous elite's access to Western education had contributed to the development of a sense of Incan nationalism, which manifested in the production of nostalgic and romanticized plays and poems in written Quechua, and which ceased after the Spaniards' defeat of a major Indigenous rebellion in 1780 and the ensuing annihilation of the Incan aristocracy (69–70).

Following Peruvian independence, during the nineteenth century there were diverse efforts to record oral Quechua folklore in written form, though, according to Noriega Bernuy, these were largely motivated by a desire to appropriate Indigenous discourse and thereby legitimize *criollo* rule over the new nation (*Escritura quechua*, 70–71). From early in the twentieth century, new forms of Quechua literature began to emerge. Meneses Morales' literary production formed part of the "boom" in Southern Quechua literature that occurred in Peru between the 1920s and 1960s. The rapid multiplication and stylistic diversification of written Quechua literature that characterized this period was born of major transitions occurring in Peruvian society at the time. While still defined by a quasi-feudal structure in the first few decades, the mid-twentieth century also witnessed growing peasant movements, centralization of political power, and the strengthening of ties with the coast (Durston 13).

The Quechua literary boom was, in many ways, a response by the Quechua-speaking elite to the challenges and opportunities that these transitions presented (Durston 13). Nonetheless, it remained a largely urban pursuit among the lettered classes, removed from the vast majority of native speakers, for whom Quechua was (and continues to be) an entirely oral language. At the risk of oversimplification, one can speak of two main corpuses of Quechua literature in addition to religious material: the oral literature of the rural majority and the written literature of a few aficionados among the urbanized literati; while the former has often acted as a substrate for the latter, the influence has been almost entirely one-way, and the work of Meneses Morales is no exception.

Huanta and Teodoro Meneses Morales

Meneses Morales was one of three writers (with Porfirio Meneses Lazón and Mauro Salvador Pérez Carrasco) who formed what Durston calls the *Grupo Huanta* (Huanta Group), given that they all hailed from this town in south-central Peru and interacted closely. According to Durston,

Meneses Morales represented a high degree of geographical mobility yet also significant local identification with Huanta (15). This paradox will be important in my argument that "Pacha manchariptin" is at least partly autobiographical in expressing a sense of dislocation from the land. Compared to most native speakers of Quechua (but like many members of the Quechua literati), Meneses Morales had a relatively privileged background, his mother's family owning a moderate amount of land in Huanta (Durston 81–82). Huanta itself was comparatively egalitarian, as reflected by the several alliances that took place between *hacendados* and the Indigenous population and the near-universal adoption of Quechua (81). Meneses Morales, for example, was largely monolingual in Quechua until the age of eight. At fifteen, he left Huanta to continue his schooling in Lima, where he would eventually study the new program in Quechua philology at Universidad Nacional Mayor de San Marcos (82). He devoted the rest of his life to teaching and researching Quechua language and theater. While better known for his academic work, Meneses Morales wrote several narratives and poems in Quechua that were of such originality that Durston considers him to have been one of the great literary innovators in the language (14).

Durston rightly states that, of the *Grupo Huanta*, "debemos preguntarnos ... en qué medida, y cómo, el contexto migratorio influyó en sus proyectos escriturales" ("we should ask ... to what extent, and how, the context of migration influenced their writing projects") (81), and suggests that, for mid-twentieth-century Quechua writers in general, "el hecho de vivir en Lima sirvió de aliciente para el nostálgico proyecto de recrear textualmente el lejano terruño" ("living in Lima was an incentive for the nostalgic project of textually recreating the distant homeland") (38). While nostalgia was plausibly a major motivation for Meneses Morales too, in the specific case of "Pacha manchariptin" what is really expressed is not the "distant homeland" but its dissolution and fragmentation, or, as Noriega Bernuy puts it, "la destrucción del universo y del hombre andinos" ("the destruction of the Andean universe and its people") (*Escritura quechua*, 128). From this standpoint, Meneses Morales' depiction of the natural environment as "hostil e incluso letal" ("hostile and even lethal") (Durston 93) is a radical attempt to break away from "la imagen bucólica del campo que predominaba en la literatura indigenista" ("the bucolic image of the countryside that predominated in *indigenista* literature") (93).

Discussing Quechua literature of the 1960s, Durston and Noriega Bernuy note how the theme of migration in this later period is "marcado

Landscapes of Heterogeneity

por la experiencia del desarraigo, [y] rompe con el 'estrecho marco local o regional andino'" ("marked by the experience of upheaval [and] breaks with the 'tight local or regional margins of the Andes'") (Noriega Bernuy, *Escritura quechua*, 95, cited in Durston 118). Durston notes how Meneses Morales' poetry anticipates this period (94), and I would similarly argue that the above characterization of 1960s Quechua literature also explains "Pacha manchariptin." This is indicated by my close reading of selected stanzas in this chapter as well as by the paradox that, while the 1940s and 1950s constituted a "Golden Age" in the study of Quechua folklore (Durston 37), the 1940s also witnessed an accelerating decline in the Quechua-speaking population due to migration, urbanization, and the expansion of formal education in Spanish (27). It is within this general context of transition that the profound sense of dislocation expressed in "Pacha manchariptin" must be interpreted.

Theoretical Framework

Two theoretical perspectives will aid the development of my argument. The first is Cornejo Polar's concept of "heterogeneity," which emerged from his analysis of Peruvian literature and, in particular, the often-antagonistic relationship between Quechua and Spanish. Key to his theory is the understanding that any subject is formed "en su relación con el mundo" (15) ("in its relationship to the world" [9]), yet reality is also partially constructed by the subject's efforts to create a "morada apacible" (15) ("peaceful dwelling place" [9]). The reality of mid-twentieth-century Peru, however, was one in which "se intersecta[ba]n conflictivamente dos o más universos socio-culturales" (10) ("two or more socio-cultural universes intersect[ed] in conflict" [5]), manifesting in situations that were "dispersas, quebradizas, inestables, contradictorias y heteróclitas" (10) ("scattered, brittle, unstable, and contradictory and heterogeneous" [5]).[3]

Heterogeneous situations produce heterogeneous subjects, "la inestable quiebra e intersección de muchas identidades disímiles, oscilantes y heteróclitas" (14) ("formed by the unstable fissures and intersections of many dissimilar, oscillating, and heterogeneous identities" [9]). Meneses Morales' psychological inhabitation of the Andean hinterland yet physical inhabitation of Lima (and a Western education system) epitomizes heterogeneity, as is reflected in his use of alternative names.[4] He maintained his Spanish names for his scholarly writing but used Quechua names for his creative work. "Pacha manchariptin" is signed under the name of Pumaqasapi Harawikuq (Bard of Pumaqasa) in reference to the street in

168   CHARLES M. PIGOTT

Huanta on which its author grew up (Durston 93). Rather than "pseudonym," in the context of Cornejo Polar's theory I prefer the term "heteronym," which goes beyond connotations of "truth" and "falsity" by evoking the multiplicity and partialness of Meneses Morales' diverse identitarian allegiances.

Cornejo Polar's perspective can be productively integrated with the geocritical approach of the French literary theorist Bertrand Westphal, who describes space as "hétérogène" ("heterogeneous") and "hétérotopique" ("heterotopic") rather than forming a stable, homogeneous unity. As such, a place is constantly emerging and becoming, and is as much temporal as it is spatial ("Approche géocritique"). Literature, moreover, has a key role in the reconfiguration of space: "Les relations entre littérature et espaces humains ne sont donc pas figées, mais parfaitement dynamiques" ("the relationships between literature and human spaces are therefore not fixed, but perfectly dynamic"), with the result that "une véritable dialectique" ("a veritable dialectic") is maintained through which "l'espace se transforme *à son tour* en fonction du texte" ("space is *in turn* transformed in function of the text") (Westphal) (my translations, italics in original). Just as particular places inform literature, so literature reciprocates by reconstituting the places themselves. From this standpoint, place can be understood as a constantly shifting semiotic constellation in time and space, rather than just a geographical location.

Combining the above theories, I will argue that, in "Pacha manchariptin," the heterogeneity that Cornejo Polar identifies in Peruvian society manifests in a configuration of space as equally conflictive, tumultuous, and uncertain. However, rather than the conflict between different cultural epistemologies resulting in different *interpretations* of space, following Westphal the point is rather that space is *itself* produced by virtue of this dialectic, being neither subjective nor objective but *intersubjective*. From this perspective, the drought alluded to in the poem (an event that is far from unprecedented in the Andes) acquires such potency because it is semiotically integrated into a wider context of heterogeneity where everything is called into question and, in this way, the natural disaster becomes a symbol of a more far-reaching sense of instability. The confluence of multiple transitions – cultural, economic, and environmental – transforms the very fabric of time and space, as old threads become loosened and new ones entangled in an uneven patchwork of conflicting patterns.

"Pacha manchariptin" is arranged in three parts. The first sets the general scene and describes people's reactions; the second continues the description of reactions and includes two contrasting explanations; the third (a single stanza) expresses the poetic subject's sympathy for his

Landscapes of Heterogeneity 169

community. My analysis will focus on the first and fifth stanzas of the first part and the fourth, fifth, sixth, and seventh stanzas of the second part.

Quechua and Spanish Titles

The epistemological frictions in the poem are evident right from the beginning, in the contrast between the Quechua and Spanish titles. The Spanish title ("Cuando cesan las lluvias coincidiendo con calamidades sociales") ("When the Rains Cease, Coinciding with Social Calamities") separates the "social" and the "natural" as two distinct phenomena and correlates them in objective, quasi-scientific terms. The Quechua version ("Pacha manchariptin") ("When the World Is Fearful") could not be more different, with the term *pacha* emphasizing holism rather than differentiation. Estermann defines *pacha* as "el todo de lo que existe en forma interrelacionada, el universo ordenado mediante una compleja red de relaciones, tanto en perspectiva espacial como temporal; la relacionalidad es su característica constituyente primordial o axiomática" ("everything that exists in an interrelated manner, the universe as ordered by a complex network of relations, both spatially and temporally; relationality is its primordial or axiomatic characteristic of being") ("Ecosofía," 4).

Salomon describes *pacha* as denoting "a moment or interval in time and a locus or extension in space ... at any scale" (14). For Gonzales, *pacha* "is characterized by being animated, sacred, variable, harmonious, diverse, immanent, and consubstantial," in such a way that "[e]verything is alive – a mountain, a rock, water, women, and men – and everything is incomplete" (203). Such incompleteness constitutes the basis for "dialogue and reciprocity in all aspects of existence" (203). The interpretation of the world as *pacha* differs substantially from the more instrumental, objectively oriented approaches of the West that were becoming increasingly dominant in 1940s Peru and that can be glimpsed in the Spanish version of the title.

The second word, *manchariptin*, comprises the verb root, *mancha-* (to fear), followed by *-ri*, a suffix of incipient or sudden action, and the subordinating particle *-pti*, translating roughly as "when (pacha) is suddenly afraid." The Quechua title, therefore, conveys the sense that the natural environment includes humanity, has agency, and is even able to experience emotion, perspectives that are widespread in animistic philosophies such as those of the Andes: "what characterizes animistic beliefs is precisely an empathetic concern for places and things which are considered to have social identities (although not always 'human-like')" (Sillar 370). The sense that *pacha* is fearful, however, suggests that the fabric of relationality that binds

170 CHARLES M. PIGOTT

the cosmos together is in deep danger. Given the holistic sense of *pacha*, the focus of the poem is not on cause and effect (although various hypotheses are given toward the end) but on a general breakdown of solidarity between humanity and its wider environment.

The Desiccation of Maize and Rupture with the Past

The first stanza sets the scene of the catastrophe:

Ñam iskay chunka punchaw hinaña	Hace ya como veinte días que en este mes de enero todavía no llueve,	Already for about twenty days in this month of January it has not rained,
kay enero killapi manaraq paramunchu,	y las sementeras en las chacras	and the maize sown in fields,
chakrakunapi sara tarpuykunapas hunta wiñarimuchkaynillanpim tiwtispan qawirqullachkankuña.	apenas en el inicio de su plena floración desmedradas se están secando quemadas por el sol.	about to grow towards its full height, is weakening and desiccating in the sun.

(Noriega Bernuy, *Poesía quechua*, 392, 393)

By foregrounding the length of time, the first two lines emphasize how the natural environment has become unknowable, unpredictable, and unreliable. While the Spanish version refers only to *sementeras* (crops), the Quechua version specifies the crop as *sara* (maize). Maize is far more than a food-source. Particularly in the form of the fermented drink, *chicha*, it is a key marker of Indigenous cultural allegiance. Duke notes how "maize *chicha* was highly important in the economic, ritual, political, military, and social functioning of both the elite, and common people of the Inka Empire" (265), so much so that the fermenting agent used in the drink's production (*aqha mama*) was an alternative name for Cuzco (Hastorf and Johannessen 118). As Duke observes, this appellation "shows the centrality placed on *chicha* by the Inka to the very process of ruling: without Cuzco, there would be no Inka and without *chicha* there would be no Cuzco" (265). One might add that, without maize, there would be no *chicha*.[5] Today, *chicha* "remains the central alcoholic beverage in indigenous ritual life" (267) and, given its relatively low cost and rural associations, it is a symbol of "being lower in the hierarchy" (268) and, by extension, solidarity. Sillar describes how "*chicha*-drinking is a communal activity" as well as "a form of communication with the ancestors and animate world," as reflected in ideological images on *chicha* drinking vessels, which

Landscapes of Heterogeneity

convey "symbolic messages [that] are directed not just at other people but at the animate world to whom the *chicha* offerings are made" (Sillar 373).

In the light of Sillar and Duke's comments, the description of maize as "puny" (*tiwti/desmedrado*) signals more than the risk of physical death from starvation but, even more seriously, the withering of an entire cosmology, the severing of people from the wider universe. In a holistic, interconnected philosophy like *pachasofía* (to use Estermann's term), cultural heterogeneity has implications far beyond humanity itself. Given that humanity forms part of *pacha*, human conflicts and contradictions manifest as an equally erratic environment. The fragmentation of humanity opens up seismic ruptures that shatter abiding relations of solidarity between humans and nonhumans. In this light, the reference to maize "about to grow towards its full height" (or "flowering" in the Spanish version) could refer to the emergence of a new cultural and literary movement that is nonetheless threatened by such dramatic changes.

The second, third, and fourth stanzas describe the community's fruitless imploration to God and how "The elders gaze in vain above and below (at the clouds)" ("Machukunam hanayta urayta qawaykachanku yanqallaña / Los viejos ya en vano hacia arriba y abajo otean las nubes") (fourth stanza), indicating the loss of efficacy of Andean epistemology (Noriega Bernuy, *Poesía quechua*, 392–393). The sense that *pacha* has diverged from normal patterns is reinforced in the fifth stanza:

Llakillatañam tayta Milchu uytupakun, ñari ancha hunta para chayamunanpi kay chika punchawña chirawchakuptin. – "Awrikuy taytalla llakim qatiwasun, manam rikuy kaynaqchu qayna watakunaqa."	Y don Melchor ya únicamente de penas se alimente, porque siendo ésta la mejor época en que debía llover ya muchos días se han hecho veraniegos. – "Así pues, don Melchor, la desdicha nos perseguirá, pues nunca sucedía esto en los años pasados."	With sadness, father Milchu hobbles along, since, at a time when rain should fall in abundance, for many days it has been sunny. "Certainly, father, sadness will pursue us, for this never happened in years gone by."

(Noriega Bernuy, *Poesía quechua*, 392, 393)

Evident here is the importance of oral tradition as a vehicle of memory and, implicitly, continuity with the ancestors. The Quechua version brings out these associations more clearly where don Melchor is "tayta Milchu," tayta meaning "father" in contrast to the Spanish title, *don*, which as well as age and respect can also connote a sense of class-based hierarchy that could be misleading in the context of the poem. Howard describes how the "cultural function of remembering in Andean ways of thinking is a regenerative one, whereby the past provides the symbolic resources for making sense of the present and projecting toward the future, in a way that allows at once for continuity and change" ("Spinning," 46). In the above stanza, however, this pattern is inverted: the sense of rupture with the past accentuates the degree of foreboding for the future, even if this foreboding is, paradoxically, strengthened through Andean epistemological practices such as divination based on memory. More than a temporary fluctuation, in the unstable context of heterogeneity a meteorological aberration is reinterpreted as heralding the start of an era where abiding relationships between humanity and the cosmos can no longer be relied upon.

The Breakdown of Traditional Ways of Knowing

The first part of the poem having set the general scene, the second part conveys people's unsuccessful attempts to remedy the situation. The fourth stanza of part two is especially noteworthy in depicting the breakdown of traditional epistemology:

Imañamá kay pachapa taqlan parquyninqa.	¡Qué es ya pues esta defección de la naturaleza!	What is this defection of nature!
Manañam kunanqa tutapas tutañachu,	Ahora, ya ni la noche es noche;	Night is no longer night; our eyes cannot shut to sleep,
manañam ñawiykupas qimllayta atinchu,	tampoco nuestros ojos pueden cerrarse para dormir,	coca no longer sweetens in our mouths;
manañam kukapas simiykupi miskiyanchu,	ni la coca ya sabe a gusto en nuestras bocas;	and everyone puzzles at what can possibly have happened.
lliwpas yuyaymanankum imanasqaraq kaynasqanmanta.	y todos cavilan de por qué el tiempo hace estas mudanzas.	

(Noriega Bernuy, *Poesía quechua*, 394, 395)

While the first line of the Quechua version describes the particular issue – the lack of water to irrigate (*parquy*) crops – the Spanish version could not be a stronger affirmation of the loss of solidarity between humanity and the nonhuman environment, diagnosing a "defection of nature" ("defección de la

Landscapes of Heterogeneity

naturaleza"). Yet, ironically, the very phrasing of the Spanish version already constructs a separation between humanity and "nature" that makes no sense in the holistic philosophy of *pacha*. The use of exclamation rather than question marks emphasizes the sense of despair but equally the fruitlessness of asking for answers in the absence of meaningful communication between the human and nonhuman worlds, with the result that the question becomes rhetorical.

This sense of unknowability is reinforced throughout the stanza. Now that night-time is not truly night, people are unable to sleep. In the Andes, the significance of this goes beyond the effects of sleep deprivation:

> In the Inca empire, dreams were believed to be instruments of divination, and specialists in the interpretation of dreams, or "dreamers" (*musoc* [musq'uq]), were called upon to make forecasts (Arriaga 1968:206) .... A semantic overlap between the Quechua words *muskuy* (musq'uy) (to dream) and *musyay* (to divine) seems also to evoke, at a linguistic level, a close link between dream and revelation (Taylor 1987). (Cecconi 404)

Given the crucial role of dreams in Andean practices of learning about the world, the inability to sleep (and therefore to dream) both signals and perpetuates the crumbling of Andean epistemologies and, consequently, a fundamental shift in the relationship between humanity and the cosmos. The stanza recalls a Bolivian Quechua play, *Atau Wallpaj p'uchukakuyninpa wankan* (*Tragedy of the Death of Atawallpa*), that would be published by Jesús Lara in 1957 and translated by Meneses Morales himself in 1983. In the play, the Inca's shaman is no longer able to interpret his own dreams, an omen of the demise of the Incan empire and the emergence of a new era that cannot be accounted for by traditional epistemological methods (Howard "Yachay," 29).

Even more significant is the negative allusion to coca, one of the most culturally important plants in the Andes. Allen notes how the "act of chewing coca leaves is an unequivocal statement of cultural loyalties. Coca chewing identifies one as a Runa (Quechua person)" ("To Be Quechua," 157). Describing a regular coca-sharing ritual known as *hallpay*, Allen further explains that the "rules for performing the ceremony express the fundamental Quechua concept of *ayllu*, which is community rooted in a sense of common origin in, and orientation toward, certain sacred places" (157). The *ayllu* is "a major source of self-identification and emotional stability" (165) and is predicated on reciprocity between humans, deities and landscapes (159, 165–166). Allen describes how coca also connects people with the wider landscape through the ritual of *kuka pukuy*, which involves blowing on coca leaves to communicate with sacred places (162–

163) and how the "essence of Quechua social organization lies in this relationship, close and continually felt, of Runa with *Tirakuna*" (165) or "earth-beings." Given that the *Tirakuna* not only safeguard people's health but also influence weather patterns (162), maintaining respectful engagement with them is essential for individual and communal wellbeing or *allin kawsay* (165).

In de la Cadena's analysis, such relationships mean that "place" and "people" should not be considered distinct categories. Rather, "place is the event of in-ayllu relationality from which tirakuna and runakuna also emerge – there is no separation between runakuna and tirakuna, or between both and place. They are all in-ayllu, the relation from where they emerge *being*" (101). The "in-ayllu" existence means that "persons are not from a place; they are the place that relationally emerges through them, the runakuna and other-than-humans that make the place" (102). By interpreting place not as a context *within* which relationships happen but as the very network of relationships itself, de la Cadena's analysis resonates with my theoretical synthesis of Cornejo Polar's insights on heterogeneity and Westphal's geocritical perspective: if humans are integral elements of place, then transformations of humanity are equally transformations of place (as *pacha*).

That coca should no longer taste sweet and that the seasons have flipped are signs that the semiotic threads connecting humans with other elements of place are weakening, and, consequently, that the very fabric of place (as previously understood) is unraveling. Everything points toward a loss of solidarity between human and nonhuman agents of the *ayllu*. It is not just the epistemological dissonance of heterogeneity that leads to the dissolution of place but the unequal power relationships that heterogeneity involves. Given the pervasive and discriminatory associations of indigeneity with "backwardness," Peruvian society has long been characterized by a desire to reject one's Indigenous ancestry in favor of the customs of the West, of which the dramatic reduction of the Quechua-speaking population from the 1940s onward is symptomatic. Given that "the rejection of coca signifies a transfer of loyalties from the Quechua to the Hispanic cultural traditions" (Allen, "To Be Quechua," 166), the sense that coca is no longer sweet (*miski*) may signal a deliberate attempt by some people to disown their community, or perhaps the influence of formal education in creating a generational divide. While Meneses Morales dedicated his life to the promotion of Quechua, it is also true that he did so from the urban context of Lima and within a Western academic framework. It is hard, therefore, not to read the stanza as at least partly autobiographical, as an expression of the author's sense of irreconcilability between the two cultural universes he inhabited.

Landscapes of Heterogeneity

An autobiographical interpretation is also supported by the possessive suffix in the Quechua words, *ñawiyku* (our eyes) and *simiyku* (our mouths). Quechua languages have two forms of the first-person plural; in Ayacucho Quechua, these are *noqanchik* (inclusive of the addressee) and *noqayku* (exclusive of the addressee). By using the exclusive form (*–yku*), the poetic subject is constructing a boundary between his own group and that of the addressee,[6] in contrast to the quoted speech of community members who use the inclusive suffix (*–nchik*). The sense that these lines may be directed toward somebody outside the community hints at the ambiguous affiliation of the poetic subject. On the one hand, he constructs himself as part of the community, in contrast to the addressee; on the other hand, he never interacts with the voices of the community, describing them in the third-person plural as an observer rather than a direct participant.

The fifth stanza of the poem's second part mirrors the fifth stanza of the first in voicing oral tradition:

– "Aurikuy mama Petuca, chiqampaqmi kay pacha sarusqanchiksi tikrakuchkanña; qayna watapas kaynallam karqa, mapas yuyariy, qayna huk watamantañam para suchurinpuni enero killapi."	– "Así es pues Sra. Petronila, es muy cierto como dice, que esta tierra que pisamos ya está revolviéndose; el año pasado fue casi igual a esto. Ve, recuérdelo, es desde hace un año atrás que en el mes de enero precisamente las lluvias se retiran."	"That's the way it is, mother Petuca, it's very true that this land we stand on is writhing; last year was almost the same. Remember, truly, that since last year the rains have suddenly gone away in January."

(Noriega Bernuy, *Poesía quechua*, 394, 395)

Particularly noteworthy is the second line, which describes *pacha* as *tikrakuchkanña* (*revolviéndose*, "writhing"). What this phrase alludes to is the notion of *pachakuti*, which Estermann explains as follows:

> En sentido ético, el *pachakuti* es el último y más radical remedio para restituir el equilibrio severamente dañado. El desorden cósmico, resultado de una serie de infracciones muy graves contra el principio de reciprocidad (tal como ocurrió en la Conquista), sólo puede convertirse nuevamente en orden (*pacha*) mediante una "vuelta" (*kutiy/kutiña*) violenta y radical. (*Filosofía andina* 291, n. 38)

> In an ethical sense, *pachakuti* is the last and most radical remedy for restoring a severely damaged balance. Cosmic disorder, the result of

a series of very grave infractions against the principle of reciprocity (such as occurred in the Conquest), can only be transformed again into order (*pacha*) by means of a violent and radical "turning" (*kutiykutiña*).

In the case of the poem, however, the world is far from being restored; on the contrary, what is described is a sense of profound disorientation for which no remedy is in sight.

The Quechua version strongly emphasizes this disorientation through the use of emphatic suffixes, especially evidentials, which convey varying degrees of certainty or intensity. As Dedenbach-Salazar Sáenz states, Quechua evidentiality "reflects both the actual evidential situation of the narrator and his attitude toward the narrated account" (164). In the above stanza, the affirmative suffix, *–m(i)*, occurs after three words or phrases: *chiqampaq-mi* (truly), *kaynalla-m* (this situation), and *qayna huk watamantaña-m* (since last year already). In the last line, another suffix, *–puni*, adds greater emphasis to the phrase, *para suchurin* (the rains suddenly went away). Combined with the individual words, *mapas* and *chiqampaq*, which both roughly translate as "truly," this avalanche of epistemic markers conveys a sense of undeniability yet disbelief at the wholesale dissolution of *pacha*. The phrase *Kay pacha sarusqanchik* (this land on which we stand/step) could be read both as a lament about the prior solidity (and solidarity) of the landscape and as a recognition of its disrespectful "trampling" by a people now distanced from traditional rituals.

The Local and the Global: Spatial Reconfigurations

The last two stanzas of the poem's second part mark a shift in tone, as two different speakers offer contrasting interpretations of the catastrophe:

– "Karu llaqtakunapis rikuy huknananaq runa masinchikkuna warawaranqanpi sipinakuchkanku awqanakuypi, ichapas chaymanta kay pacha mancharin, Diosninchik runapaq piñakun."	– "Dicen pues que en los pueblos lejanos, una infinidad de gentes, los semejantes nuestros, se están matando en guerra cruel, por millones; quizá sea por eso, que este tiempo está como atemorizado; seguramente pues nuestro Dios está molesto para las gentes."	"They say that in faraway towns infinite numbers of people like us are killing themselves by millions in battle; maybe that's why this world is afraid; our God is surely angry because of people."

– "Manam chaychu, siñu Andres, Huanta hatun plazapiqa, lliwmi rimachkanku: Huarpa mayus Avilakunata aparqunman kasqa suela cargayuq asnullankuta aysachkaqta. ¡Dios te perdone runamasillanchikkunata!" – "¡Ay, chayhina llakillam wakchakunapaqqa!"	– "No es eso, don Andrés; lo que en el mercado de Huanta todos están hablando es que el río de Huarpa se los ha cargado a los hermanos Ávila cuando lo vadeaban halando su burro cargado de suelas. ¡Que Dios les perdone a nuestros pobres semejantes!" – "¡Ay!, así únicamente pesares son para los pobres …"	"No, that's not the reason, Mr. Andrés; in Huanta town square, they're all saying that the river Huarpa carried the Ávila brothers away when they were trying to cross it with their donkey loaded with shoe soles. May God forgive our poor fellow men and women!" "Oh! For the poor there is only suffering …"

(Noriega Bernuy, *Poesía quechua*, 394–397)

From a geocritical perspective, what is particularly fascinating about these stanzas is the renegotiation of space. While the penultimate stanza of part two offers a global explanation, the section's final stanza locates the cause firmly in the local environment. In the context of 1941, the war alluded to in the previous stanza is probably World War II. While the notion that far-off actions can have profound local effects is already expressed by the concept of *pacha*, which is both immediate and cosmic, the stanza also hints at the changing conceptions of space ushered in by the expansion of communication networks, whether physical transport or telecommunications. Indeed, the phrase "our fellow men and women" ("runa masinchikkuna/los semejantes nuestros") suggests a widening of the parameters of the *ayllu* to a planetary scale, while the Quechua imperative *rikuy* ("look") indicates the increasing approximation of previously unknown contexts.

While this could be read as an expression of common humanity, it also conveys a sense of fear at the encroachment of an unknown, unpredictable, and unstable "global community" that will disrupt the *ayllu* at a local level. At the same time, the idea that human misdeeds could result in divine punishment represents a confluence between biblical notions and the Andean concept of *ayni* (a form of reciprocity). Allen notes how, at "the most abstract level, ayni is the basic give-and-take that governs the universal circulation of vitality. It can be positive, as when brothers-in-law labour in each other's fields; or it can be negative, as when the two men quarrel and exchange insults" ("When Pebbles," 76). By expressing the notion that

178   CHARLES M. PIGOTT

the world rebels against its mistreatment, the stanza can be interpreted as reasserting the epistemological validity of Andean philosophy at a time when the efficacy of this philosophy is seen to be waning.

The global explanation given by the first speaker is, however, refuted by the second. There, we not only discover the previous speaker's name (which grounds the communication in an immediate, local context) but also learn that the setting is Huanta, reinforcing the plausibility of an autobiographical reading of the poem. While Don Andrés widens the sphere of engagement to an almost unimaginably large scale, the second speaker locates the communicative arena firmly in Huanta itself and, even more specifically, in the marketplace or main square. The explanation is equally local: instead of untold numbers in far-off lands, the cause is attributed to a particular family and river, both of whose names are given.

At the same time, there are important similarities between the stanzas. Both hint at the hardships born of injustice: war in the first and poverty in the second. In this way, while standing in opposition at one level, at another level they could be interpreted as local and global refractions of a generalized reality, particularly in view of the local and cosmic reach of *pacha*. Indeed, the desire for the Ávila brothers to be pardoned and the allusion to the large number of shoe soles they carried may suggest a deviation from Andean laws of reciprocity that results in punishment by the sentient landscape, in a similar way to divine retribution for World War II. In this interpretation, both stanzas would reinforce the organizing principle of *ayni* as a means to restore order in a tumultuous context of heterogeneity. Given that the contrast between local and global explanations is itself a manifestation of heterogeneity, in the poem it is never resolved in favor of one or the other but instead constitutes one of the multiple fissures around which the poem is organized.

In this chapter, we have seen how "Pacha manchariptin" heralds the emergence of a new, unsettling era where the natural environment is only partly knowable by traditional means. While far from unprecedented in Andean history, in a context of heterogeneity, drought becomes resignified as an emblem of deeper fears that express a loss of trust in traditional ways of knowing. My analysis has highlighted some of the key ways that Meneses Morales communicates this new reality: the contrast between the Quechua and Spanish titles and, especially, the concept of *pacha*; the withering of maize, a key component of Andean ritual; the growing inefficacy of traditional practices of divination; the inability to gain insight through dreams; the bitterness of coca, a crucial social adhesive in Andean communities; the allusion to a cataclysmic *pachakuti*; the ambivalence of inclusive and exclusive

Landscapes of Heterogeneity 179

identity markers; and the ambiguity of local and global explanations. As Westphal's geocritical approach reveals, these signs are not mere representations but integral aspects of the transformation of place. With the fragmentation of solidarity between humans, and between humans and the world at large, new cosmologies must be forged from the fault lines of a world in transition.

Notes

1. Durston (92) notes how Meneses Morales reworked his poems over the course of his lifetime. Given the constraints of this chapter, I focus only on the version published in Noriega Bernuy's anthology, *Poesía quechua* (392–397). Noriega Bernuy took the Quechua version from Meneses Lazón, Meneses Morales, and Rondinel Ruiz's *Huanta en la cultura peruana* and the Spanish version from Romualdo's *Poesía peruana*.
2. English translations are my own and seek to strike a balance between the Quechua and Spanish versions. I privilege literalness over style. I have modified the spelling of certain Quechua words in accordance with the modern orthography to avoid confusion in my linguistic analysis.
3. In the passage, Cornejo Polar applies these adjectives to Andean literature, but his point is that the literature reflects the wider heterogeneity that has long characterized Andean society.
4. See Noriega Bernuy (*Escritura quechua*, 108–110) who makes a similar point in his discussion of the poet Alencastre.
5. While other ingredients can be used to make *chicha*, it is maize *chicha* that has such symbolic importance across the Andes.
6. The poem is dedicated to "la señora Andrea Valencia de Ávila, matrona campesina de Huanta" ("Mrs. Andrea Valencia de Ávila, a midwife from Huanta") (Noriega Bernuy, *Poesía quechua*, 392), though it is questionable whether this person is the addressee given the use of the exclusive suffix combined with the mention of her Huanta origins.

Works Cited

Allen, Catherine "To Be Quechua: The Symbolism of Coca Chewing in Highland Peru," *American Ethnologist* 8.1 (1981): 157–171.
"When Pebbles Move Mountains: Iconicity and Symbolism in Quechua Ritual." In *Creating Context in Andean Cultures*. Ed. Rosaleen Howard-Malverde, pp. 73–84. Oxford: Oxford University Press, 1997.
Cecconi, Arianna. "Dreams, Memory, and War: An Ethnography of Night in the Peruvian Andes," *The Journal of Latin American and Caribbean Anthropology* 16.2 (2011): 401–424.

Cornejo Polar, Antonio. *Escribir en el aire: ensayo sobre la heterogeneidad socio-cultural en las literaturas andinas,* 2nd ed. Lima: CELACP, Latinoamericana Editores, 2003. (*Writing in the Air: Heterogeneity and the Persistence of Oral Tradition in Andean Literatures.* London: Duke University Press, 2013.)

de la Cadena, Marisol. *Earth Beings: Ecologies of Practice across Andean Worlds.* London: Duke University Press, 2015.

Dedenbach-Salazar Sáenz, Sabine. "Point of View and Evidentiality in the Huarochirí Texts (Peru, 17th Century)." In *Creating Context in Andean Cultures.* Ed. Rosaleen Howard-Malverde, pp. 149–167. Oxford: Oxford University Press, 1997.

Duke, Guy. "Continuity, Cultural Dynamics, and Alcohol: The Reinterpretation of Identity through *Chicha* in the Andes." In *Identity Crisis: Archaeological Perspectives on Social Identity: Proceedings of the 42nd (2010) Annual Chacmool Archaeology Conference, University of Calgary, Calgary, Alberta.* Ed. Lindsay Amundsen-Meyer, Nicole Engel, and Sean Pickering, pp. 263–272. Calgary: Chacmool Archaeological Association, University of Calgary, 2011.

Durston, Alan. *Escritura en quechua y sociedad serrana en transformación: Perú, 1920–1960.* Lima: Instituto Francés de Estudios Andinos, and Instituto de Estudios Peruanos, 2019.

Eberhard, David, Gary Simons, and Charles Fennig (eds.). *Ethnologue: Languages of the World.* 22nd ed. Dallas: SIL International, 2019. www.ethnologue.com.

Estermann, Josef. "Ecosofía andina: un paradigma alternativo de convivencia cósmica y de Vivir Bien," *Revista de filosofía afro-indo-abiayalense* 2.9–10 (2013): 1–21.

Filosofía andina: sabiduría indígena para un mundo nuevo. *Quito: Ediciones Abya-Yala,* 2015.

Gonzales, Tirso. "The Cultures of the Seed in the Peruvian Andes." In *Genes in the Field: On-Farm Conservation of Crop Diversity.* Ed. Stephen Brush, pp. 193–216. Rome: IPGRI, Ottawa: IDRC, and Boca Raton: Lewis Publishers, 2000.

Hastorf, Christine and Sissel Johannessen. "Pre-Hispanic Political Change and the Role of Maize in the Central Andes of Peru," *American Anthropologist* 95.1 (1993): 115–138.

Howard, Rosaleen. "Spinning a Yarn: Landscape, Memory, and Discourse Structure in Quechua Narratives." In *Narrative Threads: Accounting and Recounting in Andean Khipu.* Eds. Jeffrey Quilter and Gary Urton, pp. 26–49. Austin: University of Texas Press, 2002.

"*Yachay*: The *Tragedia del fin de Atahuallpa* as Evidence of the Colonisation of Knowledge in the Andes." *In Knowledge and Learning in the Andes: Ethnographic Perspectives.* Eds. Henry Stobart and Rosaleen Howard, pp. 17–39. Liverpool: Liverpool University Press, 2002.

Meneses Lazón, Porfirio, Teodoro Meneses Morales, and Víctor Rondinel Ruiz (eds.). *Huanta en la cultura peruana: edición antológica bilingüe con extensa selección de literatura quechua.* Lima: Editorial Nueva Educación, 1974.

Noriega Bernuy, Julio. *Escritura quechua en el Perú*. Lima: Pakarina Ediciones, 2011.

(ed.) *Poesía quechua escrita en el Perú: antología*. Edición bilingüe Lima: Centro de Estudios y Publicaciones, 1993.

Romualdo, Alejandro (ed.). *Poesía peruana, antología general: poesía aborigen y tradicional popular*. *Tomo 1*. Lima: Ediciones Edubanco, 1984.

Salomon, Frank. "Introductory Essay: The Huarochirí Manuscript." In *The Huarochirí Manuscript: A Testament of Ancient and Colonial Andean Religion*, translated by Frank Salomon and George Urioste, pp. 1–38. Austin: University of Texas Press, 1991.

Sillar, Bill. "The Social Agency of Things? Animism and Materiality in the Andes," *Cambridge Archaeological Journal* 19.3 (2009): 369–379.

Westphal, Bertrand. "Pour une approche géocritique des textes." In *La Géocritique mode d'emploi*. Limoges: Presses Universitaires de Limoges, colloquium "Espaces Humains" (2000): 9–40. https://sflgc.org/bibliotheque/westphal-ber trand-pour-une-approche-geocritique-des-textes/: page consulted August 3, 2022.

CHAPTER 11

Beyond the Nation Frame
Rethinking the Presence of Indigenous Literatures in the Spanish American Novel circa 1950

Estelle Tarica

Indigenous peoples appear in practically all the national literary traditions of Spanish-American countries since Independence, but rarely, if ever, are they granted the status of literary creators. Instead, their histories and lifeways, their verbal and other arts, are taken up as primary material for non-Indigenous authors. The corpus of mid-twentieth-century fiction is no exception. One thinks of Rosario Castellanos' *Balún Canán* (*The Nine Guardians*, Mexico, 1957), Gamaliel Churata's *El pez de oro* (*The Golden Fish*, Bolivia/Peru, 1957), or Augusto Roa Bastos' *Hijo de hombre* (*Son of Man*, Paraguay, 1960), as well as the two acclaimed examples that will be discussed here, Miguel Angel Asturias' *Hombres de maíz* (*Men of Maize*, Guatemala, 1949) and José María Arguedas' *Los ríos profundos* (*The Deep Rivers*, Peru, 1958). Each of these novels reflects the author's appreciation for the literary traditions of Indigenous peoples.[1] We can hear Mexica and Inca hymns of praise and remembrance in them, or the voices of Maya books such as the *Popol Vuh*, or the lyrics of Quechua songs sung in the Andes today. These mid-twentieth-century novels are different from earlier *mestizo* or *criollo* works inspired by Indigenous verbal arts because this aesthetic appreciation is meant to be understood in sociopolitical terms: it expresses solidarity with those who have been excluded from the national community and recognizes the importance of their voices despite centuries of dispossession. These novels are examples of what critic Martin Lienhard calls "alternative written literatures," which emerge at the interface of Indigenous oral literatures and the alphabetic writing imposed by European invaders (16–17). He notes that these alternative literatures experience a renaissance in the middle of the twentieth century when writers "seize" the metropolitan novel, much as one might expropriate ill-gotten property, and put its assets to better use, that of expressing the discourse of marginalized sectors (275). Such works emerged from the

182

Beyond the Nation Frame 183

broader currents of revolutionary social thought that marked the first half of the twentieth century and led to far-reaching transitions across the region.

Yet if we understand "solidarity" as involving mutuality and a common interest, then the literary solidarity these authors sought to express is a deeply flawed one because it circulates in a discursive sphere from which Indigenous people, as living writers, artists, and thinkers, have been routinely excluded. Across Spanish-American literature, non-Indigenous authors speak for the Indigenous and integrate them into cultural and political projects that Indigenous peoples did not participate in shaping on equal terms. This situation gives rise to the Latin American literary system described by Peruvian critic Antonio Cornejo Polar, one that reproduces the race-class divisions of the broader social system: the people who read and write literature inhabit a world that is culturally different from, and socially antagonistic to, the Indigenous people they are writing and reading about (13).[2] The mid-twentieth-century novels discussed here participate in that divided system. These works therefore do not elude the colonial legacies that have obliged Indigenous peoples to cede control of their words to others, and to cede control, furthermore, of the contexts that make these words meaningful.

In the 1970s and 1980s, pioneering Latin American criticism by Cornejo Polar and Angel Rama grappled with the mutual imbrications of literature and colonialism. They were among the first to define a subset of narrative works within the broader field of Spanish-American fiction but distinct from it because of their strong connection to Indigenous voices and use of literary strategies that attempt to confront the colonial inheritance. Cornejo Polar referred to this corpus as "heterogeneous literatures," which embed a "plurality of socio-cultural signs" at multiple levels: form, content, circulation, reception (12). Angel Rama classified them as "trans-culturated narratives," drawing on the work of Cuban anthropologist Fernando Ortiz. He showed that the authors of these novels and short stories were able to integrate "modern," Western literary aesthetics with "traditional" or "popular" ones drawn from Latin America's rural, Indigenous, *mestizo*, and Afro-descended groups, creating a new subgenre of fiction that modeled an integrated national identity (32–57, 252).

From today's perspective, these approaches require revision, for two reasons. One, because they are too narrowly focused on whether the integration of Indigenous voices into these works contributes to forging a modern national or Latin American identity. This obscures the other contexts that make Indigenous arts meaningful in the novel (Rowe 215).

What is needed is a criticism that is liberated from some of the conceptual horizons of postcolonial national independence, one that is no longer beholden to an idea of "the Indian" as a symbol of cultural authenticity that makes Spanish America recognizably different from Spain and the neocolonial powers. Bolivian Indigenous scholar Silvia Rivera Cusicanqui has referred to this as an "emblematic" identity, a display of alterity that is divorced from the fluid realities of Indigenous experiences (*Ch'ixinakax*, 58).[3] Two, because the literary system that Cornejo had described in the 1970s is no longer intact, given today's new-media landscape and the greater reach of Indigenous movements for self-determination. Indigenous peoples are vocal participants in the sphere of global discourse. The Latin American literary system is no longer as closed a circuit as it once was. The year 1992 – the 500th anniversary of the "discovery of the Americas" – symbolizes this transition, which was marked by a resurgence of inventive self-naming by Indigenous writers across the Americas.[4] Indigenous poets, scholars, activists, and political leaders have fought for their place on the world stage, and offer compelling visions for self-determination, for alternative planetary political and cultural projects, and for new kinds of citizenship (Arias 614). Indigenous literary scholars, meanwhile, have developed new critical paradigms for approaching their literatures.[5]

We can therefore take this present moment as a needed vantage point from which to reevaluate the mid-twentieth-century narrative canon in Latin America. If we can better perceive the possibility of a more genuinely mutual conversation between Indigenous and non-Indigenous creators, what new constellations of old texts might emerge? A return to "transculturated" novels allows us to explore these possibilities and listen anew to the Indigenous literatures these writers included in their novels. This involves being attuned to, and seeking to resist, the tendency to constrain indigeneity to the emblematic role of "representing" an authentic Latin America or a static Indigenous cultural totality. Native American literary critic Daniel Heath Justice reminds us that the stories Indigenous peoples tell about themselves "give shape, substance, and purpose to our existence and help us understand how to uphold our responsibilities to one another and the rest of creation, especially in places and times so deeply affected by colonial fragmentation" (2). Such stories are intimately linked to native projects of self-determination, notes Gordon Brotherston, and they help us "to envisage native polities that live in body and in memory" (*Book*, 39). To what extent have Latin America's *mestizo* authors been able to honor these

Beyond the Nation Frame

contexts of Indigenous literatures, the meanings they impart, and their continuing relevance today?

This essay will first explore how Spanish-American novelists circa 1950 came to know Indigenous literatures as such and to find them newly relevant. It then moves on to examine Asturias' *Hombres de maíz* and Arguedas' *Los ríos profundos*, asking whether the Indigenous literary voices that these non-Indigenous authors integrate into their novels have been liberated from indigeneity as emblem. The dual structure of the analysis allows us to contemplate two historical transitions that bookend the twentieth century and frame the works under discussion. First, the transition, via *indigenismo*, toward the horizon of a national identity discourse more centered on "the Indian." Second, the transition away from that emblematic figure, via the actions of Indigenous peoples, toward the horizon of greater self-determination. In taking up Indigenous literatures, to what extent can these Spanish-American novels, product of the first transition, be harnessed to that second transition in order to offer a window onto native ways of conceiving Latin American space and time?

Indigenismo and the "Mini-Boom" in Indigenous Texts

Why did mid-century novelists turn toward Indigenous literatures, and how did they come to know about these works in the first place? It is thanks to *indigenismo* that a new appreciation for Indigenous peoples – past and present – became more widespread in the first half of the twentieth century. *Indigenismo* was a discourse centered on the idea that "the Indian" and "Indianness" – "lo indio" or "lo indígena" – are integral to national identity and modern development. It provided a counter-discourse against prevailing views of "Indian" inferiority. *Indigenismo* flourished across diverse fields of intellectual inquiry, artistic experimentation, and government policy. Particularly in Mexico and Peru, *indigenismo* was at the heart of national movements for modernization and social renewal, and had an activist and polemical orientation. *Indigenista* intellectuals, artists, and policymakers understood themselves to be acting in solidarity with native peoples against the entrenched social structures that carried colonial legacies of racism and exploitation into the present day. Yet as the century advanced, it became increasingly clear that *indigenismo* reproduced many of the colonial legacies instead of overcoming them. These were deeply embedded in *indigenismo*'s political aims and in its conceptual apparatus and rhetorical modes, such as its weakening of Indigenous cultures through the pursuit of national modernization via economic integration

186   ESTELLE TARICA

and cultural assimilation, or its paternalistic forms of address toward Indigenous peoples, its desire to speak "for" them.[6]

Indigenismo had a lasting impact in the field of literature, and not just in terms of the production of "*indigenista* literature" per se. Its impact can also be measured in terms of the greater exposure to Indigenous literatures it enabled. Starting in the 1930s, we see a small yet significant publishing "boom" that brings out translations into Spanish of Indigenous texts in Quechua, Nahuatl, and the Maya languages. Many such works had earlier appeared in French, English, and German translations. By the mid-twentieth century, Spanish versions had become an established feature of publishing houses in Latin America. Two separate editions of the Maya "Book of Counsel," the *Popol Vuh*, were brought out in Mexico in the 1930s and 1940s, both published by Mexican state institutions and both based on translations by Miguel Angel Asturias. The Yucatec *Libro de Chilam Balam de Chumayel* (*The Book of Chilam Balam of Chumayel*), translated by Mexican writer Antonio Mediz Bolio, appeared in 1930 in Costa Rica and was then subsequently issued in Mexico in 1941, again by state imprint. Nahuatl literature also experienced a mini-boom, due largely to the efforts of Father Angel María Garibay, the most prominent expert in Nahuatl in his time. He produced multiple works containing translations of pre-Conquest Mexica poetry and other genres: *La poesía lírica azteca* (*Aztec Lyric Poetry*, 1937), *Poesía indígena de la Altiplanicie* (*Indigenous Poetry of the Highlands*, 1940), the monumental *Historia de la literatura Nahuatl* (*History of Nahuatl Literature*, 1953), and various others. In the Andes, meanwhile, we see contemporary and classical Quechua poetry and song anthologized and translated into Spanish by Peruvian and Bolivian authors: José María Arguedas' *Canto kechwa* (*Quechua Song*, Peru, 1938); Jorge Basadre's *Literatura Inca* (*Inca Literature*, published in Paris for a Peruvian press in 1938); J. M. B. Farfán's *Poesía folclórica quechua* (*Quechua Popular Poetry*, Argentina, 1942); Jesús Lara's *La poesía quechua* (*Quechua Poetry*, Bolivia, 1947); Farfán and Arguedas' *Apu Inca Atawallpaman: Elegía quechua anónima* (*To Mountain Spirit Inca Atahualpa: Anonymous Quechua Elegy*, Peru, 1955); and Jorge Lira's *Himnos sagrados de los Andes* (*Sacred Hymns of the Andes*, Peru, 1959), to name but a few.

These anthologies participated in *indigenismo*'s general current because they attempted frontally to refute some ideas about the inferiority of "the Indian." In some cases, they justified a turn to Indigenous literatures on grounds that these would strengthen national identity. Via the Romantic connection between literature and the national spirit, they saw these works

Beyond the Nation Frame

as pathways into "the national soul" (Garibay 11) and "the national genius" (Arguedas, *Canto*, 13). In all cases, they sought to expand prevailing concepts of aesthetic beauty to encompass Indigenous texts and incorporate them into a *mestizo* literary canon. The *Chilam Balam* is "more beautiful" and "more profound" than we might have imagined (Mediz Bolio ix, xiv). Nahuatl poetry is "as beautiful" as biblical and classical texts in Hebrew and Greek, clearly not the work of a "barbarous" people (Garibay 9, 20). Indigenous artists produce works "of aesthetic content" filled with as much "soul" or "genius" as any art (Arguedas, *Canto*, 10).

These translations would be hugely influential for novelists of the mid-twentieth century. As we will see, Asturias drew extensively from Garibay's Nahuatl anthologies, from Mediz Bolio's *Chilam Balam*, and from his own translation of the *Popol Vuh*. We will also see that Arguedas' *Canto Kechwa* established the approach to Indigenous song that he would use in *Los ríos profundos*. *Indigenismo* thus in a sense laid the groundwork to transcend some of its own limits by orienting writers toward Indigenous voices and lending the study of Indigenous verbal arts a positive significance that ended up encouraging creative work in new directions.

Novel Recontextualizations in *Hombres de maíz*

Hombres de maíz is structured across six episodes, beginning with the story of Gaspar Ilóm. He leads a Maya resistance against invading settler farmers whose slash-and-burn style of intensive agriculture threatens the millennial maize-based lifeways of the region's native inhabitants; Ilóm is assassinated through an act of treachery. This part of the novel is based on historical events occurring in Guatemala around 1900 (Asturias, *Hombres*, 282, n. 2).[7] Subsequent episodes chronicle the aftereffects of Ilóm's defeat, moving diachronically across the generations to describe how those who were involved in his death, as well as their descendants, die violently by shamanic means. The novel's later episodes chart a more expansive geography that is recognizably "national" in its breadth and stitches together the shared symbolism of a common cultural imaginary. By the last and longest episode of the novel, focused on a mail carrier and his pilgrimage to the underworld, the connection to Ilóm's Maya uprising has loosened almost beyond all recognition, until it is brought back in at the novel's close. Throughout, Asturias showcases a playfully poetic language. Indeed, language itself can be said to be a protagonist of the novel. It is a protean shape-shifter that calls attention to itself, reminding us of the novel's status as a self-consciously literary invention and setting up an interesting tension

188   ESTELLE TARICA

between the referential elements of the novel, which reach across the time-space of twentieth-century Guatemala, and the sheer linguistic inventiveness of Asturias' prose, which generates more than a few moments of surrealist opacity.

Hombres de maíz is profoundly marked by the impact of Asturias' encounter with classical Mesoamerican texts such as the *Popol Vuh*, the *Anales de los Xahil*, the *Chilam Balam of Chumayel*, and the pre-Conquest Nahuatl "poetry" translated by Garibay. Critics Gordon Brotherston and Gerald Martin have studied the direct and indirect presence of these works in *Hombres de maíz*; Martin's critical edition of the novel is indispensable in this regard. The novel adopts some of the poetic structures characteristic of these classical works, such as the repetition of phrases that are nearly identical, as Martin has shown (*Hombres*, 283, n. 4). Asturias explained the importance of this parallelism in his Nobel Prize speech in 1967, stressing Maya literature's poetic commitment to the nuances of language to achieve altered states of consciousness ("La novela"). Images and ideas from these works permeate the novel, not least the title itself, a direct reference to the *Popol Vuh*, which narrates the human creation out of yellow and white corn by "Bearer / And Engenderer, / Majesty / And Quetzal Serpent, as they are called" (*Popol Vuh*, 147).

The novel references all these sources and creates from this practice a textured and polyphonic poetic language. Let us look at a striking instance, from the novel's "Gaspar Ilóm" section, which describes how Ilóm, after having initially resisted the call to defend his people's land from the new settlers, takes up arms against them and is celebrated by his people:

> El Gaspar es invencible, decían los ancianos del pueblo. Los conejos de las orejas de tuza lo protegen al Gaspar, y para los conejos amarillos de las orejas de tuza no hay secreto, ni peligro, ni distancia. Cáscara de mamey es el pellejo del Gaspar y oro su sangre – "grande es su fuerza," "grande es su danza" – . . . La huella de sus dientes en las frutas y la huella de sus pies en los caminos sólo la conocen los conejos amarillos. Palabra por palabra, esto decían los ancianos del pueblo. (*Hombres*, 10)

> Gaspar is invincible, said the old folk of the town. The rabbits with maize-leaf ears protect Gaspar, and for the yellow rabbits with maize-leaf ears there are no secrets, no dangers, no distances. Gaspar's hide is mamey skin and gold his blood – "great is his strength," "great is his dance" . . . Only the yellow rabbits know the mark of his teeth in the fruits and the mark of his feet along the path. Word for word, that is what the old folk of the town said. (6–7)

Beyond the Nation Frame 189

In this excerpt's initial line, the novel's main narrator cedes to "the old folk" and creates a lengthy indirect discourse in their voice. The syntax, rhythm, and word choice of this discourse suggest a prophetic mode, while the content explains how Gaspar's body takes its power from the land and reinforces the theme of "harmony between human and vegetable flesh" that Brotherston has identified as fundamental to classical Maya texts (*Emergence*, 32). Yet this apparently new voice of the elders is not new at all but rather a continuation of the narrative voice that came before, repeating themes that had been introduced in the pages prior. Asturias effectively blends together his primary narrator with the collective "old folk" narrator, such that we are not sure where one leaves off and the other begins.

The rabbits who help Ilóm in his war, meanwhile, constitute an indirect citation of the *Popol Vuh* (Brotherston, *Emergence*, 33): they help the heroes Hunahpu and Ixbalanque escape from Xibalba, the underworld, in chapter 21 of the *Popol Vuh*. Their yellow color is also significant, being associated with the pathway out of the underworld, toward the dawning East, as noted in Asturias' translation of the text (*Popol Vuh*, 160, n. 62). This creates a parallel between the historical hero of the novel (Gaspar Ilóm) and the legendary heroes of the classical text. Furthermore, when the old folk intone the sonorous phrases "great is his strength, great is his dance," we see quotation marks around their words, signaling an intertextual citation and thereby creating yet another layer of discourse. Martin explains that these words were suggested by the *Anales de Xahil*, which Asturias and J. M. González de Mendoza had translated while working with French Mayanist Georges Raynaud in Paris (*Hombres*, 295, n. 70). When, a few paragraphs later, the phrase repeats, now with a slight difference, Asturias has slyly removed the quotation marks; what started out as an intertextual allusion to the Maya text has now become the verbal matter of the novel itself.

There is a strong dose of historical irony to the fact that Asturias would have turned to these Indigenous texts as a source of aesthetic renewal at so many levels of his literary creation. In 1923, his university thesis on the "problem of the Indian" recycled the most racist clichés of its day about native peoples (Arias, "Algunos," 558). In Guatemala this fact shadows his legacy. Maya writers have criticized him for using "the Indian" as a literary resource "to construct national identity" (Chacón 130), and K'iche' poet Humberto Ak'abal refused to accept the Miguel Angel Asturias National Literary Prize when he was awarded it in 2003, citing "the racism permeating Asturias's early writing" (Chacón 2–3).

There is no doubt that *Hombres de maíz* is the result of his profound encounter with classical Mesoamerican poetics. But these voices do little to make Indigenous people present as protagonists in their own right, as "characters who are shown both to remember their past and to exist in the modern world" (Brotherston, *Emergence*, 37). He communicates that millennial Maya words and beliefs permeate Guatemalan society like an essential cultural fluid, but one that is inexplicably disconnected from living Indigenous communities and their struggles. Thus, although Asturias demonstrates the powerful beauty of Indigenous literary aesthetics, he takes them up in a surrealist and *indigenista* vein: they have become collectible motifs rather than expressions of Maya peoples' "singular way of experiencing the world" (Chacón 7). Only in "Gaspar Ilóm," the novel's first magnificent section, does he show how the Maya confront the present day with an alternative vision nourished by what Gloria Chacón calls "the double gaze" of Maya vision, which "advances the project of indigenous autonomy in the present based on its preclassic and post-classic legacies" (17–18). In *Hombres de maíz*, Asturias more often than not limits the novel to the idea of "the Indian" as "national soul," "the very essence of the country," or as access point to a fantastical experience of surrealist beauty (Arias, "Algunos aspectos," 560–561; Asturias, "La novela").

Los ríos profundos and the Song-Paths of Memory

Los ríos profundos centers on the experiences of a *mestizo* adolescent, Ernesto, in the Southern Peruvian Andes of the early twentieth century. After a period of travel with his father, Ernesto must adapt to life in a conservative boarding school in the provincial town of Abancay. Through his eyes we see the realities of Peru's colonial legacies, most especially the dehumanizing dispossession of Indigenous peoples that Ernesto witnesses on the brutal sugar plantations surrounding Abancay, which run on the forced labor of Indigenous communities whose lands have been stolen. Throughout the novel, in scenes from the school, from Abancay, and from his journeys across highland Peru, Ernesto reveals an insidious, utterly naturalized anti-Indian racism permeating all aspects of Andean life. It injects cruelty and contempt into the most intimate personal relations. At its core, Ernesto's work in this novel – Arguedas' work – is to show us that this violence can be resisted if we draw on the alternative social awareness learned from Indigenous sources.

Beyond the Nation Frame

Sometimes this resistance happens frontally, as in the novel's celebratory depictions of how Ernesto confronts the worst bully at school or local women rise up against a corrupt municipality. But its primary and most radical resistance is of a subtler nature. It resides in the novel's memory work, and it is in this domain that we can locate the importance of the Indigenous literatures that Arguedas makes present in *Los ríos profundos*. Elsewhere I have shown that an Inca hymn to the creator god constitutes an important intertext for *Los ríos profundos* (Tarica, *Inner Life*, 129–133). In fact, contemporary Quechua verbal artistry is of far greater importance in the novel, which contains numerous Quechua song-poems. Sometimes the narrator cites remembered fragments of song, as happens in one of the novel's most famous scenes: he is inspired by the stones of an Inca wall in Cuzco to remember a refrain from Quechua songs, "yawar mayu" (26) ("river of blood" [7]), and to riff on these words in response to the simmering energy of the ancient wall. Examples of this kind abound in the novel. So too do examples of songs that appear with their lyrics fully transcribed in Quechua alongside Arguedas' poetic translations into Spanish. Some examples include: "Killinchu yau" (54) ("Kestrel, hear me" [29]); "Ay warmallay warma / yuyaykunkim, yuyaykunkim!" (71) ("Do not forget, my little one, / do not forget!" [42]), and "Ay siwar k'enti!" (77) ("O, hummingbird!" [46]).

Whether reproduced whole or in fragments, these song-poems are intimately linked to memory. The narrator notes he as listens to them:

> Acompañando en voz baja la melodía de las canciones, me acordaba de los campos y las piedras, de las plazas y los templos, de los pequeños ríos adonde fui feliz. (77)

> As I accompanied the singing in a low voice I would think about the fields and stones, the squares and churches, and the streams where I had once been happy. (46)

In the novel's tenth chapter, which takes place in a bar and is titled "Yawar mayu" so as to connect back to that earlier ur-song remembered in Cuzco, we find a veritable cascade of Quechua songs, each linked to a particular Andean geography that the narrator and other listeners mentally invoke.

Arguedas' devotion to Quechua songs dates back to two decades before this novel. In the 1930s he worked with his wife Celia Bustamante and her sister, the visual artist Alicia Bustamante, to promote contemporary Indigenous arts in Lima. Arguedas and the Bustamantes served as what Javier García Liendo calls "cultural organizers," using public interventions into established cultural spaces to question existing configurations of cultural power (8). Through social gatherings, and later through radio (García Liendo 138–146), they sought to validate the artistry of Indigenous singing, dancing, and handicrafts and bring them to a wider audience. As part of these efforts, in 1938 Arguedas published the book *Canto kechwa*, a collection of Quechua songs with illustrations by Alicia Bustamante. It serves as a good example of how *indigenismo* caught Indigenous verbal arts in order to release them into the broader stream of national culture. In his introduction, Arguedas uses an exalted tone to speak of the new national self that will come into being once Indigenous peoples are recognized as artistic creators in their own right (*Canto*, 13), and offers an image of the national spirit unified around Indigenous music (*Canto*, 12).

But Arguedas' introduction to *Canto kechwa* also reflects a thinking that goes beyond the national theme and that will be carried over into *Los ríos profundos*. He explains that Indigenous song is a call and response to its environment that casts the listeners' awareness to nearby rivers and rocks (*Canto*, 5). He brings us repeatedly to a concept of the "Andean landscape," not as a figure or theme for artistic depictions, but rather as something "deeply felt" by those who inhabit it, who identify with it and live with it intimately – art as a form of interrelationship with this environment (13), and song as an expression of love for it (16). He then goes on to establish a link between this sentimental voice and the more forceful voice of contemporary Indigenous struggles for land justice. Arguedas describes the voices of the peasant leaders he had heard just the year before, at a political mobilization by Andean *ayllus* (16). By connecting the poetry of the Quechua songs to these political acts of self-determination, and by linking the living land – rivers and rocks that respond to people-song – to agrarian land, Arguedas opens the door to an understanding of Indigenous creativity that is not bounded by the aesthetic sphere or the concept of art. Rather, it is embedded in the daily reproduction of communal life and in Indigenous peoples' negotiations with hegemonic power structures to wrest back control over their lives. In his attempts here to describe an art that is deeply connected to its local physical environment and to the historical actions of Indigenous peoples in defense of it, he relies on Romantic terms in order to point to an Indigenous art that is not Romantic at all.

Returning to *Los ríos profundos* with *Canto kechwa* in mind, we can appreciate that the songs are more than just vectors for individual memory. Rather, in the novel these Quechua song-poems function as Andean "memory paths." A memory path consists of the ritualized invocation of sacred places that maps out a mental "journey across the living landscape" (Abercrombie 6). These sacred places are *wak'as*: "Andean numina [who] lodge in places or placed objects: mountains, springs, lakes, rock outcrops, ancient ruins, caves, and any number of humanly made objects in shrines: effigies, mummies, oracles, and so forth" (Salomon 16). *Wak'as* are the other-than-human beings whose actions across time, in consonance with human action, have shaped the world as we know it. The Spanish considered them "diabolical idols" and destroyed them by the thousands. The term *wak'a* does not appear in *Los ríos profundos*, yet they are present whenever the narrator turns toward the poetics of Quechua song in order to achieve a mental journey across the landscape that connects the past to the present; this memory work constitutes an alternative historical consciousness.

Rama reads the Quechua songs in the novel through the lens of his concern with the formation of a *mestizo* national culture; he proposes that the songs represent an Indigenous past that is salvaged once it is integrated harmoniously to a modern, Western aesthetic form, the novel (252). Yet the song-poems are integral to all levels of Arguedas' writing, not an external element that requires integration. William Rowe has argued that they are the stuff of which the novel is made, because it is through these invocations that Arguedas inaugurates a writing practice that links words to the spatial environment (235). In this, Arguedas drew not just on Quechua language poetics, such as the preference for sound symbolism (onomatopoeia), but also on the dense interrelations between different visual, verbal, and kinesthetic arts (Rowe 225), whose reference points include the surrounding environment and inscribe that landscape into communal history. In Indigenous memory practices, the verbal artistry that is required to generate a memory path is inseparable from multiple nonverbal ways of making meaning, such as dancing and weaving. These "nonwritten and unvoiced forms of social memory," notes Thomas Abercrombie, "were erased from Spanish accounts of the Andean past" (13). But they are a living practice that Arguedas was steeped in, even though he himself was not Indigenous. *Los ríos profundos* does not simply depict the practice of memory paths; it follows it, creating it anew.

The memory pathways that we follow in Arguedas involve an extraordinary degree of "sensory complexity," as Karen Spira has noted (73), and contribute to what she calls, drawing on the work of Jacques Rancière, a "politics of perception" that provides a new "distribution of the sensible" (Spira 85; Rancière 12). Recently, Rivera Cusicanqui has revitalized the memory path as a critical concept for anticolonial thought. She explains the reterritorializing and reparative power of memory paths, which "connec[t] distant spaces in a pan-Andean frame that re-actualizes the gestures ... and semantic practices that decipher and penetrate through the crevices of colonial violence, rearticulating that which is deranged, joining forces to repair the 'pierced fishing net' that the cosmos became for the peoples of the Andes" ("The Potosí Principle").[8] From this perspective, we can appreciate how *Los ríos profundos* emerges from, and seeks to sustain, Indigenous memory work as a living practice of social commentary that names the world on its own terms.

Conclusion

Critic Gloria Chacón proposes that we move "beyond national literatures" in order to study the Indigenous literatures of Latin America (4), and this essay follows her lead, but now in reference to canonical "transculturated" novels of the mid-twentieth century. It proposes that by moving beyond a national frame of interpretation, we can better perceive and learn from the Indigenous literary voices that these writers studied and found inspiring. Here I do not propose that we entirely jettison that national frame, which undoubtedly continues to hold extraordinary relevance for how we approach these works and, indeed, for how their authors conceived them. It is due precisely to national frames that these authors and others were able to engage in close encounters with native literatures. But this essay asks that we see "the national" as a mode of interpretation that tends to block Indigenous frames of interpretation from view. "It is not an accident," writes Chacón, "that all archeological sites are considered the patrimony of the nation-state, and that indigenous peoples have to petition to revere their ancestors" (17). By decentering these novels away from the patrimonial question of the nation-state and its literary canon, we can better approach them through Indigenous literatures old and new. Such an approach requires that we rely on ethno-historical knowledge, from both native and non-native sources, to help us understand those literatures in their various contexts and perceive "what such texts can and do mean in the world now" (Brotherston, *Emergence*, 39), especially as they relate to Indigenous efforts at greater self-determination. What critical and interpretive keys will continue to emerge when we constellate Indigenous literatures with the mid-twentieth-century Spanish-American novel?

Notes

1. Use of the capital "I" for "Indigenous people" follows Daniel Heath Justice: "the capital 'I' is important here, as it affirms a distinctive political status of peoplehood, rather than describing an exploitable commodity, like an 'indigenous plant' or a 'native mammal'" (6).
2. The reader will notice that this essay refers at times to "Spanish America" and at times to "Latin America." These two frames offer distinct yet overlapping ideas about what binds together the diverse nations of this world region into a coherent entity in the period following their formal Independence from European powers. "Spanish America" in this essay refers to an entity united by shared connections to Spain and Spanish – and a shared ambivalence about those connections, one might add. Hence "Spanish-American narrative" signals a body of literature written primarily in Spanish that participates in the ongoing project of postcolonial independence from Spain. "Latin America" refers to a broader hemispheric entity composed of Brazil, Spanish America, and much of the Caribbean, one that is united in its difference from "Anglo America" (i.e., the United States) and expresses a shared resistance to imperial and colonial domination. "Latin American literature" and "Latin American literary criticism" – terms that take on new vitality in the Cold War period – signal a multilingual body of work invested in that ongoing work of differentiation and resistance. Neither frame has sufficiently addressed its own internal colonialism vis-à-vis Indigenous peoples.
3. Rivera Cusicanqui's work on this point cites historian Rosanna Barragán's study of Republican Bolivia (Barragán, "Entre polleras").
4. The term "Abya Yala" is one instance of renaming that has seen widespread use (see Arias, Cárcamo-Huechante, and Del Valle Escalante 10). The rise of contemporary Indigenous social movements of course dates to several decades before 1992, but became especially visible in 1992.
5. See, for example, Craig Womack, *Red on Red*.
6. For more on *indigenismo*, see Coronado; Taylor; Tarica.
7. I refer here to Gerald Martin's invaluable critical edition of *Hombres de maíz* and to the footnotes by Martin that accompany the text.
8. In using the phrase "pierced fishing net," Rivera Cusicanqui references a Nahuatl metaphor for colonial destruction and thereby engages in a pan-Indigenous memory pathway herself.

Works Cited

Abercrombie, Thomas. *Pathways of Memory and Power: Ethnography and History among an Andean People*. Madison: University of Wisconsin Press, 1998. Project Muse.

Arguedas, José María. *Los ríos profundos*. Buenos Aires: Losada, 1998 [1958].
  Deep Rivers. Trans. Frances Horning Barraclough. Austin: University of Texas Press, 1978.

Canto kechwa: Con un ensayo sobre la capacidad de creación artística del pueblo indio y mestizo. Dibujos de Alicia Bustamante. Lima: Ediciones "Club del Libro Peruano," 1938.

Arias, Arturo. "From Indigenous Literatures to Native American and Indigenous Theorists: The Makings of a Grassroots Decoloniality," *Latin American Research Review* 53.3 (2018): 613–626. DOI: 10.25222/larr.181.

"Algunos aspectos de ideología y lenguaje en *Hombres de maíz*." In Miguel Angel Asturias, *Hombres de maíz*. Ed. Gerald Martin, pp. 553–569. Paris: ALLCA XX/Fondo de Cultural Económica "Colección Archivos," 1996.

Arias, Arturo, Luis Cárcamo-Huechante, and Emilio Del Valle Escalante. "Literaturas de Abya Yala," *Lasa Forum* 43.1 (2012): 7–10. https://forum .lasaweb.org/files/vol43-issue1/OnTheProfession2.pdf.

Asturias, Miguel Angel. *Hombres de maíz*. Ed. Gerald Martin . Paris: ALLCA XX/ Fondo de Cultural Económica "Colección Archivos," 1996 [1949].

Men of Maize. Trans. Gerald Martin. New York: Dell Publishing, 1975.

"La novela latinoamericana: testimonio de una época." Nobel Lecture. December 12, 1967. Nobelprize.org.

Barragán, Rosanna. "Entre polleras, lliqllas y ñañacas: Los mestizos y la emergencia de la tercera república." In *Etnicidad, economía y simbolismo en los Andes: II Congreso Inernacional de Etnohistoria, Coroico.* Ed. Silvia Arze, Rosanna Barragán, Laura Escobari, and Ximena Medinacelli, pp. 85–127. La Paz: HISBOL-IFEA-SBH/ASUR, 1992.

Brotherston, Gordon. *Book of the Fourth World: Reading the Native Americas through Their Literature.* Cambridge: Cambridge University Press, 1992.

The Emergence of the Latin American Novel. Cambridge: Cambridge University Press, 1977.

Chacón, Gloria Elizabeth. *Indigenous Cosmolectics: Kab'awil and the Making of Maya and Zapotec Literatures.* Chapel Hill: The University of North Carolina Press, 2018. Project Muse.

Cornejo Polar, Antonio . "El indigenismo y las literaturas heterogéneas: su doble estatuto socio-cultural," *Revista de Crítica Literaria Latinoamericana* 7–8 (1978): 7–21.

Coronado, Jorge. *The Andes Imagined: Indigenismo, Society and Modernity.* Pittsburgh, PA: University of Pittsburgh Press, 2009.

García Liendo, Javier. *El intelectual y la cultura de masas: argumentos latinoamericanos en torno a Angel Rama y José María Arguedas.* West Lafayette, IN: Purdue University Press, 2017. Project Muse.

Garibay, Angel María. *La poesía lírica azteca: Esbozo de síntesis crítica.* Mexico City: Bajo el signo de "ábside," 1937.

Justice, Daniel Heath. *Why Indigenous Literatures Matter.* Waterloo, Ontario: Wilfred Laurier University Press, 2018.

Lienhard, Martin. *La voz y su huella: Escritura y conflicto étnico-social en América Latina (1492–1988).* Havana: Casas de las Americas, 1990.

Beyond the Nation Frame

Mediz Bolio, Antonio. "Introducción." In *Libro de Chilam Balam de Chumayel*. Trans. Antonio Mediz Bolio, pp. ix–xiv. Mexico City: Universidad Nacional Autónoma de México, 1973 [1941].

Mediz Bolio, Antonio. *Popol Vuh: Libro del Consejo de los Indios Quichés*. Trans. Miguel Angel Asturias and J. M. González de Mendoza, based on the French version by Georges Rayneaud. Buenos Aires: Losada, 1965 [1927].

The Book of Counsel: The Popol Vuh of the Quiché Maya of Guatemala. Trans. Munro S. Edmonson. New Orleans, LA: Middle America Research Institute, Tulane University, 1971.

Rama, Angel. *Transculturación narrativa en América Latina*. Mexico City: Siglo XXI Editores, 1982.

Rancière, Jacques. *The Politics of Aesthetics: The Distribution of the Sensible*. Trans. and introduction by Gabriel Rockhill. London: Continuum, 2004.

Rivera Cusicanqui, Silvia. "The Potosí Principle: An Other View of Totality," *emisférica* 11.1 (2014). hemisphericinstitute.org.

Ch'ixinakax utziwa: una reflexión sobre prácticas y discursos descolonizadores. Buenos Aires: Tinta Limón, 2010.

Rowe, William. "Sobre la heterogeneidad de la letra en *Los ríos profundos*: una crítica a la oposición polar escritura/oralidad." In *Heterogeneidad y literatura en el Perú*. Ed. James Higgins, pp. 223–251. Lima: Centro de Estudios Literarios Antonio Cornejo Polar, 2003.

Salomon, Frank. "Introductory Essay." In *The Huarochirí Manuscript: A Testament of Ancient and Colonial Andean Religion*. Trans. Frank Salomon and George L. Urioste, pp. 1–24. Austin: University of Texas Press, 1991.

Spira, Karen. "Toward an Aesthetics of the Abject: Reimagining the Sensory Body in Arguedas's *Los ríos profundos*," *Revista Hispánica Moderna* 67.1 (2014): 73–89. www.jstor.org/stable/43285261.

Tarica, Estelle. "Indigenismo." *Oxford Research Encyclopedia: Latin American History*. Ed. William H. Beezely. March 2016. latinamericanhistory.oxfordre.com.

The Inner Life of Mestizo Nationalism. Minneapolis: University of Minnesota Press, 2008.

Taylor, Analisa. *Indigeneity in the Mexican Imagination: Thresholds of Belonging*. Tucson: University of Arizona Press, 2009.

Womack, Craig. *Red on Red: Native American Literary Separatism*. Minneapolis: University of Minnesota Press, 1999.

CHAPTER 12

Femininity in Flux
Gabriela Mistral's Madwomen

Amanda Holmes

In Gabriela Mistral's renowned poem from *Tala* (*Felling*, 1938), "Todas íbamos a ser reinas" ("We Were All to Be Queens"),[1] the speaker catalogues the feminine dreams of little girls from the poet's childhood home in the Elqui Valley of Chile. The musicality of the verses recalls that of nursery rhymes, while the poem singsongs through the girls' desires to find husbands and raise children as they each seek their future fortunes far from their desert valley home in "cuatro reinos sobre el mar" ("four kingdoms on the sea") (2). The poem recounts the sad fates of each woman: Rosalía grows up to marry a sailor who dies in a shipwreck; Soledad raises her younger siblings and has no time to start her own family; Efigenia leaves her homeland with a foreigner, destined never to return. Only Lucila finds a happiness that, as the poem declares, emerges from insanity: "Y Lucila, que hablaba a río, / a montaña y cañaveral, / en las lunas de la locura / recibió reino de verdad" ("And Lucila who talked to the river / and the mountain and fields of cane, / under moons of madness / received a kingdom of her own") (53–56). Lucila, the birth name of the poet, Lucila Godoy Alcayaga,[2] finds her kingdom in her imagination as she deciphers the natural wonders that she encountered in her verses. An accomplishment that the speaker equates with dreams of motherhood and marriage – "En las nubes contó diez hijos" ("In the clouds she counted ten sons") (58), "en los ríos ha visto esposos" ("in the rivers she saw her husbands") (59) – this kingdom develops from an insanity construed through her femininity – "las lunas de la locura" ("under moons of madness") (55) – her moonlit moments associated with the menstrual cycle lead Lucila to her creativity and her voice. It is not only Lucila, the fourth of the queens from this poem, who finds opportunity in her madness. The sixteen poems published under the title *Locas mujeres* (*Madwomen*) in the anthology *Lagar* (*Winepress*, 1954) represent women at their most authentic and most complex. Mistral's madwomen are

Femininity in Flux

caught in a state of transition from social convention to unbridled liberty; their "madness" lies in their lack of subjective definition.

Mistral's poems of "insane" women constitute a transition from feminine images in her earlier works, while they also counter a misconstrued image of the poet, reinforced during the Augusto Pinochet dictatorship, as upholding patriarchal norms for women's societal role. Known as Saint Gabriela or the Mother of America, the professional Mistral, in her image sustained by the dictatorship (Sepúlveda 23), is portrayed in a number of photographs dressed in an austere conservative fashion holding a motherly pose as she greets a crowd of school children. Born in 1889 in Vicuña, and raised in the remote village of Montegrande, from the age of fourteen Mistral worked as a rural teacher and principal in a number of primary and secondary schools across Chile, then as director of a prestigious private high school in Santiago, finally to be invited by the Mexican minister of education, José Vasconcelos, to help reform the education system in this North American country from 1922 to 1924. From there, Mistral lectured, taught, and wrote in the United States and Europe, she served as cultural representative for Chile in the United League of Nations in the 1920s, and she was consul for Chile in cities across the United States and Europe. Her remarkable rise from a modest childhood in a remote village in the fertile Elqui valley to international representative of culture and education could perhaps not have been improved upon if it were not for her receipt of the Nobel Prize in literature in 1945. That the first Latin American author to receive this prize was a woman is stunning and was followed by the Premio Nacional de Literatura de Chile six years later in 1951. Mistral's fraught relationship with her country, tarnished by affronts that aimed to restrict her professional advancement in her youth, led her to live outside of Chile; after she left for Mexico in 1922, she only returned to visit Chile three times in thirty-five years. While she died in New York, her body was repatriated, and her last poetic work was dedicated to her birth country. *Poema de Chile* (*Poems from Chile*), published posthumously in 1967, records the natural beauty of Chile and the speaker's continued feelings of endearment toward her childhood land.

Viewed through a feminist lens, Mistral's poetry and person have been the source of both condemnation and pride. Hjalmar Gullberg's Nobel citation of her work refers to Mistral as "the great singer of mercy and motherhood," while scholars have noted her alignment with the Christian ideals of motherhood in her early volume, *Ternura* (*Tenderness*, 1924) (Zubizarreta; Concha). Apparently too conservative, her proliferation of the image of motherhood in her poetry and person was off-putting for feminist readers (O'Connor; Peña), spawning, in part, a disengagement with her poetry in scholarship. Mistral even claimed early on in her introduction to *Lecturas para mujeres* (*Books for Women*, 1923) that: "*Para mí, la forma del patriotismo femenino es la maternidad perfecta. La educación más patriótica que se da a la mujer es, por lo tanto, la que acentúa el sentido de la familia*" ("*For me, perfect motherhood best represents female patriotism. The most patriotic education that is given to a woman is, therefore, one that accentuates the importance of family*") (13, italics original). More recently, as Magda Sepúlveda exclaims, Mistral's image has been transformed radically in the second decade of the 2000s to be characterized by "una subjetividad lésbica desafiante" ("a defiant lesbian subjectivity") (23). In this vein, Sepúlveda calls attention to the 2018 book jacket illustration of Jorge Baradit's *Historia secreta de Chile III* (*Secret History of Chile III*) in which Mistral is portrayed in punk fashion with the name of her partner, Doris, tattooed on her neck (23).

Mistral's characterization of women in her poetry finds resonance in the poet's own understanding of her societal role, as Claudia Cabello Hutt underlines in her analysis of Mistral's newly accessible correspondence: "Mistral se perfila como un sujeto excepcional que no se ajusta a lo que la sociedad de su época espera de una mujer pobre de provincia" ("Mistral portrays herself as an exceptional subject who does not fit into what the society of the era expected of a poor woman from the country") (21). In line with her self-image as gleaned from her letters, Mistral repeatedly focuses on the unconventional female subject in her verses. Even in the early prose poetry, "Poemas de las madres" ("The Mothers' Poems"), from *Desolación* (*Desolation*), the mothers depicted by Mistral are untraditional. Most importantly, the mothers in these pieces are allowed agency and are celebrated in their pregnant conditions. The expectant mother seeks community in women from different economic statuses for practicalities such as breastfeeding, if her breast is barren ("La hermana" ["The Sister"]), or from her own mother, to understand the new stage of womanhood ("La madre" ["The Mother"] and "Cuéntame, madre" ["Tell Me, Mother"]). Most clearly, the "Poemas de la madre más triste" ("Poems of the Saddest Mother") illustrate the young woman who conceives out of wedlock and is turned away from her family home on the cusp of giving birth. The poem evokes pity for this sad mother's circumstances and condemns the patriarchal social norms that permit such atrocities. Mistral's own experience of childhood raised by a single mother of two girls – the father left the family when Mistral had just turned three – resonates in the mothers depicted in

Femininity in Flux   201

these poems. That Mistral never had biological children but adopted and raised her nephew, and that she was in an amorous relationship with the US writer and translator Doris Dana, all point to the poet's personal understanding of womanhood as one that counters the tight boundaries defined by the conservative patriarchal state (see Fiol-Matta; Cabello Hutt; Mistral, *Gabriela Mistral's Letters*).[3]

While Mistral's early pieces already begin to represent a fuller scope of the woman's experience, her later poetry volume, *Lagar* (1954), demonstrates a transition in her representation of women. The final volume to be published during her lifetime, *Lagar* follows three anthologies, *Desolación* (1922), *Ternura* (1924), and *Tala* (1938). In the first two volumes, Mistral establishes her poetic voice as a spokesperson for motherhood and education, while in her most complex volume, *Tala*, the representation of women evolves to reveal intersectional identities. Finally, in *Lagar*, Mistral's focus shifts to present a wider spectrum of women's experience.

Unlike Mistral's earlier volumes, which were published in New York, Madrid, and Buenos Aires, respectively, *Lagar* was printed in Santiago in the Chilean press, Editorial del Pacífico, in 1954. In Mistral's discussion of this publishing decision in her personal correspondence, her conflictive relationship with Chile emerges: "Se hará en Chile y lo repartirá muy mal. Pero me han fabricado allá una leyenda de descatada y tengo que darles *Lagar*" ("It will be done in Chile and they will distribute it very badly. But they have fabricated a story there that I am ungrateful and I have to give them *Lagar*") (quoted in Couch 16). Previously, between 1941 and 1943, nineteen poems from the volume had been published in the Buenos Aires newspaper, *La Nación*. These contributions were sent from Brazil following the suicide of Mistral's good friends, the writer Stefan Zweig and his wife in 1942, and of her seventeen-year-old adoptive child, Juan Miguel or Yin-Yin, in 1943. Biographical readings of the *Madwomen* poems have supported the comments of Mistral's friend and collaborator, Palma Guillén, who described them as portraits of "todos los estados de ánimo por los que [Mistral] fue pasando después de la muerte del último de los suyos" ("all the emotional states through which [Mistral] passed after the death of the last of her own") (Guillén xxxvi).[4]

Lagar's fifteen sections with seventy-four poems in total include twelve pieces that celebrate nature principally from the Americas, four historical poems that contemplate aspects of war, and seven poems under the heading "Luto" ("Mourning") that explore the emotions of loss – clearly referencing Juan Miguel by name in "Aniversario" ("Birthday") and "Los dos" ("Both of Us"). Different aspects of religion are underscored in the nine poems of the section "Religiosas" ("Devotees"), while "Vagabundaje" ("Vagrancy") records responses to moving homes such as "Puertas" ("Doors"), a piece that explores the symbolism and advantages of doors, and "Patria" ("Homeland") that constructs dual homes in Montegrande and Mayab. Less serious poems are interspersed in the anthology, including "Ocho perritos" ("Eight Puppies"), which celebrates the pleasure of puppies, and the four brief poems in the section "Tiempo" ("Time") that impart thoughts on the four periods of the day. The volume closes with two poems: "Recado terrestre" ("Earthly Message"), written to Goethe on the commemoration of the bicentennial of his birth, which places the German poet on the level of the divine and requests his presence and his wisdom during this difficult time after World War II; and "Último árbol" ("Last Tree"), a piece that turns to nature to relate the narrator's thoughts on life and mortality.

The sixteen poems that constitute *Locas mujeres* from 1954 illustrate Mistral's appreciation of the large scope encompassed by the woman's perspective, her sentiments, her social condition, and her unrecognized abilities.[5] As translator of *Locas mujeres* into English, Randall Couch affirms in his introduction from 2008 that "These madwomen are strong, intensely human beings confronting situations to which no sane response exists" (2). Grínor Rojo, in his earlier analysis (1997) of these poems, refers to Elaine Showalter's *The Female Malady* (1985), Michel Foucault's *Madness and Civilization* (1961), and Sandra M. Gilbert and Susan Gubar's *Madwoman in the Attic* (1979), among others, to review how madness has been a category attributed to women especially in psychoanalysis, but also in other areas of Western thought. He acknowledges that this attribution diminishes women's agency and experience, and that Mistral surely understands this and counters it in her poetry. Lorena Garrido Donoso builds on Rojo's analysis to argue that the madwomen should be construed through the lens of the artist as the poet's doubles: Mistral "describe para poder, así, definirse a sí misma" ("describes in order to, in this way, define herself") (185).

While it is tempting to locate the insanity of these women in their experience of creative liberty, like Lucila in "Todas íbamos a ser reinas," the repeated incorporation of doubles in *Locas mujeres* reveals a more complex understanding of their madness. Although connected to their doubled identities, their madness is constituted by their condition of flux that emerges from the fact that these women maintain a state of transition between convention and liberty. In their attempts to embody the duality of their identities between those aspects that are prescribed by convention and those that are released from these prescriptions, these women embrace

Femininity in Flux   203

"madness." Mistral's madwomen demonstrate the impossibility for the woman to reconcile fully self and other; in seeking this reconciliation, these women lose their socially defined sanity inside the state of transition.

The first poem of the series, "La otra" ("The Other"), illustrates this dire predicament and sets the stage for the other female characters to illustrate further examples of women's double identity conflict. The speaker of "La otra" is uncomfortable with and dislikes a part of herself; she explains that she allowed this part of her to die and would like others to forget it too. Simultaneously, however, she maintains a unique connection to this other:

Era la flor llameando	She was the blazing flower
del cactus de montaña;	of the mountain cactus;
era aridez y fuego;	she was drought and fire,
nunca se refrescaba. . . .	never cooling her body. . . . (1–7)
La dejé que muriese,	I left her to die,
robándole mi entraña.	robbing her of my heart's blood.
Se acabó como el águila	She ended like an eagle
que no es alimentada. . . .	starved of its food. . . . (23–26)
Yo la maté. ¡Vosotras	I killed her. You women
también matadla!	must kill her too! (35–42)

The poem begs the question: who or what lived inside her; whom did the speaker allow to die? Clearly connected to an arid mountain landscape, reminiscent of the Elqui Valley of Mistral's youth, in its comparison with the mountain cactus and the eagle, this "other" was not nurtured; it was burned, unfed, and encouraged by the speaker to die. As the first poem in the collection, "La otra" leads the reader to understand the complexities of the women's "foreignness" in the fifteen poems that follow. Opening the series with this poem implies, tongue-in-cheek, that the woman who is not mad and who tries to fit into patriarchal prescriptions should shun and kill these "others" within herself to make way for a more harmonious and reputable female existence that would adhere to societal norms. However, after reading the poems that follow in the series, the definition of "madness" becomes hazier. The madwomen of the poems do not represent the "other" of the opening poem. Rather, their identity imitates that of the opening poem: it is caught in the uncomfortable place of transition between embracing the Self while still feeling connected to the Other.

It is almost as if "La otra" were written in direct response to Helene Cixous' call for feminist writing penned two decades later in her essay "The Laugh of the Medusa" (1976; French original, 1975). While Mistral claims in this poem that the speaker has killed the woman that she was, Cixous finds that women have been "reduced to being the servant of the militant male, his shadow," and pronounces that "we must kill the false woman who is preventing the live one from breathing. Inscribe the breath of the whole woman" (880). Cixous' women who write do not fear essential characteristics that allow them, like the mythological Medusa, to repel and fight against men. They embody the "monster" that society has forced them to tame and suppress. The French feminist exclaims that "we" women do not genuinely uphold society's perceptions and prescriptions: "We're stormy, and that which is ours breaks loose from us without our fearing any debilitation. Our glances, our smiles, are spent; laughs exude from all our mouths; our blood flows and we extend ourselves without ever reaching an end; we never hold back our thoughts, our signs, our writing; and we're not afraid of lacking" (878). Mistral's madwomen are uncomfortable in their new positions outside the prescriptive confines. They return to conventions for self-definition, while they also find liberty in their self-expression, constructing their identities within a state of transition.

The unexpectedly rigid organization of the *Madwomen* series underscores this state of transition. The fifteen poems that follow "La otra" in the series follow an organization that corresponds to that of a list or catalogue. The types of women are placed in alphabetical order beginning with "La abandonada" ("The Abandoned Woman") and concluding with "Una piadosa" ("A Pious Woman"). By placing into conventional organization that which cannot be structured, the series pokes fun at prescriptive social systems. A catalogue of women's experience in alphabetical order becomes arbitrary; the reader soon finds that the surface organization of the poems belies a resistance to categories. The titles, as well, designate women who appear to lack complexity. Frequently, they are defined in the titles by a single attribute – "abandoned," "unburdened," "happy," "fervent," "pious" – but the poems that capture them reveal the depth and multifaceted nature of these women's identities. Before closely analyzing two poems from the series, a brief overview of the main themes of the poems will reveal that these women's interactions with men play a determining role in their "madness" in many cases. Their self-definition becomes unclear when they measure themselves within the male–female relationship.

The first three poems depict women who are overly influenced by men, be it through the pain of abandonment ("La abandonada"), through overwhelming concern for his wellbeing ("La ansiosa" ["The Anxious Woman"]), or by unfulfilled desire for the lover's appearance ("La desvelada" ["The Sleepless Woman"]). While dreaming of a life without

Femininity in Flux 205

responsibilities, "La desasida" ("The Unburdened One") realizes that she must still cope with her worldly relationships. "La dichosa" ("The Happy Woman") portrays a woman who has found happiness in her life with her husband, but who has removed herself from her past. She notices the ambiguity in her identity, as was the case for "La otra": "La dichosa" also finds that "me sé y me desconozco" ("I know and I don't know myself") (36), leaving the reader to understand the inner conflict that seems to drive this woman's happiness.

Revealing a similar pain caused by men as the first poems, the next five pieces depict women who are not in a relationship and must endure loneliness. "La fervorosa" ("The Fervent Woman"), "La fugitiva" ("The Fugitive Woman"), and "La granjera" ("The Farm Woman") find strength in their solitude. "La fervorosa" feels connected to her family who are with God; "La fugitiva" relates to the trees and likens herself to the pine, "pino errante sobre la tierra!" ("pine wandering over the earth!") (42); "La granjera" works the farm alone, longing to join her loved ones in death. On the other hand, "La humillada" ("The Humbled Woman") is almost overwhelmed by her solitude; she attempts to protect herself from the intensity of the love that she feels by withholding certain intimacies (her breast and her prayers), only to be conquered by "el árbol de azufre y sangre" ("the tree of sulphur and blood") (33).

The first of the final four poems of the series describes the faithful bonds between biblical sisters, "Marta y María," while the next two elaborate on women who experience profound relationships with men. "Una mujer" ("A Woman") describes a woman who lives in mourning, while "Mujer de prisionero" ("Prisoner's Woman") portrays a wife's connection with her incarcerated husband. The series of poems concludes with the search for religious meaning in "Una piadosa" ("A Pious Woman"), a poem that depicts a woman who seeks the divine illumination of the lighthouse keeper, symbol of Jesus.

Two poems that have been omitted from this analysis until now, "La bailarina" ("The Dancer") and "La que camina" ("She Who Walks"), underscore the transitory nature of these women's identities, the dualities they seek to reconcile, and the madness they embrace as a result. In both pieces, the women express themselves, and their madness, through movement: the fervent dance and the constant walk. Both women have lost the ability to reconcile their dual identities and choose that of unbridled movement to appropriate their loss of sanity.

"La bailarina" grieves her past life and seeks the means to come to terms with her contradictory responses to her experiences. She leaves behind all that she was, including the essence of her Self represented by her own face and her name – "su propio rostro / y su nombre" ("her own face / and name") (6–7). Her conflicting sentiments lead her to dance: "lo que avientan sus brazos es el mundo / que ama y detesta, que sonríe y mata" ("what her arms fan away is the world / that loves and detests, that smiles and kills") (12–13). While the dancer both loves and hates, both encourages and destroys, the community also finds itself expressed in her dance in the final stanzas of the poem. The ballerina's sad but lively expression embodies an insanity that belongs to all of us:

Somos nosotros su jadeado pecho,	We are ourselves her panting breast,
su palidez exangüe, el loco grito	her bloodless pallor, the mad shout
tirado hacia el poniente y el levante	thrown out to the west and the east,
la roja calentura de sus venas,	the red fever of her veins, the neglect
el olvido del Dios de sus infancias.	of the God of her childhood days. (44–48)

Tremendous suffering drives the ballerina's dance that becomes a universal corporeal cry. Through artistic expression (the dance, the poem), the woman is able to expose her power and express the universality of women's experience. Her madness, like that of many of the madwomen, develops in the transition from an identity steeped in society to one that is detached from, released from, or unburdened by convention. She dances in an attempt to reconcile the two.

Of the sixteen women portrayed in the series, "La bailarina" most directly harnesses the power that Cixous would later call on women writers to assume. Cixous decries the place that has been assigned to women in psychoanalysis and patriarchal society: "They riveted us between two horrifying myths: between the Medusa and the abyss" (885). Mistral's dancer releases a force that, if exposed, is marked insane or even monstrous by patriarchal conventions. The poem even includes a reference to snakes in its description of the dancer's liberty: "y baila así mordida de serpientes / que alácritas y libres la repechan" ("and so she dances, struck by snakes / that free and eager climb her") (34–35). Like Cixous' representation of Medusa, the ballerina hides a power that is released in her dance. According to Cixous, "You only have to look at the Medusa straight on to see her. And she's not deadly. She's beautiful and she's laughing" (885). Mistral's dancer represents a solidarity with us all as we encounter the irreconcilable contradictions between embracing our authentic identities and living according to societal prescriptions.

As "La bailarina" transitions from prescribed identity in her unbridled dance, the woman from "La que camina" immerses herself in a never-ending

Femininity in Flux

walk to escape the chains of convention. Connected to the nature that surrounds her, the solitary woman walks her well-trodden path to weave her fate through her travels – she is alone "como un árbol / o como arroyo de nadie sabido" ("as a tree / or as a creek nobody knows") (40–41). The route she travels is capitalized in reference to the divine – "camina la Única" ("she walks the One") (8) – a path that is paralleled by her prayer to God: "solo en su oración dice el del Único" ("only in prayer speaks that of the One") (47). Like many of the madwomen from the volume, she has released herself from her prescribed identity and embraces her Self in her movement. Her despairing relationship to her identity is summarized with the lines that recall the doubles in "La otra": "Tanto quiso olvidar que ya ha olvidado. / Tanto quiso mudar que ya no es ella" ("She wanted to forget so much that she's forgotten. / She wanted to change so much she's no longer herself") (48–49). Moving between life and death or between "un fin y un comienzo" ("an end and a beginning") (42), this woman walks as if she were ageless or within a dream, "como sin edad o como en sueño" ("as if ageless or in a dream") (43), detached from social conventions.

As in "La bailarina," in which artistic expression envelops Mistral's dancer, in "La que camina," the woman embraces both the unending walk and a particular word that implies artistic expression through language:

esa sola palabra ha recogido	she has salvaged that single word
y de ella vive y de la misma muere.	and she lives on it and dies of the same. (19–20)
Otras palabras aprender no quiso	She wanted to learn no other words
y la que lleva es su propio sustento	and the one she bears is her proper food;
a más sola que va más la repite	the more alone she is, the more she repeats it (25–27)

This word, which seems to be the name given to her at birth, stays with her like a twin: "Ninguna más le dieron, en naciendo / y como es su gemela no la deja" ("They gave her nothing else at birth, / and since it's her twin, she won't leave it") (35–36). Therefore, as she walks toward death, she holds onto her name that links her to her creation, to divinity, and eventually to the afterlife. Finally, the narrator becomes involved in the walking woman's plight. In solidarity with her, as if to help her, the narrator recites all names instead of just one. In contrast with the woman who walks, accompanied by a single word, who finally rests in the "sueño fabuloso" ("fabled sleep") (64), the narrator moves, "sin descanso recitando / la letanía de todos los nombres" ("I recite without rest / the litany of all the names") (57–58). The juxtaposition of these two expressions points again to the impossibility of reconciling one's complete identity with the conventional prescriptions.

The unbridled dance and the never-ending walk mark the women of both poems as they release themselves from social conventions. Their transition from constrained to free taints them with madness as they realize the impossibility of reconciling their dual identities. Both women also move in solidarity with others: the "we" of "La bailarina" feels similarly released by her fiery dance, while the narrator of "La que camina" seeks to empathize with the walking woman by offering up more words than just the one that ironically seems to have imprisoned her. In both cases, creativity represented by movement permits these women a freedom that has otherwise been unavailable to them in their social and "sane" womanly roles.

Returning to the question raised by the opening poem of the mad-women series, "La otra": if the catalogue of women represents the images from the poem of the cactus flower that does not know how to bend, and the eagle who is independent, should they be forgotten and killed – "olvidadla. / Yo la maté. ¡Vosotras / también matadla!" ("I killed her. You women / must kill her too") ("La otra," 36–42)? The fifteen women characterized in the poems that follow represent those who have allowed the "Other" to live: the abandoned one, the dancer, the wanderer, and the other female protagonists of these poems all characterize women who challenge their socially prescribed masks, or the "divine composure" of the "well-adjusted normal woman" (Cixous 876). These individuals represent women who seek to embrace the independent and genuine child of their youth – the unbending cactus flower and the independent eagle – but who find themselves, like "La otra," caught in the transition between their authentic and their conventionally defined identities. Like the never-ending dancer and the eternal walker, these women seek meaning in self-expression, a madness that represents the only possible response to an attempt to reconcile contradictory and opposing identities.

Mistral's personal life underscores the dual identities she straddled: in her career as she transitioned from rural schoolteacher to pedagogical adviser and diplomat on an international level; through her clandestine lesbian identity that contrasted with the feminine image she espoused professionally as Latin American mother and teacher. As Mistral transitioned in her career and lifestyle between social convention and authenticity in her identity, her poetry's representation of women also shifted. From "Poemas de las madres" to "Todas íbamos a ser reinas" and, finally,

Femininity in Flux 209

Locas mujeres, the woman transforms from the mothers who define their identity through childbirth; to the "reinas" who resign themselves in sadness to their lost dreams; to the madwomen who realize that the only way to reconcile these contradictory identities is to embrace a form of insanity.

Notes

1. Translation by Doris Dana (88–93).
2. Mistral explained that her pen name was in tribute to Italian poet Gabriele D'Annunzio and the French poet Frédéric Mistral, as well as the Archangel Gabriel, and the Mistral wind of Provence (Aizenberg 119).
3. As Velma García-Gorena affirms in her introduction to the correspondence between Dana and Mistral: "the poet was not a chaste, traditionally Catholic spinster; Gabriela Mistral was in love with Doris Dana and never expressed a desire for a heterosexual relationship. Moreover, although Mistral embraced aspects of Catholicism, she also wrote about feeling a connection to her Jewish ancestors as well as an admiration for Buddhist ideas and practices" (Mistral, *Gabriela Mistral's Letters*, 3).
4. Yenny Ariz Castillo analyzes the changes introduced in *Locas mujeres* through their trajectory of creation and publication.
5. Beyond the sixteen *Madwomen* poems in the 1954 volume, in *Lagar II*, published posthumously in 1991, are added eight more poems that were retrieved from Mistral's unpublished manuscripts. I have chosen to analyze the series as it appeared in the first volume that follows Mistral's publication choices to not enter, in this brief chapter, into the debates surrounding the poet's completion of the poems given their posthumous publication.

Works Cited

Aizenberg, Edna. *On the Edge of the Holocaust: The Shoah in Latin American Literature and Culture.* Waltham, MA: Brandeis University Press, 2015.

Ariz Castillo, Yenny. "Las 'Locas mujeres' de Gabriela Mistral publicadas por *La Nación* de Buenos Aires (1941–1943)," *Revista Chilena de Literatura* 99 (2019): 145–176.

Cabello Hutt, Claudia. *Artesana de sí misma: Gabriela Mistral, una intelectual en cuerpo y palabra.* West Lafayette, IN: Purdue University Press, 2018.

Cixous, Hélene. "The Laugh of the Medusa," *Signs* 1.4 (1976): 875–893.

Concha, Jaime. *Gabriela Mistral: Colección los poetas 68.* Madrid: Ediciones Iucar, 1987.

Couch, Randall. "Introduction." In *Madwomen: The "Locas Mujeres" Poems of Gabriela Mistral, a Bilingual Edition.* Trans and ed. Randall Couch, pp. 1–28. Chicago, IL: University of Chicago Press, 2008.

Dana, Doris, trans. *Selected Poems by Gabriela Mistral.* Baltimore, MD: Johns Hopkins University Press, 1971.

Fiol-Matta, Licia. *A Queer Mother for the Nation: The State and Gabriela Mistral.* Minneapolis, MN: University of Minnesota Press, 2002.

Garrido Donoso, Lorena. *"No hay como una contadora para hacer contar": mujer poeta en Gabriela Mistral.* Santiago: Editorial Cuarto Propio, 2012.

Guillén, Palma. "Introducción." In *Desolación-Ternura-Tala-Lagar* by Gabriela Mistral, 1973. Mexico City: Porrúa, 2006. ix–xlviii.

Mistral, Gabriela. *Gabriela Mistral's Letters to Doris Dana.* Ed. Velma García-Gorena. Albuquerque: University of New Mexico Press, 2018.

Madwomen: The "Locas Mujeres" Poems of Gabriela Mistral, a Bilingual Edition. Trans. and ed. Randall Couch. Chicago, IL: University of Chicago Press, 2008.

Tala / Lagar. Ed. Nuria Girona. Madrid: Ediciones Cátedra, 2001.

Lecturas para mujeres. 2nd ed. Ed. Palma Guillén de Nicolau. Mexico City: Editorial Porrúa, 1969.

O'Connor, Erin E. *Mothers Making Latin America: Gender, Households, and Politics Since 1825.* Hoboken, NJ: Wiley, 2014.

Peña, Karen Patricia. *Poetry and the Realm of the Public Intellectual: The Alternative Destinies of Gabriela Mistral, Cecília Meireles, and Rosario Castellanos.* London: Legenda, 2007.

Rojo, Grínor. *Dirán que está en la gloria—: Mistral.* Santiago: Fondo de Cultura Económica, 1997.

Sepúlveda, Magda. *Gabriela Mistral: somos los andinos que fuimos.* Santiago: Editorial Cuarto Propio, 2018.

Zubizarreta, John. "Gabriela Mistral: The Great Singer of Mercy and Motherhood," *Christianity and Literature* 42.2 (1993): 295–311.

CHAPTER 13

The Representation of Afro-Cuban Orality by Fernando Ortiz, Lydia Cabrera, and Nicolás Guillén

Miguel Arnedo-Gómez

The 1930s in Cuba unleashed a transition toward a more pronounced cultural solidarity toward Afro-Cubans on the part of Cuban writers and intellectuals. This responded to the fact that the first Republican constitution of 1901 had granted equal opportunities to all Cubans and Afro-Cuban culture had begun to symbolize national distinctiveness for its uniquely Cuban-Spanish-African hybridity. This chapter examines transitions in the ethnographic and literary representation of Afro-Cuban orality as reflected in the representational strategies employed by Fernando Ortiz, Lydia Cabrera, and Nicolás Guillén. Their different approaches challenge the unequal power relations reproduced through traditional ethnographic discourse to varying degrees but, as will become evident, their methodologies cannot be taken as an accurate measure of the true extent of their affiliation to, and immersion in, Afro-Cuban culture.

African Survivals and Fernando Ortiz's Representation of Afro-Cuban Orality

In his 1950 study *La africanía de la música folklórica de Cuba* (*Africanness in the Folkloric Music of Cuba*), Fernando Ortiz felt he needed to furnish his readers with a basic understanding of African music to then contrast it with truly national Cuban music, which he conceived as a mixture of the African and the European (27, 150). To explain African music, he decided to use examples from the musical forms and oral texts employed in the rituals and cultural practices of Afro-Cuban religions, which he believed to be perfectly preserved forms of African culture, or *supervivencias africanas* (African survivals) (154). Such a notion – probably drawn to some extent from survival theory in folklore studies[1] – is hard to reconcile with a Cuban history of intense Spanish-African cultural interpenetration,

211

a phenomenon that Ortiz's own 1940 definition of the term transculturation partly addressed by positing that interacting cultures always produce new, hybrid cultural forms (Ortiz, *Contrapunteo*, 96–97). Although Ortiz's conception of Afro-Cuban religions as African survivals has received little critical attention, it complements critiques of his detachment from Afro-Cuban culture by Lienhard (26–28) and Rodríguez-Mangual (25–58). For example, Lienhard argues that Ortiz's tendency to provide transcriptions of lyrics from religious chants in African languages distances him from a vast compendium of secular and spontaneous Afro-Cuban oral texts, which means he does not really dialogue with Afro-Cubans but with their sacred traditions of African origins. Because of this, Lienhard categorizes Ortiz's methodology as a vertical ethnography, and he demarcates it from Lydia Cabrera's horizontal, and thus less hierarchical, approach.

Nevertheless, the notion of a vertical ethnography occludes the fact that Ortiz's transcriptions of supposedly pristine African oral forms often end up reflecting their Cuban features. For instance, in his 1951 study *Los bailes y el teatro de los negros en el folklore de Cuba* (*Black Dance and Theater in the Folklore of Cuba*), Ortiz transcribes two Abakuá oral forms through which adepts orally and spontaneously interacted with their Cuban surroundings in between religious ceremonies. These oral forms were songs of mutual defiance known as *inúas*. The practice of oral dueling, present in several Afro-Cuban traditions, involves singers addressing their immediate environment and audience. Although Ortiz's two transcribed *inúas* do not feature Spanish words, their local origins are clear as they invoke the creation of Efik Ebutón, the first Cuban Abakuá society, in the Havana neighborhood of Regla. The *inúas* also reflect the creation of new terms in the Abakuá language to designate Cuban phenomena, as they include the names given in Abakuá to this neighborhood (Itiáro Kánde) and to Havana (Núnkue) (74–75). Thus modified from their original African versions in order to include these Cuban phenomena, these *inúas* point toward Afro-Cubans' elaboration of neo-African identities, a process Stephan Palmié terms "ethnogenesis" (338).

Ortiz was acquainted with conquered people's capacity to appropriate cultural elements of dominant cultures, and he even characterizes this strategy as a form of transculturation on some occasions. In the third chapter of *La africanía*, he argues that pygmies from Central Africa "quickly transculturated white music in order to adapt it to their own system," thus turning it into "authentically black music" (215). Ortiz dampens this strategy's subversiveness, by contrast, when he turns to the analysis of Black American musicians' handling of European musical

The Representation of Afro-Cuban Orality   213

influences. These musicians do not turn European music into Black music; instead they "tropicalize" it, according to the scholar (216). This terminological choice is symptomatic of Ortiz's failure to acknowledge that forms of Black culture and Black or Afro-Cuban identities continued to exist in Cuba despite cultural mixture. Tellingly, in another section of *La africanía* Ortiz does not even mention the term "transculturation" when discussing a similar display of cultural resistance in magical spells used in Cuba by the *tata nganga*, who, as Dodson explains, are elders and spiritual leaders for Cuban adherents to the Palo Mayombe religion (97). While Ortiz sees this religion as an African survival, his transcription of a magical spell is a clear example of African-Spanish linguistic hybridity. On this occasion, Ortiz does mention the text's linguistic duality but swiftly dismisses it as not worthy of extended analysis (301–308). This dismissal is consistent with his professed aim of illustrating African culture using local African survivals. Like functionalist anthropologists such as Bronislaw Malinowski, then, Ortiz filtered out foreign elements from African cultural forms in an archaeological search for pristine forms in their pre-contact state.[2]

In another passage from *La africanía*, Ortiz describes a noteworthy example of Afro-Cuban cultural resistance in the realm of written literature. He claims to be in possession of a curious nineteenth-century poem written in the Abakuá language but with the meter of the Spanish *décima*. Ángel Rama's landmark study *Writing Across Cultures* suggests that incorporation into written literature of non-Western cultures at the level of form was the accomplishment of twentieth-century writers such as José María Arguedas, Gabriel García Márquez, and Juan Rulfo. Ortiz's Abakuá poem suggests that instances of formal fusion between non-Western cultures and the dominant literary tradition predated the work of these narrative transculturators, as Ángel Rama called them. And yet, Ortiz does not analyze this text or even transcribe it for his readers. He also swiftly affirms that penetration of African languages into the dominant language and literature of Cuba was not significant despite including lexical, syntactical, and prosodic aspects, and that African influences on Cuban mainstream culture were much more pronounced in Cuban music (318).

Why did Ortiz so often seem to diminish the interactions between Afro-Cuban traditions and the dominant European-derived culture? To some extent, the answer is linked to his ultimate allegiance to Western culture and civilization and his concomitant understanding of transculturation as a process that would culminate with a single mulatto composite that excluded African belief systems (Duany 24; Ortiz, "Por Colón," 5, 23; Ortiz, "La religion," 146–147). The related notion that Afro-Cuban religions were doomed to extinction because of their inadaptability fitted this conception of Cuban development. Despite this outlook, Ortiz's aspiration to ethnographic objectivity and accuracy stopped him from completely ignoring the Spanish-African hybridity of Afro-Cuban religions. The above examples are his rhetorical attempts at resolving this tension.

While the arguments thus far point to some of the limits of Ortiz's solidarity with his subjects of study, certain descriptions of his own real-life interactions with Afro-Cubans seem at odds with his fossilizing rhetoric. At one point in *La africanía*, the scholar explains that he was asked several times to be a witness in legal proceedings against Cuban musicians who had plagiarized Afro-Cuban religious melodies (189). Logically, such proceedings were initiated by Afro-Cuban religious practitioners (which means they were more actively engaged with the dominant sociocultural system than Ortiz's bell-jar anthropology suggests). Therefore, Ortiz's intervention in these legal cases evinces that Afro-Cuban adepts considered him a knowledgeable and legitimate source of authority on their religion. Moreover, in Ortiz's subsequent explanations a peculiar break from his customary scientific detachment may signal a greater degree of immersion in Afro-Cuban culture than is generally attributed to him. He goes on to explain that musicians who plagiarized Afro-Cuban religious melodies tended to die shortly after their theft and that he was informed that it was the orishas who killed them. "We would not dare support this explanation," he writes,

> but the orishas would not have looked kindly upon those who commit simony with their property. Any other individuals with similar intentions should take heed ... the usurpation of ritualistic chants to turn them into vulgar cabaret music will incite the ire of Changó, the god of music; and the goddess Oyá is a fearsome executor of his punishments. (189)

While expressing cautious detachment from this irrational argument in the first sentence, Ortiz's narrative stance transitions into an Afro-Cuban worldview in the rest of the extract as he adopts the perspective of someone who holds no doubt about the orishas' ability to influence reality. Another section of *La africanía* presents a similar transition to a perspective from which events normally relegated to the realm of magic are perceived as factual. Ortiz starts this section by approaching Afro-Cuban animist beliefs from a rational-scientific perspective. He argues that Afro-Cuban animism consists in humanizing inanimate objects and relating to them "as if they were real." However, he then narrates the real-life case of an Afro-Cuban

The Representation of Afro-Cuban Orality

drum in a *cabildo* of "a certain Cuban city" who "refused to be taken to the funeral of a renowned Afro-Cuban drummer." He adds that "the drum was so saddened it increased its own density until becoming so heavy that nobody could lift it." Eventually, a drummer convinced the drum to play at the funeral by striking it with leaves from a Royal Palm tree (274). As can be seen, Ortiz writes about this event as if the drum were a living being, thus siding with Afro-Cuban magic once again. In view of such moments of authorial assimilation of the Afro-Cuban worldview, attractive hypotheses can be formed based on a claim by certain Cuban scholars that Ortiz must have been an Abakuá to obtain so much information about the secretive society, and that such affiliation precluded him from broaching sensitive issues on race, such as the 1912 massacre of Black protesters known as the Guerrita del 12 (María Poumier as cited in Coronil xlix). Something like this could also explain Ortiz's recurrent vagueness about specific Afro-Cuban cultural actors, religions, and real-life episodes of Afro-Cuban magic such as the one cited above. Why "a certain Cuban city"? Which *cabildo*? Who was the Afro-Cuban drummer who persuaded the drum? Perhaps one could approach Ortiz's ethnographic persona as a rhetorical mechanism that projected the appearance of detached observer to hide the true extent of his Afro-Cuban religious beliefs.

Lydia Cabrera and the Afro-Cuban Re-oralization of *El Monte*

Whereas Ortiz tends to isolate Afro-Cuban culture from Cuba's dominant culture of Spanish origins, Lydia Cabrera's 1956 *El monte* (*Afro-Cuban Tales*, 2004) (a study of the Afro-Cuban religion *Santería* or *Regla de Ocha*) foregrounds the interactions of a white creole woman with the Afro-Cuban worldview of her Afro-Cuban informants. At the start of this book, Cabrera's introductory explanations about Afro-Cubans and their beliefs betray her reliance on Western rationality. After mentioning one of her informants' visions of a Black man's head with feet covered in hair in the forest (*monte* in Cuban Spanish), Cabrera tries to make sense of it for the non-Afro-Cuban reader. She warns against assuming it was a mere fantasy, adducing that these types of experiences are very real for Black people because "para un negro creyente pronto se convierten en realidad, como todo lo que sueña o imagina" ("for a Black believer, they soon become real like everything he or she dreams or imagines") (18). They are inclined to lie, she adds, but they are not insincere; they merely convince themselves of the actuality of magical events. She claims that a Black person's capacity for autosuggestion "nos explica muchas particularidades de su alma, de su gran emotividad religiosa de su credulidad; y desde luego, la influencia persis-tente, incalculable, que el hechicero y la magia ejerce" ("explains several peculiarities of their soul, of their profound spirituality, of their credulity, and of the constant influence that witchcraft and imaginary spiritual beings exercise over them") (18). But, in line with her aim of letting her Afro-Cuban informants guide her through their religious universes (11), Cabrera follows these explanations with the verbatim testimony of her informant Gabino Sandoval. Sandoval remarks that Blacks go to the forest to commune with the dead and the saints just like whites go to church to ask for protection from Jesus Christ or the Virgin Mary (18–19). This could be taken as his way of reminding Cabrera that irrational thought underpins Catholicism too, which questions her preceding binary opposition between white rationalism and Afro-Cuban magic. The ease with which Sandoval's explanation conflates the two faiths is symptomatic of Cuban Blacks' success at commodifying Christian religious beliefs within their African-derived religions. In these pages of *El monte*, thus, distinct rhetorical traditions and communication styles enter a dialogic relation of sorts, establishing a pattern that resurfaces throughout the rest of the book.

Such treatment of Afro-Cuban oral discourses has garnered critical praise for Cabrera. Edna Rodríguez-Mangual unfavorably compares Ortiz's ethnography to *El monte*, stressing the book's disarticulation of the traditional ethnographic gaze in ways that pre-empt the conceptual shift advocated by James Clifford thirty-two years later (Rodríguez-Mangual 62; Clifford 1–26). She also praises the book's questioning of the notions of truth, meaning, and authenticity, as well as its dismantling of "the rigid categories of anthropology, the testimonial novel, and fiction in general" (98). Rodríguez-Mangual sees *El monte* as a "construction for a space of otherness" and "a space that blurs the dividing lines between the researcher and the object of study, between the voice of white people and that of blacks, which has the effect of placing the reader in the midst of an Afro-Cuban cosmogony, black or mestizo" (73, 93, 104). However, Erwan Dianteill and Martha Swearingen's research provides ammunition for a less celebratory interpretation of Cabrera's relationship with Afro-Cubans, along the lines of critiques of Latin American *testimonio* as "exploitation of the marginal Other as raw anthropological material to be processed for consumption" (Emery 17–18). Some of their findings suggest Cabrera engaged in a form of "salvage ethnography" as characterized by James Clifford; that is, as a problematic practice allowing ethnographers' self-legitimation as transcribers of vanishing oral traditions (Clifford 112–113).

The Representation of Afro-Cuban Orality   217

Indeed, they draw attention to one of Cabrera's statements in which she warns of the impending disappearance of Afro-Cuban oral traditions, and she advocates for an urgent written transcription of the vanishing teachings of Afro-Cuban elders (Dianteill and Swearingen 275; Cabrera, *Koeko Iyawó*, 6). For these critics, this assertion suggests that "*santeros* are confined to a purely oral world of religious practices and that Cabrera considered herself to be a witness of an endangered tradition" (Dianteill and Swearingen 275). They go on to demonstrate that this underestimated the level of literacy of Afro-Cuban religious practitioners, who in fact made ample use of reading and writing to record and expand cultural information related to their religions. They outline several types of such writing practices and resulting written forms. These include a booklet of prayers purchasable in the streets or at markets, a booklet for followers of Allan Kardec's Spiritism – which was intertwined with African religions in Cuba (*La africanía*, 259) – and a Spanish book of witchcraft (*Book of San Ciprián*) that *santeros* used as a source of magical recipes. They also mention the *libretas de santería*; notebooks in which, as Rogelio Martínez Furé explains, *Santería* practitioners transcribed hundreds of myths, fables, refrains, glossaries, and spells (Martínez Furé 211). According to Dianteill and Swearingen (276), Cabrera knew of these Afro-Cuban texts and even relied on the *libretas de santería* as sources, openly acknowledging them on at least five different occasions in *El monte* (275, 358, 367, 399, 520). But she also appears to have purposely downplayed their existence and this may have helped consolidate her status as author of Afro-Cuban literature (Dianteill and Swearingen 280). It was particularly Afro-Cuban religious myths that Cabrera sought to appropriate with her writing, and for this reason she consciously glossed over the already written versions produced by practitioners: "She emphasized their oral origin and claimed the art of writing for herself. This allowed her to modify the original texts found in the *libretas*, which were not intended to be published and whose authors had no literary ambitions" (Dianteill and Swearingen 278).

Is Cabrera's *El monte* a usurpation of Afro-Cuban writing that falsely relegates Afro-Cubans to orality, then? It could be argued that this impression is undermined by the few pages of *El monte* analyzed above. The prominence of Sandoval's testimony and its juxtaposition to Cabrera's ethnocentric depiction of Afro-Cubans as fantasy-prone beings suggest *El monte* was conceived as a heterogeneous and polyphonic text rather than as a totalizing narrative. It is also important to note that if we were to draw up a classificatory system for a broad concept of Afro-Cuban literature comprising all forms of writing connected to Afro-Cuban culture, *El monte* and the *libretas de santería* would fall under different categories. The former is an erudite work of written literature with a clear literary aesthetic that can only be fully appreciated through reading. The latter, by contrast, consist of rudimentary notations of essential religious information, and they serve as mnemonic devices in live ritual practices. As Dianteill and Swearingen assert, *Santería* manuals are today's equivalent of the *Santería* booklets as their purpose is "to help the practitioner perform rituals" (288).

It is productive to consider another of Dianteill and Swearingen's findings, which is that after *El monte* was published it was used as the main source for a contemporary *Santería* manual entitled *Manual de santero*, written by an anonymous author (281). In a meticulous comparison between both texts, they outline how the manual re-oralizes the ethnographic information collected in *El monte* so that it can be used in rituals. This includes the use of anonymous authorship, a colloquial register, and an abbreviated writing style. The information from *El monte* is also re-oralized through a re-organization of Cabrera's alphabetical plant and herb lists according to the order in which their corresponding orishas appear in rituals (283–286). If we accepted the image of *El monte* as appropriation of Afro-Cuban writing, we would have to also acknowledge that *Manual de santero* re-appropriates *El monte* in some ways. In any case, Cabrera's study has already been widely re-appropriated in Afro-Cuban religious practice, as many *santeros* in Cuba and the United States use it as a source of reference for their religious practices (Dianteill and Swearingen 274, 287). Incidentally, this shows *santeros* allocate some value to Cabrera's representation of their culture, although it is not *El monte*'s cross-cultural features that interest them but its unadorned Afro-Cuban cultural knowledge. It is possible to find an array of approaches to Afro-Cuban religions in Cabrera's work and, in fact, her study *Koeko iyawó* could be more susceptible to accusations of appropriation and plagiarism than *El monte* because it is "clearly organized as a manual for initiates, which is precisely the function of a *libreta*" (Dianteill and Swearingen 277). Still, a critique of this kind would need to consider that *Koeko iyawó* was published by Cabrera once she was in exile in Miami and that it was driven by her concern about Miami Cubans' progressive loss of their Cuban cultural heritage, which for her included both African and Spanish traditions (*Koeko iyawó* 1–2).

Admittedly, Cabrera's *El monte* would have been surpassed in terms of cultural immersion by Afro-Cuban religious practitioners' own literary expressions. But the book does not hide its true nature as the work of an educated, privileged *criolla* addressed to white educated Cuban readers. Moreover, it foregrounds perspectives of Afro-Cuban informants that

The Representation of Afro-Cuban Orality   219

undermine Cabrera's ethnocentric authorial voice. While she may have manipulated her Afro-Cuban written and non-written sources to pursue her own literary goals, *El monte* has contributed to the spread of an unjustly suppressed and marginalized Afro-Cuban religion.

Afro-Cuban Orality and a New Afro-Cuban Subjectivity in the Poetry of Nicolás Guillén

Nicolás Guillén's explanations about his first book of Black poetry *Motivos de son* (1930) present similarities to the approach to popular culture in folklore studies, the discipline also informing Ortiz's and Cabrera's books and whose original European formulation responded to the need "to root the formation of new nations in the identity of their past" (García Canclini, *Hybrid Cultures*, 150). Guillén declared that what truly interested him was "the study of the Cuban folk" and "the search for their inner identity." He added that he used his *son* poetry to advocate and promote "the only thing that is still truly ours" (as cited in Madrigal 62–63). Like Cabrera, Guillén insisted on the accuracy of his representations of Afro-Cuban orality. Mirroring Cabrera's claim in *Koeko iyawó* that she did not alter the thought, concepts, feelings, or oral expression of her informants, Guillén affirmed in a 1930 speech that he had not invented a single characteristic of the Black characters that speak in his *motivos* (*Koeko iyawó*, 3; Guillén, "Motivos literarios," 30–31).

Guillén at this early stage focused on the immediate presence of Afro-Cuban orality in everyday Cuban life, as opposed to the fossilized texts of Afro-Cuban religious chants that interested Ortiz. Rather than appearing as a vanishing tradition in need of salvaging through writing, the orality of lower-class Blacks represented in *Motivos* was a living force permeating everyday reality. In recreating it through written poetry, Guillén sought to draw attention to the fact that the distinctive orality of lower-class Havana Blacks was an undeniable part of Cuban culture, and that it was infecting all Cubans. As he wrote in the above-mentioned speech, "the characters I am referring to are around us every day, they play a role in our lives, and they even (why continue to deny this?) infect us with their exuberant ways of thinking" (31).

After *Motivos* Guillén began to engage with a different kind of Black orality that was omnipresent at the time: the lyrics of the Afro-Cuban musical genre known as *son*. Moore explains that *son* was "the first black street genre to gain national acceptance and to be performed commercially without excessive stylistic alteration or transformation" (89). Its popularity

220 MIGUEL ARNEDO-GÓMEZ

was especially noticeable in the period from 1925 to 1928, "a turning point in the history of *son*, one in which it was transformed from a marginal genre of dubious origins into the epitome of national expression" (Moore 104). The radio played a fundamental role in disseminating *son* throughout the nation, with radio transmitters being "a common feature in homes, corner stores, barbershops, cafés, and nightclubs" (Moore 103). Guillén's choice of *son* music as source material was key in avoiding the trappings of salvage ethnography. As the verbal constituents of *son* invaded the households and streets of Havana, he no longer needed to alert his readers to the presence of Afro-Cuban orality, and any concern about preserving it through writing could be cast aside. This allowed him to abandon the technique of misspelling Spanish words to imitate Black lower-class speech, which he had used in *Motivos*. It also gave him the freedom to think beyond transcription and to engage in creative reconfigurations of the verbal constituents of *son*.

A perfect example of Guillén's conscious interplay with this Afro-Cuban form of orality is his poem "Secuestro de la mujer de Antonio" ("The Kidnapping of Antonio's Wife"), as it is a reworking of "La mujer de Antonio" ("Antonio's Wife"), a popular *son* piece from the late 1920s written by Miguel de Matamoros and performed by his band, the Trío Matamoros (Orovio 289; Ledón Sánchez 85). The poem's title already draws attention to its paratextual relationship with the song through the word *secuestro* (kidnapping). In the poem the speaker essentially threatens to kidnap Antonio's wife, but what is also suggested by the title is Guillén's own appropriation of Matamoros' song. This possibility could be taken seriously since Guillén was a middle-class intellectual from a privileged background working with cultural materials developed by lower-class Blacks (Arnedo-Gómez xvi–xvii). Differences between the two texts are so extreme as to invalidate any possibility of an appropriation, though, and they derive to a large extent from their different systems of production, especially at the stage García Canclini refers to as "the step of circulation," as this brings into play how the intended audience and channel of distribution of any cultural form significantly shapes its formal make-up.[3] When composing the lyrics, Miguel de Matamoros employed language with basic rhymes whose meaning could be immediately apprehended by the listener upon first hearing them. The lyrics' formal simplicity is also partly a function of their intended actualization in musical performances that comprise a broad array of musical codes. In contrast, Guillén's "Secuestro de la mujer de Antonio" employs the language of erudite written poetry, with complex metaphors and similes that require attentive reading.

The Representation of Afro-Cuban Orality

Guillén's transformation of the lyrics into an erudite literary text could elicit comparisons with Cabrera's attempt to upgrade the *libretas* to more sophisticated written versions, an implication of her statement that they were useless because they were badly written (Cabrera as cited in Dianteill and Swearingen 277). But Guillén always seemed to maintain the distinction between *son* and his *son* poetry. He stated that his poems could be put to music but that he had not written them with that objective in mind (as cited in Augier 129). Unlike Ortiz and Cabrera, he did not set out to preserve Afro-Cuban orality in writing, which implies a substitution of orality with literature. On the contrary, his poem "Secuestro" actually relies upon the parallel existence of the song "La mujer de Antonio," and upon a reader who was familiar with it. The prominence of *son* lyrics in the Cuban imaginary at the time meant there were many Cuban readers familiar with Matamoros' song. For this reason, the poem would have activated a dual process, with the memory of the original song and its lyrics arousing certain associations and Guillén's verse others. The memory of the original *son* song by Matamoros evoked the idea of an authentic, rural Cuban tradition, largely attributable to Afro-Cubans but also anchored in the nation's bicultural origins. Such a conception of *son* was certainly expressed by 1930s Cuban intellectuals, who were inspired by the music's widespread appeal. For instance, the Afro-Cuban writer Regino Boti wrote that "our *son* comes from Cuba's eastern region, it is autochthonous to the region of Baracoa and it has sprouted within our singing traditions, free of foreign contamination and displaying a simplicity we could call traditional" (85). These qualities of *son* suited Guillén's aim of promoting Afro-Cuban culture as a central component of Cuban identity. Over this symbolic substratum of national authenticity, the verbal discourse of "Secuestro" introduces a highly personal take on race and the nation that concerns the predicament of a new Cuban subject represented by the poet: the male, urban, mulatto intellectual seeking a place within the conflictive social fabric of 1930s Cuba. What makes this evident is the contrast between Guillén's treatment of Antonio's mulatto wife and her representation in the song, which can also be read in terms of a transition from a collective consciousness in the song to a different type of Afro-Cuban subjectivity.

In the song, Antonio's mulatto wife is not the main thematic focus. The lyrics merely mention the attention her walk receives and evoke it through the repeated chorus "camina así" ("she walks like this"). Other than that, there are references to contemporaneous national and international events: the politics of then president of the Republic Gerardo Machado and Charles Lindbergh's successful crossing of the Atlantic Ocean in 1927. By contrast, Guillén's poem is exclusively about the *mulata* and is addressed to her directly. Its speaker is an individualized male who wants to sexually possess and consume her, metaphorically sequestering her from her husband Antonio. In the first stanza, he already declares he will drink her as if she were a glass of rum. He further describes her as "cintura de mi cancion" ("hips of my song"), which makes her seem a mindless accessory for his art. In the fourth stanza he reinforces her subjection to his will, asserting she will not leave to go home or to the market and will instead remain where she is so that "molerán tus ancas / la zafra de tu sudor" ("your legs grind the harvest of your sweat"). In the last stanza, although still addressing the *mulata*, the speaker expresses a macho challenge to her husband Antonio, telling him he will need to walk away (*Summa poética*, 85–86). As Roberto Méndez Martínez rightly notes, the poem produces an overall sensation of violent male chauvinism (568). This is the discourse of an urban *mulato* expressing a new form of Afro-Cuban subjectivity within the modern social order by ill-using the figure of that other social subject who threatened the Black male ego: the socially ambitious *mulata* whose sexual appeal facilitated her relationships with white men. There is ample evidence in Guillén's poetry of his disapproval of the *mulata*'s racial crossovers. For instance, in "Mulata," a Black speaker reprimands a *mulata* for demeaning him because of his Black physiognomy. He not only admonishes her for this but also expresses his preference for a blacker woman, thus undermining the whitening ideology that her behavior responded to and presenting Black women who have no problem with having Black partners in a positive light (Guillén, *Obra*, 92). In "Puente," the *mulata*'s relations with a white old man are portrayed in a similarly negative light (Guillén, *Obra*, 398). Against the backdrop of Cuban Blacks' contestation of *mestizaje* as a whitening ideology in the 1930s (Arnedo-Gómez 23–38), it could be argued that in "Secuestro" Guillén once again desires to punish the *mulata* for her complicity in the nation's *blanqueamiento* (whitening). Particularly troublesome is that such punishment is expressed through an image connecting the *mulata*'s body and sexuality to the harvest and production of sugar, thus mirroring a tendency in Cuban white poets' demeaning representations of Black women at the time (Anderson 25). Thus, despite avoiding the trappings of Ortiz's and Cabrera's salvage ethnography in terms of its relationship with Afro-Cuban orality, this poem expresses a new Afro-Cuban subjectivity that draws upon white-dominant mechanisms used to oppress Black Cuban women.

Conclusion

The representational transitions identified in the writings of these three Cuban intellectuals may be seen as expressions of a growing cultural solidarity with Cuban Blacks and their Afro-Cuban cultures on the part of Cuba's early and mid-twentieth-century literary intelligentsia. On the whole, Cabrera's ethnography best avoids imposing authorial control over the oral discourses of her Afro-Cuban informants, letting them "speak for themselves" to a much greater degree than Ortiz and even Guillén. Curiously, despite its non-ethnographic status, it is Guillén's poem that best avoids the discourse of salvage ethnography as characterized by Clifford because it avoids transcription and fossilization of *son* lyrics and engages with them dialogically, which is what facilitates expression of his Black middle-class mulatto subjectivity. But the analysis also reveals that it is not easy to ascertain the extent of each of these writers' solidarity with Cuban Blacks from their representational strategies. Indeed, as shown, Ortiz's rhetorical detachment from Afro-Cuban culture may have been a strategy to distract from his close affiliation to Afro-Cuban religious beliefs in real life. Similarly, the less hierarchical modes chosen by Cabrera and Guillén do not manage to avoid misrepresentations that reflect some sense of cultural or moral superiority over Afro-Cubans.

Notes

1. Survival theory can be traced back to E. B. Tylor's 1871 book *Primitive Culture*, in which Tylor put forward the concept of cultural survivals, "culture traits which have lost their original function: meaningless customs and the like" (Tylor as cited in Kongas 74). Another significant proponent was Potter, who in 1949 defined folklore in the following way: "Folklore is the survival within a people's later stages of culture of the beliefs, stories, customs, rites, and other techniques or adjustment to the world and the supernatural, which were used in previous stages" (Potter as cited in Kongas 75).
2. As Sykes explains, Malinowski sought to retrieve as close a vision of the pre-colonization version of the Trobriand natives' culture as possible, believing that "the presence of colonial administration, missionaries, and other Europeans endangered the accuracy of the account of 'native' life" (46).
3. García Canclini advocates an approach to the study of culture as production, which implies considering "not only the act of production but every step in a productive process: production, circulation and reception" (*Transforming Modernity*, 13).

Works Cited

Anderson, Thomas, F. "Inconsistent Depictions of Afro-Cubans and Their Cultural Manifestations in the Early Poetry or Marcelino Arozarena," *Afro-Hispanic Review* 27.2 (2008): 9–44.

Arnedo-Gómez, Miguel. *Uniting Blacks in a Raceless Nation: Blackness, Afro-Cuban Culture and Mestizaje in the Prose and Poetry of Nicolás Guillén*. London: Bucknell University Press, 2016.

Augier, Ángel. *Nicolás Guillén: Notas para un estudio biográfico-crítico*, I. Havana: Editora del Consejo Nacional de Universidades, 1965.

Boti, Regino E. "El verdadero son." In *Recopilación de textos sobre Nicolás Guillén*. Ed. Nancy Morejón, pp. 247–249. Havana: Casa de las Américas, 1974.

Cabrera, Lydia. *El monte*. Havana: Editorial Letras Cubanas, 1993.

Koeko iyawó: Aprende novicia – Pequeño tratado de regla lucumí. Miami: Ediciones C. R., 1980.

Clifford, James. "Introduction: Partial Truths." In *Writing Culture: The Poetics and Politics of Ethnography*. Ed. James Clifford and George E. Marcus, pp. 1–26. Los Angeles: University of California Press, 1986.

Coronil, Fernando. "Transculturation and the Politics of Theory: Countering the Centre, Cuban Counterpoint." In Fernando Ortiz, *Cuban Counterpoint*, *pp*. ix–lvi. Durham, NC: Duke University Press, 1995.

Dianteill, Erwan and Martha Swearingen. "From Hierography and Back: Lydia Cabrera's Texts and the Written Tradition in Afro-Cuban Religions," *Journal of American Folklore* 116.461 (2003): 273–292.

Dodson, Jualynne E. "Encounters in the African Atlantic World: The African Methodist Episcopal Church in Cuba." In *Between Race and Empire: African Americans and Cubans before the Cuban Revolution*. Eds. Lisa Brock and Digna Castañeda Fuertes. Philadelphia, PA: Temple University Press, 1998.

Duany, Jorge. "Reconstructing Cubanness: Changing Discourses of National Identity on the Island and in the Diaspora During the Twentieth Century." In *Cuba, the Elusive Nation*. Ed. Damián J. Fernández and Madeleine Cámara Betancourt, pp. 17–42. Gainesville: University Press of Florida, 2000.

Emery, Amy Fass. *The Anthropological Imagination in Latin American Literature*. Columbia: University of Missouri Press, 1996.

García Canclini, Néstor. *Hybrid Cultures: Strategies for Entering and Leaving Modernity*. Minneapolis: University of Minnesota Press, 1997.

Transforming Modernity: Popular Culture in Mexico. Austin: University of Texas Press, 1993.

Guillén, Nicolás. "Motivos literarios." In *¡Aquí estamos! El negro en la obra de Nicolás Guillén*. Ed. Denia García Ronda, pp. 28–31. Havana: Editorial de Ciencias Sociales, 2008.

Summa poética. Ed. Luis Íñigo Madrigal. Madrid: Ediciones Cátedra, 1990.

Obra poética: 1922–1958. Ed. Ángel Augier. Havana: Editorial Letras Cubanas, 1980.

The Representation of Afro-Cuban Orality 225

Kongas, Elli-Kaija. "The Concept of Folklore," *Midwest Folklore* 13.2 (1963): 69–88.

Ledón Sánchez, Armando. *La música popular en Cuba*. Oakland, CA: El Gato Tuerto, Intelibooks, 2003.

Lienhard, Martín. "El fantasma de la oralidad y algunos de sus avatares literarios y etnológicos," *Les Langues Neó-Latines* 11.297 (1996): 19–33.

Madrigal, Luis Íñigo. "Introducción." In *Nicolás Guillén: Summa poética*, pp. 13–48. Madrid: Ediciones Cátedra, 1990.

Martínez Furé, Rogelio. *Diálogos imaginarios*. Havana: Editorial Arte y Literatura, 1979.

Méndez Martínez, Roberto. "Nicolás Guillén, vanguardia poética, vanguardia plástica." In *Nicolás Guillén: Hispanidad, vanguardia y compromiso social*, pp. 557–574. Cuenca: Ediciones de la Universidad de Castilla-La Mancha, 2004.

Moore, Robin, D. *Nationalising Blackness: Afrocubanismo and Artistic Revolution in Havana, 1920–1940*. Pittsburgh, PA: University of Pittsburgh Press, 1997.

Orovio, Helio. *Diccionario de la música cubana biográfico y técnico*. Havana: Editorial Letras Cubanas, 1992.

Ortiz, Fernando. "La religión en la poesía mulata." In *Fernando Ortiz: Estudios etnosociológicos*. Ed. Isaac Barreal Fernández, pp. 141–175. Havana: Editorial de Ciencias Sociales, 1991.

"Por Colón se descubrieron dos mundos." In *Fernando Ortiz: Estudios etnosociológicos*. Ed. Isaac Barreal Fernández, pp. 1–9. Havana: Editorial de Ciencias Sociales, 1991.

Los bailes y el teatro de los negros en el folklore de Cuba. Havana: Editorial Letras Cubanas, 1982.

Contrapunteo cubano del tabaco y el azúcar. Caracas: Biblioteca Ayacucho, 1978.

La música afrocubana. Madrid: Júcar, 1975.

La africanía en la música folklórica cubana. Havana: Ministerio de Educación, Dirección de Cultura, 1950.

Palmié, Stephan. "Ethnogenetic Processes and Cultural Transfer in Afro-American Slave Populations." In *Slavery in the Americas*. Ed. Wolfgang Binder, pp. 337–363. Würzburg: Konigshausen and Neumann, 1993.

Rama, Ángel. *Writing Across Cultures: Narrative Transculturation in Latin America*. Durham, NC: Duke University Press, 2012.

Rodríguez-Mangual, Edna M. *Lydia Cabrera and the Construction of an Afro-Cuban Cultural Identity*. Chapel Hill: The University of North Carolina Press, 2004.

Sykes, Karen. *Arguing with Anthropology: An Introduction to Critical Theories of the Gift*. London: Taylor and Francis, 2005.

PART IV

Aesthetics and Innovation

CHAPTER 14

Eros
After Surrealism and Before the Revolution (1945–1967)
Sarah Ann Wells

After Surrealism, Before the Revolution

This chapter examines multiple surrealisms that surfaced in South America during the period following World War II in the work of women across literature and the visual arts. Beginning in the 1940s, a newfound interest in dreams and the unconscious joined changing patterns in consumer culture and new media formats to foster surrealisms that were often more massified and less narrowly political, but also potentially more democratic, than their predecessors. These changes coincided with shifting sexual norms that slowly whittled away at prohibitions against premarital sex and non-heteronormative relationships; at the same time, women's bodies were increasingly disciplined, displayed, and self-fashioned. If earlier surrealisms have often been read as a conflicted response to the trauma of World War I, the postwar feminine surrealisms examined here speak to the increasing encroachment of capitalist modernity into daily life, with specific implications for gendered bodies, habits, and practices. Surrealism's most provocative legacy in South America, I argue, can be found in those women artists and writers who took up its promise of eros and expanded it into unfamiliar zones, while simultaneously keeping our eyes on the *longue durée* of gendered violence.

My title delineates the period before the idea of radical sexual liberation that emerged under the banner of 1968, a moment of paradoxical transition. In this sense, the preposition *before* is chronological, but it also suggests how the promise of liberation remains incomplete and deferred into the present. The *after* in my title also has a dual sense, both chronological and aesthetic: these surrealisms emerged in the wake of historical surrealism, the movement that arose in France in the mid- to late 1920s and remained active and influential until World War II. But *after* also suggests "in the manner of," a citational quality that entails a certain distance from earlier surrealisms even as it embraces some of their unfulfilled promises. For its part, *eros* is not reducible to descriptions of sex but rather entails a search for alternative economies that query instrumentality and reproductivity, privileging instead unexpected couplings and excess. Eros is surrealism's engine and its telos, its specific approach to the broader avant-garde project to question the relationship between art and life (Bürger). Yet the eros I examine here is not uncritically celebrated – given the political and economic position of women throughout the long twentieth century, it is necessarily fraught.

Ultimately, an attention to the surrealisms of this earlier period also provides us with an alternative approach to the literary history this volume considers. It provides a corrective to the tendency – especially prevalent in Anglo-Americanist readings of Latin American literature – to overgeneralize non-realist approaches under the framework of either modernism or, alternatively, the "Boom" of the 1960s/70s, which brought the region global recognition. Teasing out the relationship between eros and surrealism in Latin America affords new approaches to transition in the mid-century by taking seriously what has been referred to, often in passing, as the *consolidation*, *automation*, or *gentrification* – but not the death – of the avant-gardes beginning in the 1930s (Wells). It also provides us with an entry point for writers and artists – for example, Silvina Ocampo (Argentina, 1903–93) and Hilda Hilst (Brazil, 1930–2004) or filmmakers Narcisa Hirsch (1928–) and Nelly Kaplan (1931–) – who are more difficult to locate in our inherited histories and taxonomies.

Surrealism has a long history in South America, beginning in the late 1920s – or even earlier, if we consider retrospectively consecrated precursors, most prominently the French-Uruguayan Isadore Ducasse (known as Lautréamont).[1] However, it is in the postwar period that it expands substantively to impact writers of both poetry and prose, as well as visual artists. This expanded surrealism included, increasingly, the contribution of postcolonial intellectuals and/or women writers and artists. As it migrated to Latin America and the Caribbean, it shifted: the focus on proper names and specific polemics (e.g., André Breton versus Georges Bataille) gave way to a more expansive approach. Thus, while scholars have tended to see historical surrealism as ossifying in the 1930s, of all the historical avant-gardes it arguably has the most robust half-life in the postwar period (Nicholson; Speranza). From the late 1940s and up until the 1970s, we find an outpouring of surrealist-inflected literature and visual arts – unhooked to a movement, undefined by a leader, and increasingly interwoven with broader processes of sociohistorical and economic

Eros 231

transformation. While I focus here on writers and artists from Brazil, Argentina, and Uruguay, the specific features of this late surrealism resonate with other contexts in and beyond Latin America – most notably the case of Mexico.

Surrealism is also a slippery and contentious term, and only becomes more so as it expands its geographic and historical borders. This notorious bagginess is nevertheless undergirded by a visceral identity: anti-utilitarian, surrealism loves chance, dreams, the unconscious, the irrational, the unfathomable, and, above all, eros. It saw itself not merely as a specific artistic movement but a way of being in the world and as a connection machine, bringing together disparate or even opposing objects, experiences, and thinkers (most notably Marx and Freud). This capaciousness is both its downfall and its lifeblood, ensuring its continued flexibility and openness to new kinds of voices and experiences, even while it becomes increasingly bound up with the capitalist and patriarchal norms it sought to overcome.

Surrealism's Gender Problem

In its desire to see the world anew and its search for connectivity, historical surrealism privileged above all the unexpected image, which emerged through the juxtaposition of words or things that rejected a causal-logical connection. And yet many of its most prominent images remained deeply familiar, even numbingly repetitive – in particular, the dismembered female body, limbless and/or faceless. Surrealist dismembering is most prevalent in visual art, but it also appears in literature and seeps into the discursive paratexts that surround how women surrealists were depicted, as in "the head of a lioness, mind of a man, bust of a woman" (Mahon 10). Here Julien Levy, among the most important promoters of surrealist art in the 1940s, describes artist Leonor Fini (Argentina 1907–Paris 1996) through surrealism's signature juxtaposition, echoing the innumerable cut-up, jerry-rigged bodies of the surrealist woman muse. Yet Fini's own work – which included paintings, book illustrations, costume, furniture design, and performance – affords one of the more robust critiques of the misogyny of historical surrealism.

When surrealism emerged as a force in postwar Latin American literature and art, the dismemberment of the female body and the opacity of "its" particular experiences persisted. Consider one of its most graphic iterations, in the famous prologue to the novel *El reino de este mundo* (*The Kingdom of this World*, 1949) by Cuban writer – and erstwhile surrealist – Alejo

Carpentier. Here Carpentier casts off the influence of historical surrealism, deeming it feeble and depleted. (He fails to mention that many historical surrealists had already declared Latin America and its writers and artists constitutively surreal.) In its place he privileged a vital "marvelous real" indigenous to the Americas. Carpentier's claim hinged on a peculiar example: "Today there are still too many 'adolescents who find pleasure in raping the cadavers of beautiful women who have recently died' (Lautréamont), without realizing that the marvelous would reside in raping them alive" (29).[2] Surrealism's necrophilia is diagnosed and rejected, but its cherished metaphor of rape refuses to budge.

Carpentier's graphic imagery can be found echoed, in various ways, in his Latin American successors, the Boom novelists (including Mario Vargas Llosa, Gabriel García Márquez, and Carlos Fuentes). Not a single woman writer is present in the pantheon of the Boom, just as most anthologies of Latin American surrealism are predominantly, and at times exclusively, male. Many Boom novels are engraved indelibly on the imagination of readers of world literature, often for their surrealist eroticism. Following in the footsteps of Georges Bataille, the Boom writers were deeply invested in the coupling of a male transgressor and female transgressed or sacrificial victim. Julio Cortázar's ambitious novel *Rayuela* (*Hopscotch*, 1963) seeks to reinhabit the feminized Paris of Breton and his *Nadja* (1928), the surrealist's woman-child. It is in *Rayuela* that Cortázar coined his infamous opposition between the "accomplice-reader" and the "female-reader," the former an active critical thinker who accompanies the avant-garde writer on a homosocial adventure, the latter his sentimental foil, passively over-identifying with facile literature.

The sense of an unfulfilled promise – of surrealism's postcolonial aperture, only to be rerouted into an all-too-familiar misogyny – shapes the surrealisms of Latin American women writers and artists. Surrealism had promised to transgress familiar scripts, yet often fell back into familiar norms. This regression lends women's surrealisms their peculiar tension. A movement that claimed to transgress gender norms while turning on long-familiar gender scripts became an impetus for those left out of these same scripts. They investigate and extend surrealism's pursuit of eros to bodies and experiences it conveniently shuttered. These midcentury surrealist sisters, many of whom were single and/or childless, were also interested in alternative models of family and couplings. They shaped an eroticism that questioned the faith of their predecessors and contemporaries in the utopia of a free libido, which inevitably seemed to require an object to be fragmented. Surrealism had often presented itself as a mechanism for fraying binary oppositions: day/night, in/out, sleep/wakefulness, subject/object. And yet, as these artists showed, it often remained stubbornly wedded to a different set of oppositions: oppression/liberation, passive/active, and a pressure valve model of tension/release. It is this last set of binaries that the surrealists examined here call into question.

In literature, this feminine erotic surrealism is characterized not only by privileging short fiction and poetry over the novel but also by miniaturizing, inverting, or otherwise deflating the narrative world-building of the Boom. Like their peers in the visual artists, they favor short, often abrupt deviations, eruptions, or transformations, as well as intimate architectures and interior designs that, like an M. C. Escher drawing – the example of midcentury surrealist kitsch is intentional – seem at once entrapping and infinite. Many of these figures also worked as both visual artists and writers, creating feedback loops of intensified images across verbal and visual planes. They recast surrealism's feminine gallery – the woman-child, the raped mannequin, the dismembered nude – as new avatars: the surrealist spinster, the geriatric pornographer, the lesbian vampire, and other, less anthropomorphic, figures. Their production allows us to consider competing forms of autonomy throughout the twentieth century: of the art work, the body, and of public and private space. In what follows, I will trace the specific instantiations of surrealist eros in four figures: visual artists Grete Stern and Maria Martins and writers Marosa di Giorgio and Alejandra Pizarnik.

Capitalist Dreaming: The Photomontages of Grete Stern

In the postwar period the emergence of sophisticated advertising techniques and consumption patterns constructed a gendered body that women were taught to both be and desire. The midcentury also witnessed the vernacularization of psychoanalysis – which the historical surrealists had pursued less for therapeutic than for aesthetic and political purposes. In Buenos Aires in particular, psychoanalysis quickly found its way into popular art and mass culture, as well as avant-garde artforms and literature. The work of former Dada artist Grete Stern (Germany 1904–Argentina 1999) for the Argentine popular periodical *Idilio* (*Idyll*) from 1948 to 1951 is arguably the most arresting example of the popularization of both surrealism and psychoanalysis. In this singular project, women sent descriptions of their dreams to the editors. In the resulting column, "El psicoanalásis te ayudará" ("Psychoanalysis Will Help You"), their dreams were decoded by a psychoanalyst, with Stern creating a surrealist photomontage to iconographically capture the dreamwork. Her production grapples with and displays new, and often contradictory, forms of social mobility and anxiety that emerge under Peronism's particular approach to the working, consuming, and desiring modern woman.

In adopting surrealist image techniques, Stern's photomontages make explicit that the fantasy of an unmediated unconscious must also grapple with mass culture's shaping and codifying force in the highly gendered space of the interior – understood here as both the domestic space and the self. In this context, the 140 photomontages Stern created for *Idyll* both inflate and denaturalize gender codes, showing their seams (Uslenghi), and construct a rich range of images from emancipatory fantasies to the limiting binds of the second shift. Many stage the dilemmas and desires of a new class of working women – anticipated by the popular cinema of the 1930s (e.g., Manuel Romero, *Mujeres que trabajan* [*Women Who Work*, 1938]). Given the centrality of domestic work in the developmentalist imaginary of Peronism, such desires were ambiguous. Others index the postwar boom in consumer appliances in Argentina, staging contradictory visual metaphors about modern women's role as a labor-saving device. In "Artículos eléctricos para el hogar" ("Appliances for the Home"), a seated women faces the camera with closed eyes, her sinuous curves positioned as a lamp; behind her, a preternaturally large male hand looms, his face and body unseen. In another ("Made in England," 1950), a different woman has become all head, her body a brush for house-painting. As in her surrealist predecessors, the woman's body is fragmented, but to quite different ends: as critique, rather than extension, of her instrumentalization. In "Made in England," the decapitation inverts the surrealist topos – Stern's model is pure head, rather than faceless torso. Moreover, the fragment also exhibits a more explicit critique of capitalism. Through the *Idyll* project, the anxieties and fantasies of anonymous, non-elite women – here, agentic source material – entered the public sphere as privileged objects of inquiry.

Contorted Encounters: The Sculptures of Maria Martins

André Breton begins his essay on sculptor Maria Martins (Brazil, 1894–1973) with a phrase that represents his own shift toward Latin America and the Caribbean during World War II: "During these last few years, the winds of the human spirit have not ceased to blow from warm latitudes." This Southern spirit will suture modernity's divisions: between man and earth, "the psychological upon the cosmological" (*Maria* 47). Along with his compatriot Benjamin Péret and others in the midcentury period,

Breton locates Brazil as a land of the future and Martins as its artist and its synecdoche ("She could not have come from anywhere else on the globe," writes Péret; her works "foretell a world that does not yet exist"). Péret, the historical surrealist with the most extensive relationship to Brazil, finds in the country "an unfinished image that wanted to be immobilized" (*Maria* 53). Both historical surrealists depict Martins as uniquely privileged to capture the dynamism of the Amazon: a site of sacrifice, ecstasy, and ritual, as well as an obscenely fertile nature. Under the sign of late surrealism, Martins becomes a synecdoche for Brazil; both the woman and her art – a fecund-feminine lying in wait in the Amazonian depths – will maternally usher in a renewed avant-garde origin.[3]

Martins' relationship to Brazil was in fact more complicated than these fans acknowledged. Her striking sculpture *Don't Forget I Come From the Tropics* (1945) was, like many of her works, titled in French, and she spent extensive parts of her life abroad. While she began exhibiting her sculpture in the late 1930s, it is in the postwar period that her work shifts toward her unique approach to eroticism, and when her subject matter turns increasingly toward Brazilian cosmologies and materialities, at times employing tropical wood (*jacaranda, imbuia, peroba*). During this period Martins is also embraced by international surrealism, forming friendships with exiled Europeans and their patrons in New York, appearing in the journal *VVV* (1942–4) and in the Parisian exhibition "Surrealism in 1947" (Ades; Geis).

During this period, Martins' re-elaboration of matriarchal Amazonian cosmologies renders a much more fraught approach to fecundity than we might expect. Her goddess-figures – often ambitious in size and featuring puckered textures that translate jungle foliage and animal skins into bronze – are destructive, frequently self-contained sinuous desiring machines without beginning or end. *Cobra Grande* (1943) casts an Amazonian river-dwelling queen as a sinewy, headless snake with four breasts, the nipples peaked and detailed. Martins described her as possessing the "cruelty of a monster and the sweetness of wild fruit"; Breton saw the figure as embodying the sovereignty of desire, "raised to a panic pitch," "so that for the first time in art it succeeds in awarding itself absolute license" (*Maria*, 42). In the contemporaneous *Boiuna*, a different river goddess consumes men, again in Martins' words, "sucking their blood, draining their strength" (*Maria*, 14–15). Like the liana, another key figure in her work, Martins' cobras are agents of paralytic ecstasy – as she writes in an unpublished poem where the "I" seeks to coil around her lover's body, suffocating him.

Martins' sculptures chafe against a harmonious understanding of eros or reproduction, and underscore gender difference while also imagining new possibilities, as in the phallic cobra with multiple breasts. Loosely feminine figures splay their legs, and eagerly unfurl their arms, flames darting from pelvises. It is precisely in their anti-anthropomorphic, contorted figures that we find a difference with the historical surrealists' female body. In Martins, the dismembered feminine figure has found claws; those pelvises might shoot out not just flames but tentacles for feeling and grasping. Her sculptures are at once organic and warped, thrusting and thwarted, at times in a near-Baroque twisting ecstasy – a world away from the manipulable dolls of the most renowned sculptor of historical surrealism, Hans Bellmer.

Martins' rejection of physiognomies, moreover, has a near-opposite effect of the historical surrealist tendencies to efface the woman's face altogether, or replace it with birdcages or vaginas. Martins – like the avant-garde painter Tarsila de Amaral before her – uproots the physiognomy from its privileged position, its center in the humanist tradition of Western art (Aguilar); she asks us to see limbs and claw/hands as sites of meaning-making and sensory production, creating a new kind of desiring body, contorted and mobile while fixed in bronze. Many of her sculptures depict an auto-erotic ecology, as in *Sem Eco* (*Without Echo*, 1943) or the unusual *Trés Avide* (*Very Voracious*, 1949), a smaller sculpture, its pelvic bowl playing on the notion of the sacred jewel-box, protected by its own set of tentacles, of a single, supple (rather than textured) bronze. When Martins depicts two distinct figures, we find a taut straining at a union perpetually deferred, most famously in *The Impossible* – completed and exhibited in 1944 and remade by Martins in subsequent years. In this large, disturbing piece, two unidentifiable figures face off; depending on the angle of the viewer, one or the other seems the aggressor. In *Impossible*, the face is at once a void and a site that projects outward through its tentacles or antenna, which do not touch but almost interlace. Their bodies face each other but are strangely inert: all the energy of the sculpture lies in those faceless faces. Hers is less the creation of new species through birth than a tense encounter of nonhuman amalgamations, on the cusp of something that might be equally utopic or destructive.

Marosa Di Giorgio: Savage Domesticities

Like Martins, the surrealism of poet Marosa di Giorgio (Uruguay, 1932–2004) is marked by an interest in interspeciesism. While her central figures may possess physiognomies (and possessive pronouns), that is merely because the entire world – animal, mineral, and vegetable – does too. In an inversion of Giuseppe Archimboldo, the sixteenth-century Italian painter and surrealist

Eros 237

precursor who created human faces out of vegetation, in her poetry potatoes have heads, squashes possess horns, mushrooms have flesh and shriek. Eschewing any humanist prerogative for one of the more unusual erotic bodies of work in Latin American literature, di Giorgio also tests the limits of the creaturely body in a stealthy assault on the cherished family home.

Reading her decades' worth of poems, one has the sense of an ongoing exploration rather than a finished product. She grouped her collected poems under her suggestive title, *Los papeles salvajes* (*The Wild Papers*), and the choice of "papers" over "works" or "poetry" indexes the unclassifiable nature of her production; commentators frequently note her work's irreducibility to any specific school, style, or periodization in or beyond Uruguay, including its only surrealist collective, founded in 1965. For its part, the adjective *salvajes* ("wild" or "savage") suggests an amalgamation of the erotic and the terrestrial, as embedded in di Giorgio's childhood in the countryside, where the sexual coexisted alongside lovingly detailed animal, mineral, and vegetable worlds.

Many of her poems take the form of a mutation or encounter that place pressure on the poetic "I." Nearly always feminized, this "I" is engulfed, infiltrated, or transformed into others, including nonhumans: as in #34 from *The History of Violets* (1965) where she becomes, without any shifters to warn us, the hare her father is hunting (74–75). Her writing grew more brazenly erotic as she grew older, when stranger creatures emerge to engulf the "I." The late collection *Rosa mística* (*Mystic Rose*, 2003), one of five volumes of erotic tales published during this period, opens with a story of the narrator's deflowering by the incisors of a large rat-like creature; teeth and tongue become one of many instruments for the collection's continued exploration in her longstanding interest in the relationship between "sexual pain and sexual pleasure" (9). In many ways, di Giorgio's interest in masochism suggests how this mode may allow women in patriarchal cultures a means to describe and experience pleasure indirectly, by rechanneling it. In the process, her signature grammatical and temporal experiments grow even stranger with these interspecies encounters, as sex becomes the name for the unclassifiable; for example, the "I" might couple with "a not-very-large being," "the color of sapphire, gloomy, formless, in the shape of a cone" (27). The erotic object is often impossible to pin down, abusing taxonomies; love and desire might be depicted as pure motion, a surging something, never identified through form (*I Remember Nightfall*, 44–45).

At other times the "I" herself becomes devourer of the creatures of the world, which takes on a homey cannibalism. In another poem from *Violetas*, she encounters beings called *animalejas* (an intriguing neologism for feminine animal-like creatures that possess humanoid features and ornaments). The poem ends when one of these creatures is killed, seasoned, and consumed at the family dinner table, still alive; it possesses human hands, which are now mimetized in the poet's own, in the poem's shivery last line, "The ring I now wear was once hers" (*I Remember Nightfall*, 48–49). Is this a black mass, an interspecies marriage ceremony, or a ritual of primitive accumulation?

Indeed, di Giorgio's poetry often suggests multiple and seemingly conflicting forms of love and violence, even exploitation – and a cruelty that contrasts with her image, reaffirmed in interviews, as an enchanted girl-child in a pastoral setting. Di Giorgio, who never married or had children, continually foregrounds virginity, puberty, and initiation in her poetry. With their sadistic and masochistic rituals of play, her poems at times stage the surrealist legacy of the game, often signaled by abrupt shifts between singular and plural first person. Thus the enchanted, girlish, childlike kingdom always has a lie or trick or violence behind it.

The backdrop for these encounters is the family home, which features rituals rarely marked by productivity or reproductivity. Setting in di Giorgio is far from an inert container but a pulsating and alive framework that shifts the relationship between context and figure, foreground and background. Her poetry underscores and unfurls spatial-temporal thresholds and territorial boundaries that emerge only to unhinge the respective coherence of each; her privileged affect is an invasive intimacy. The outside encroaches upon the space of grandmothers, mothers and hearths, but that ostensibly cozy, feminine space is always already shot through with violence. Outsiders and foreigners are ultimately no less terrifying than the "sinister games" of her beloved father and mother (from *Magonia* [1965], in *I Remember Nightfall*, 104–105). In this way her works tend to corrode the property and propriety at the heart of the family terrain, frequently invoked with references to exchanges of land, bounty, or dowries. Often her poetry feels ahistorical, with its rustic setting, yet she is a near-obsessive observer of the rites and results of the gendered division of labor in social reproduction, all the while muddying and cannibalizing them.

Alejandra Pizarnik: Autonomous Zones

In contrast to di Giorgio, Argentine writer Alejandra Pizarnik (1936–72) established a much more extensive and intimate relationship to historical surrealism and its tenets; in this sense, she more closely resembles Martins. Her exposure to surrealism began early in Buenos Aires, when she was a student of the surrealist painter Juan Batlle Planas. In 1960, she took the first of two trips from Buenos Aires to Paris, where she met Max Ernst and Bataille, and reconnected with Argentina's most passionate advocate of surrealism, Cortázar. As a late surrealist or surrealist on the edge, Pizarnik is best understood as a writer who took the movement very seriously in order to invert some of its fundamental precepts (Aira; see also Lasarte). What she would call, in an interview shortly before her suicide, her "innate surrealism" refers not only to her acclaimed poetry but also her work as a translator and critic; that is, to her roles as both writer and a reader. Her literary friendships with Cortázar, Argentine poet Olga Orozco, and Octavio Paz, Mexico's principal literary surrealist; her translations of works like Breton and Paul Éluard's *The Immaculate Conception* (1930); and, as I explore below, her ornate gloss of an unusual surrealist text, run alongside her poetic production. They also inform the process by which she created a life, a *bios*.

While in Paris, inspired in part by Bataille's *The Tears of Eros* (1961) and by a book by the French surrealist Valentine Penrose (*La Comtesse Sanglante* [*The Bloody Countess*], 1962), Pizarnik began to explore a specifically feminine sadism, its aesthetic and techniques of the body. "La condesa sangrienta" ("The Bloody Countess"), first published in Mexico in Paz's periodical *Diálogos*, and later in book form, is contemporaneous to her pivotal poetry collection, *Los trabajos y las noches* (*Works and Nights*, 1965) and anticipates both the later volumes *Extracción de la piedra de locura* (*Extraction of the Stone of Madness*, 1968) and her last work, *El infierno musical* (*A Musical Hell*, 1971). The early to mid-1960s witnessed yet another surrealist revival: in 1963, Breton's *Nadja*, apparently Pizarnik's favorite book, was reissued in France and translated into Spanish; and Cortázar published *Rayuela*, his homage to *Nadja*. "La condesa sangrienta," Pizarnik's contribution to this renewed interest in surrealism, is slippery and singular. It is a work of prose from a poet who wrote very little of it; critics have diverged in their definition of the text, alternately labeling it a prose poem, commentary, gloss, article, scenes, vignettes, or pastiche. Pizarnik herself characterized it as "notes." As a surrealist heir of Lauréamont (and Borges), she had no qualms about genre-bending and, in the process, eschewing an authorial signature, choosing replication over reproduction.

"La condesa sangrienta" echoes historical surrealism's fascination with true crime in its detailing of the case of Erzébet Báthory, a Hungarian aristocrat who, in the late sixteenth century, tortured and murdered over 600 girls. As surrealists who eschewed heteronormative relationships, both Penrose and Pizarnik were drawn to the brutal, near-camp excess of this historical figure, who murdered with relative impunity, in perverse rituals designed to prevent her body from aging. Pizarnik's text consists of very short chapters, each with its own title and epigraph, many of which seek to inscribe both Báthory and herself into the pantheon of surrealist writers and precursors (e.g., Breton, Bataille, Sade, Paz, Artaud). These chapters are more episodic than narrative. In contrast to Penrose's homonymous study, Pizarnik prevents us from reading for the plot: episodes are privileged over narrative connective tissue and context, chronology, or causality; detailed depictions of lineages, emblems, intrigues, and social structures of feudalism are excised, along with any hint of naturalistic or psychoanalytic explanation.

Pizarnik reduces the role of the Countess' husband even further than Penrose, emphasizing her "exclusively feminine universe" (384), populated by seamstresses, servants, and tortured girls. This setting is also activated by specifically feminine techniques – the occult know-how of her servant-witches, her "instruments" – with specifically feminized ends: to maintain the Countess' one true possession, her hyperbolic beauty, by halting the flow of time and decay through the gush of youthful "fluido humano" ("human fluid") (388). In both her person and her acts, she embodies Breton's privileged concept "convulsive beauty," explicitly invoked in the text (373), but here as sovereign despot rather than muse. Coming from a tradition of Latin American women's writing, and poetry in particular, where the essentializing figure of the mother had been hegemonic, this fierce, destructive individualism, with a disregard for futurity, has a unique sting.

"La condesa sangrienta" burrows into Báthory's castle and its different corners or cells, sites for premodern "happenings" that recall the surrealist commitment to games. Eros here is a shocking series of situations – cruel, audacious experiments – which together sketch the figure of the Countess, approximating her without ever capturing her. Among them are a lethal cage that impales its victims when they try to flee and an iron maiden who locks them in a deadly embrace. As in the Countess' music box that springs to vibrant, spastic life before ceasing to move, in these experiments there is a play between frenzied activity and immobility, between an ecstatic present that witnesses temporary metamorphoses – the iron virgin becomes the penetrator; the Countess' white dress becomes red with blood, an image that suggests a blank page blooming with sadistic scribble – and the monotonous, nearly bureaucratic time of daily life, inscribed in the imperfect tense.

The castle's sites play with the seizing up and flow of time in "cuadros vivos" (76) ("tableaux vivants" – "living pictures" [380]). (The text's striking graphic quality also inspired a 2009 graphic novel by Santiago Caruso.) In specular, Baroque fashion, this form of entrapment is reflected on different scales: of the body, the literary world, the domestic space. For example, the Countess has an "espejo de la melancolía" ("melancholy mirror") designed especially for her body that allows her to contemplate her own image for hours on end (see Gregory; Molloy). Pizarnik speculates that this mirror is her attempt to design a dwelling – *morada*, a privileged noun in her poetry (384) – something she was unable to do as a woman, despite her aristocratic lineage. In this sense, the Countess' death after her sentence is the most fitting of ends for this figure without a future: "*La prisión subía en torno suyo. Se muraron las puertas y las ventanas de su aposento. En una pared fue practicada una ínfima ventanilla*" (391) ("*Around her the prison grew. The doors and windows of her chamber were walled up; only a small opening was left in one of the walls*" [86]). This small opening echoes the gashes, crevices, and fissures that mark the walls in Pizarnik's contemporaneous poems, such as "Nombrarte" ("Naming You") and "Cuarto solo" ("Single Room," 2016; 16, 32).

From the depths of her premodern dwelling, Pizarnik's Countess thus elicits the problem of sexual limits and autonomy that would increasingly occupy writers and artists in the late 1960s: her lesbianism, auto-eroticism, body-experimentation/body-hacking, and the rituals that end in black-outs, theatrically put on display. The Countess, that is, embodies the excessive contortions and extremes that result from a life lived in the singular pursuit of aesthetic, erotic forms. In her posthumously published diaries and her letters, Pizarnik herself grapples with the art–life divide central to the surrealists: she experiments in bed with men and women; she subjects her body to tests with hunger, alcohol, cigarettes, pills, and insomnia; and she seeks to collapse the gulf between living a life and writing a life. She also writes about sex as the only truly independent act: "Se puede hacer el amor con cualquiera sin que intervengan conceptos como amistad, amor, familia, etc." ("One can have sex with anyone, without the intervention of concepts like friendship, love, family, etc."). To describe this potentially limitless freedom, she draws on the language of confine-ment: she calls sex "una especie de zona cerrada por un círculo" ("a special zone enclosed by a circle," *Diarios* [*Diaries*], 2009): a figure for the paradoxical autonomy required to open up the self in life and in art, neither a life that collapses into literature nor a reiteration of the fantasy of an artist in control.

In fact, when grappling with women's surrealism, we run up against a particular problem: how to discuss the problem of the art–life divide without reinscribing women into the zone of raw, unmediated experience – the way in which the historical surrealists long approached them: paradigmatically, in Breton's *Nadja* or Cortázar's la Maga, but also in critical reappraisals – as when, for example, scholars underscore Maria Martins' affair with Duchamp as testament to her avant-garde status. To make art, and a life, unhooked from this kind of legitimation was a problem for these late surrealists. I have been interested precisely in the period before the revolution (May 1968), in many ways one of greater tension – that is, of transition – when women artists in particular mobilized surrealism to explore and display a sexuality that was fraught and constrained, yet also gradually shifting, if never entirely. When surrealism became key for the experimental art, philosophy, and activism of the late 1960s and early 1970s in Latin America and globally, the body as a monadic unit dependent upon scripted roles and performances would be called into question more explicitly. And yet, as for the historical surrealists, even during this later period the understanding of sexual liberation was often, if not exclusively, enacted upon the marked-up and fragment bodies of women – revealing the ways in which the revolution continued to be incomplete.

Surrealist Futures

Already in 1930, Peruvian poet César Vallejo declared surrealism obsolete in his "Autopsia del superrealismo" ("Autopsy of Surrealism," 1930). In a 1954 essay on Maria Martins, Brazilian writer and surrealist Murilo Mendes wrote: "Outmoded as a system and a doctrine, doesn't surrealism escape – by definition – any attempt at systematization?" (*Maria* 54). Indeed, throughout the twentieth century, scholars and artists have continually claimed that, precisely because it emerged with the attributes of a corpse, surrealism can never really die. "Stillborn," dead on arrival, and yet continually renewable: this paradox runs through approaches to surrealism beginning in the postwar period and continuing through the twentieth century. Today, surrealism – and surrealist women writers and artists in particular – appears to be undergoing yet another iteration, as recent international solo exhibitions of Leonor Fini, Remedios Varo, Leonora Carrington, and Frida Kahlo suggest, along with recent feminist literature that recalls the work of writers such as Pizarnik, di Giorgio, and Silvina Ocampo, each the subject of recent translation and retranslation projects into English. On this view, surrealism continues to provide one of the more powerful modalities to query sex as the site where art, violence, and new ways of feeling comingle.

Eros 243

Notes

1. In Buenos Aires, 1928, Aldo Pellegrini founded the first surrealist group and journal in Latin America; others would spring up soon after in Peru, Chile, and Mexico. Already in his famous "Cannibalist Manifesto" (1928), Brazilian avant-gardist Oswald de Andrade had "digested" the Surrealist Revolution (39).
2. This problematic prologue, central to Latin American literary history, is omitted from the most recent English translation, replaced by one by Haitian-American writer Edwidge Danticat.
3. Both essays appeared in her solo show at the Julien Levy Gallery in New York, 1947.

Works Cited

Ades, Dawn. "Criaturas hibridas." In *Maria*. Ed. Maria Martins, Charles Cosac, Vicente de Mello, et al. Sao Paulo: Cosac & Naify, 2010.

Aguilar, Gonzalo. "Abaporu de Tarsila de Amaral: saberes del pie." *Por una ciencia del vestigio errático (Ensayos sobre la antropofagia de Oswald de Andrade)*, pp. 35–46. Buenos Aires: Grumo, 2010.

Aira, César. *Alejandra Pizarnik*. Rosario: Beatriz Viterbo, 2012.

Andrade, Oswald de. "Cannibalist Manifesto." Trans. Leslie Barry. *Latin American Literary Review* 19.38 (July–December 1991): 38–47.

Bürger, Peter. *Theory of the Avant-Garde*. Trans. Michael Shaw. Minneapolis: University of Minnesota, 1986.

Carpentier, Alejo. "Prologue to *The Kingdom of This World*," *Review: Latin American Literature and Arts* 26.47 (1993): 28–31.

di Giorgio, Marosa. *I Remember Nightfall*. Trans. Jeannine Marie Pitas. New York: Ugly Duckling, 2017.

Los papeles salvajes. Buenos Aires: Adriana Hidalgo, 2008.

Rosa Mística. Relatos eróticos. Buenos Aires: Interzona, 2003.

Geis, Terri. "'My Goddesses and My Monsters: Maria Martins and Surrealism in the 1940s." In *Surrealism in Latin America: Vivísimo Muerto*. Ed. Dawn Ades, Rita Eder, and Graciela Speranza, pp. 153–159. Los Angeles, CA: Getty Research Institute, 2012.

Gregory, Stephen. "Through the Looking-Glass of Sadism to a Utopia of Narcissism: Alejandra Pizarnik's *La condesa sangrienta*," *Bulletin of Hispanic Studies* 74:3 (1997): 293–309.

Lasarte, Francisco. "Más allá del surrealismo: la poesía de Alejandra Pizarnik," *Revista Iberoamericana* 49.125 (1983): 867–877.

Mahon, Alyce. "Leonor Fini: Theatre of Desire." In *Leonor Fini: Theatre of Desire, 1930–1980*. Ed. Melanie Cameron and Kendy Genovese, pp. 6–8. New York: Museum of Sex, 2018.

Maria: The Surrealist Sculpture of Maria Martins. New York: André Emmerich Gallery, 1998.

Molloy, Sylvia. "From Sappho to Baffo: Diverting the Sexual in Alejandra Pizarnik." In *Sex and Sexuality in Latin America*. Ed Daniel Balderston and Donna J. Guy, pp. 250–258. New York: New York University Press, 1997.

Nicholson, Melanie. *Surrealism in Latin America: Searching for Breton's Ghost.* New York: Palgrave Macmillan, 2013.

Pizarnik, Alejandra. *Extracting the Stone of Madness: Poems, 1962–1972.* Trans. Yvette Siegert. New York: New Directions, 2016.

Diarios. Ed. Ana Becciu. Barcelona: Lumen, 2009.

"La condesa sangrienta." *Obras Completas. Poesía & Prosa*, pp. 371–392. Buenos Aires: Corregidor, 1994.

"The Bloody Countess." *Other Fires: Short Fiction by Latin American Women.* Ed. Alberto Manguel, pp. 70–87. Trans. Alberto Manguel. New York: Crown, 1986.

Speranza, Graciela. "Wanderers: Surrealism and Contemporary Latin American Art and Fiction." In *Surrealism in Latin America: Vivísimo Muerto.* Ed. Dawn Ades, Rita Eder, and Graciela Speranza, pp. 193–208. Los Angeles, CA: Getty Research Institute, 2012.

Uslenghi, Alejandra. "A Migrant Modernism: Grete Stern's Photomontages," *Journal of Latin American Cultural Studies* 24.2 (2015): 173–205.

Wells, Sarah Ann. *Media Laboratories: Late Modernist Authorship in South America.* Evanston, IL: Northwestern University Press, 2017.

CHAPTER 15

The Return of the Galleons
Transitions in the Work of Alejo Carpentier

Graziella Pogolotti
Translated by Par Kumaraswami

ALEJO CARPENTIER: SOME BRIEF BIO-BIBLIOGRAPHICAL NOTES

Rafael Rodríguez Beltrán
Translated by Par Kumaraswami

Alexis Carpentier Blagoobrazov was born on December 26, 1904, in Lausanne, Switzerland. His father was a French architect who had settled there and his mother was a Russian medical student. When Alexis was a small child, the Carpentier family moved to Havana and the future writer began his primary education, while getting some musical education at home. Family circumstances took them back to Europe, to Russia, Austria, Belgium, and France, where he studied for a while in a Parisian high school.

By 1915, the family had returned to Cuba, settling on the outskirts of Havana, in the hope that the boy's health (he was a chronic asthmatic) might improve. Alexis' father introduced him to the work of some of the great French authors, such as Balzac, Flaubert, Zola, and Anatole France. Carpentier soon began writing novelettes and short stories, very much in the style of Anatole France. He then studied at the Institute of Secondary Education in Havana, while also taking classes in music theory.

In 1922, Carpentier passed the entrance exam to enroll in Havana University's School of Engineering to study architecture. However, his father left home to live in Colombia, and Carpentier abandoned his studies in order to contribute financially to supporting his family. He began writing for the press under the pseudonym of Lina Valmont, but, from November that year, began using his Hispanized name, Alejo.

In the following year, he joined the Grupo Minorista, a group of intellectuals close to the Cuban cultural avant-garde, who proposed new ways of addressing the issue of national culture, which they considered too anchored in nineteenth-century traditions. Carpentier's journalistic production at that stage was already considerable, covering general themes in art, literature, theater, music, the plastic arts, and film. His articles appeared in various well-known Cuban publications such as the newspapers *La Discusión*, *El País*, and *El Diario de la Marina*, and the magazines *Social* and *Carteles*.

In 1926 he traveled to Mexico where he met several intellectuals, developing a particular admiration for the work of the muralists Diego Rivera and José Clemente Orozco. On his return, alongside the Cuban composer Amadeo Roldán, he organized concerts of new music where works by Stravinsky, Poulenc, Satie, and Ravel, among others, were premiered in Cuba.

The following year, as one of the signatories of a trade union document, he was arrested and imprisoned. Soon after, while Cuban signatories to the document were released on parole, foreigners (including Carpentier) were deported. In prison, he began writing his first novel, which would only see the light of day several years later. Meanwhile, his mother, with the help of friends, was able to draft a document by which he was declared Cuban by birth. That enabled him to leave prison, while remaining on parole.

During a Prensa Latina conference in Havana in March 1928, he met the surrealist poet Robert Desnos, who provided him with the necessary papers to leave Cuba, so Carpentier traveled to France on the same boat as the European conference delegates. In France, he initially linked up with the group of intellectuals around André Breton, an influence that represented a further step in an aesthetic renewal that was already glimpsed in his journalistic writings and his literary creativity. He soon began a period of intense journalistic activity, mostly in Cuban and French publications. He also produced scripts for ballets and lyrical and symphonic works; he became editor-in-chief of his own magazine, *Imán* (*Magnet*), published in Paris; he finished his first novel, *¡Écue-Yamba-Ó!* (*Praised Be God!*), wherein a commitment to that early avant-garde influence was discernible; and he became director of the recording studio Foniric Studios, therefore also becoming involved in the medium of radio script-writing. He meanwhile participated in protests against the dictatorship of Gerardo Machado in Cuba and went on to join the movement of intellectuals supporting the Spanish Republic. Following his participation in the II International

The Return of the Galleons

Conference of Writers in Defence of Culture, held in 1937 in Valencia, he published a series of articles under the title "España bajo las bombas" ("Spain Under Bombardment").

In 1939, on the eve of the Nazi invasion of France, he returned to Cuba where he continued his public cultural activity by participating in conferences, developing scripts, and setting film documentaries to music. He also continued to write for different newspapers and magazines, including the series "El ocaso de Europa" ("Europe's Sunset"), about Europe in World War II. Simultaneously, he began writing a second novel, *El clan disperso* (*The Dispersed Clan*), which remained unfinished but did contribute to other later works. However, he managed to publish two of his short stories: "Viaje a la semilla" ("Journey Back to the Source") and "Oficio de tinieblas" ("Twilight Profession").

In 1943 he traveled to Haiti, where his emerging fascination with the island motivated his next novel. However, as life in Cuba gave him little time for writing projects, he went to Venezuela in 1945 at the invitation of a Venezuelan publicist. There, work with the advertising firm Ars allowed him to continue his journalism, a period when his column "Letra y Solfa" ("Letters and Music") in *El Nacional de Caracas*, and his remarkable essay "La música en Cuba" ("Music in Cuba"), won him fame. Above all, he completed a series of works of fiction that are now classics of Latin American literature: in 1949 he published *El reino de este mundo* (*The Kingdom of This World*); in 1953, *Los pasos perdidos* (*The Lost Steps*); in 1958, *Guerra del tiempo* (*The War of Time*), which included the novella *El acoso* (*The Pursuit*); and also in 1958, the three stories "Viaje a la semilla," "Semejante a la noche" ("Like the Night"), and "El camino de Santiago" ("The Road to Santiago"). These works laid out a new path for Latin American literature that would mean moving from domination by European literature's aesthetic and conceptual traditions toward an entirely new vision of the artistic work of the Americas.

On January 1, 1959, the Cuban Revolution began and Carpentier soon returned permanently to Cuba to participate fully in the revolutionary process beginning in Cuba. He brought from Venezuela the manuscript of the great novel that would emerge in 1962: *El siglo de las luces* (*Explosion in a Cathedral*). Once settled in Cuba, he participated in a great many cultural initiatives, representing Cuba in international forums. During the 1960s he gave lectures in Cuba and abroad and published a collection of essays: *Tientos y diferencias* (*Counterpoints and Differences*). From 1968, he was a diplomat at the Cuban Embassy in Paris, as Minister-Counsellor for

Cultural Affairs, where he continued his long project of disseminating Latin American, and particularly Cuban, culture in Europe, and of updating the Americas' knowledge of European culture.

In the 1970s, he published another book of essays, *Razón de ser* (*Reason for Being*), and four novels that stand as milestones in the literatures of the New World: *El recurso del método* (*Reasons of State*) and *Concierto barroco* (*Baroque Concerto*), both in 1974; *La Consagración de la primavera* (*The Rite of Spring*) in 1978, the year he was awarded the Miguel de Cervantes Prize, Spain's greatest literary distinction; and *El arpa y la sombra* (*The Harp and the Shadow*) in 1979, with its brilliant decolonizing discourse.

Carpentier died in Paris on April 24, 1980, while preparing his novel *La verídica historia* (*The True History*), whose protagonist is the revolutionary intellectual Pablo Lafargue, who, although born in Santiago de Cuba, was principally active in France and Karl Marx's son-in-law.

The following essay by the renowned Cuban intellectual Graziella Pogolotti, the title of which is a metaphor for her way of understanding Alejo Carpentier's work, shows step by step how Carpentier was an example of the transformation of Latin America's literary production over the course of the twentieth century, a transition from a literary mentality mediated by the European canon and thus partly "colonized" to an openly decolonizing discourse, conceived and developed from Cuba.

The Return of the Galleons
Transitions in the Work of Alejo Carpentier

According to Alejo Carpentier, Christopher Columbus rounded, rounded off and rounded up the planet. The cost was very high for the indigenous cultures of 'nuestra América' [our America]. Gradually, a new culture was founded made of all possible hybrids, that came from Europe, Africa and Asia. Carpentier himself also stated that, in order for the novel to exist, there must be a tradition of the novel; the first narrative manifestations were for domestic consumption: we would have to wait for the mid-twentieth century to begin what would soon become an avalanche. It was the return to Europe of the ships that once left Palos de Moguer, the carriers of another culture.

Several concomitant factors contributed to this reception in Europe. In post-war Europe, new curiosities were being awakened. André Malraux published his Musée imaginaire, thereby breaking the traditional Eurocentric hierarchy that gave Europe a civilizing mission in the face of the barbarism represented by the unfamiliar. The dominance of fictional literature, somewhat exhausted by the weight of tradition and by the now-tired formulas of the avant-garde, was supplemented by an interest in the documentary, promoted by advances in photography and by the technical development of printing which could now reproduce colour with the greatest fidelity.

On the other hand, in Latin America a renewed approach to the novel had been generated via the role of storytelling, the expression of a different reality that articulated the particular with the universal. The historical novel was transformed. It demonstrated, together with a partially unexplored physical world, the questions that unsettle humankind in any context.

Given the limits of space here, it is impossible to encapsulate the whole of Carpentier's work, so I will simply try to point out the landmarks that helped to earn a place for Latin American narrative in readers at the other end of the voyage of the galleons. On the face of it, the beginning of what we might call the Carpenterian novel was in line with established novelistic tradition, despite his early work rejecting the prevailing influence of nineteenth-century realism and naturalism. Later disowned by

Carpentier the mature writer, *¡Écue-Yamba-Ó!* (*Praised Be God!*) is a starting point worth considering in order to understand the contexts shaping his initial impulses as a writer. The slave-owner regime characterizing Cuba's colonial period left a nefarious economic, social, and cultural legacy; and, far from disappearing under the neocolonial Republic, it was reaffirmed via other forms of oppression, such as limited access to education and abundant employment, alongside the demonization of religions of Afro-Cuban origin. In society at large, and throughout the lettered city, the contrast between civilization and barbarism prevailed. The intellectual generation born with the Republic sought to transform reality into a process consistent with progressive political radicalization: writers and artists from a broad ideological spectrum constituted the Grupo Minorista, becoming visible and participating widely in public life.

Meanwhile, currents in music were adapting to the general air of modernity. Debussy and Igor Stravinsky, especially, brought fertile revelations allowing us to read passionately the musical scores that arrived from Europe. Carpentier the musicologist, however, was not content to be simply the observer of a changing reality; he became fully involved in the creative work of the musical innovators Amadeo Roldán and Alejandro García Caturla. Interested in the rhythmic values of Cuba's African heritage, they brought those popular expressions to symphonic composition. They strove to penetrate a mythical world that, while persecuted by the authorities, preserved clandestinely its people's particular worldview. The binary of civilization and barbarism was beginning to rupture through the workings of culture, and the same motivations led Carpentier to develop ballet projects that could not be performed until the revolutionary government came to power. His prison experience in 1927 then put him in contact with the underworld of the marginalized.

¡Écue-Yamba-Ó! is the result of that constellation of experiences. With the North American sugar mill as the backdrop, the novel's protagonist, Hermenegildo Cué, is dispossessed of his piece of land. Deprived of future possibilities after being compromised by an incident with a Haitian, he migrates to the city in the hope of an easier life and quick fortune. His role models are successful baseball players and gamblers. However, he is killed after being involved in a *ñáñiga abakuá* society, the most secret of all secret societies. A few years earlier, in 1912, thousands of Blacks (the exact figure is still not known) were killed by the official army in what was called the *guerrita de los negros* (little Black war). Research into the world of religions of African origin, often associated with petty crime and corruption, was still only rudimentary; while Fernando Ortiz was still moving from his

The Return of the Galleons 251

period as a criminologist, with Lombrosian training, toward his period as an ethnologist, his major research had not yet taken shape. Everything seems to indicate that Carpentier, dissatisfied with the available scholarship research at that point and in search of valid perspectives, found himself faced with an impasse. His friendship with Michel Leiris and other rebels from the André Breton school brought him to anthropology, and to a questioning of history and an obsession with the theme of time.

After returning to Cuba, he also returned to literary work, although the definitive leap forward came with a visit to Haiti. His reacquaintance with the Caribbean had been sharpened by Aimé Césaire's *Retour au pays natal* (*Return to the Native Land*), which coincided with the return of Carpentier and then of the painter Wifredo Lam. That new encounter helped to mature his vision. Although scarcely known outside Haiti, Haitian anthropologists had conducted important research on their country. In Haiti, Carpentier also found an old friend from the age of surrealism, the writer Pierre Mabille. He was able to benefit from productive dialogue while marveling at a cultural landscape that revealed the unexpected consequences of the colonial legacy in the clash of cultures. From that revelation came the prologue, intended only for Spanish-language editions, about *lo real maravilloso* (the marvelous real), which, paradoxically, has led to Byzantine discussions of all kinds, leaving the work's more revealing aspects in the shadows. Years later, Carpentier himself changed his original point of view. In an essay published in *Tientos y diferencias*, in a summary of a long journey from Prague to China and then returning via the Soviet Union, he addressed the problem of how to approach other cultures. For the observer, China was admirable but simultaneously indecipherable. With no reference points, we came up against an impossibility because we knew that it would take years to acquire them. In Prague, however, Carpentier recognized the memory of Jan Huss and evoked the conflicts between the Reformation and the Counter-Reformation. Despite not knowing the language, Petrograd seemed somehow familiar, in the relationship between Catherine and Diderot, and in the common treasury of a vast Russian literature, from Pushkin to Chekhov and Mayakovsky to Tolstoy and Dostoyevsky.

Alejo Carpentier always took extreme care when giving titles to his major works. His editors found it difficult to convince him of the need for any modification that might take account of the characteristics of potential readers; only twice did they succeed: in the French version of *Los pasos perdidos* (*Le partage des eaux* [*The Parting of the Waters*]), the original title being too close to a well-known text by André Breton; and in the English translation of *El siglo de las luces*, replaced by *Explosion in the*

Cathedral, because the original was seen as too associated with essay writing or historical research. In the latter case, it was a concession made very reluctantly by Carpentier, because the key to his work was precisely in the ambiguity between essay and fiction, a formula underlining his writing's transcendentalist projection. It is worth remembering the sequence of his most recognized titles: *Los pasos perdidos* (*The Lost Steps*), *El reino de este mundo* (*The Kingdom of This World*), *El recurso del método* (*Reasons of State*), *Concierto barroco, El arpa y la sombra* (*The Harp and the Shadow*), and the semi-confessional *La consagración de la primavera* (*The Consecration of Spring*).

The point of view is located on *this* side of the Atlantic, in the environment of specific landscapes and historical situations. The local gives way to the universal because questions touch on problems affecting everyone. They include the dialogue between cultures and the possibilities of understanding the culture of the other, as well as the problems around the convergence of myths, the role of grand narratives, the sense of the life of the common man aware of his ephemeral condition when faced with the mystery of the cosmos, and its possible interventions in the events defining his destiny.

In *El reino de este mundo* this is obvious, but it also manifested itself with varying degrees of nuance in his other texts. Regardless of any specific religious practice, the legacy of the Judeo-Christian tradition is a fundamental component, a common denominator of Western culture that, since the Conquest and despite the resulting painful experience, has been integrated to a considerable extent. At the same time, the book subverts the principles underpinning the historical novel, even in examples such as *La comédie humaine* (*The Human Comedy*), which extrapolated that conception to address contemporary reality. The narrative does not attempt to reconstruct the complexities and conflicts of the Haitian Revolution; it is based on the subjective vision of Ti-Noel, who tries to decipher the indecipherable from a culture forged in the remotest confines of the land of Voodoo. His reading of reality, by nature subversive given his background, contrasts with the imaginary of those who dominate. Between the two universes, the barriers are impassable. Born of a profound truth, his interpretation of the signs that identify trades is prophetic: there will be severed heads and blood will run because, despite appearances, Mackandal survives transformed, in an act of public incineration. After the revolt, Ti-Noel travels with his master to Santiago de Cuba. After an indeterminate number of years, he returns alone. He explores what is now a country unknown to him, where surveyors measure the land, but ends up in the realm of Henri Christophe, where two cultures fuse inorganically and violently under a new form of slavery, where men have to carry materials

The Return of the Galleons   253

to build La Citadelle. Ti-Noel's consciousness collapses into the inability to understand things. In the second part of the work, the subjectivity of the self ("I") has surreptitiously become "we," encapsulated in the myth of Sisyphus. The human figure grows in stature: the greatness of man in the kingdom of this world is defined by his commitment to do and to work against all obstacles and adversity.

The drama of finding a reason to be runs through *Los pasos perdidos* in an impossible journey toward the dawn of a new day. The narrator makes a double journey back to the origins: after a dazzling journey to the unknown depths of the jungle, he goes through space and time to reach the fourth day of creation, when primitive society begins to take shape. In Rosario, he discovers the authentic woman, the female procreator, still close to nature and to the truths of the earth. Along the hazardous route, through vast flows of water, until, in a place where newly discovered oil wells burn away, he hears Beethoven's Ninth Symphony coming from an old radio in a small tavern. Shortly before that, when he lived in the great city, working away at the manufacture of cultural products for propaganda and commercial purposes, he had rejected it; now it provides him with another journey through memory. Rootless, by association he digs up a fragment of Combray, the memory of his parents and the evocation of a childhood in nameless place, which is undoubtedly Havana. At the crossroads between the two journeys, an encounter with a possible lost paradise, the rebirth of a lost creativity will emerge. The fever of artistic creation, the writing of a lamentation inspired by Prometheus Unbound, imposes itself on everything else. He needs paper, scarce in such a far-flung place. Intent on returning, he happily boards the plane that comes to rescue him. He answers the call of the great city not just because he will find the material he needs but also because of the call of tastes, smells, meals, a way of life, and a daily routine he thought he had left behind. We are, it seems, also molded by those who build cities. We cannot escape the time in which we have to live, in the civilization that has shaped the contexts for who we are. Returning to the reality that belongs to him, the narrator suffers from difficulties of all kinds. The narrow gate to allow entry into the origin of all things has been closed forever. Rosario has been made pregnant by a man made to fit the circumstances of the world in which he lives, capable of shooting without hesitation at the leper despite the victim's pleading gaze. In a half-open denouement, the musician will have to test his strength, caught as he is between Ruth's vengeance, Mouche's superficial snobbery, and the temptations of alcohol.

Lonely, sunk in the deepest abandonment, misery, and bewilderment, Ti-Noel had found a fleeting refuge in the ruins of his master's mansion. In search of somewhere to sit, he had piled up the volumes of the *Great Encyclopedia*, the intellectual nutrient of the Enlightenment. Carpentier always kept his belief in the notion of progress, a hymn of hope incanted to a happiness arising from the rapid transformation of material existence suggested by the conquests of science. He distanced himself from the positivism still dominant in Cuba while he was young.

We have to approach *El siglo de las luces* with caution. Its title has an ironic element, a new kind of subversion of the historical novel by the ambiguous substrate of the narrative. Carpentier puts the reader on guard when, after Victor Hughes' arrival, followed by a hurricane, Carlos comments on the ghost who is roaming across Europe. In the fabric formed by the repercussions in Latin America of the French Revolution, he weaves a reflection on history and on man's commitment to revolutionary upheaval and his ability to intervene in them. We are not looking at a reconstruction of what actually happened, but a stage performance. The protagonists of the conflict are Sofia, Stephen, and Victor, and Carlos simply raises and lowers the curtain.

Armando Raggi, while researching in the archives of the Fundación Alejo Carpentier in Havana, discovered the first sketches of what would become *El siglo de las luces*. They were part of the drafts of *El clan disperso*, a project that occupied years of Carpentier's life and which, though never completed, nevertheless became a recognizable basis for later texts. The idea of an eccentric life making the night into day was inspired by the family of Dulce María Loynaz, winner of the Premio Cervantes (Cervantes Prize), where many talents that arose never fully materialized. More than simply a few anecdotes about the Loynaz family, loaded with irony, what stands out is Carpentier's latent preoccupation with understanding the Grupo Minorista generation that burst onto the scene, tinged by defeatism (a consequence of the US intervention in Cuba's War of Independence) with the purpose of breaking a stalemate, renewing artistic discourse, and assuming the active role of public intellectuals. Once again defeated by the US mediation's role in the overthrow of the tyrant Machado, they then enabled the dictator Batista to seize power. They adapted to circumstances and cut short a promising work in the making. The discovery of the existence of Victor Hughes, a minor historical figure with enough dark areas in his little-known biography to offer the novelist a vast space, opened up the possibility of constructing a framework with a universal scope. The route of those leaving France at the dawn of the Revolution took them to America, their involvement in slavery then raising questions, valid for all, about the commitment of the intellectual.

Located both inside and outside a precise chronology, *El siglo de las luces* is the dramatic representation of the intellectual's debate with the Grand

The Return of the Galleons

Narrative that is emerging, a kind of parenthesis of the theater within the theater, with the wake-up call from Victor Hughes. Play is learning and training for life. That is where everything begins: old clothes become a stage dressing room. Through the roles assumed, we see the life ambitions of the characters. Released by the death of their father, they have an appetite for knowledge. They import the latest devices invented by technology, which then remain on the shelf. Victor Hugues, bearer of the new truths, restores order, starts up the disused machinery, and introduces the ideas of Freemasonry. As a representative of the Grand Narrative, he changes the lives of the young people, being seen by them firstly with admiration and then with a gradual critical distance. The real protagonists of the conflict are Esteban and Sofía. Their names have not been randomly chosen. Carpentier was born on Saint Stephen's day and Sofía evokes the term's etymological root. With a change of costumes, a transition from the image of the Incorruptible to Bonapartism, yesterday's Freemason shows the decay of the mask and the profile of an opportunist, eager for wealth and power. Abolished by the Revolution, slavery has re-imposed itself in America. Esteban goes from disbelief to disappointment. Working as a clerk in the service of Victor Hughes, the mutilation of slaves in cold blood by the appropriate surgical instruments restores his confidence in the word. On the way back to Havana, he leaves the manifestos in unknown hands; someday they may fulfill his role.

For Carpentier, wisdom consists in the right balance between reason and passion. The ties that bind Sofia and Victor Hughes have this double origin. He is the bearer of new ideas and the man who has led her to an understanding of the fullness of womanhood. Implicated in the first Cuban conspiracies against colonial dependency and widowed after fulfilling her duties as a wife, Sofía escapes in search of a long-awaited meeting. She has not wanted to hear the stories told by a disillusioned Esteban; foreshadowing what will befall her, she knows that the woman who awaits her man dressed in finery ends up in the mire. Little by little she becomes aware of the deterioration of both the man and his personality and of her own condition as a kept woman, far away from the affairs of public life. The end is abrupt. Together with Esteban in a house in Madrid, his health broken by prison in Ceuta, she resurrects the ambiguous maternal relationship of their youth. When rebellion breaks out against Napoleon, it is left to Sofia to "do something." With antiquated weaponry at their disposal, they disappear.

For the moment, the narrative is over. It is an episode in the confrontation between the intellectual and the Grand Narrative. Much later, in *La consagración de la primavera*, there would be many Cubans fighting in defense of the betrayed Spanish Republic, a tragic prelude to World War II.

Carlos manages to go to the Madrid house to collect his belongings, close the house, and lower the curtains. *El siglo de las luces* still hangs there, a premonition with something of a surreal atmosphere. With space and time paralyzed, the fractured columns supporting the building seem to be suspended in the air, a synthetic vision of the struggle between the new and the old, between a future project and the remains of an underlying past. Both clinging to similar ethical values, Esteban clings to the absolute values of what should be, while Sofía assumes the being of reality with all its contradictions. Driven by Carpentier's theoretical work, the Baroque theme complements the hyperbolization of the "reality of wonder." There is no doubt about the Baroque, but the whole of Carpentier's work refers to the pristine sense of the term, defined by Italian architecture, that is the construction of spaces where the real and the illusory are confused. That space grows larger over time as the dialogue between here and there increases as the games with perspective multiply.

The shift is evident in Carpentier's last narrative triad, consisting of *El recurso del método*, *Concierto barroco* and *El arpa y la sombra*. From the early 1970s, Carpentier knew that the timing of the end of his life was fixed and his term was fulfilled with almost arithmetic accuracy. However, he never modified the rigid work discipline he had imposed on himself from his time in Caracas. He fulfilled his diplomatic duties as Cultural Counsellor of the Paris Embassy. He received visitors, responded to numerous interviews, and delivered lectures whenever his presence was required. That work was intensified by the honors granted him as he reached his seventies. Those tributes led him to Venezuela and emotional meetings with the friends he had gathered around him during his long and fruitful stay there over fourteen years. However, he never desisted from the systematic and daily blurring of pages. Throughout his literary trajectory, he had frequently employed irony. In that final stage, humor, sometimes pushed to the limits of farce, became a central subversive instrument.

Literary commentators have written extensively on an alleged agreement between several Latin American writers to write texts on the subject of the dictator. There was already one classic antecedent, regrettably now forgotten: Miguel Ángel Asturias' *Señor Presidente*, inspired by Estrada Cabrera and his power over an entire society. Carpentier had known the writer well since the 1930s when the two lived together in Paris. However, his own purpose, driven by the ideas of decolonizing emancipation, was quite

The Return of the Galleons

different: he was endeavoring to show the fragility of power when subordinated to domination by an imperial power. Capable of committing the most brutal crimes when his control seems threatened by internal enemies, his dictator turns out to be disposable material when he loses the ability to fulfill the mission entrusted to him. In addition to being a puppet-dictator, the nameless First Magistrate is an interloper, always arriving late to the European cultural trend of the time, managing to penetrate, with the money he sheds, one part of the cult to the Verdurins, although he does not enter the inner circle of the Guermantes. All doors will be closed to him when newspaper photos spread irrefutable evidence of his criminal behavior. His oratory, a late vulgarization of Renan's model, oscillates between emptiness and kitsch. He is powerless under the clear gaze of the rebellious student. He becomes farcical when, like the tyrant Machado, he erects a monument to the Republic. Brought from Italy, as is appropriate considering the magnitude of the work transported in fragments, the massive size of its feminine forms amuses the workers who unload it at the port. Expelled from the house that has become alien to him, he takes refuge in the servants' rooms, where the Indian woman, the only faithful companion he has left, recommends rediscovering the flavors and smells of his homeland. He returns to his origins. However, in the fluid space that joins the two continents, history is written differently. The Grand Narrative comes from "there," while the events "here" have little resonance. They are separated by time and space.

With space and time ambivalent by nature (a game of masks), a Mexican and his companion, a Black Cuban descendant of Salvador Golomón (the hero of *Espejo de paciencia*, the founding work of Cuban literature), have gone, following the sound of silver, to the Venice carnival. The representation of Vivaldi's opera inspired by the figure of Moctezuma will be unveiled. The Mexican is outraged at the misrepresentation of the true story, a collateral issue that has no interest for those involved. The triumph of the cultural counteroffensive is seen in the great musical orgy of the Ospedale della Pietà, where the Black man's improvised percussion, using instruments of daily life, draws all the participants to follow the rhythm of the chorus "Calabazón, son, son." Symbolically, a nun hands a trumpet to the Cuban musician. Time and space break apart and fragment; the walls that separate illusion and reality are broken. Over a sumptuous breakfast in the cemetery, Vivaldi and Handel look at Stravinsky's grave and comment on his work. Wagner's funeral cortege parades nearby. The party is over. Always dissatisfied, the Mexican returns to his land. At the railway station he says goodbye to the Cuban who, trumpet in hand, is off to attend a Louis Armstrong concert in Paris. The story continues to be told wrongly; the counter-culture of "here" has penetrated "there."

To round off the planet from the cultural point of view, *El arpa y la sombra* interrogates the way that history is constructed. As happened with *El siglo de las luces*, the narrative uses theatrical resources. It does so even more patently, such that the reader finds themself with the distanced perspective of a spectator. Divided into three acts and an epilogue, each part appeals to different narrative forms. It begins with a chapter conceived in a linear way. A narrator recounts the journey of the young Massai, an aristocrat from a downtrodden family and a future pope. After an arduous journey through the Argentine pampas, he gets to know Chilean society up close. When independence came to Latin America, the newly created republics were not subject to the agreements that united the interests of the monarchy and the Vatican; therefore, the hold of Catholicism over the inhabitants of those lands is in danger. Devotion to local saints like Rosa de Lima persists, but it would be better to find a unifying personality to attract everyone's adherence. In this case, he thinks, the beatification of Columbus (we might add, the discoverer who established civilization against the ignorance of the original peoples) would strengthen the power of the Church. Elected pontiff, after much thought, he begins the process of beatification. In the second act, Columbus, dying, awaits his confessor. While the confessor arrives, the Grand Admiral has had to lie about his origins and his seamanship, having to make credible the gamble taken on an expensive adventure to win the complicity of Isabel la Católica, the political strategist of the kingdom of Spain, eager for expansion after having expelled the Arabs from the Peninsula.

In the third and decisive act of the farce, the masks are removed. The ghost of Columbus contemplates the spectacle of his last judgment. Nobody cares about the value of his person, of the feat of having set foot on the shores of America, of having contributed, after the first seeming failure, to the supply of gold and silver that will decisively shape the development of European capitalism. Nor does anyone count the enormous human and cultural cost that the conquest of a continent incurred. In the heterogeneous and timeless parade of the characters empowered to express their opinions and make decisions, the confrontation takes place around personal politics, primary fundamentalisms, and ambitions to become pre-eminent. Only the epilogue is missing. The ghosts of Andrea Doria and Christopher Columbus cross in the Plaza de San Pedro, the most paradigmatic of all Baroque spaces, where, according to one's point of view, several columns are hidden behind the illusion of there being only one.

The Return of the Galleons

Despite everything, the labor that went into each of Carpentier's works remains visible, changing according to the times and the prevailing ideological tendencies. At the mercy of fickle judgment, human work leaves its mark, because from labor and men's will to transform comes the faith driving tasks of a vast size exceeding our ephemeral and small stature. We all know that one day death will happen, as our common predetermined destiny. Marked by cancer, his voice almost inaudible, Carpentier had a date marked on the calendar. As instructed by his doctor, he maintained his full dignity to the end, by fulfilling his duty as a man. At dawn on that last day, he worked on the pages of *La verídica historia*, perhaps yet another new twist seen through the life of the Cuban Pablo Lafargue, a man who came from "here" to promote a great emancipatory revolution, available for all over "there," the often-dissenting son-in-law of Karl Marx. Later, Carpentier attended some engagements at UNESCO. He shared the first night with his friends Fina García Marruz and Cintio Vitier, poets of the Cuban Catholic group Orígenes, once led by José Lezama Lima. As he was just about to go to bed, he collapsed.

Round the planet in the circumstances of a neoliberal and homogenizing globalization, Carpentier built a fluid Baroque space, made of truth and illusion, of interpenetration between the two Atlantic shores, driven by an essential emancipatory spirit in defense of human life. The "I" of Ti-Noel is transformed into "we," the subordinates, determined to decipher the keys of the world that surrounds and shapes us. There is also something of every one of us in Christopher Columbus, moved by the appetite for success and gold, but subject to the judgment of history. The triumph of Carpentier with the publication in France of *El reino de este mundo* and *Los pasos perdidos* helped to introduce the new Latin American narrative to the distant "there." Now, as the twenty-first century marches on by seven leagues, when the audio-visual domain tarnishes the old literary tradition, we must return to Carpentier's work with a new gaze, abandoning the worn-out clichés that were justified at a time that now already seems remote. Literature must be restored to its transcendental vocation, the one that inspired the spirit of Don Quixote and Gargantua and Pantagruel, closing our doors to the temptations of popularization and marketing. In this renewed Baroque space, the intellectual must claim his rightful place, based on an ethical commitment that involves his work and his civic responsibility. The debate on modernity and on the survival of the species was now open.

CHAPTER 16

"Un Híbrido de Halcón y Jicotea"
Testimonio *and Its Challenge to the Latin American Literary Canon*

Par Kumaraswami

This chapter reexamines the commonalities and tensions between two coexisting modes of writing Latin America – magical realism and testimonial writing – in the first two decades of the 1959 Cuban Revolution. The rapid inclusion of magical realist texts and the "boom" authors in international canons of literature tells us much about the central role of editorial decisions and policies (implemented primarily from Spain and the United States) in putting Latin American literature on the map. Equally prominent in scholarship are the acrimonious debates between writers and intellectuals that were provoked by the 1968–71 *caso Padilla* (Padilla Affair) and subsequent schism of "los cien intelectuales" ("the 100 intellectuals") from the Cuban Revolution and played out in Latin American publications such as *Plural* and *Vuelta*; all of this was explored in forensic detail in Jorge Fornet's *El 71: Anatomía de una crisis* (2013).

However, this chapter proposes a different focus, and one that is much less explored: it charts the conceptualizations in Cuba (and more generally via Casa de las Américas in left-wing Latin American and developing postcolonial nations) of the hybrid mode of *testimonio* in the 1960s and 1970s, revealing how sustained cultural policies to create via *testimonio* a new kind of literature – built on the foundations in post-1959 Cuba of near-universal literacy and the massification and socialization of literary culture – presented a challenge to the literary establishment in Latin America and beyond. Through examining some key theoretical and policy-based texts from the first two decades of the Cuban Revolution, the chapter argues that the horizon of expectation for *testimonio* in these early conceptualizations shared many commonalities with those of magical realism but also some important differences based on positionality and intention. As such, the 1968–71 schism between the Cuban Revolution and Latin American intellectuals represented not only

260

"*Un Híbrido de Halcón y Jicotea*" 261

a mostly irrecoverable political fracture but also a tipping point, or moment of transition: after 1971, the lasting legacy of Latin American literatures in continental and global terms would be magical realist writing rather than testimonial. However, the testimonial writing promoted from Cuba (and also as a Latin American form, principally via Casa de las Américas) continued to lay claim during the 1970s and 1980s to becoming the iconic representation of Latin American literature that would provide a new set of qualities, values, and functions for literature in the new Cuba and the new Latin America. The chapter demonstrates that, alongside complicating the realist novel, as magical realism aimed to do, *testimonio* went a step further and provided an anti-colonial stance that aimed to put "la gente sin historia" ("people without history"), as the intellectual and writer Miguel Barnet described them, at the center, and as subjects, of their own realities (Sklodowska, "La visión de la gente"). In this way, it proposes that what appear to be exclusively moments of rupture can also be understood as evidence of continuity and transformation; that is, of constant transitions and evolutions in the complex and heterogenous field of Latin American literatures.

In 1992, Barnet described the complex responsibilities attached to the task of creating a new way of writing, the *novela testimonial* (testimonial novel). The explanation for his own role in this endeavor featured a lively and expressive simile that crystallized what was both original and valuable about this hybrid kind of literature: "Soy algo así como un híbrido de halcón y jicotea" ("I am something akin to a hybrid of the falcon and the tortoise"), wrote Barnet ("Alquimia de la memoria," 76).[1] The first result of this endeavor, the story of 113-year-old ex-slave Esteban Montejo, published in 1966 as *Biografía de un cimarrón* (*Biography of a Runaway Slave*), and soon translated into several other languages, quickly became a flagship text of the Cuban Revolution, providing as it did the apparent (although ultimately fleeting) proof that it was possible to create authentic postcolonial narratives and simultaneously appeal to national, continental, and international audiences. Importantly, it signaled that the revolutionary concept of *Cuba rebelde* (rebel Cuba) that explained Cuba's history from the nineteenth-century wars of independence to the present meant radical changes to the question of whose stories were important, whom they were important for, and, crucially, how those stories might be gathered and represented. Specifically in relation to the issue of gathering and processing these voices and stories, Barnet's metaphor encapsulated several key ideas: the writer of the *novela testimonial* had to be able to listen to the small individual voices of history (as the *jicotea*) but also represent a more

262   PAR KUMARASWAMI

universal or bird's-eye perspective of humanity's story (as the *halcón*). To do this, testimonial writing had to be truly revolutionary: it had to embrace hybridity and heterogeneity in terms of genre, epistemology, and academic discipline. Stories such as Montejo's announced that the anti-colonial future, Calibán's revenge in the terms of Roberto Fernández Retamar's 1968 essay, was imminent; however, rather than continue to exhaust Fernández Retamar's much-used metaphor, we can turn to Barnet's imagery as a way of understanding how common this anti-colonial stance was in Cuba.

Despite the importance of *testimonio* to the revolutionary project in Cuba and Latin America, and despite these imaginative attempts to configure a new, hybrid, way of writing in Latin America, the most visible debates on *testimonio*, from within and beyond Latin America, have barely engaged with the ideas that were formulated and expressed in the crucible of the first two decades of the Cuban Revolution. As a result of common perceptions of Cuban literature as being subordinated, after 1968, to the precepts of Soviet socialist realism, international debates about *testimonio* did not emerge until the 1980s, and preferred to trace the testimonial mode in that decade (most publicly – and acrimoniously – with the Rigoberta Menchú controversy) and focus on its apparent decline in the 1990s. Thus, international scholarly approaches to Latin American *testimonio* had, by the 1990s, exhausted the possibility for testimonial writing to provide solutions to the social, political, and economic violence ushered in by the end of the Cold War and Fukuyama's much-publicized end of history. Many of these changing positions were presented in Georg Gugelberger's 1996 collection of essays on Latin American *testimonio*, *The Real Thing*, the introduction of which set out the current reception of *testimonio* in the West. Gugelberger's approach indicated that the idea of *testimonio* was now defunct: "Obviously the euphoric 'moment' of the *testimonio* has passed, and it is now time to assess in a more self- and metacritical spirit its reception by the critical and academic disciplines" (1). Gugelberger viewed the first stages of reception of *testimonio* as taking place in the 1980s, and through the channels provided by international networks, as the hope of establishing a politics of solidarity with developing countries that reflected the need for liberal US academics to reject the reactionary and interventionist policies of their government. As Gugelberger expressed it: "the desire called *testimonio* was the desire called Third World literature" (1). This hope, answering Gayatri Spivak's doubt that the subaltern really could speak, was termed by Gugelberger "the salvational dream of a declining cultural left in hegemonic countries" (7).

"*Un Híbrido de Halcón y Jicotea*" 263

Other theorists, however, saw *testimonio* in more literary terms, as having emerged as a cultural response to the elitist narratives of the Latin American "boom." Linda Craft, in the excellent introduction to her 1997 study of Central American narratives of testimony and resistance, glossed John Beverley and Marc Zimmerman by seeing *testimonio* as a development or "refunctioning" of the "boom" literature of the 1960s and 1970s rather than a blunt negation or rejection of it, and saw in *testimonio* narratives a reworking of a "perceived overpreoccupation with signifiers, aesthetics, formalistic experimentation, fantasy, and authorial command and celebrity" (18). Indeed, she referred to the now notorious pronouncements of Dinesh D'Souza on the inclusion of Menchú's testimonial text in a general undergraduate course on culture at Stanford University, implying that in some sectors of high culture, *testimonio* was regarded as the antithesis of culture, "to be of inferior quality linguistically, stylistically, and literarily" (1).

Throughout these late periods of conceptualization, theorization, and lively debate, however, Cuban testimonial writing, and its conceptual frameworks, remained virtually invisible. A possible explanation for the continued neglect of Cuban testimonial writing, along with the long shadow cast by Cuba's *caso Padilla* and the subsequent *quinquenio gris* (Grey Five Years), could lie in the desire of the US liberal academy to incorporate and assimilate those texts that reflected their own political and ethical agendas, thus fulfilling the hermeneutic circle of canonization: according to Craft, developing-country testimonial texts had been co-opted to fill the conflicted space of capitalism/democracy in the United States (2). However, the positionality of the scholar is also key: Craft's interpretation of the evolution of testimonial writing in post-revolutionary societies revealed her own assumptions about the essentially subversive or contestatory function of writing, and the belief of many critics that testimonial writing in particular was characterized by its oppositional stance. Naming Cuba and Nicaragua as post-revolutionary societies where *testimonio* had been institutionalized, she wrote: "it has lost its subversive punch and perhaps its critical objectivity as an outsider looking in – and even, we might suggest, its moral high ground as the discourse of the marginalized" (191).

At the same time, Elzbieta Sklodowska reminded us of the role of the reader in the struggle for the conferral of meaning to the *testimonio*. Quoting Stanley Fish's famous essay of 1980, "How to Recognize a Poem When You See One," she proposed that it is not the text that triggers acts of recognition in the reader but rather "the paying of a certain kind of attention" that elicits the emergence of textual and poetic qualities in the reader (84). With reference to the exposure and reception of testimonial writing and its importance for Latin America, she continued:

> Some rarely explored islands of Spanish American letters, such as women's autobiography, subaltern autobiography, and minority experience, have come to be evaluated with "testimonio-seeing eyes" .... The fact that we, the interpretive community of academic critics, have agreed to "recognize" *testimonio* and give it institutional legitimation is, arguably, one of the most important events of the past two decades in Spanish American literary history. (84)

Sklodowska's underlining of the subjective or socially and ideologically sanctioned nature of processes of literary recognition reveals most convincingly the neglect of Cuban conceptualizations: by the 1980s, *testimonio*'s importance seemed to exist only when it was visible from the outside, from a critical distance, with particular "*testimonio*-seeing eyes" that were primed to expect resistance, contestation, and inconformity.

Furthermore, a survey of the debates certainly seems to suggest that self-reflection on the part of the distant reader, rather than action emanating from the context of writing, had become the primary purpose or function of many testimonial texts. For instance, Gugelberger's conclusion to his introduction indicated a considerable level of self-interest on the part of academic readers in more developed countries: "But, and this cannot be emphasized strongly enough, without the insights gained and problems faced while discussing the *testimonio*, we hardly would be where we are now, looking for new ways of expression that deterritorialize our disciplines and breathe new life into them" (17). Although traces of Barnet's multidisciplinary self-image are evident here, Gugelberger's conclusion suggested that the appropriation of the peripheral or subaltern was no longer an act of solidarity, or even of charity, but rather had become an act of appropriation and consumption serving the needs of the center. As such, by the end of the 1980s, Barnet's role as the *halcón* appeared to be the dominant model for producing and reproducing testimonial writing: that is, via an educated and powerful mediator, whether interviewer, transcriber and editor, publisher, translator, or critic.

The functions and contexts of the production and reception of writing are, therefore, key to understanding the paths that *testimonio* and magical realism took between the 1960s and 1980s and the subsequent trajectory of their reception. At the same time as the new model of the hybrid writer was emerging from revolutionary Cuba, and Barnet was publishing *Biografía de un cimarrón*, another hybrid form, magical realism, was coming to the fore on the continent and internationally, most notably in international terms with the publication of *Cien años de soledad* (*One Hundred Years of Solitude*) in 1967. The novel, which has propagated its own mythology about the writing process, immediately gained international appeal, winning the Prix de Meilleur Livre Étranger in France in 1969 and the Premio Rómulo Gallegos in Venezuela in 1972. By 1970, it had been published in its first English version (translation by Gregory Rabassa) and in 1982, of course, Gabriel García Márquez was awarded the Nobel Prize for Literature. Within the space of fifteen years, then, magical realism established itself as the literary voice of Latin America, and its principal proponents (García Márquez, Carlos Fuentes, Julio Cortázar) were feted outside Latin America as the new literary celebrities of the continent, often choosing to reside and work temporarily in Europe and meeting each other along the international circuits for literature. In that sense, their role as the *halcón* or predator, ripe with "authorial command and celebrity" and, one might argue, illustrating the "overripe subjectivity" that, according to John Beverley (*pace* Frederic Jameson), was the trademark of both the *bildungsroman* and traditional autobiography, reinscribed the peoples of their respective nations and of the continent as a whole as the object of representation, the raw material, the prey (28).

However, rather than argue that these two modes of writing constituted separate and mutually exclusive genres, emerging through some unusual coincidence from the same continent at the same time, it may be more productive to understand each as different ways of understanding the solution to the same problem: that is, two forms of postcolonial and continent projects of self-representation that suggest a matter of degrees of difference of production, promotion, and reception. In this way, the simile of falcon and tortoise takes on new facets as it is operationalized in different contexts.

Examining the broader landscape for Cuban *testimonio* is a vital part-precursor to understanding its claims. In pre-1959 Cuba, the lack of a readership among the educated middle and upper classes (who were attracted more to foreign cultural models), coupled with a lack of material resources, had produced a national literature that was individualistic, sporadic, and diffident. Lourdes Casal, among others, described the consequences for writers and readers of the impoverished state of the 1950s literary context: a lack of publishing houses, with writers consequently being obliged to finance from their own funds the limited publication of their work, very few incentives (only one literary prize, the *Hernández Catá* for the short story, was awarded regularly and fairly), and a general attitude that saw literature as an effete and socially irrelevant activity (456). The perception and self-perception of the literary figure, then, was reduced to that of a highly individualized and self-contained role, divorced from social realities (and especially unable to engage with the realities of underdevelopment) and devalued or ignored by society at large. The social values, which formed the larger context for this self-perception, were based on institutionalized discrimination and social fragmentation.

The debates over the function of the writer and the direction of cultural change in revolutionary Cuba rested on the conflict between a lack of self-definition, a range of embryonic self-definitions being produced by a wide range of writers, and definitions imposed from a burgeoning range of revolutionary individuals and institutions; and all of these in dialogue with the rest of the world, itself in constant transition. Implicit in the sometimes-chaotic debates in Cuba were not only aesthetic questions but, more significantly, a range of ethical, moral, social, and ideological issues on which writers would eventually have to state their position: the relationship of the writer to society, to their readership, their non-literary revolutionary duties, and the nature of their revolutionary work, all of which pointed to the larger question of the function of art and the artist within a new value system. The analogy of the *halcón* and *jicotea* was thus a universal problem for all kinds of writing in the new Cuba. And, as the desire for change became a reality for the Cuban nation in the early 1960s, the spectrum of responses from writers and intellectuals to a nascent but already radical cultural policy was, at least initially, inevitably diverse.

Nevertheless, and as reflected in Barnet's theorization and practice, the testimonial novel's first shape was less radical than we might expect, and thus shared many features with the magical realist novel: to demystify official histories; to find a language proper to the subject matter, based on research, which nevertheless engaged the creative imagination; to recognize and record the collective memory of the continent and to position this politically. In this sense, the *novela testimonio*, as first essayed by Barnet in 1967, itself represented a midpoint – a transition in Cuban terms – between the first attempts at including the *pueblo*'s voice in literature and the end point: producing literature by the masses. While magical realism began to be celebrated and translated outside Latin America, the idea of the writer and of writing that was being promoted and shaped by the Cuban Revolution was beginning to emerge. The 1961 Cuban Literacy Campaign had created a nation of nascent readers in the space of nine months: if for some this meant being only functional readers, for others it meant access to education and, eventually, to national, continental, and world literatures. The pains to which the Cuban government went, soon after 1959, to create an infrastructure for publishing Cuban and world literatures have been evocatively described by intellectuals such as Ambrosio Fornet and Fernando Martínez Heredia, detailed in Parvathi Kumaraswami and Antoni Kapcia's *Literary Culture in Cuba* (2012), who were tasked with coordinating the collection and translation of foreign literatures and the publication of national, continental, and world literatures on the now defunct private printing presses that had served the pre-1959 press. In addition, the infrastructure for reading was soon followed by a network of spaces for writing: the national movement of *talleres literarios* (literary workshops) and an ever-increasing system of literary prizes. Fidel Castro's 1961 warning to established writers in the "Palabras a los intelectuales" that a new generation of revolutionary artists and intellectuals was soon to step forward hinted that the rules of the game of literature in Cuba had reached a crucial moment of transition.

What, then, of established writers? In accordance with the general euphoria and naivety of the first two years of the Revolution, the first articulations of the nature of the revolutionary writer detached them from their literary work: merely to be a *miliciano* made one a revolutionary writer. However, from 1961 onward, it was evident that the role of the writer required sharper self-definition, and there began a period of intense debate surrounding the importance of aesthetic and ideological elements (and their relationship to each other). In the midst of this, of course, were the writers, with a spectrum of self-images ranging from the self-contained and self-obsessed existential antihero to the self-sacrificing servant of the Revolution. As Mario Benedetti expressed it in the late 1960s:

> En su mayor parte, son artistas que concurren voluntariamente a las labores agrícolas y cumplen su función en la milicia ciudadana. Otros, en cambio, defendían virtualmente el derecho de contemplar el trabajo ajeno, y sin embargo vivir de él. Pero la Revolución tiene a su vez el derecho de no entenderse con ese tipo de contemplativos, y hasta de ser injusta con ellos. ("Situación actual de la cultura cubana," 32)

> On the whole, there are artists who participate voluntarily in agricultural work and fulfill their function in the urban militias. There are others, on the other hand, who defended virtually the right to contemplate the work of others, and nevertheless live off that work. But the Revolution itself has the right not to get on with that kind of navel-gazing figure, and even to be unfair toward them.

In other words, the revolutionary writer could not take refuge in an ivory tower; they must confront the same traumatic process of conflict, adaptation, and evolution, of *desgarramiento* (rupture), that the collective was

268 PAR KUMARASWAMI

experiencing. As an extension of this elementary fact, one can identify figures, representative of both orthodox and liberal sides of the debate, whose approaches brought them into public conflict. The rejection of the ivory tower paradigm – the position from which the falcon surveys its prey – was a common theme: a paper presented to the 1961 Congreso de Escritores y Artistas advocated what some might consider to be a somewhat militaristic approach to culture. The literary critic José Antonio Portuondo suggested:

> Nacionalizar las egoístas torres de marfil, enviando al campo a los artistas. No hay que abolir las becas para estudiar en el exterior, sino mandar al interior primero a los artistas mejor dotados y enviarlos después a descubrir el mundo con una conciencia nacional íntegramente formada. Como en el caso de los jóvenes destinados al Servicio Exterior y en el de los maestros, que no salga ningún artista becado sin antes haber subido cinco veces al Turquino. (60)
>
> We should nationalize the self-seeking ivory towers, sending artists out to the countryside. There is no need to abolish study-abroad grants, but we should first send the most talented artists into the countryside and then send them out to discover the world with a fully formed national consciousness. Just like the young people destined for foreign missions and the teachers, no artist should leave Cuba with such a grant without first having scaled the Pico Turquino five times.

The notion of the artist as humble servant of the people, the lowly *jicotea*, also found an early expression in Portuondo's paper: "Los escritores y artistas, por nuestra parte, debemos esforzarnos por entender los tiempos nuevos y adoptar una justa actitud de humildad. Convencernos de que nos toca ahora aprender, antes de enseñar. Que no somos guías del pueblo, sino sólo su expresión" (60) ("We writers and artists should make an effort to understand these new times and to adopt a just attitude of humility. We should convince ourselves that our time has come to learn, rather than teach. That we are not the *pueblo*'s guide but rather its mere expression"). This reformulation of the relationship between writer and masses would later be reinforced by the Declaration of the 1971 Congreso de Educación y Cultura, where the people, not the intellectual, would be identified as the "conciencia crítica" ("critical consciousness") of revolutionary Cuban society.

Despite, or perhaps because of, the public debates over the role of the intellectual, the Cuban writer was no longer writing in the vacuum of solitude and neglect. With a new cultural community within which to share ideas – a new readership demanding new cultural products – the communicability, functionality, and intentionality of art were seen as

"Un Híbrido de Halcón y Jicotea"
269

paramount if the dialogue with the people was to be successfully established and maintained. Not only did the public participate through its newly acquired access to culture but it was also invited to judge, critique, and participate actively in the art that was being produced. And, as cultural and educational levels rose, the *pueblo* would initiate the dialogue and become the subject of its own representation. The ideal, then, was a model of culture where artist and public communicated freely and influenced one another in an endless dialogue, eventually erasing the demarcations between *halcón* and *jicotea*, between subject and object. However, the relationship was bound to be conflictive, mediated as it was by ideological and institutional forces. With in the context of the *caso Padilla*, the closing declaration at the 1971 Congress underlined the extent to which the Western or "First World" figure of the intellectual had lost prestige in revolutionary Cuba, and privileged the role of the people rather than that of the writer in this dialogue: "Rechazamos las pretensiones de la mafia de intelectuales, burgueses seudoizquierdistas de convertirse en la conciencia crítica de la sociedad. La conciencia crítica de la sociedad es el pueblo mismo y, en primer término, la clase obrera" ("Los intelectuales extranjeros," 152) ("We reject the pretensions of the mafia of pseudo-left-wing bourgeois intellectuals to become the critical consciousness of our society. The critical consciousness of our society is the *pueblo* itself and, most of all, the working class"). The intellectual's role was ancillary, to "coadyuvar a esa crítica con el pueblo y dentro del pueblo" ("contribute to that critique with the *pueblo* and from within the *pueblo*") (154). Did the future, then, promise an entire society where individuals could exercise their right as both *halcón* and *jicotea* in the search for an independent and autochthonous identity and, therefore, forms of expression?

For the revolutionary project was not merely about transforming the future; it was also concerned with recovering history and incorporating it into the contemporary cultural reality by constructing a revised concept of national identity, or *cubanía*. In this respect, it shared many similarities with the Latin American search for identity and its representational forms in which magical realism played a part. Despite personal and ideological conflicts, there was a real sense in which cultural representatives were united in the recovery of a lost heritage and the construction of an identity suppressed by colonialism and neocolonialism (this new identity was also charged with recognizing the reality of underdevelopment).

It was this factor – the recognition of underdevelopment and a desire to contribute to the creation of an authentic Cuban and Latin American cultural identity – that provided some common ground in a context of

270 PAR KUMARASWAMI

polarization and conflict. Writing in 1967, Fernández Retamar summed up the enormous complexity and ambitious aspirations of the first decade of revolution with ironic understatement: "Se trata de hacer un arte de vanguardia en un país subdesarrollado en revolución" ("We are attempting to create vanguard art in an underdeveloped country in the process of revolution") (182). Within the context of the "siege" atmosphere of underdevelopment prevalent in the late 1960s, writers such as Mario Benedetti rejected the recent interventions of foreign intellectuals in relation to Padilla as evidence of "cierto aire feudal" ("a certain feudal air") (El escritor latinoamericano, 59), which aimed to judge and dictate the direction of cultural life in Cuba from the cozy ivory towers of the European and Latin American metropolis. Moreover, Benedetti's acerbic analysis of "los 62" – the foreign intellectuals who had denounced the treatment of Padilla – portrayed them as cowardly and ineffective intellectuals who rejoiced in the purity of the failed revolution of May 1968 in France but could not comprehend the complexities of a real (and sometimes dirty) revolution. For Benedetti, their cowardice had led them to take refuge in Eurocentric and bourgeois notions of aestheticism and freedom of expression, concepts that were anathema within the new cultural practice and policy of revolutionary Cuba:

> Para el intelectual europeo, o para el latinoamericano que secretamente aspira a serlo, las revoluciones frustradas tienen la ventaja innegable de que no originan los desagradables, incómodos, trabajosos problemas que enfrenta una revolución en el poder . . .. Lástima que, por lo común, las revoluciones no se emprenden por motivos estéticos, sino por razones de justicia social. (El escritor latinoamericano, 64)

> For the European intellectual, or for the Latin American who secretly aspires to be one, revolutions that are frustrated have the undeniable advantage that they don't generate the unpleasant, uncomfortable, arduous problems that are faced by a revolution in power . . .. It's a shame that, on the whole, revolutions are not undertaken for aesthetic motives, but rather for reasons of social justice.

More importantly for the purposes of this chapter, *Biografía de un cimarrón* emerged during this period as an iconic *testimonio* that prefigured a new mode of writing Latin America, albeit a new mode with a long and complex genealogy. The decade of the 1960s therefore promised to be a moment of profound and radical transition for Cuban literature, a tipping point that, through the implementation of cultural and social policies, envisioned a more sovereign, anti-colonial, and egalitarian mode of writing literature. In the 1970s, it promised the same for Latin America, and was promoted through the creation of the Casa de las Américas prize category in 1970, alongside the many infrastructural mechanisms for writing as a mass activity in Cuba. Thus, in a context where the traditional role of the writer, artist, and intellectual was no longer valid currency, the newly emerging boom of magical realist texts was too conservative, too influenced by power differentials and colonialist expectations, and simply too extractive, too predatory, to garner prestige in the new Cuba. Cuban testimonial writing was produced eventually neither by the *halcón* nor by the *jicotea* but by a hybrid of both that provided the ideal autochthonous form for a radical sociocultural and political project that rested on unity of purpose, anti-colonial development.

In the essay in which the metaphor first appears, Barnet positioned the new mode of *testimonio* as the ideal alternative to resist the cultural neocolonialism of the two powers, which, as argued eloquently for nearly a century by intellectuals such as Rodó and Marti, continued to subjugate Cuba and determine its cultural directions: Europe and the United States. *Testimonio*, ultimately authored from the ground, by resisting both the elite literary models of modernity and the lure of the market made visible by the emerging boom could offer Cuba – and, by extension, the entire continent – a new direction for development and self-representation. Indeed, *testimonio* was just one mechanism in the project of Cuban cultural anti-colonialism: other key Cuban cultural texts from the era covered similar ground in terms of illustrating ways of undertaking anti-colonial development: Fernández Retamar's 1968 essay "Calibán" offered a defiant rereading of *The Tempest*, with the slave using language as a weapon against his dual masters; Nicolás Guillén offered equally militant challenges to the "First World" through poems such as his 1972 "Problemas del subdesarrollo" ("Problems of Underdevelopment"), which shifted the ontological bases of knowledge to the southern hemisphere. Tomás Gutiérrez Alea played out the same problems in his 1968 *Memorias del subdesarrollo* (*Memories of Underdevelopment*), most notably in the footage of the Casa de las Américas panel on literature and underdevelopment, with Barnet himself seated a short distance from Jack Gelber, the US playwright who unproblematically asks his question in English, and the film's protagonist, Sergio.

By the 1970s, with the massification of writing now established and formalized through expanded training, prizes, and publishing infrastructure, Raúl González de Cascorro framed *testimonio* in a confident way, as a stance against alienated capitalist culture and, therefore, as an ideal form of autochthonous revolutionary culture: "Esa literatura reaccionaria va a encontrar un rechazo rotundo por parte de los escritores y lectores revolucionarios. Y es el género *testimonio* el que habrá de oponerse con más fuerza y eficacia a esa enajenante literatura" (80) ("That reactionary literature is going to be roundly rejected by revolutionary writers and readers. And it is the testimonial genre that will oppose that alienating literature most strongly and effectively").

However, even within the new Cuba, and not least in light of the *caso Padilla* and the increasing success of the boom writers, there were also strong signs that the inferiority complex that characterized cultural colonialism had not been exorcized. For example, the social and ideological relevance of the genre was seen by some as more appropriate to the disciplines of politics, history, and sociology than to literature. A host of roundtables and commentaries in the 1970s and 1980s by practitioners, critics, and theorists of Cuban testimonial writing interrogated and ultimately defended the genre against accusations of *panfletismo* (propagandism). These included the "Mesa Redonda sobre el *testimonio*" 1983, published in *Revolución y Cultura* in 1983; Alberto Batista Reyes' "Los testigos cómplices," published in *El Caimán Barbudo* in the same year; and Ambrosio Fornet's "Mnemosina pide la palabra" in *Revolución y Cultura* in 1984. Víctor Casaus, in his aptly titled collection of essays *Defensa del testimonio* (*In Defense of Testimonio*), was clearly writing from a position of defensiveness as he outlined the unique characteristics of the genre and its undervaluation by the literary establishment. The essay (written in the 1970s), which gives the volume its name, for example, begins with an anecdote that illustrates the suspicion the genre had aroused among writers of literature. On reading one of Casaus' testimonial texts, Casaus' writer friend returned the manuscript with generally favorable comments, but then added: "Claro, este es un libro de servicio. Seguramente estás escribiendo también algo tuyo" ("Obviously, this is a commissioned work. No doubt you're also writing something for yourself") (45). In other words, the referential, external, and collective orientation of the genre had led critics to emphasize its conformity to sociocultural prescriptions articulated by the political establishment; moreover, the suspicions articulated by Craft in the late 1990s had already been anticipated in the context not only of pre-1959 literary conventions but also of the emerging profile of the boom writers. Undoubtedly, with the increased attention of the Soviet bloc to Cuba, the mistrust was additionally based on the fear that the phantom of socialist realism had once again appeared, this time in the form of testimonial writing.

In this sense, then, testimonial writing was seen contradictorily as the epitome of the new literature of Cuba, but also the "poor cousin" or the "official version," according to different voices in the debates of the 1960s and 1970s. Although the genre continued to gain prizes

"Un Híbrido de Halcón y Jicotea"

throughout the 1970s and 1980s, then, there was already a feeling that the *halcón* would overcome the *jicotea* once again, and the rising profile of magical realism, as it began to be translated into English, would lead to the rapid marginalization, ossification, and eventual demise of *testimonio*.

By the late 1980s and early 1990s, and with a different political landscape developing in the context of the end of the Cold War, the end of history, the move from left-wing radicalism to left-wing liberalism, and the post-structuralist turn in literary criticism, scholars such as Beverley attempted to underline that the importance of *testimonio* lay in its stance "against literature" (1993). While his important study was hugely instrumental in helping us understand how *testimonio* forced us to question the assumptions on which conventional literary genres were based, the possibility for the *jicotea* to be heard outside Cuba was quickly transforming into the salvational dream highlighted by Gugelberger in the 1990s. Meanwhile, the canonization of magical realism continued apace, prolonging the genre's status as a reaction to the local, nationalist, and regionalist realism of the first half of the twentieth century, and firmly embedding Latin American literature on a global scale as the metropolitan and even cosmopolitan view from Paris or Barcelona of the rural underbelly of Latin America.

Nevertheless, it may be more fruitful to view the evolution of both *testimonio* and magical realism as dialogic processes in the search for an authentic way of representing Latin America. While the metaphor of the *halcón* and the *jicotea* – the possibility of embracing hybridity – seemed at first to be of equal interest to proponents of both ways of writing Latin America, internal and external political, economic, and cultural forces, themselves played out in the context of the Cold War, radicalized both forms of writing. The much-examined *caso Padilla*, then, seen by some as a tipping point, can also be understood as no more than a visible landmark, the tip of the iceberg, in the complex collision and transition of literary and political projects.

Notes

1. All English translations are by the chapter author.

Works Cited

Barnet, Miguel. "La novela testimonio: Alquimia de la memoria," *La Palabra y el Hombre* 82 (1992): 75–78.

274 PAR KUMARASWAMI

"La novela testimonio: Socio-literatura." *La fuente viva*, 12–42. Havana: Editorial Letras Cubanas, 1983.

Biografía de un cimarrón. Havana: Academia de Ciencias de Cuba/Instituto de Etnología y Folklore, 1966.

Benedetti, Mario. *El escritor latinoamericano y la revolución posible*. Buenos Aires: Editorial Alfa Argentina, 1974.

"Situación actual de la cultura cubana." In *Literatura y arte nuevo en Cuba*. Miguel Barnet et al., pp. 7–32. Barcelona: Editorial Estela, 1971.

Beverley, J. "The Margin at the Center: On *Testimonio* (Testimonial Narrative)." In *The Real Thing: Testimonial Discourse and Latin America*. Ed. G. Gugelberger, pp. 23–41. Durham, NC : Duke University Press, 1996.

Casal, Lourdes. "Literature." In *Revolutionary Change in Cuba*. Ed. C. Mesa-Lago, pp. 447–469. Pittsburgh, PA: University of Pittsburgh Press, 1971.

Casaus, Víctor. *Defensa del testimonio*. Havana: Editorial Letras Cubanas, 1990.

Craft, Linda J. *Novels of Testimony and Resistance from Central America*. Gainesville: University Press of Florida, 1997.

Fernández Retamar, Roberto. "Hacia una intelectualidad revolucionaria en Cuba." In *Ensayo de otro mundo*, pp. 159–188. Havana: Instituto del Libro (Colección Cocuyo), 1967.

González de Cascorro, Raúl. "El género Testimonio en Cuba," *Unión* 4 (December 1978): 73–89.

Gugelberger, G. M., ed. *The Real Thing: Testimonial Discourse and Latin America*. Durham, NC: Duke University Press, 1996.

"Los intelectuales extranjeros: Declaración del Primer Congreso Nacional de Educación y Cultura, 30 de abril de 1971." In *Mon Informe secreto sobre la Revolución cubana*. Ed. C. A. Montaner, pp. 147–153. Madrid: Ediciones Sedmay, 1971.

Portuondo, José Antonio. *Estética y Revolución*. Havana: Ediciones Unión (Ensayo), 1963.

Retamar, Fernández. "Vanguardia artística, subdesarrollo y revolución." In *Estética y marxismo*. Ed. Adolfo Sánchez Vásquez, Tomo II, pp. 333–342. Mexico City: Ediciones Era, 1970.

Sklodowska, Elzbieta. "Spanish American Testimonial Novel: Some Afterthoughts." In *The Real Thing: Testimonial Discourse and Latin America*. Ed. G. Gugelberger, pp. 84–100. Durham, NC : Duke University Press, 1996.

"La visión de la gente sin historia en las novelas testimoniales de Miguel Barnet" (PhD thesis), Washington University, 1983, p. 5.

CHAPTER 17

Literature and Revolution in Transition
An Aesthetics of Singularity

Bruno Bosteels

Threshold

Transition is a strange critical term with which to approach the topic that I want to address in this chapter, that is, literature and revolution in Mexico. Hardly a label that writers would voluntarily ascribe to themselves, let alone a badge of honor to wear with pride as in the case of other period terms such as *modernismo* or the avant-garde, the term nonetheless can count on a respectable pedigree in two other fields of study to which literary and cultural criticism continues to be strongly indebted, namely philosophy and political theory.

On the one hand, modern European philosophy has struggled with the concept of transition from Hegel to Heidegger and beyond. For the author of the *Phenomenology of Spirit*, perhaps nothing is more characteristic of the power of the concept than its dialectical capacity for "going over" or "passing over" from one historical moment to the next in the uninterrupted forward march toward absolute knowing, while for the author of the posthumous *Contributions to Philosophy (Of the Event)*, the only task worthy of thinking consists in preparing the "leap" or "transition" into the "other beginning," that is, other than the "first beginning" of metaphysics with Plato and Aristotle. Even though in the first case the history of notional transitions is already supposed to have reached its end, while in the second the destination can only be intimated in silent glimpses of a future that is still to come, both scenarios revolve around a philosophy of history in which the logic of the transition is pivotal.

On the other hand, political theory since at least the early 1980s, especially in the Spanish-speaking world, has been busy defining the "transition to democracy" after decades of armed struggle and military dictatorships. Political theorists such as Guillermo O'Donnell in Argentina or José Joaquín Brunner and Norbert Lechner in Chile built much of their international reputation around the comparative study of the origins of the new authoritarianism and the wave of transitions to democracy in Latin America, while some of their compatriots such as León Rozitchner in Argentina or Nelly Richard and Tomás Moulian in Chile would go on to cast serious doubts upon the alleged purity of the break that would have occurred between the military regimes of terror and the democratic rule of law of the post-dictatorship.

In these reflections, whether philosophical or political, the category of transition works, even as an object of critical suspicion, because there exists an underlying consensus about the before and the after. With regard to the problems to be addressed in any theory of transition, O'Donnell observes: "The first of these problems revolves around some conceptual clarifications of the 'wherefrom' and the 'whereto' implied in the very idea of a process of political transition" (5, my translation). If political scientists are in agreement that the transition moves from military-bureaucratic authoritarianism to parliamentary democracy and if philosophers are preparing the leap from metaphysics into post-metaphysical thinking, however, no such consensus about the before and the after is likely to have been on the minds of the Latin American authors writing in the period of the mid-twentieth century who are the subjects of the present volume. On the contrary, we ought to accept that, at least in the field of literary studies, the very notion of transitional literatures is strictly speaking an invention of the critics. By and large, moreover, we are dealing with a posthumous invention, insofar as most of the writers under consideration have long passed away. But then the next question becomes: what exactly is supposed to define the before and after between which literary critics today are interested in situating a period of transition? And can the definition of this before and after shed light on the peculiar hopes and desires but also the deceptions and disappointments that speak through the newfound interest in the specificity of the period that lies in between?

My hypothesis in this regard holds that the period of the mid-twentieth century allows a growing number of critics retrospectively to uphold the ideals of a new aesthetic paradigm of singularity that obeys the rules of neither the realist-avant-garde tradition of the first two decades nor the experimental novel of the 1960s and 1970s in the so-called Boom. This also means that the before and after do not constitute the wherefrom and whereto of an actual transition; instead, the period of the midcentury is singled out as a potential alternative to the aesthetic programs of the realist-avant-garde and the Boom, now considered outdated and in need of a radical overhaul. In other words, the point of focusing on the literatures

Literature and Revolution in Transition 277

of transition is not just to include unduly forgotten names in the existing canon, following the same criteria available for the traditions that came before or after. Rather, in the process of reevaluating the literary production of the mid-twentieth century, it is precisely the aesthetic value system with which contemporary critics approach the texts of their choice that undergoes a profound mutation. But then, in an inevitable ricochet effect, this transformation in aesthetic sensibilities at the same time comes to impact the way in which a previously dominant political and ideological category such as the revolution – specifically, the Mexican Revolution for the realist-avant-garde tradition and the Cuban Revolution for the tradition of the experimental novel of the Boom – ends up being displaced if not completely transmogrified in the name of a new transitional aesthetic.

Behind the interest in transitional literatures, no less than in the case of the transitions dealt with in continental philosophy and political theory, there lurks another debate concerning the fate of the revolutionary ideal. Thus, thinking in the aftermath of the French Revolution and the National-Socialist Revolution, the world-historical shock of which they could not fail to absorb in their respective philosophies, Hegel and Heidegger each in their own way had to come to terms with a problem of transition. For the author of the *Phenomenology of Spirit*, this meant asking how the dialectic of history could continue after the senseless deaths of the Terror of 1793–4 in France; for the author of *Being and Time*, on the other hand, it meant taking a step back from the overly subjectivist and decisionist elements present in his own thinking that could have led him in 1933 to support the Nazi regime. But in the debates of political theory about the transitions from authoritarian rule, too, the underlying alternative between dictatorship and democracy entails a decisive if mostly unspoken displacement of the centrality of the reference to the revolutionary ideal. I would not go so far as to argue that the idea of the transition is anti-revolutionary by definition, but in the specific ways this category has been mobilized in philosophy, political theory, and now also in literary history and criticism, there can be no doubt that the sensibilities and desires have shifted away from the grandiose and world-historical elements associated with the revolutionary imagination toward the much more modest values of the singular and the site-specific.

To illustrate this shift in the realm of literature, I propose to take another look at Nellie Campobello's *Cartucho* (1931, second expanded and revised edition 1940; English translation in 1988 as part of *Cartucho and My Mother's Hands*) in order to study how the Mexican Revolution by the midcentury produced a singular aesthetic in the form of the unique short story, poetic vignette, or narrative sketch. My aim is to come to an understanding of how the collective revolutionary experience, both of what transpired and of what was transmitted, becomes singularized and receives a new aesthetic form. This process involves a violent segmentation of the common, in tandem with a no less forceful production of the singular. While Campobello, like Juan Rulfo in *El llano en llamas* (*The Burning Plain*, 1953) some twenty years after her, evidently taps into the resources of collective storytelling, the transformations to which they subject these oral materials conform to a process of aestheticization whose operating principle lies in producing an image of self-standing beauty or singularity rather than community. Literature, even when its topic is the personal, affective, or subjective aftermath of the Revolution, seems to run counter to the latter's supporting ideals of collectivization or communization. Even the most excruciating scenes of violence and death become transposed into well-rounded vignettes, as pointed and striking as bullets lined up in a cartridge belt. Similarly, the chain of oral storytellers is typically interrupted with the appropriation of orality on behalf of an individual author with a unique signature and instantly recognizable trademark style of writing.

In light of Campobello's *Cartucho* and, to a lesser extent, Rulfo's *El llano en llamas*, we might begin to wonder if there ever even existed anything like a "novel of the Mexican Revolution" to begin with: not only because their narrative sketches and short stories hardly can be considered novels but also because their modes of writing reveal that what we have learned or come to appreciate in the literature of the Mexican Revolution amounts rather to a narrative of the counter-revolution. As Horacio Legrás observes in a central chapter of his *Literature and Subjection* dedicated to "Literary Strategies in the Face of Revolution":

> Authors as diverse as Martín Luis Guzmán, José Vasconcelos, Agustín Vera, Rafael Muñoz, and Mariano Azuela, and later Juan Rulfo, Carlos Fuentes, and others, found it extremely difficult to compose anything other than condemnations of the movement. In their words, the revolution is resolved through a language of abjection and a whirlpool of whimsical decisions portrayed as the fruits of petty passion and unrestrained ambition. Most express such dismay at the lack of moral or ideological convictions involved in the revolution that one is forced to wonder in what sense these are novels *of* the revolution. (112–113)

What remains to be seen is how authors such as Campobello, whom Legrás together with a growing number of recent critics singles out for their ability to escape the clutches of the hegemonic machine for writing the

Literature and Revolution in Transition 279

Revolution in Mexico, become the preferred icons of a new transitional aesthetic on the basis of a series of categories such as singularity that in reality are anything but revolutionary.

Beyond the Mexican context, this line of questioning would have to be extended to see if the ideals of modern aesthetics, based on values of beauty and sublimity that themselves are rooted in a moral and ontological paradigm of autonomy and singularity, do not derive from historical and material processes that disrupt the continuum of social existence in favor of the disconnected lives of isolated individuals. What philosophically can be described as the epochal changeover from realism to nominalism in the scholastic sense thus coincides not only with the change of taste in literary forms from allegories to novels, as Jorge Luis Borges once suggested. It also further highlights and in retrospect casts doubt upon the source of the validity – whether moral, aesthetic, or ontological – of what we as critics and theorists today take to be the universal appeal of pure singularity.

Defeat

Earlier I used the hyphenated category of "realist-avant-garde" to describe the period before the transition. This may appear to have been a sign of indecision on my part, as if somehow I did not manage to keep my terms of literary history in order. For anyone trained in literary history, even if only in Fredric Jameson's Marxist version, the sequence was supposed to be straightforward at least for the past two centuries: romanticism, realism, naturalism, modernism, postmodernism. The historical avant-garde in this scheme was supposed to come after and in direct opposition to the conventional mimetic pacts of realism and naturalism. However, in order to understand the newfound appreciation that in recent years has befallen later authors such as Campobello as emblematic of transitional literatures, I believe it is important to grasp in what way an earlier classic such as Mariano Azuela's *Los de abajo* (1915–20, translated as *The Underdogs*) owes its canonical status precisely to a certain indecision within the novel between its realist tendencies and its experimental avant-garde techniques. This indecision is not the fault of the critic but belongs to the innovation of the text itself. More importantly, while its realist credentials allow the novel to lay claim to a certain proximity to the events of the revolution themselves that could be lived, so to speak, in real time (thus, before being rebaptized *novela de la revolución*, the original subtitle was *Cuadros y escenas de la revolución actual*, or *Frames and Scenes from the Current Revolution*), we should note that the technical experimentation that becomes increasingly radical in the novel's development corresponds historically speaking to the downward spiral of the revolutionary process.

Azuela's novel in fact combines what we might call a logic of incorporation with a logic of disintegration. By this I do not intend to refer only to the author's well-established doubts about the process of the revolution, or what he himself refers to as "mis resentimientos de derrotado," or "my feelings of resentment as defeated" (quoted in Ruffinelli 103, my translation). Rather, what interests me is the structure of the operations whereby the Mexican Revolution becomes a unified process that we can invoke as a historico-political referent in the first place. Especially in the first and longest of its three parts, the main ideological operation at work in *Los de abajo* consists in the creation of a passage from the individual to the collective, from family to nation, and from personal revenge to social justice. By contrast, no sooner does the Revolution show signs of decline and disintegration in the second and third parts than the reader begins to be bombarded with violent depictions of battle scenes in which it is no longer possible to make a whole out of the particular elements. Ironically, though, this is exactly the kind of fragmented and cinematographic writing that has been praised as the novel's greatest innovation: the experimental breakthrough that sets apart the better parts of *Los de abajo* from its otherwise outdated indulgence in a certain late-Romantic *modernista* taste for elaborate portrayals of the Mexican landscape. This suggests that we contemporary readers are better attuned to the style of the revolution in decline than to the verbosities of its upward momentum. Concomitant with this change in aesthetic sensibilities, however, there has occurred a profound change in the way in which we evaluate the success or failure of political movements in general. In fact, my basic hypothesis for understanding the value attached to the transitional literatures of the mid-twentieth century holds that these two processes must be seen as inextricably linked.

From today's vantage point, the passage from the particular to the universal still operative in Hegel's philosophy of history can be seen as having been interrupted not as the result of a contingent political failure but because of an inevitable structural impossibility. The problem, then, is no longer that the particular failed to be subsumed under a general ideological cause, because all such mechanisms of subsumption have now become suspect beyond repair, based on the idea that they betray the rights of the singular. When the revolutionary logic begins to break down, therefore, this no longer must be seen as a shortcoming to be remedied by an alternative political program at

Literature and Revolution in Transition

the level of the nation-state. Instead, such a breakdown in the eyes of many contemporary critics seems to lay bare the place where the prerogatives of difference and singularity may be asserted over and above all hegemonic desires.

In the literature of the Mexican Revolution, this radical change in perspective is perhaps nowhere more evident than in the renewed appreciation for the accomplishments of Campobello's *Cartucho: Relatos de la lucha en el Norte de México* (*Cartucho: Tales of the Struggle in Northern Mexico*). Though sometimes mistakenly referred to as a novel, this is a collection of relatively autonomous stories or vignettes, titled after the nickname of one of its many unknown heroes drawn from Pancho Villa's Northern Division. Based in part on recollections from her mother from when the author herself was barely a child or adolescent (depending on where we place the still uncertain year of her birth) during the cruelest stages of guerrilla warfare in Chihuahua between 1916 and 1920, *Cartucho* has only recently attracted widespread critical praise for its bold style and breathtaking concision. Theoretically savvy critics have exalted the collection's ability to sidestep the Revolution's overarching ideological ambitions in order to zoom in on the singular and often anonymous lives of those affected by the violence. For Jorge Aguilar Mora, in an extensive introduction to the most recent paperback edition, the fifty-something prose pieces of *Cartucho* thus evoke nothing so much as the general philosophical mood of our post-revolutionary times as Campobello draws her reader's attention to a minute detail here and a single gesture there. Without the intellectual's pretension to speak *for* or *on behalf of* them as the character of Luis Cervantes does in *Los de abajo*, these gestures and details restore the dignity of each and every existence touched by the Revolution. "They were dispossessed, they were scum, they were bandits, but nobody could take from them the dominion over their way of dying," Aguilar Mora comments, drawing a parallel with Rafael F. Muñoz's *¡Vámonos con Pancho Villa!* (*Let's Join Pancho Villa!*) published in the same year as *Cartucho*'s first edition. "Muñoz and Campobello, deviating their gaze away from power and toward the defeated bandits, knew how to return to the tragic destiny its singularity and its innocence. And its greatness" (24, my translation). And Legrás, expanding upon Aguilar Mora's interpretation, sees in this privileging of the immanence of a singular life a trend that would be uniquely in tune with contemporary theories of political autonomy not just from the state but from all projects to subsume the voices of the subaltern under the heading of some grand hegemonic cause.

However, instead of joining the chorus in solidarity with those who aesthetically sing the praises of the Revolution only at the moment of its political downfall, we could ask ourselves: at what cost for the cause of collective emancipatory action today do we celebrate the beauty of each of these singular gestures and laconic sayings of the defeated, the betrayed, or the convicted in the face of death? What is the violent prehistory hidden behind these close-ups, the heavy price ticket attached to their perceived dignity and autonomy, in a sense that is indistinguishably both moral and aesthetic?

Just as Azuela's style reaches breathtaking heights only in the wake of the Revolution's ideological breakdown, Campobello's repeated gesture of eternalizing the beauty of this or that unique detail in a character's resigned acceptance of his or her fate presupposes a complete reversal in the incorporative logic of the revolution. Here, contrary to what *Los de abajo* promised through the words of its intellectuals, we move back from nation to region to family: "By the year 1915 and after, the Revolution had turned from a civil war into a regional war, and worse, into a local war and even in a war between families" (Aguilar Mora 29, my translation). But this further implies that the aesthetic and ideological values being put forth devolve from the collective myth to the individual anecdote, from the meaningful totality to the isolated fragment, and from the process of subsumption under a universal cause to the exaltation of an unsubsumable singularity.

As the age of revolutions comes to an end and critical theory and philosophy begin to lay bare the aporias inherent in the intellectual's typical gesture of speaking for the subaltern, it is not surprising to see that the critical appeal of Campobello's stories skyrocketed to the point of becoming part of a new literary and artistic canon. "I think it is fair to say that the relentless assertion of local autonomy encapsulated in this eulogy of an unsubsumable particularity is the element that lies at the source of contemporary fascination with Campobello's work," Legrás observes about *Cartucho*. "The novel would thus work as the recovery of a singularity that has been left untouched by the busy scriptural machine of the revolution" (144). And about "Las cinco de la tarde," one of the *Cartucho*'s shortest narrations that is part of the section "Fusilados," the same critic adds:

> Nellie Campobello vindicates Villa in the singularity of experience, in the "this" or "that" of which history and literature know nothing, because they are born of their disavowal. What is an afternoon of the revolution – one already forgotten as Campobello writes – to the powerful discourses that order the brute facts of existence into the transcendentalism of a design? For the people who experienced the everyday of the revolution, as Campobello

Literature and Revolution in Transition 283

did, this afternoon is all they have. To narrate such an unsubsumable afternoon (to sustain the gap between the locally lived and narrative subsumption) offers the possibility of living the temporality of the event not from the perspective of an extra in the crowd, but as part of the unanimous and inalienable experience of the everyday. (146–147)

It is symptomatic of the larger problem that I want to address in these pages that Legrás repeatedly mischaracterizes *Cartucho* as a "novel" and on the other hand uses adjectives such as "unsubsumable," "intractable," "incommensurable," and "inalienable" to qualify the absolute singularity of the real that would be captured in Campobello's text. About the former mislabeling, we could repeat Aguilar Mora's mordant judgment when he recalls the similarly imprecise use of the term *novela* in Mexican literary criticism to describe texts as disparate as José Vasconcelos' *Ulises criollo* (*Native Ulysses*) or Martín Luis Guzmán's *Las memorias de Pancho Villa* (*The Memoirs of Pancho Villa*): "Literary criticism with aspirations of aesthetic purity or theoretical laziness has opted for the simplest misleading solution: to consider all these texts as 'novels'" (Aguilar Mora 14). But the use of adjectives is potentially even more revealing insofar as "inalienable," for instance, in the various declarations and constitutions that accompanied the bourgeois revolutions in France or the United States, more typically describes the political rights and freedoms of the individual than the demands of the collective. Thus, what we would obtain by turning to the transitional literatures that emerge at the end of the age of revolutions ironically would bring us back to the inalienable singularity of a life that would resist becoming dialectically subsumed or sublated into some grand collective project.

Instead of simply taking the value of these (mis)characterizations for granted, could we not further question the association of the novel with the singular and the concomitant (re)emergence of freedom and autonomy as the principal criteria for judging the merits of literary or aesthetic projects? What lies behind these summary judgments and associations?

Singularity

If we assume that the organizing principle of the modern novel coincides with a principle of individuation, the novel being the genre of the individual subject par excellence, we may ask ourselves: what are the historic conditions of existence for this aesthetic mode to emerge, together with the lyric poem, as the dominant literary forms of modernity in the West?

284 BRUNO BOSTEELS

No one described these presuppositions more succinctly if also still idealistically than Jorge Luis Borges in an *inquisición* or "inquiry" titled "De las alegorías a las novelas" ("From Allegories to Novels," first published in 1949 in *La Nación* before being included three years later in *Otras inquisiciones*). For the Argentine, the rise of the modern novel can be understood through the scholastic debates in the late Middle Ages between the *antiqui doctores* of realism, for whom universal ideas are somehow real, and the *moderni* of nominalism, for whom universals are conventions that at best exist in name only. With his typical flair for provocation, Borges goes so far as to propose a single year in which nothing less than modernity begins as the era of the individual subject who therefore no longer finds expression in allegory but has recourse to the narrative forms of the novel:

> The passage from the allegory to the novel, from the species to the individual, from realism to nominalism, required several centuries, but I shall attempt to suggest an ideal date when it occurred. That day in 1382 when Geoffrey Chaucer, who perhaps did not believe he was a nominalist, wished to translate a line from Boccaccio into English, *E con gli occulti ferri I Tradimenti* ("And Treachery with hidden weapons"), and he said it like this: "The smyler with the knyf under the cloke." (Borges 157)

Though he is right to point out that this process took several centuries, Borges fails to mention the material conditions under which individuals rather than species and genera begin to shine forth as value-laden entities in the first place. Yet the assumption that only individuals exist and always have existed is part of the general ideological illusion projected by the history of modernity in the West, whereby "modernity" no less than "the West" should be understood as euphemisms for the age of capitalism inaugurated in the violent process of what Marx discussed under the heading of "so-called primitive accumulation" (871–940). It is this process that gives rise to the historic phenomenon of isolated individuals who are, as Marx says, *Vogelfrei* – that is, free as a bird – but free mainly to sell their labor power. For this profoundly ambiguous process of the "freeing up" of individual labor to be possible, all previous bonds must be severed; peasants must be ripped from their lands and thrown en masse onto the burgeoning urban centers as a reserve army of disposable labor under the constant threat of unemployment so that new laws will have to be promulgated to keep them away from the life of crime, vagrancy, and idleness; and, in general, the commons will have to be enclosed according to the logic of private ownership – with the individual self henceforth constituting the first and most fundamental possession in a proto-Lockean fashion.

Literature and Revolution in Transition 285

Now, this process of primitive or originary accumulation ("so-called" because it would be better to speak of a process of dispossession and expropriation) also plays itself out in the domain of literary writing. In fact, actively contributing to the establishment of this very domain, especially in the Spanish-language tradition, it is what first gives rise to the structure of the modern novel and its mode of subjectivity in the form of the picaresque – with Lazarillo de Tormes, as John Beverley explains, being the prototypical figure of the petty delinquent roaming the streets and outskirts of Salamanca or Toledo, offering his services to one corrupt master after another at the risk of running into trouble with the law, and therefore explaining himself in the first-person singular to the standard-bearer of legal authority mentioned only as "Vuestra Merced" ("Your Honor").

Through the case of *Lazarillo de Tormes*, which he claims "*is* the first modern novel," Beverley proposes to show how the rise of the novel and the rise of capitalism are inextricably linked: "Lazarillo's Spain – and in a larger sense the whole social world of the early picaresque novel in Europe – offers a concrete instance of that general process of transition between the feudal and the capitalist modes of production which Marx called 'the primitive accumulation of capital'" (34). Beverley justifies this claim in terms that should reverberate throughout the history of the Mexican Revolution:

> Lazarillo is the product of that still familiar disintegration of the family unit as it passes from an agrarian milieu, where its functions and forms are consecrated by centuries of tradition, into the city life of a marginal sub-proletariat. His predicament presupposes a separation from agrarian community life and mutual aid systems like the *compadrazgo*; he is, from puberty onwards, "on his own." As such he constitutes a new form of freedom and mobility, but also of degradation, made possible by market society: the individual. (37)

To this provocative insight, two further hypotheses could be appended whose implications are potentially even more far-reaching for our understanding of the literatures of the transition. The first, already implicit in Beverley's argument, concerns the fact that this development entails an epochal change not only in the mode of production but also in the mode of subjection or subjectification, in a recurrent process that continues to this day. As Rosalind Morris observes:

> It is premised on the assumption that the separation of persons from the means of production is never fully accomplished at the level of the mode of

286 BRUNO BOSTEELS

production, and that instead this procedure must be recursively enacted within the lifetime of every person who is subjected *to* capitalism by being made a subject *of* capitalism – over and over again, in every generation. (30)

Capital, subject, and value, in other words, are the effects of a process of co-originary accumulation and expropriation. But they are effects that, as a result of this process, appear as if they were the spontaneous causes of themselves. "¡Válete por tí!" ("Value yourself!"), Lazarillo's mother exclaims, before sending him off to his first master, the blind beggar who promptly teaches his young apprentice a life lesson by hitting his head against the statue of a bull: "Parecióme que en aquel instante desperté de la simpleza en que como niño dormido estaba. Dije entre mí: 'Verdad dice éste, que me cumple avivar el ojo y avisar pues solo soy, y pensar cómo me sepa valer'" ("It appeared to me that in that moment I woke up from the simplemindedness in which I was slumbering as a child. I told myself: 'This much is true, that I must open my eyes and be alert, for I am on my own, and have to think how to make myself valuable'," my translation) (108–110). Here, not only does the child learn how to enter into the value relation of a new mode of production, but the value form itself becomes embedded in a new mode of subjection that, together with its dominant literary forms of expression, is being constituted at the same time.

How this process unfolds in the case of Campobello is something we can perceive in her own account of her discovery of the "freedom" and "technique" required to become a writer. I am referring to a small vignette in the prologue she wrote for the volume *Mis libros* (*My Books*) in which in 1960 she collected most of her writings:

> I felt my first breath of liberty one day when they straddled me on a horse. But do not think that I took off, no, I did not go running, but the horse simply went, step by step, walking around the interior patio of our old maternal house, and led by the bridle by someone whom I must have loved immensely. That walk, which only lasted for a few moments, made me feel an almost permanent security of well-being. I captured a new air, believing that I had been in an unknown world, immense and free. None of the direct stares of reproach, nor the psychological oppression, nor the fierce author-ity, nor the tight clothing, nor any other obstacle to the free action of my mental and physical movement could stop the impulse of feeling that I had the part of well-being that belonged to me. (340, my translation)

In Campobello's self-understanding, this passage functions as a kind of primitive scene of the author's subjectivization – her entrance as a child into a form of liberty of her own. Ever so slightly complicating the linear passage from allegories to novels, the fragment offers a mini-allegory of the

Literature and Revolution in Transition 287

coming into being of the free individual subject without which the structure and field of modern literature would not have been able to come into existence. This is a liberty that belongs to the author and defines her most intimate well-being, but it is a liberty gained within and against the constraints of a strict enclosure: the horse's bridle held by a beloved yet unnamed guide, the tight clothing, the moral judgment implicit in the eyes staring at her, and, above all, the physical and emotional confines of the maternal house's interior patio. But the scene also encapsulates the recursive effects of the process of primitive accumulation at the level of the child's individual subjectivity: her way of carving out, enclosing, and appropriating a free space for herself, as a result of which this freedom retrospectively acquires the appearance of an impulse that always already would have been there beforehand, ready to be set free, even though in a strange loop back upon itself it is actually the product of an intensely material and even physical process of segmentation and appropriation.

A second hypothesis to be appended to this discussion concerns not just the type of subjectivity inaugurated in the modern novel but the definition of aesthetic beauty in general as rooted in the violent origins of capitalist modernity – origins that are erased and forgotten in the same retroactive process whereby capital, subject, and value appear as autonomous apparitions of the magician's own making – like so many iterations of Munchausen pulling himself up from his own hair. This second hypothesis holds that the rebellious or rogue subject of modern literature, in the freedom of their self-valorization both inside and outside the system, presents us at the same time with the fundamental matrix of the liberty and autonomy of aesthetic beauty, which much later will become codified in the philosophy of Immanuel Kant.

In his *Critique of Judgment*, Kant in this regard distinguishes between two types of beauty, which he calls "merely adherent" (*bloss anhängende Schönheit*) and "free" (*freie Schönheit*), respectively, in Latin: *pulchritudo adhaerens* and *pulchritudo vaga*. As exemplary of the second type of beauty, which he considers the only pure and therefore true kind, Kant cites a cut flower; more specifically, a tulip. Not the botanical species, genre, or class of wildflowers but, here and now, *this* or *that* singular tulip. Jacques Derrida comments on this passage in *The Truth in Painting*:

> The tulip is not beautiful inasmuch as it belongs to a class, corresponding to such-and-such a concept of the veritable tulip, the perfect tulip. *This* tulip *here*, this one alone is beautiful ("a flower, for example a tulip"), it, the tulip of which I speak, of which I am saying here and now that it is beautiful, in front of me, unique, beautiful in any case in its singularity. . . . This is the

288 BRUNO BOSTEELS

> paradox (the class which-immediately-sounds the death knell of uniqueness in beauty) of the third *Critique* and of any discourse on the beautiful: it must deal only with singularities which must give rise only to universalizable judgments. (93)

Once we forgo the structure of interpellation whereby an individual incorporates themselves into the collective by somehow standing for the species, as in *Los de abajo*, what is left if not the unique beauty of the singular, as in the cases that make up the series that Nellie Campobello called "mis fusilados," hers to put into a class or series like *cartuchos* in a *cartuchera*, even though in each case the beauty or sublimity being sought after must be as unique as a singleton? And, given the style of Campobello's *Cartucho*, should we then be surprised that another section in Derrida's *The Truth in Painting* is called "Cartouches"? Whereas, during the upward movement of the Revolution, there may still have been a tension toward some higher end, as soon as the momentum shifts to fragmented instances of sheer violence and death, this tension is cut short like a flower: "But this tension, this vection, this rection is absolutely interrupted, with a clean blow. *It has to be* thus interrupted: by having to be, purely, absolutely, removing all adherence to what it cuts itself off from, it liberates beauty (free, wandering, and vague)" (Derrida 98). But what if this free, wandering, and vague beauty is not as pure or innocent as it seems? What if it is a type of beauty that shines forth only as the result of a centuries-long process of destruction of every bond or adherence that might connect life to its collective surroundings? What if this independence – the freedom of isolated singularities – is gained only at the price of a recursive process of expropriation and subjection? Does not the tradition of the picaresque, from which the modern novel is born, show us that behind every appearance of autonomous beauty, individuality, and singularity there lurks a process of originary destruction?

Shall we draw from this the sweeping conclusion that today, as we turn to the transitional literatures of the mid-twentieth century, we are still (or once again) imprisoned in the same moral, political, and aesthetic framework derived from the values and virtues of this "free" and "singular" beauty? We who are in the business of the "liberal arts," in this post-revolutionary age of ours defined by incredulity toward all projects for the subsumption of the particular under the universal, are we not still (or once again) enthralled by the beauty and dignity of a freestanding individuality – only now rebaptized with the philosophically dignified codename of singularity? And is the free-spirited subject of the modern novel, even when distilled and eternalized into the detail of a single scene or anecdote

Literature and Revolution in Transition 289

cut to the size of a minimal narrative sketch or short story, not still the quintessential expression of this aesthetic autonomy – free as a bird, detached as a clean-cut flower, or spent as the shell of a bullet used to execute the defeated revolutionaries?

Works Cited

Aguilar Mora, Jorge. "El silencio de Nellie Campobello." In *Cartucho: relatos de la lucha en el Norte de México*. Nellie Campobello, pp. 9–43. Mexico City:Era, 2000.

Anonymous. *La vida de Lazarillo de Tormes y de sus fortunas y adversidades*. Ed. Joseph V. Ricapito. Madrid: Cátedra, 1985.

Beverley, John. "'Lazarillo' and Primitive Accumulation: Spain, Capitalism and the Modern Novel," *The Bulletin of the Midwest Modern Language Association* 15:1 (1982): 29–42.

Borges, Jorge Luis. "From Allegories to Novels." In *Other Inquisitions, 1937–1952*. Trans. Ruth L. C. Simms, pp. 154–157. Austin: University of Texas Press, 1993.

Campobello, Nellie. "Prólogo a *Mis libros* (1960)." In *Obra reunida*, pp. 337–376. Mexico City: Fondo de Cultura Económica, 2007.

Derrida, Jacques. *The Truth in Painting*. Trans. Geoff Bennington and Ian McLeod. Chicago, IL: The University of Chicago Press, 1987.

Legrás, Horacio. *Literature and Subjection: The Economy of Writing and Marginality in Latin America*. Pittsburgh, PA: University of Pittsburgh Press, 2008.

Marx, Karl. *Capital: A Critique of Political Economy*. Vol. 1. Trans. Ben Fowkes. London: Penguin, 1976.

Morris, Rosalind C. "*Ursprüngliche Akkumulation*: The Secret of an Originary Mistranslation," *boundary* 2 43.3 (2016): 29–77.

O'Donnell, Guillermo. *Notas para el estudio de procesos de democratización política a partir del estado burocrático-autoritario (Documento de trabajo)*. Buenos Aires: Centro de Estudios de Estado y Sociedad, 1979.

Ruffinelli, Jorge. *Literatura e ideología: el primer Mariano Azuela (1896–1918)*. Mexico City: Ediciones Coyoacán, 1994.

CHAPTER 18

Divergence and Convergence
Avant-Garde Poetics in Twentieth-Century Spanish America and Brazil

Odile Cisneros

Literary historians have generally acknowledged certain key turning points in the development of innovative poetics in Latin America from the end of the nineteenth to the late twentieth century. Some transitions, while independent phenomena, took place almost simultaneously across the Spanish- and Portuguese-language contexts. For instance, Symbolism and Parnassianism, renewal trends from Europe, gave way to the radical emergence of Brazilian *Modernismo*. Likewise, Spanish American *Modernismo*, considered by many the region's literary declaration of independence from Europe, was challenged by the *Vanguardias*. In both cases, writers reacted to nineteenth-century models, mostly borrowed from Europe, developing avant-garde vocabularies adapted to their local context. These coincidences are remarkable if we consider that, for the most part, Spanish America and Brazil lacked sustained literary interaction. This lack of mutual awareness, as has been noted, is evident in the fact that Brazilian writers of the 1922 Week of Modern Art in São Paulo chose the term "Modernismo" to refer to their innovations, while in Spanish America that term had already been used in the nineteenth century by Rubén Darío, leader of a movement that had adopted Symbolism and Parnassianism, the main tendencies the Brazilian *Modernistas* were keen to counter. In the 1920s and 1930s, the *Vanguardias* and Brazilian *Modernismo* responded to historic and literary conditions that drove a similar search for innovation, displaying cosmopolitan, experimental, and contentious attitudes in their aesthetic production (Unruh 22–23).

The migration of European artistic and literary avant-gardes to Latin American contexts, which gave rise to the *Vanguardias* and *Modernismo*, was the catalyst for poetic innovation in the region for the better part of the twentieth century. After a brief examination of such avant-garde trends, this essay looks at the transitions or turning points in poetic innovation

290

from the 1930s to the 1980s, particularly those that fostered divergence and convergence in Brazil and Spanish America. Significantly, despite a similar enthusiastic embrace of European avant-garde experimental trends in the region, a major change occurred in the 1930s, when divergent receptions of Surrealism in Spanish America and Brazil meant the dominance of a discursive, less formally oriented lyric poetry in Spanish America. In contrast, with time, Brazil witnessed a preference for anti-lyrical, shorter forms employing spatial syntax and visuality, as opposed to Spanish America's partiality for formally traditional, *engagé* poetry. In a new transition, the postwar period up until the 1980s produced a convergence evident in poetic forms driven by constructivist tendencies. In the last quarter of the twentieth century, the neo-baroque, another transition signaling further convergence, gathered a plurality of experimental poetic practices that challenged and decentered traditional national and linguistic boundaries.

Vanguardias and *Modernismo*: Laying the Groundwork

Perhaps the most momentous turning point in poetic renewal worldwide took place in the years between the two world wars. Radical artistic groups in Europe questioned not only the preceding artistic movements but also, as Peter Bürger argues in *Theory of the Avant-Garde*, the very status of the work of art and the nature of artistic institutions. The aftershocks of the European avant-gardes were equally felt in Spanish America and Brazil. Between about 1922 and 1940, Spanish America saw "a period of radical and violent experimentation" (Quiroga 303). A plethora of experimental groups emerged, including *Estridentismo*, *Contemporáneos*, *Amauta*, *Ultraísmo*, *Martín Fierro*, *Revista de Avance*, and *Negrismo*. The situation in Brazil was similar: The Week of Modern Art, staged in São Paulo in February 1922, ushered in to *Modernismo*. Their common denominator was a rejection of the past and the embrace of new avant-garde vocabularies native to Europe yet transplanted to Latin American soil.

The movements were as ground-breaking as they were prolific. Hugo Verani notes that "[i]n Latin America, the *Vanguardia* included a remarkable constellation of poets who moved beyond established conventions toward radical linguistic and formal experimentation, aware of the inadequacy of traditional artistic means of communication, to reflect the complex, disjointed, and changeable world of the twentieth century" (118). In Spanish America, key figures such as Vicente Huidobro, Jorge Luis Borges, Oliverio

Girondo, César Vallejo, and Pablo Neruda exemplify these trends. Steeped in the European vanguards, Huidobro favored a constructivist and visual poetry that emphasized imagination over expression and representation. *Horizon carré* (1917) and four collections from 1918 that employed visuality, juxtaposition, and simultaneity (*Tour Eiffel* and *Hallali*, in French, and *Ecuatorial* and *Poemas árticos*, in Spanish) eventually gave way to his masterpiece, the long poem "Altazor o el viaje en paracaídas" ("Altazor or a Voyage in a Parachute," 1931). Jorge Luis Borges shared Huidobro's focus on creation when he established a chapter of the Spanish vanguard *Ultraísmo* in Buenos Aires. Poetry volumes such as *Fervor de Buenos Aires* (*Fervor of Buenos Aires*, 1923), *Luna de enfrente* (*Moon Across the Way*, 1925), and *Cuaderno San Martín* (*San Martín Chapbook*, 1929) were also steeped in the local – specifically, Buenos Aires – appropriating its vernacular for poetic purposes. Oliverio Girondo's *Veinte poemas para ser leídos en el tranvía* (*Twenty Poems to Read on the Streetcar*, 1922) and *Calcomanías* (*Stickers*, 1925) burst into a humorous, earthy celebration of urban life, while his later volume *En la másmedula* (*In the Moremarrow*, 1957) sought to dismantle and recreate language at the level of the word. César Vallejo, a key, paradoxical figure of the avant-garde, "denounced – but did not renounce – poetic experimentation and invention" (Verani 127). Efraín Kristal notes that Vallejo's masterpiece, *Trilce*, featured a kind of "jaggedly abstract writing ... full of non-sequiturs" that also experimented with the space on the page and transformed language (12). Though Neruda's work is seen as marking a transition in the avant-gardes, his own position in that movement, like Vallejo's, remains uncertain: "both poets spurned the frivolous traits of the -isms, but internalized the innovative techniques inherent to the various movements" (Verani 134). Neruda's early career as a love poet with *Veinte poemas de amor y una canción desesperada* (*Twenty Love Poems and a Song of Despair*, 1924) was followed by *Tentativa del hombre infinito* (*Venture of the Infinite Man*, 1926), where he charts the epic journey of a subject across time and space. Later collections, *Residencia en la tierra* (*Residence on Earth*, 1933), *Alturas de Machu Picchu* (*Heights of Machu Picchu*, 1944), and *Canto General* (1950), featuring expansive views of subjectivity and history in a discursive and more referential mode, came to garner him worldwide acclaim. His protean poetry would develop into an ever-renewing project that "features a radically different poetic modality, a disjointed, dissonant, and prosaic verse, flowing inward, self-reflexively, thus instituting a new diction in Latin American poetry" (Verani 136).

Movements in Mexico, the Caribbean, and Central America also witnessed the rise of new poetries that conveyed local and political themes via

Divergence and Convergence

experimental language. Manuel Maples Arce's urban-inspired poetry in *Andamios interiores* (*Inner Scaffoldings*, 1922) combined Cubism and Futurism with *épater-le-bourgeois* attitudes and was followed by the more politically aligned *Urbe: Super-poema bolchevique en 5 cantos* (*Metropolis*, 1924). Introduced in Cuba by the Spanish poet Juan Ramón Jiménez, pure poetry, an attempt to purify poetic language via abstraction, was embraced by Eugenio Florit, Emilio Ballagas, and Mariano Brull. Brull exploited sonic possibilities in his *jitanjáforas*, the closest thing to Dadaist sound poetry ever produced in Latin America. *Jitanjáforas* were also linked to a nationalist desire to foreground Afro-Cuban dance and music heritage, an interest shared by Nicolás Guillén, who inaugurated the trend known as *Negrismo*. He incorporated Afro-Cuban language and imagery in *Sóngoro cosongo* (1931) before moving into more politicized work. In Puerto Rico, Luis Palés Matos combined Afro-Antillean motifs with sound experimentation in *Tuntún de pasa y grifería* (1937), and in Nicaragua, the *Vanguardia* poets such as Pablo Antonio Cuadra irreverently broke with Darío's nineteenth-century *Modernismo*. Significantly, all these contexts converged in an avant-garde poetics that aimed to invent a national idiom.

In Brazil, Mário de Andrade and Oswald de Andrade led a similar charge within *Modernismo*, a movement that produced an exceptionally gifted generation of innovative poets and laid the groundwork for future poetic generations. A poet and a dynamic intellectual, in *Paulicéia desvairada* (*Hallucinated City*, 1922), Mário launched a home-grown poetics rooted in the European avant-garde transplanted to the modern metropolis of São Paulo. Oswald de Andrade, a cosmopolitan poet who lived briefly in Paris with his wife, the artist Tarsila do Amaral, devised a concentrated, irreverent collage form he called the *poema-piada* (poem-joke) in his collection *Pau Brasil* (*Brazilwood*, 1925). The "Manifesto da Poesia Pau-Brasil" ("Brazilwood Poetry Manifesto"), named after Brazilwood, the first commodity to be exported from Brazil, called for a "poetry for export." His tongue-in-cheek "Manifesto Antropófago" ("Cannibalist Manifesto," 1928) proposed an imaginative reversal of Native Brazilians' ritual cannibalism as anti-colonial aesthetics. Remarkably, the convergence in formal and political agendas in the Spanish American and Brazilian contexts happened in parallel, without significant cross-cultural contact. Ultimately, regardless of their wide geographical reach and endless variety, avant-garde poetic endeavors throughout the region also converged in their preoccupation with the renewal of vocabularies on a formal level as well as the incorporation of local realities.

The ideologically charged and at times playful poetic experimentalism of the 1920s largely fizzled out by the mid- to late 1930s, which ushered in

294   ODILE CISNEROS

a more discursive poetry, often linked to social and political concerns. The 1929 market crash, rising fascism in Europe, military coups, and the emergence of communist parties in Latin America are the historical circumstances surrounding this transition.

Divergence: The Varying Impact of Surrealism

Assessing the legacy of the Spanish American poets of the historical avant-gardes is no easy task. Huidobro, Vallejo, and Girondo were bold in their explorations of form, visuality, syntax, and lexicon, yet the poets of the following generation were mostly the heirs of Neruda and the discursive, metaphoric, and free-association style he developed. After Neruda's brief excursion into avant-garde techniques, his shift to the discursive long poem coincides with the advent of Surrealism in Latin America in the late 1920s and early 1930s. This transition marked an important divergence in the development of innovative poetics in the region. While Spanish America assimilated its influence widely for decades to come, Brazil's reception of Surrealism was at best lukewarm.

Surrealism's impact on Spanish American poetry is complex, varied, and difficult to chart. Early on, it provoked strong reactions. For instance, Huidobro's pioneering manifestos were written as a riposte to Breton, and, in Peru, José Carlos Mariátegui, founder of the avant-garde journal *Amauta*, fostered the dissemination of surrealist ideas, but his compatriot Vallejo wrote the scathing critique "Autopsia del superrealismo" ("Autopsy of Superrealism," 1930). Still, it touched many poets on a variety of levels, contexts, and moments, arguably creating an enduring legacy. Argentina, among other contexts, proved more welcoming. In Buenos Aires, Aldo Pellegrini founded the review *Que* (1928–30), which published the first self-avowed surrealist works, though its activity was short-lived. Braulio Arenas edited the journal *Mandrágora*, which generated another group in Chile in 1938. Meanwhile, Neruda, in *Residencia en la tierra* and beyond, made use of dream-like free association reminiscent of Surrealism but did not actually subscribe to the surrealists' technique of automatic writing. Latin America would not fully come under the sway of Surrealism for at least another decade.

The 1940s introduced a different poetic mood that in Spanish America was historically marked by the impact of the Spanish Civil War. There was a reaction to the rhetorical nature of Neruda by the poets originally gathered around the review *Contemporáneos* in Mexico. Particularly, Xavier Villaurrutia's *Nostalgia de la muerte* (*Nostalgia of Death*, 1938) and Jorge Gorostiza's *Muerte sin fin* (*Death Without End*, 1939) are considered landmark works that explore existential themes in the discursive style of Surrealism. Villaurrutia's *Nostalgia* touches on homoerotic desire, while Gorostiza's highly structured *Muerte* (with ten sections of ten parts each) broaches phenomenological questions of form and matter. Only the Peruvian César Moro, who lived in France and published in French, was a direct participant in the surrealist movement. In Mexico, where he befriended Villaurrutia and several artists, he also acted as promoter of surrealist art, organizing several exhibits. His volume *La tortuga ecuestre y otros poemas 1924–1949* (*The Equestrian Turtle and Other Poems*), published posthumously in 1957, delves into oneiric and homoerotic themes.

Emerging from the generation of *Contemporáneos*, Octavio Paz is the core figure that for decades came to define innovation in Spanish America. As a young man, Paz traveled to Spain in the midst of the Civil War to participate in the Congress of Anti-Fascist Writers, where he became acquainted with important figures of the avant-garde such as Huidobro, Neruda, and Vallejo. On his way back, he met the European Surrealists in Paris, including Benjamin Péret. In later sojourns in Paris as a diplomat, Paz befriended André Breton, who exerted a profound influence on him. Some early work includes the lyric poems of *Luna silvestre* (*Wild Moon*, 1933) and *Raíz del hombre* (*Root of Man*, 1937) as well as volumes devoted to the Spanish Republican cause. Initially, Paz was caught between the *Contemporáneos'* ambivalent attitude toward Surrealism and the social commitment and nationalist ideals espoused by his review *Taller* (1938–41). *Libertad bajo palabra* (*Freedom Under the Word*, 1949), which Paz considered his "true first book," began to explore more distinctly a poetics allied to Surrealism (including the unconscious and eroticism), along with meditations on history and Mexican identity. Over the course of his life, Paz republished several heavily revised editions of *Libertad bajo palabra*, where he included other works such as the prose poems *¿Águila o sol?* (*Eagle or Sun?*, 1951) and *Piedra de sol* (*Sunstone*, 1957).

Piedra de sol's title refers to the Aztec calendar, a carved stone on display at Mexico City's Museum of Anthropology. A veritable tour de force, the poem's 584 hendecasyllabic lines allude to the days in the synodic cycle of the planet Venus, a significant astronomical phenomenon in ancient Mesoamerica. Though following a metrically traditional form and referencing Mexico's pre-Columbian past, *Piedra de sol* signals Paz's unambiguous endorsement of Surrealism in its free-association assembly of oneiric images and its exploration of the erotic, time, history, and the artistic vision. In *Piedra de sol*, Paz embraced what he saw as the great Spanish American tradition of the long poem as practiced by Huidobro, Neruda, Villaurrutia,

296   ODILE CISNEROS

and Gorostiza. With this gesture, Paz also deliberately inscribed himself in a lineage of world modern poets such as Pound, Eliot, Stevens, Apollinaire, Saint-John Perse, Pessoa, and Mayakovski. His adoption of Surrealism likewise served as a model for a younger generation of poets in Latin America, particularly the Argentines Juan Gelman, Enrique Molina, Olga Orozco, and Alejandra Pizarnik. Emerging from a different poetic lineage, other Spanish American poets coming of age in this period include Alberto Girri, Jaime Sabines, Cintio Vitier, and Roberto Juarroz.

The concurrent developments in Brazil mark a divergence from the Spanish American context. The 1930s in Brazil, a period critics associate with the second phase of Brazilian *Modernismo*, saw important lyric poets such as Manuel Bandeira, Cecília Meireles, and Carlos Drummond de Andrade come into their own. Drummond's *Alguma poesia* (*Some Poems*, 1930) is noteworthy for its recourse to the *poema-piada* and the quotidian in search of transcendence. A gradual change of mood characterized by introspection and a preoccupation with universal themes (Pontiero 254–256), coupled with a diminished drive for innovation, effectively brought *Modernismo*'s "heroic phase" to a close.

The 1940s ushered in the consolidation of the Vargas administration and, in literary terms, another divergence from the experimentalism of preceding years. *Modernismo*'s radical linguistic experimentation ended with Mário de Andrade's untimely death in 1945. A new world order emerged at the end of World War II, affecting poetic sensibilities and producing a renewed emphasis on form. The traditionalist *Geração de 45*, headed by Lêdo Ivo, editor of the journal *Orfeu* (*Orpheus*), retrenched from *Modernismo*'s free-wheeling innovation. Also, unlike their Spanish American counterparts who embraced open, free-association forms, the Brazilian poets of this generation called for a return to structure, the sonnet, in particular, signaling "a triumph of *poematic* form, as opposed to the looser poetic formats of the *modernista* tradition" (Merquior 377). They also abandoned the combative nationalist spirit of 1922, espousing instead more timeless and universal concerns.

From the perspective of Surrealism's impact, from the 1930s into the 1940s, Brazilian poetry charted a course that diverged from Spanish America's. The surrealist style was adopted by only a few poets in Brazil. Some inkling of Breton's ideas on the power of the unconscious had filtered through into Oswald de Andrade's *Revista de Antropofagia* in the late 1920s, but only Jorge de Lima and Murilo Mendes came to effectively embrace the style. Mendes's first book, *Poemas* (*Poems*, 1930), reveals dreamlike qualities associated with Surrealism. His conversion to Catholicism in

Divergence and Convergence 297

1934, in a period of intense political turmoil, set him apart from other writers who turned instead to leftist causes. He found kinship in a fellow Catholic, Jorge de Lima, with whom he collaborated on *Tempo e eternidade* (*Time and Eternity*, 1935), confessional poems addressing aesthetic concerns. Other works in this mode include *A poesia em pânico* (*Poetry in Panic*, 1938), a record of Mendes's struggle with conflicting religious and poetic loyalties, and Lima's biblically inspired *A túnica inconsútil* (*The Seamless Tunic*, 1938). The works that would come to seal these two poets' reputations would be Mendes's *Poesia Liberdade* (*Poetry Freedom*, 1947), where he explores a pessimistic outlook, and Lima's *Invenção de Orfeu* (*The Invention of Orpheus*, 1952), an ambitiously long poem incorporating material from classical authors.

Mendes and Lima's surrealist poetry was, however, the exception. Surrealism was but one of two main poetic tendencies at the time in Brazil, and certainly not the one that eventually came to dominate, a clear divergence from the situation in Spanish America. As José Guilherme Merquior argues, the "vatic neo-Cultism of the later Jorge de Lima and the cool, objectivist quatrains of [João] Cabral [de Melo Neto] both [remain] largely alien to Spanish American trends at the same time, despite all the common denominators in terms of Surrealism or [Nicanor Parra's] 'anti-poetry'" (377). Although Merquior is right to point to the divergence in poetic tendencies between Brazil and Spanish America in this period, he also seems to suggest a degree of affinity between the surrealist-influenced poems practiced by Lima and long poems such as Paz's aforementioned *Piedra de sol* (1957). He likewise points to a parallel between Cabral's anti-lyrical stance and Nicanor Parra's debunking of poetry in *Poemas y antipoemas* (*Poems and Anti-Poems*, 1954). However, Parra's self-ironic posture admittedly differs in mood from Cabral's hard-edged poems. In all, Surrealism seems to have been the main driver of innovation in Spanish America from the 1920s and 1930s through the postwar period and into the 1960s. The long poem and oneiric associative poetics left a powerful mark on the region, from the poets of *Contemporáneos* to Octavio Paz, passing through César Moro. Brazil proved a less fertile ground for Surrealism, influencing important figures such as Lima and Mendes, but not effectively charting the course for subsequent innovators such as João Cabral de Melo Neto.

Convergence: Formalist and Political Concerns

In contrast with the divergent reception of Surrealism by Spanish American and Brazilian poetry in the postwar period, there were instances

298   ODILE CISNEROS

where the agendas also converged. We see this in the case of experimental-
ists whose formalist and political concerns came together either through
direct contact, as was the case of concrete poetry, or independently, as with
João Cabral de Melo Neto in Brazil and Nicanor Parra in Chile. The most
important innovator to emerge from Brazil in the 1940s, Cabral was
responsible for a transition away from the *Geração de 45*. *Pedra de sono*
(*Stone of Sleep*, 1942), an early work, adopts a quasi-surrealist diction he
soon abandoned in favor of calculated poetic form. Cabral hailed from
Pernambuco in northeastern Brazil, a region of arid landscapes known as
the *sertão*, and his poems often thematically evoke the plight of its impoverished inhabitants in an unsentimental way. Cabral was indeed greatly
concerned with the mechanics of a clear and precise poetry, a hard and
sharp "poetry of things," emblematized by the figures of the stone and the
knife-edge. *O engenheiro* (*The Engineer*, 1945) and *Psicologia da composição*
(*Psychology of Composition*, 1947) evince Cabral's distinct anti-lyrical and
constructivist poetics that came to influence postwar literary movements in
Brazil, notably concrete poetry. He also drew from popular forms, to
which he brought new life: the play *Morte e vida severina* (*Life and Death
of a Severino*, 1955) employs the heptasyllabic meter and style of popular
cordel literature to portray a Northeastern migrant's journey in search of
a better life, and, in an homage to the medieval Spanish poet Gonzalo
Berceo, *Quaderna* (1960) alludes to *quaderna vía*, the popular four-line
stanza characteristic of Berceo's work.

Cabral came to formally revolutionize the poetic landscape in a way
that parallels Nicanor Parra's break with a less form-oriented tradition in
Spanish America. A physicist and mathematician by training, Parra came
into contact with the surrealist group *Mandrágora* early in his career. His
first collection, *Cancionero sin nombre* (*Nameless Ballads*, 1937), which
echoes Federico García Lorca's *Cancionero gitano* (*Gypsy Ballads*, 1928)
and which Parra later disowned, was influenced by surrealist poetry.
Published seventeen years later, *Poemas y antipoemas* (1954) was a turning
point for Chilean poetry. Parra's iconoclastic *antipoesía* reacted to
Huidobro's lofty experimentalism, Gabriela Mistral's traditionalism,
and Neruda's elevated rhetoric. He adopted everyday topics in a more
colloquial, conversational language and spurned the view of the poet as
visionary. His use of Chileanisms and words in Indigenous languages also
points to a rejection of a poetry he saw as overly dependent on foreign
models, including Surrealism. Still, as Nicholson notes, his poetic practice was marked by some of Surrealism's ideals of freedom (189–190). In
1952, with the poets Enrique Lihn and Alejandro Jodorowsky, Parra also

engaged in a short-lived experiment in visual poetry titled *Quebrantahuesos*. They created collages of newspaper headlines and exhibited them in shop windows and other public places. These compositions did not aim at the unexpected or poetic so dear to the surrealists, but rather at humorous and coarse effects. A subsequent project similarly focused on the material, *Artefactos* (*Artifacts*, 1972), consisted of tongue-in-cheek poems printed on postcards. Parra developed an idiosyncratic, irreverent style that also embraced a black sense of humor. Other works in this vein include *La cueca larga* (1958) and *Versos de salón* (1962). Parra lived to the ripe old age of 103, and, in his long career, his poetry developed in different directions but retained some characteristics of his work of the 1950s.

Another convergence emerged in the late 1950s and 1960s, during a transition marked by the waning influence of Surrealism in Spanish America and the growing formalist concerns of Brazilian poets. I noted above how, at the time Octavio Paz was making his forays into Surrealism in the late 1940s and early 1950s, Brazil's poetic landscape was moving toward a very different conception of poetry. Whether it was the *Geração de 45*'s revival of traditional forms such as the sonnet or Cabral's original, unadorned "poetry of things," the general direction of Brazilian poetry was formalist. Following the high point of *Piedra de sol*, Paz's Surrealism took a radical turn in *Blanco* (1967), a simultaneist poem where he also incorporates the visual. Printed on a single long folded sheet, *Blanco* is made up of three distinct columns in different fonts and colors that can generate multiple poems and readings. *Blanco* not only became a touchstone of the avant-garde, but, as we will discuss, it also served as a catalyst for contact with concrete poetry, Brazil's most radical poetic innovation in the postwar period.

Taking Cabral's lapidary poetics to heart, concrete poetry burst onto the Brazilian poetry scene in the 1950s, taking it by storm. In 1952, the Campos brothers, Haroldo and Augusto, along with Décio Pignatari, founded the experimental poetry journal *Noigandres*, and in 1956 they joined the first exhibition of concrete art held in São Paulo's Museum of Modern Art. In 1958 they issued the manifesto "Plano-piloto para poesia concreta" ("Pilot Plan for Concrete Poetry"), where they launched a poetic program based on the staples of the international avant-gardes (Mallarmé, Pound, Joyce, and Apollinaire) and Brazilian masters (Cabral and Oswald de Andrade) but adapted to a new era of mass communication and cybernetics. The opening lines daringly declared the "historical cycle of verse" as "closed," calling for its replacement by an ideogrammatic syntax and verbi-voco-visual signs. Concrete poetry foregrounded the constructed nature of the

300   ODILE CISNEROS

poem, the disappearance of the lyrical "I," and the materiality of language, among other features. The concrete poets also brought Brazil into contact with other postwar avant-gardes in Germany, Switzerland, Britain, and Japan, effectively realizing Oswald de Andrade's dream of a "poetry for export."

The concrete poets' experimentation with graphic space and other material properties of language led to a revolution in Brazilian poetry that soon gained many followers. Two journals, *Noigandres* (1952–62), named after a mysterious Provençal word in Ezra Pound's *Cantos*, and *Invenção* (*Invention*, 1962–7), were the main forums of their poetic production. Haroldo de Campos's works were later gathered in *Xadrez de estrelas* (*Chess of Stars*, 1976). *Poetamenos* (*Minuspoet*, 1954) was Augusto de Campos's first book of concrete poetry, printed in color and inspired by Anton Webern's *Klangfarbenmelodie*. Other concrete poems by Augusto first published in various little magazines were collected in *Viva vaia* (1979) and *Despoesia* (*Dispoetry*, 1994). A tireless innovator, Augusto went on to experiment with other media such as billboards, videotext, neon, hologram and laser, computer graphics, and multimedia events. Décio Pignatari, who first published in a journal associated with *Geração de 45*, joined the Campos brothers in 1952 and became a key promoter of concrete poetry at home and abroad. His poems, scattered in journals, were published eventually as *Poesia pois é poesia 1950/1975* (*Poetry Thus Is Poetry*, 1977) and *Poesia pois é poesia e Po&tc 1976/1986* (*Poetry Thus Is Poetry and Po&tc*, 1986). Theoretical texts on concrete poetry were gathered in the collectively authored *Teoria da Poesia Concreta* (*Theory of Concrete Poetry*, 1965). Though the impact on Spanish America of this type of tendency was minimally felt at the time, the relationship the *Noigandres* poets built with Octavio Paz is noteworthy. Haroldo corresponded with Paz regarding his interest in translating Paz's *Blanco*. The correspondence led to Haroldo's translation *Trans-Blanco* (1984) and a poem series Paz titled *Topoemas* (*Topoems*, 1968), an homage to, among others, Haroldo de Campos and the young Brazilian poets of *Noigandres*.

The formally revolutionary poetics of concrete poetry also generated splinter groups and resistance from poets who sought a firmer commitment to political concerns. This transition again produced a convergence with *engagé* poets in Spanish America. From 1955 to 1957, Ferreira Gullar participated in the movement started by Augusto de Campos and Haroldo de Campos. He broke off with concrete poetry, inaugurating neo-concretism, a trend seeking a more participatory poetics. Both the Cuban Revolution in 1959 and the military coup in Brazil in 1964 are the

Divergence and Convergence

historical and political backdrop to the developments in these years of polarization and convulsion. Gullar actively engaged in cultural politics, eventually going into exile in Argentina, where he wrote his most important work, *Poema sujo* (*Dirty Poem*, 1976). In this 2,000-line poem, while preserving some of concrete poetry's material play, Gullar denounces political persecution and evokes his youth in Maranhão. Gullar's *engagé* poetry finds a relative parallel in the revolutionary lyric of the Salvadoran Roque Dalton and the Nicaraguan modernist epics of Ernesto Cardenal.

Alongside highbrow poetic innovation, starting in the 1970s and in sync with cultural resistance movements, a popular and revolutionary art also emerged throughout Latin America. In this vein, *Violão de rua* in Brazil to an extent parallels *Nueva canción* in Argentina, Chile, Cuba, and Uruguay. The Brazilian counterculture movement *Tropicália*, led by the pop musicians Caetano Veloso and Gilberto Gil, was contemporaneous to the popular poetry of *Poesia marginal*. Characterized by cheap or mimeograph printing and low-brow topics geared at controversy, *Poesia marginal* included poets such as Glauco Mattoso, Ana Cristina César, Paulo Leminski, and Francisco Alvim.

From the 1940s to the 1970s, thus, we witness convergence in formal and political concerns in both contexts. João Cabral de Melo Neto's antisentimental focus on form mirrors Nicanor Parra's self-deprecating *antipoesía*, which rejected the lyrical and rhetorical tradition of his compatriots Huidobro, Mistral, and Neruda. This convergence did not necessarily imply interaction, but in the case of Octavio Paz in Mexico and the concrete poets in Brazil, Haroldo and Augusto de Campos, and Décio Pignatari, there was mutual awareness and exchange. This led to productive dialogue and mutual influence. A further convergence, this time in political terms, can be seen in subsequent *engagé* poets emerging from Brazilian concretism, as the aforementioned case of Ferreira Gullar's poetry which mirrors the political concerns of Central Americans like Dalton and Cardenal. Both contexts also spawned fertile popular politically oriented poetry and song movements.

Convergence Redux: The Neo-baroque

Going in a different direction, when the "high-definition" era of Brazilian concrete poetry was winding up, Haroldo de Campos began the first drafts of what would arguably become his most original and innovative work, *Galáxias* (1984). A clear transition from brief texts employing purely visual or spatial syntax, *Galáxias* is a long prose poem that experiments instead with the uninterrupted flow of language. Divided into fifty cantos printed on a single side of the page, *Galáxias*, in the guise of a travel log, deploys a poetics that experiments with sound, morphology, allusion, syntactic ambiguity, and multilingualism, following the lead of Joyce's *Finnegans Wake*. Though an independent development, *Galáxias* partakes in, and converges with, the most compelling innovation to emerge in the complex and diverse landscape of Spanish American poetry from the 1970s and into the 1990s: *el Neobarroco* (the neo-baroque). The poetics of the neo-baroque reach back to Golden Age Spain, particularly Luis de Góngora, via Lezama Lima's complex and highly ornate rhetoric. To understand the neo-baroque, we must return to the scene of origin – the vanguard movements of the 1920s and 1930s.

A fundamental figure to arise in Cuba in the late 1930s and early 1940s, José Lezama Lima shared an admiration for Juan Ramón Jiménez's poetry with poets such as Ballagas and Brull, but his own work took a very different course than their *jitanjáforas* and abstraction-inspired work or, for that matter, Guillén's *Negrista* poetry. *Muerte de Narciso* (*Death of Narcissus*, 1937), a personal retelling of the Greek myth written when Lezama was twenty-two, marked the beginning of a new rhetorical style full of classical allusions, elaborate metaphors, and complex syntax. *Enemigo rumor* (*Enemy Rumor*, 1941) contained shorter poems that dealt with the nature of poetic creation and carried on his exploration of a style inspired by Spanish Golden Age poetry and the New World baroque. Lezama, as did Alejo Carpentier, identified the baroque with the cultural liberation of the Americas, a topic broached in Lezama's essay *La expresión americana* (1957). Lezama was also the chief animator of the group gathered around the review *Orígenes* (1942–56), one of the main conduits of Cuban literary and cultural life for more than a decade. His semiautobiographical poetic novel *Paradiso* (1966) is arguably his masterwork and the culmination of his neo-baroque aesthetics.

Building on Lezama Lima's theorization and adoption of the baroque as a New World aesthetic, the neo-baroque first appeared self-consciously in Severo Sarduy's experimental novel *Cobra* (1972) and his essay *Barroco* (*Baroque*, 1974). An avid reader of Lezama, Sarduy exiled himself in France after the Cuban revolutionary government came to power. He participated in the avant-garde group *Tel Quel*, also assimilating their (post)structuralist sensibilities. Combining elements of the baroque in a postmodern context, neo-baroque writing is expansive: it revels in proliferating and exploiting (and exploding) the possibilities of the signifier, which ultimately remains inaccessible. The neo-baroque enacts a dynamic play of signifier and signified, where syntax has been restored yet powerfully altered. The

Neobarroso – as the Argentine Néstor Perlongher later dubbed it, alludes to the mud of the River Plate, where it also had a controversial presence. It is characterized by a language that "'abandons' (or relegates) its communicative function, to unfold instead as pure surface, thick and iridescent, that 'shines in itself': 'literatures of language' that betray language's purely instrumental, utilitarian function to gloat over the meanders of sound and sense" (Perlongher 22). Preceded by *Transplatinos* (*Transplatinians,* 1990) and *Caribe transplatino* (*Transplatinian Caribbean,* 1991), *Medusario* (*Medusary,* 1996) is the most important collection of neo-baroque poetry, bringing together Spanish- and Portuguese-language poets from many countries in Latin America. With Lezama Lima as tutelary spirit, *Medusario* includes work by Gerardo Deniz, Rodolfo Hinostroza, José Carlos Bezerra, David Huerta, Mirko Lauer, Arturo Carrera, Marosa di Giogio, Raúl Zurita, Marco Antonio Ettedgui, Tamara Kamenszain, Eduardo Milán, Oswaldo Lamborghini, Haroldo de Campos, José Kozer, Roberto Echavarren, Wilson Bueno, Néstor Perlongher, Coral Bracho, Reynaldo Jiménez, Eduardo Espina, Gonzalo Muñoz, and Paulo Leminski. *Medusario* marks perhaps the last and most important turning point in Latin American poetry at the close of the twentieth century.

Conclusion

The rich poetic experimentalism of the Latin American avant-gardes of the 1920s and 1930s no doubt provided the ferment for many innovations in the subsequent decades. Their varying fates, however, can give readers pause. In Spanish America, achievements such as *Altazor, Trilce,* and *En la masmédula* remain unsurpassed. Other innovations, as the case of Borges shows, were abandoned or disavowed, with further poetic production turning away from experimentation yet forging new paths. José Quiroga argues that although Borges' poetry "seems to deny the fractured history of modernity . . . it is this disfigurement that most powerfully situates Borges as Spanish America's most modern poet" (317). Brazilian *Modernismo*'s experimentalism, in turn, proved an enduring poetic model and inspiration, surviving past the postwar period and inspiring the innovations of concrete poetry.

In this broad panorama, certain patterns emerge that allow us to make sense of poetic developments in the contexts of both Spanish America and Brazil. The heroic avant-gardes gave way to the 1930s' change in poetic mood – in Spanish America, more political; in Brazil, more inward-looking. Surrealism marked a transition from the 1930s on, and the way it was received generated divergence in the poetries of Spanish America and Brazil. Convergence in terms of formalist and political concerns was evident, particularly in the work of Cabral and Parra. Innovation reached a new high point emblematized by the dialogue between Octavio Paz and concrete poetry from the late 1950s on. But it was Lezama Lima's revival of baroque poetry that would generate the neo-baroque, another point of convergence and perhaps the most wide-ranging renewal in the decades that followed.

For the Uruguayan Roberto Echavarren, neo-baroque poetry is a reaction to both the avant-garde (from Huidobro to Girondo to Octavio Paz), which focused on image and metaphor, and the Nerudian tradition of *engagé* colloquialism, where the referent is paramount for its political value (Echavarren 11–14). The tensions in Spanish American and Brazilian poetic innovation between expression and formalism, visionary poetics and the foregrounding of language, are embodied in the neo-baroque, which is less a school than a shared sensibility. It also shed the weight of militancy and ideology, replacing it with playfulness and eroticism. Geographically, the neo-baroque also brought into productive dialogue the largely disconnected (or at least frequently disparate) poetic worlds of Brazil and Spanish America. Though the paths of innovation in the region may still wander away from each other, the neo-baroque illustrates Merquior's hope for dialogue, a "Latin American unity [that] lies in the future" as a fortunate "case of convergence within diversity" (382).

Works Cited

Bürger, Peter. *Theory of the Avant-Garde: Vol. 4. Theory and History of Literature.* Minneapolis: University of Minnesota Press, 1984.

Echavarren, Roberto. "Prólogo." In *Medusario: Muestra de poesía latinoamericana,* pp. 11–17. Mexico City: Fondo de Cultura Económica, 1996.

Kristal, Efraín. "Introduction." In *The Complete Poetry: A Bilingual Edition.* César Vallejo and Clayton Eshleman, pp. 1–20. Berkeley: University of California Press, 2007.

Merquior, José Guilherme. "The Brazilian and the Spanish American Literary Traditions: A Contrastive View." In *The Cambridge History of Latin American Literature, Volume 3: Brazilian Literature; Bibliographies.* Eds. Roberto Gonzalez Echevarría and Enrique Pupo-Walker, pp. 363–382. Cambridge: Cambridge University Press, 1996.

Nicholson, Melanie. *Surrealism in Latin American Literature.* New York: Palgrave Macmillan, 2013.

Divergence and Convergence

Perlongher, Néstor. "Prólogo." In *Medusario: Muestra de poesía latinoamericana.* Eds. Roberto Echavarren, José Kozer, and Jacobo Sefamí, pp. 19–30. Mexico City: Fondo de Cultura Económica, 1996.

Pontiero, Giovanni. "Brazilian Poetry from Modernism to the 1990s." In *The Cambridge History of Latin American Literature, Volume 3: Brazilian Literature; Bibliographies.* Eds. Roberto Gonzalez Echevarría and Enrique Pupo-Walker, pp. 247–268. Cambridge: Cambridge University Press, 1996.

Quiroga, José. "Spanish American Poetry from 1922 to 1975." In *The Cambridge History of Latin American Literature, Volume 2: The Twentieth Century.* Eds. Roberto Gonzalez Echevarría and Enrique Pupo-Walker, pp. 303–364. Cambridge: Cambridge University Press, 1996.

Unruh, Vicky. *Latin American Vanguards: The Art of Contentious Encounters.* Berkeley: University of California Press, 1994.

Vallejo, César. *The Complete Poetry: A Bilingual Edition.* Trans. Clayton Eshleman. Berkeley: University of California Press, 2007.

Verani, Hugo. "The Vanguardia and Its Implications." In *The Cambridge History of Latin American Literature, Volume 2: The Twentieth Century.* Eds. Roberto Gonzalez Echevarría and Enrique Pupo-Walker, pp. 114–137. Cambridge: Cambridge University Press, 1996.

CHAPTER 19

Cortázar's Transitional Poetics
Experiments in Verse behind Experiments in Prose

Marcy Schwartz

The camera follows him walking in Paris through iconic neighborhoods, and just after a stroll through the Galérie Vivienne, where half of his story "El otro cielo" ("The Other Heaven") takes place, Julio Cortázar pauses on the street in front of a wall covered with posters and flyers. He comments, "esta cantidad de carteles, de afiches que se van amontonando . . . para mí tiene algo siempre de mensaje, como una especie de poema anónimo porque ha sido hecho por todos, por montones de pegadores de carteles que fueron superponiendo palabras, que fueron acumulando imágenes" ("such an enormous number of flyers, of posters that pile up one on top of the other . . . for me it always sends something of a message, like a sort of anonymous poem because it's been written by everyone, by a ton of people posting signs that ended up overlapping words, accumulating images") (Bauer).[1]

This unexpected encounter with the poetry of urban public space in this scene from the 1994 documentary *Cortázar* by Tristán Bauer introduces a cluster of Cortázar's vision of poetry. He posits an individual reader's experience rooted not only in the verbal material of the text but also in the messages and colors, the context or setting that surrounds them. In the introduction to his poetry collection *Pameos y meopas*, Cortázar admits to his hesitation about publishing his poems, considering them "marginal," too intimate; before publishing them, "se me fueron quedando en los bolsillos del tiempo" ("they ended up stuck in the pockets of time") (8). But later he affirms that "la poesía está cada vez más en la calle . . . en el lenguaje de las tizas en los muros" ("poetry appears more and more in the street . . . in the language of chalk on walls") (9, 10), and he gradually accepts that his poems are examples of creative experiences that "abren cada día más al gran público el pasaje a nuevas formas de lo estético y lo lúdico" ("open the way more every day for the broad public to experience new aesthetic and playful forms") (10).

306

Cortázar's Transitional Poetics 307

Poetry serves Cortázar as a bridge between aesthetics and the world around him as his work puts innovation to the service of sociopolitical engagement.

Despite Cortázar's consistent investment in poetry – both writing verse and reading others' work – the critical literature has mostly ignored it. A critical reading of his poetry reveals aesthetic, social, and political preoccupations that echo those in his fiction and other prose work. Cortázar's playful sensibility as well as his increasingly politicized engagement flourish in his poetry, from questioning conventional societal norms (such as his continuous attacks on "la Gran Costumbre" ["the Grand Habit"]) to more direct political critique. The presence of poetry throughout his oeuvre serves as a generically transitional mode of writing that allows him to articulate his politicized positions.

In what follows, I offer examples of Cortázar's poetic work that illustrate how poetry becomes a zone of passage for expressing his life transitions, such as from expatriate to engaged political exile, as well as his aesthetic evolution. Cortázar identifies with the poet's chameleonic nature that embraces "la irrupción osmótica de la realidad" (*La vuelta*, II 190 ["the osmotic eruption of reality"]) (*Around the Day in Eighty Worlds*, 148). This chameleonism – a variable and flexible mode of being in the world – is for Cortázar a poet's responsibility rather than an excuse, and allows for his poetic expression. He exploits poetry's formal flexibility as a transformational strategy that underscores the sense of play so central to his work, to draw the reader into the game. His poetry exhibits metadiscursive maneuvers that blend the lyrical and the critical voice. The cityscapes in his poetry pave the way for his deepening social and political engagement as he relies on urban constructs to question bourgeois conventions and denounce international human rights abuses. Finally, Cortázar returns to poetry at the end of his life as he prepares his last book, a generically hybrid anthology that blends poetry and autobiographical narrative passages. A comprehensive reassessment of Cortázar's poetry confirms how his aesthetic innovation and urban metapoetics develop alongside his evolving political consciousness.

Poetry and poetics not only orient Cortázar's writing throughout his work but also frame his writing and publication history situated neatly within the timeframe of this volume. The first and last books that Cortázar wrote, planned, and published are collections of poetry (*Presencia* [*Presence*] in 1938 and *Salvo el crepúsculo* [*Save Twilight*] in 1984), and his first periodical publication was a poem ("Bruma" ["Mist"], published in the magazine *Addenda* in 1934).[2] Previous to his earliest publications, Cortázar wrote a collection of poems in 1927 at twelve years old.[3] He did not limit his poetry publications to volumes solely dedicated to verse work (best known are *Pameos y meopas*, 1971, and *Salvo el crepúsculo*) but also included poems in his "albums" (*Último round* [*Last Round*], 1969 and *La vuelta al día en ochenta mundos* [*Around the Day in Eighty Worlds*], 1967), in many of his novels (*Libro de Manuel* [*A Manual for Manuel*], *Rayuela* [*Hopscotch*], *Un tal Lucas* [*A Certain Lucas*], and *Divertimento* [*Divertissement*], among others), and in his essay collections. Furthermore, Cortázar's informal musings on poetry and poetics, scribbled on scraps of paper he referred to as "papelitos,"[4] confirm that poetry forms "una textura de fondo que sustenta toda su escritura" ("an underlying texture that sustains all of his writing") (Campra 110).

Cortázar's poetic corpus represents the wide range of his formal experimentation, from sonnets, other strophic forms, and classical and romantic themes to long-form free-verse innovations. Although he admired the sonnet and wrote many, his significant corpus of free-verse poetry gave him more formal and linguistic flexibility than prose for invention, play, humor, neologisms, and even visual interventions and collage.[5] The scant critical work on his poetry identifies some early derivative work patterned after the Romantics,[6] *Modernistas*, and vanguard poets, but concurs that his later work evidences a strong poetic voice and aesthetic innovation.

Cortázar considered himself first and foremost a poet. Although he was hesitant to publish his poetry, keeping it something of a secret, he distributed limited copies of anthologies that he created to friends. The distinction for him between poetry and fiction was less generic than relational and discursive (Bocchino 64). His fascination with the poetic process – formal, rhythmic, and linguistic – moves him to honor poetic traditions in his own verse work while simultaneously critiquing or even undermining them. He renovates language by mixing social and linguistic registers, incorporating localisms, and writing multilingually, even when relying on classic poetic forms (Campra 18–19; Mesa Gancedo 228). One critic considers his poetic voice "a medio camino entre la voz poética y la voz crítica" ("halfway between a poetic voice and a critical voice") as he develops an ambiguous lyrical "I" that turns him into a "comentarista de su propia obra" ("commentator on his own work") (Fonsalido 9, 18). This critical lyrical voice is one of the transitional, indeed liminal, aspects of his poetry writing.

Cortázar's Transitional Poetics

A poem included in *Un tal Lucas*, for example, identifies the poet as indistinguishable from a novelist or narrator:

> poeta
> porque ser escritor novelista
> narrador
> es decir ficcionante, imaginante, delirante, mitopoyético, oráculo o llámale equis,
> quiere decir en primerísimo lugar que el lenguaje es un medio, como siempre,
> pero este medio es más que medio, es como mínimo tres cuartos . . .
> no se conocen límites a la imaginación
> como no sean los del verbo;
> lenguaje e invención son enemigos fraternales
> y de esa lucha nace la literatura
> (*OC* vol. IV, 539–540)

> poet
> because being a writer novelist
> narrator
> that is, fictionant, imaginant, delirant,
> mythopoietic, oracle or call him as you choose,
> means in the firstest place
> that language is a medium, as always,
> but this medium is more than medium,
> it's three-quarters at least . . .
> there are no known limits to the imagination
> except those of the word,
> language and invention are fraternal enemies
> and from that struggle literature is born
> (*A Certain Lucas* 138–139)

Poetics for Cortázar is not generic but rather a discursive mode that infuses all of his writing (verse, fiction, essays) (Bocchino 64). His resistance to the constraints of forms and genres – even as he enjoyed experimenting with them – was a central strategy of his aesthetics. Mario Goloboff identifies in his work a "constante lucha por salirse de las formas, de los géneros . . . en la raíz de sus intentos de superar otras ataduras . . . otros confines de la expresión" ("constant struggle to escape forms, genres . . . at the root of his attempts to overcome other binds . . . other expressive confines") (9). Cortázar's metaphor of the chameleon, inspired by a John Keats letter, further links his fascination with changeable forms to the role of the poet who "renuncia a conservar una identidad" ("refuses to conserve his identity") in order to "salirse tan fácilmente de sí mismo para ingresar en las entidades que lo absorben" (*La vuelta*, II 190) ("escape from himself into the entities that absorb him") (*Around the Day*, 148). This flexible perspective on literary

310 MARCY SCHWARTZ

form – Cortázar often refers to it as plasticity – and poetic identity became something of a poetic modus operandi.

Cortázar's gradually emerging political engagement is inseparable from his aesthetic concerns; he acknowledged a shift as his work turned toward addressing major world events, exile, and his role as a Latin American intellectual. Although he identified himself unapologetically as apolitical for several decades, he clearly felt at odds with the cultural and political climate in Argentina under Peronism in the 1940s; this became one of a number of factors motivating his move to Paris in 1951. He claims that during his first years in Paris, "no tenía ningún conocimiento ni ninguna preocupación política" ("I had no knowledge or concern for politics") (Kohut quoted in Goloboff 74). He began to expand his emphasis on aesthetics as he witnessed historical events from a new vantage point, taking stock from Paris of human rights abuses, French colonialism, the Vietnam war, and the dictatorship in Argentina. His support of the Cuban Revolution, his travels to Cuba and later on to Nicaragua, and the wave of dictatorships in the Southern Cone and civil wars in Central America mark key moments of convergence between aesthetic and political vanguards that prompted him to articulate new positions (Goloboff 99). More personally, censorship under the dictatorship in Argentina banned his books and forbid his presence in the country as well. Thus another key transition that marks Cortázar's work is the shift from expatriate in Paris to political exile, a position that many intellectuals attacked him for, provoking polemical debates as he was pushed to defend himself (see Cortázar and Heker).

Although many critics trace Cortázar's evolving politics according to his fiction,[7] his poetry registers his formal experimentation alongside the emerging articulation of his sociopolitical ideology. As his poetic corpus spans his whole life and writing career, from the time he was a child until his death, it is his poetry that offers the most complete evidence of his various personal, political, and aesthetic phases and how those shifts intersect with the broader transitional period of mid-twentieth-century Latin American writing. Cortázar approached his writing as both an aesthetic and a political act (Barea 19). Cortázar's self-reflexive poetic voice fuses attention to writing with global sociopolitical concerns. In his life and work, "the political informs an aesthetics that in turn makes possible new forms of the political and the historical" (Bishop 72). Rather than a linear cause and effect, Cortázar's poetic articulation reveals a dovetailing of politics and aesthetics in a complex generative process.

Poetry as Playground

As much as Cortázar introduces games and playfulness in his fiction, particularly evident in *Rayuela*, in his poetry he takes ludic experimentation to even greater extremes. He commented extensively on the often unsettling journey of a game that in literature takes the reader into new territory, what he calls "descolocación," a neologism that combines dislocation and displacement. Games and play become strategies for steering the reader away from familiar territory and challenging conventional assumptions. In fact, Cortázar considered an alternative title for *Salvo el crepúsculo*, his most comprehensive poetic collection: "Palabras para el juego" ("Words for the Game").

The series of poems called "poesía permutante" ("interchangeable poetry") offers excellent examples of Cortázar's insistence on play and invention among the author, the text, and the reader. "Toda poesía que merezca ese nombre es un juego" ("any poetry that merits that name is a game"), Cortázar declares in a brief narrative introduction to these poems in *Último round* (*Last Round*) (ground floor, 65).[8] This collection of experimental poems invites readers to order the stanzas themselves, to participate actively in the structuring and composition of the texts. Nevertheless, these poems have never been published according to the format indicated by the manuscripts, but instead appear conventionally printed in a fixed order. Three of these poems – "Homenaje a Alain Renais," "Viaje infinito," and "Homenaje a Mallarmé" ("Homage to Alain Renais," "Infinite Voyage," and "Homage to Mallarmé") – included in the "ground floor" section of *Último round* occupy the small horizontal rectangular pages as if they were playing cards, each stanza printed on its own page with a dotted-line border (165–172, 184–188, 195–198).[9] Cortázar refers to the fragments of the poems as playing cards to be shuffled, and to the poems themselves as "ensayos" ("rehearsals") (66, 69). He also warns readers that the order of each poem does not necessarily follow the order in which it was originally written, but this does not matter "puesto que no es más que una de las múltiples combinaciones de estas estructuras" ("because it is only one of the multiple combinations of these structures") (67). The fragments in tercets or quatrains with conventional rhyme schemes reference traditional lyric poetry in Spanish, and yet the resistance to a fixed order and the active collaboration of the reader unseat those conventions. The suggestion of ordering the fragments by chance instead of according to a reader's considered determination adds another of Cortázar's favorite playful moves, the unpredictability of random luck, along with poetic allusions to Mallarmé's "Un coup de dés n'abolira jamais le hasard" ("A Throw of the Dice Will Never Abolish Chance").

Cortázar insists that the tools of literary writing are not only thematic but also include "las posibilidades de fractura, extrañamiento, desacomodación que la estructura literaria (tema/escritura) permiten [sic] operar en el receptor, en la otra punta del puente" ("the possibilities of fracture, estrangement, a lack of accommodation that literary structure [theme/writing] allows to operate on the recipient, on the other side of the bridge") (Cortázar papers, Princeton University Library). Cortázar stretches traditional writing and poetic forms to the point of "des-écriture" ("un-writing") to test the limits of speech and meaning (Mesa Gancedo 230). His persistent attention to language and literary structure fuels his metapoetic attempts to reshape them in his poetry.

"Escríbase la Vida, Simplemente": Cortázar's Metapoetics

Cortázar is known for his metafictional experimentation through the fantastic mode in his short stories and in his novels, a characteristic of the "Boom" generation fiction and of this period generally in Latin American writing.[10] He elaborates on this preoccupation with the process and materiality of writing, and even of reading, in his poetry. His metapoetics presents a "sujeto que habla de sí en su escritura pero también de una escritura vuelta sobre sí" ("a subject who talks about himself in his writing but also writing that turns back on itself") (Bocchino 65). The prose poem "Se dibuja una estrellita" ("Drawing a Little Star") likens the writing process first to a surgical procedure and then to a religious ritual – from the scientific to the sacred – referencing the stars that Cortázar was fond of drawing on his own manuscript pages and even on pages of poetry anthologies that he read:[11] "[s]e dibuja, así, una estrellita en lo alto de la página, y el campo operatorio queda claramente demarcado" (*Último round*, ground floor, 78) ("Make a little star right at the top of the page, and the field of operation will appear clearly" [*Around the Day*, 215]).[12] The materiality of the page, "the field of operation," requires the necessary tools and precision, and yet the text concludes by doubting the writer's freedom as an "esplendorosa ilusión" (79) ("blinding illusion," 215). Folon's drawing that accompanies the piece (79, 215) depicts a hybrid figure with human legs and a pair of scissors for a torso: a being that is half human and half utilitarian tool. The verbal-visual communication underscores the physical and material procedures of writing.

Along with commenting on the writing process, Cortázar also elaborates on the editing of his books – how he chooses and orders the poems. In one

Cortázar's Transitional Poetics 313

of the narrative introductions in *Salvo el crepúsculo*, he declares, "si este libro no es plástico, no es nada" ("if this book isn't plastic, it's nothing") (107). Plasticity is key to his conception of this collection; as he announces in the book's introduction, "Discurso del no método, método del no discurso .... Ninguna cronología, baraja tan mezclada que no vale la pena" ("Discourse on non-method, method of non-discourse .... No chronology, a deck of cards that is so thoroughly shuffled that it's not worth it") (11). In another narrative segment, he mentions copying a sonnet from the 1940s to add to the collection, "[a]ntes de copiarlo (el papel está amarillo y, justo signo que acato conmovido, una hormiguita de las que vagan por mi mesa se ha trepado a su frágil columna y la explora como si quisiera leerla, como si acaso lo estuviera leyendo de verdad)" ("before copying it, [the paper has yellowed and, in a perfect sign that I accept, amazed, one of those little ants that wander across my desk climbs onto its fragile column and explores it as if he would like to read it, as if he might even be actually reading it]") (116). In the passage mentioned earlier, he refers again to his writing process, musing that what he conjures up pops onto the typed page: "las cosas saltan como ranitas cadenciosas desde sus pozos de papel a la máquina de escribir que las pone en fila .... Todo aquí es tan libre, tan posible, tan gato" ("things jump like little rhythmic toads from their wells of paper to the typewriter that puts them in line .... Everything here is so free, so possible, so cat-like") (107). Language, as it moves from the poet's mind to the typed page, appears in unexpected, animal-like movements, surprising the writer who watches rather than controls the scene. Cortázar draws the reader into the entire process by making transparent, in his narrative interpolations, many elements of collating the very book that we are reading.

Cortázar's poetry registers the convergence of aesthetic experimentation and engagement with the world around him, a convergence often marked by geopolitical references and transnational urban spaces. "[L]o estético, no tiene ya para mí la fuerza irresistible que tuvo en mi juventud ... ha sido suplantado en mí por ... intereses de tipo histórico. Actualmente me interesa más el espectáculo que ves en la calle que un cuadro donde esté pintado ese espectáculo" ("Aesthetics no longer has that irresistible force that it had for me in my youth ... it has been substituted by ... historical interests. Lately I'm more interested in the spectacle that you see in the street than in a painting depicting that spectacle") (Prego 248). His deployment of a poetics of urban space stages street spectacles – from ordinary neighborhood meanderings to international urban happenings – that mesh his aesthetics and his politics.

"El Poema Que Engendra la Ciudad": Cortázarian Urban Inscriptions

Cortázar's urban preoccupations, so prevalent and extensively studied in his fiction, impact his poetry as well, and evidence the emerging articulation of his political positions.[13] The urban images that mark Cortázar's poetry vary widely to include nostalgic remembrances of Buenos Aires, human rights violations in cities around the globe, classical allusions, ruins, images of cafés, and daily street life. The modern city plays a key role in much of the literature written during this period, as the chapters in Part II of this volume, "Metropolis and Ruins," elaborate. A poem from a pivotal historical moment in Cortázar's life and work, "Noticias del mes de mayo" ("News from the Month of May"), documents the student protests in Paris in May 1968. The year 1968 is clearly a turning point in Cortázar's work, "un año clave ... otra vuelta de tuerca" ("a key year ... another turn of the screw"); witnessing the May student protests in Paris follows his engagement with the Cuban Revolution. During the decade of the 1960s his aesthetic and political visions fuse, never to turn back (García Cerdán 49; see also Sorensen). This extensive poem-collage can be considered Cortázar's most urban poem, given that it is structured around student protesters' graffiti messages, slogans, and posters on public walls. With a journalistic eye and a reporter's commitment to documentation, he identifies the street name, university building, or author or group that generated each slogan. The original publication in the journal *Casa de las Américas* and the version in *Último round* include photographs of Parisian walls covered with posters and flyers during the student protests (second floor, 46–62).

"La poesía está en la calle. Rue Rotrou" ("Poetry is in the street. Rotrou Street") (56),[14] one of the graffiti messages quoted in the middle of "Noticias del mes de mayo," echoes Cortázar's appreciation of the poetry of city streets mentioned in Bauer's documentary (cited earlier). After a brief stanza the first quote appears: "EL SUEÑO ES REALIDAD" ("DREAM IS REALITY"), situating the poem in the street by evoking the "manos livianas" that "trazaron / con la tiza que inventa la poesía en la calle" ("light hands ... traced with chalk that invents poetry in the street") (47). The poem captures the collective and public nature of the movement by interspersing the slogans with enumerations of Parisian neighborhoods and international cities and countries, and quotes by key intellectuals of the time (including student activist Daniel Cohn-Bendit[15]). At the same time that it underscores the public and collective nature of the street protests,

Cortázar's Transitional Poetics

"Noticias" draws on intimate encounters through the apostrophic dialogue with a loved one: "Escucha, amor, escucha el rumor de la calle, / eso es hoy el poema, eso hoy el amor. / El ritmo, una vez más, es el solo pasaje" ("Listen, love, listen to the street sounds, today this is the poem, today this is love. Rhythm, once again, is the only passage") (56). An effervescent energy inspired by the sentiments and activities of the political moment permeates this long poem of over 400 lines. It seems to unroll on the pages like a protest through the streets, winding among the chants and slogans that are printed in bold in varying fonts, alternating with Cortázar's interventions, all of it occupying the pages from both the left and the right margins, the way the students and other protesters who joined in occupied the streets and university buildings.[16] "Noticias" celebrates the political-poetic Word as a force for change on the ground despite entrenched institutions (educational, academic, political, social), and takes aim at "la Gran Costumbre" ("the Grand Habit") that Cortázar disparages in many of his poems. Just after citing a quote from a phrase etched on a wall at the Sorbonne campus that declares, "UN PENSAR QUE SE ESTANCA ES UN PENSAR QUE SE PUDRE" ("THINKING THAT STAGNATES IS THINKING THAT ROTS") (56), he continues:

> Lo imposible se hizo día en la Sorbona, un largo mes de día,
> Se despertó desperezó en la calle en los cafés
> Y un pueblo que no hablaba más que para callar
> . . .
> Descubrió la Palabra hizo el amor con ella
> en cada esquina bajo cada puente
> un árbol de sonrisas nació sobre el cemento
>
> The impossible dawned at the Sorbonne, a long month of daylight,
> it woke up stretched in the street in the cafés
> and the people who only used to speak to shut up
> . . .
> Discovered the Word and made love with it
> on every corner and under every bridge
> a tree of smiles was born on the cement   (56–57)

The students' messages resonate with some of Cortázar's persistent preoccupations about the emptiness of institutions, bourgeois attitudes, and codified cultural habits:

> Porque los monolitos /
> durarán mucho menos que esta lluvia de imágenes /

esta poesía en plena calle triturando el cemento /
de la Ciudad Estable.

Because the monoliths
will last much less than this shower of images
this poetry in the middle of the street tearing up the cement
of the Stable City. (62)

This critical stance toward the city emerges in a number of his urban
poems, coinciding with his essays that accompany photographs, such
as *Prosa del observatorio* (*From the Observatory*) and *Alto el Perú* (*Peru
Up High*), which takes aim at the "lettered city" and its stale institutions (see Schwartz, "Writing against the City" and "Cortázar under
Exposure").

However, Cortázar's repertoire of urban poems represents city space
differently than his novels and short stories. In the tighter verbal space of
the poem, he distills the urban *rabdomancia* (wandering) readers are
accustomed to in his fiction to propose instead tonal portraits of the city
in a particular light or mood. The poems that evoke Buenos Aires mesh
nostalgia with the tragic loss of the disappeared. A section of *Salvo el
crepúsculo*, "Con tangos" ("With Tangos"), includes poems such as
"Veredas de Buenos Aires," "Mufa," and "Milonga" ("Sidewalks of
Buenos Aires," "Bad Luck," and "Milonga"), the titles alone referencing
tango lyrics. "Por tarjeta" ("By Postcard") offers an intimate portrait of
a neighborhood rather than extensive roaming, and seems prescient (particularly since this is one of his earlier poems, originally published in
Pameos y meopas) in evoking absence in its series of negations: "no se lo
ve en la esquina de Otamendi, / empiezan a extrañarlo . . . / no se lo oyó
silbar / no le compra más *Clarín*" ("they don't see him on the corner of
Otamendi, / they start to miss him . . . / they didn't hear him whistling / he
no longer buys [the newspaper] *Clarín*") (*Salvo el crepúsculo*, 72). In
Cortázar's narrative comments following the poem, which he calls
a "guitarreada" ("a riff, an improvisation") (72), he says he wrote the
poem more than twenty years before: "Una vez más la naturaleza habrá
imitado al arte . . . hoy lo leo preguntándome si algo en mí no veía ya lo que
nos esperaba en nuestra famosa tierra de paz y prosperidad" ("once again
nature imitates art . . . today I read it wondering if I didn't see then what
was coming in our famous land of peace and prosperity") (72–73). These
poems link Cortázar's own complicated identity as an exile, his distance
from Argentina, with collective loss from human rights abuses all evoked
by the lament of the tango.

Twilight Transitions

To conclude this exploration of Cortázar's poetry as a transitional genre that allowed him the fullest range of experimentation, I return to *Salvo el crepúsculo*, the last book that he prepared for publication before his death. A decisive return to poetry prompted his comprehensive review of a lifetime of his own poetic writing, reading, and thinking about poetry: *Salvo el crepúsculo* includes numerous poems by others throughout the book and brief narrative and autobiographical comments.[17] Cortázar veers away from prose and fiction to meticulously compile and organize his poetry,[18] just on the cusp of the end of his life when he "intuye que la muerte le pisa los talones" ("senses that death is nipping at his heels") (Benedetti 38). As *Salvo el crepúsculo* appears in print posthumously, it is the book that bridges his life and his death. Mario Benedetti traces the nocturnal in this volume, beyond the title, pointing out that nearly all the poems involve nighttime scenes and many references to death. The crepuscular tone and images of night and darkness envelop the book in an interstitial mode, not quite day yet not quite night, in parallel with the ultimate (and in Cortázar's case, imminent) existential transition.

"Nocturno" ("Nocturne") (53), one of his poems that appears in *Pameos y meopas* as well as in *Salvo el crepúsculo*, begins: "Tengo esta noche las manos negras" ("Tonight I have black hands" [*Save Twilight*, 35]), and mentions a dying blind man, a forest surrounding the house, and navigating by unreliable stars. The poem paints a somber late-night still life of objects (a newspaper, other papers, bottles, a glass of milk) with a foreboding tone of uncertainty: "[m]i mujer sube y baja una pequeña escalera / como un capitán de navío que desconfía de las estrellas" (*Salvo el crepúsculo*, 53) ("my wife goes up and down a little ladder / like a sea captain who doesn't trust the stars" [*Save Twilight*, 35]).

Some of Cortázar's most evocative twilight images appear in "Resumen en otoño" ("Autumn Summary"), a poem that also links discontinuous moments in time:

> Asombra a veces que el fervor del tiempo
> vuelva, sin cuerpo vuelva, ya sin motivo vuelva;
> que la belleza, tan breve en su violento amor
> nos guarde un eco en el descenso de la noche
> . . . .
> saber que esto que resta
> fue ganado a la sombra por obra de silencio
>
> (*Salvo el crepúsculo*, 257)

It's amazing sometimes how the years' fervor
returns, returns without a body, returns for no reason at all;
how beauty, so brief in its violent love,
saves us an echo as night falls.
. . . .
You know this remnant
was wrung from the dark by the work of silence

(*Save Twilight*, 177)

The alliterative resonance between the verb "asombra" and noun "sombra" gives the poem a musically provocative and semantically rich structure. The poem begins with an image of birds filling the late-day sky, a sign of time passing and night falling. The darkness is pierced slightly, in many of these crepuscular poems, by some feeble source of light. "Resumen de otoño" concludes with a sliver of light: "la lámpara que alumbra" ("the lamp shining its light"), promising a glimmer of hope in this meditation on time, memory, and the body's frailty.

Cortázar's poetics delineates an ambiguous space of enunciation, on the border between creation and criticism, oscillating between formal and linguistic innovation and the representation of the world. These parallel objectives seemed to emerge in tension with one another, but his poetry provided them the space to coexist, where they shifted from divergence to intersection. In one of his drawings, a series of lines and arrows (labeled "A" and "B") crisscrosses two fields (designated as "1" and "2"), mapping a complex project of distinct but related axes. As in *Rayuela*'s "this side" and "the other side," Cortázar often conceptualized his creative field in parallel but intersecting zones or directions. In his growing political consciousness that compelled him to take ever-bolder stands, Cortázar considered poetry too precious or intimate initially, isolated from the global human rights concerns in which he increasingly invested. The persistent challenge of reconciling his aesthetics of literary writing with current politics and mass media explodes in works such as "Noticias del mes de mayo" and *Libro de Manuel*. Poetry seems to be his way out or forward, but also the way back to his earlier work as he incorporates it into *Salvo el crepúsculo*.

Cortázar also returns to a dialogue with the visual in *Salvo el crepúsculo* through retro print elements illuminating the pages as head or tail pieces. The last of these printed graphics, a typewriter with hearts popping out of the roller (n.p.), turns the book into a love letter to poetry. In this heterogeneous scrapbook of an anthology that reveals his best-kept secrets, he transcends the aesthetic/political binary: the book's autobiographical narrative fragments avoid any strict chronology, and the poems chosen jump

Cortázar's Transitional Poetics

among places and times, public street and private interior, language and world. Cortázarian poetics charges the reader with the task of connecting these pieces, times, and places, because the language of poetry remains "centrado en el lector en cuanto éste es, a la vez (ontológicamente) el poeta" ("centered on the reader as far as he is, simultaneously [ontologically] the poet") (Cortázar Papers, Princeton University Library). Cortázar makes us his accomplices as we read his work, connecting the dots and lines, skipping along, playing the game. Poetry allows him to sidestep the confines of language and form to embody the chameleon. He embraced poetry as a transitional mode for fusing his aesthetics and his politics.

Notes

1. All translations into English are mine unless a translated edition is referenced.
2. *Salvo el crepúsculo* was published posthumously but Cortázar meticulously organized and edited it before his death. Numerous anthologies of his selected poetry have been edited and published posthumously, as well as a multivolume complete works that devotes one volume (IV) to "poetics and poetry." Five poems by Cortázar are anthologized in the volume *200 años de poesía argentina* edited by Jorge Monteleone (306–309).
3. This notebook of nine handwritten poems is published as an appendix ("anexo") in the section of unpublished poems that the editors call "El poeta puber" ("The Adolescent Poet") (*OC* vol. IV 743–756).
4. These notes are included in Cortázar's papers at the Princeton University Library. See also *Papelitos*, a limited-edition artist's book with facsimile reproductions of selected "papelitos."
5. Cortázar's "albums" such as *Último round* and *La vuelta al día en ochenta mundos* are heterogeneous collections of fiction, essays, poetry, photography, and drawings (see Dávila). *Salvo el crepúsculo* also incorporates visual elements in the form of reproduced vintage graphics on nearly every page, as well as a section of the book that is handwritten.
6. Some critics, such as García Cerdán, see Cortázar's early poetry as "neoromantic," a poetic group in the 1940s (47).
7. Goloboff, for example, sees Cortázar's story "El perseguidor," published in 1959 in *Las armas secretas*, as a turning point in his political engagement: "el cierre de una etapa en su trabajo literario y la apertura de otra nueva" ("the close of one stage of his literary work and the opening of a new one") (86).
8. *Último round*, one of Cortázar's "book objects," is printed in an unusual format. The pages are split and separately numbered, and can be turned and read independently of one another; the lower portion forms the "planta baja" ("ground floor") and the larger pages above comprise the "primer piso" ("second floor"). All references to *Último round* indicate to which section of the book the passage pertains.

320   MARCY SCHWARTZ

9. These three also appear in *Territorios*, along with four others; another three are included in *Salvo el crepúsculo*, but printed in full, each on a single page.
10. The line "Escríbase la vida, simplemente" in this section's heading is from "De esto, la vida el tiempo," unpublished poem (Cortázar Papers, Princeton University Library).
11. In Cortázar's personal library at the Fundación March, poetry accounts for a large percentage of his books whose pages bear his idiosyncratic markings. Hand-drawn crosses and five- or six-pointed stars are frequent interventions. See Marchamalo.
12. The English translation titled *Around the Day in Eighty Worlds* includes selected texts from *Último round*.
13. The line "El poema que engendra la ciudad" in this section's heading is from "Territorio de Guido Llinás" (OC vol. IV 537).
14. All quotes from "Noticias del mes de mayo" refer to the 2013 edition of *Último round*.
15. Cohn-Bendit, a French-German sociology student at the University of Paris-Nanterre, was a leader of the May 1968 protests. He went on to become a Green Party politician and elected member of the European Parliament.
16. "Homenaje a una torre de fuego" relates the students' takeover of the Argentine residence hall on the international campus in Paris during this same period (*Último round*, ground floor, 52–56).
17. Benedetti calls *Salvo el crepúsculo* "quizá el único sucedáneo posible de la autobiografía que nunca escribió" ("perhaps the closest thing to the autobiography that he never wrote") (33).
18. Critics point out how difficult it is to define *Salvo el crepúsculo*, calling it an "extraña publicación" ("strange publication") (Bocchino 63) and a "curiosa miscelánea" ("curious miscellany") (Fonsalido 7).

Works Cited

Barea, Federico. "Manual de instrucciones para la presente bibliografía." *Todo Cortázar: bio- Bibliografía*. Ed. Lucio Aquilante and Federico Barea, pp. 19–21. Buenos Aires: Fernández Blanco y Aquilante, 2014.

Bauer, Tristán. *Cortázar*. Dir. Tristán Bauer. La Zona, 1994.

Benedetti, Mario. "Cortázar by Night." *Revista de crítica literaria latinoamericana* 18.35 (1992): 33–39.

Bishop, Karen Elizabeth. *The Space of Disappearance: A Narrative Commons in the Ruins of Argentine State Terror*. Albany, NY: SUNY Press, 2020.

Bocchino, Adriana A. "*Salvo el crepúsculo* de Julio Cortázar o volver atrás y recapitular." *Confluencia* 7.1 (1991): 63–68.

Campra, Rosalba. *Cortázar para cómplices*. Prologue Jean Andreu. Madrid: Del Centro, 2009.

Cortázar, Julio. *Save Twilight*. Trans. Stephen Kessler. San Francisco: City Lights, 2016.

Cortázar's Transitional Poetics 321

Último round. 1969. Barcelona: RM, 2013.

Papelitos. Ed. Raiña Lupa. Barcelona: Pérgamo, 2008.

Poesía y poética: Obras completas. Vol. IV. Ed. Saúl Yurkievich et al. Barcelona: Galaxia Gutenberg/Círculo de Lectores, 2005.

Around the Day in Eighty Worlds. Trans. Thomas Christensen. San Francisco, CA: North Point Press, 1986.

A Certain Lucas. Trans. Gregory Rabassa. New York: Knopf, 1984.

Salvo el crepúsculo. Buenos Aires: Nueva Imagen, 1984.

Un tal Lucas. Madrid: Alfaguara, 1979.

Territorios. Mexico City: Siglo XXI, 1978.

Libro de Manuel. Buenos Aires: Sudamericana, 1973.

Pameos y meopas. Barcelona: Ocnos, 1971.

La vuelta al día en ochenta mundos. Mexico City: Siglo XXI, 1967.

Rayuela. Buenos Aires: Sudamericana, 1963.

Cortázar, Julio and Liliana Heker. "Polémica con Julio Cortázar." *Cuadernos hispanoamericanos* 517–519 (1993): 590–603.

Dávila, María de Lourdes. *Desembarcos en el papel: la imagen en la literatura de Julio Cortázar.* Rosario: Beatriz Viterbo, 2001.

Fonsalido, María Elena. "Tres lecturas contemporáneas de una forma canónica. Borges, Cortázar, Saer y el soneto." *Olivar* 8.9 (2007): 127–145.

García Cerdán, Andrés. "La poesía de Julio Cortázar: Discurso del no método, método del no discurso." *Cartáphilus* 5 (2009): 44–57.

Goloboff, Mario. *Julio Cortázar: la biografía.* Havana: Arte y Literatura, 1998.

Julio Cortázar Literary Manuscripts, 1943–82. Benson Latin American Collection, University of Texas Libraries.

Julio Cortázar Papers (C0888). Manuscripts Division, Special Collections, Princeton University Library.

Marchamalo, Jesús. *Cortázar y los libros.* Madrid: Fórcola, 2011.

Mesa Gancedo, Daniel. "Poésie Rather Hard to Understand: Cortázar et la mantique dans la semantique." In *Cortázar, de tous les côtés.* Ed. Joaquín Manzi, pp. 217–231. Poitiers: Langues Littératures Poitiers/Maison des Sciences de l'Homme et de la Société, 2002.

Monteleone, Jorge, ed. *200 años de poesía argentina.* Madrid: Alfaguara, 2010.

Prego, Omar. *Julio Cortázar: la fascinación de las palabras.* Montevideo: Trilce, 1990.

Schwartz, Marcy. "Writing against the City: Julio Cortázar's Photographic Take of India." In *Photography and Writing in Latin America: Double Exposures.* Coedited by Marcy Schwartz and Mary Beth Tierney-Tello, pp. 117–139. Albuquerque: University of New Mexico Press, 2006.

"Cortázar under Exposure: Photography and Fiction in the City." In *Latin American Literature and Mass Media.* Eds. Debra Castillo and José Edmundo Paz-Soldán, pp. 117–138. New York: Garland Press, 2000.

Sorensen, Diana. *A Turbulent Decade Remembered: Scenes from the Latin American Sixties.* Stanford, CA: Stanford University Press, 2007.

Index

Amado, Jorge, 1, 8, 47, 49, 60
  and anti-fascism, 51
  Communist Party, 49
Appardurai, Arjun, 117
Argentina, 2, 3, 320
  Buenos Aires, 3, 5, 6, 132–136, 201, 233, 238, 239,
    243, 292, 294, 314, 316
  Journal *Sur*, 2, 3, 21, 133
  military dictatorship, 30, 68
  Nueva canción, 301
  Perón, Juan Domingo, 1, 3, 310
  Peronism, 234, 310
  political theory, 275
  Surrealism, 231, 294
  women, 7, 11, 234
  World War II, 32
Arguedas, José María, 2, 7, 9, 182, 185, 186, 187,
    190, 191, 192, 193, 213
  and the Boom, 25
  El zorro de arriba y el zorro de abajo, 25
  expectations for writers, 25
  literature and politics, 25
  Los ríos profundos, 9, 65, 182, 185, 187, 190, 191,
    192, 193, 194
Asturias, Miguel Ángel, 1, 4, 5, 7, 9, 72,
    149, 150, 182, 185, 186, 187, 188, 189,
    190, 256
  and the Boom, 25, 28, 74
  biography and context for novels, 72–74
  conferences, 21
  El Señor Presidente, 72
  Hombres de maíz, 9, 65, 72, 74, 75, 182, 185, 187,
    188, 190
  Mulata de tal, 5, 67, 73, 74–76, 77, 78
  Nobel Prize, 74

Balcells, Carmen, 66, 77
Barcelona, 26, 244, 273, 274, 321
Barnet, Miguell
  Biografía de un cimarrón, 29
BBC Latin American Service, 4, 47

Bello, Andrés, 20
Benjamin, Walter, 100
Berlant, Lauren
  slow death, 101
Bermúdez, María Elvira, 122
Bernal, Rafael, 123
Betto, Frei, 83, 84
Biografía de un cimarrón, 261, 264, 270,
    274
Bioy Casares, Adolfo, 6
  Seis problemas para Don Isidro Parodi,
    132–136
Bolaño, Roberto
  on José Donoso, 77
Bombal, María Luisa
  La amortajada, 28
Boom, 2, 5, 10, 11, 18, 23, 65, 185, 230, 232, 233,
    276, 312
  and poetry, 28
  as filling a vacuum, 25
  as idyllic collaboration, 25
  authors, 27, 28, 66, 67, 73, 74, 76
  beginning date, 26
  common cause, 25
  continental influence, 65
  culminating novel, 77
  novela total, 65
  political and cultural circumstances, 26
  the 1960s, 25
  transculturation, 70
  women authors, 28, 66
Boomito, 28
Borges, Jorge Luis, 1, 3, 4, 5, 6, 7, 10, 21, 23, 239,
    279, 284, 291, 292, 303
  "Anotación al 23 de agosto de 1944", 32, 33,
    36
  "Deutsches Requiem", 4, 39
  "El jardín de los senderos que se bifurcan", 4
  and detective fiction, 120
  and parody, 132
  and the Boom, 25, 28

322

Index

323

compared with Asturias, Miguel Ángel, 22
compared with Neruda, Pablo, 22
global recognition, 22
ideal of totality, 32
on liberation of Paris, 33
opinions on fascism, 32
Seis problemas para Don Isidro Parodi, 6, 132–136
Braga, Rubem, 50
Brazil, 3, 4, 5, 12, 56, 60, 195, 201, 230, 234, 235, 290, 291, 293, 294, 296, 297, 298, 299, 300, 301, 303, 304
Amnesty Law, 81, 82, 87, 88, 94
anti-fascism, 47–52
authoritarianism, 60
Cold War, 56
Communist Party, 81
democratic regime, 57, 81
fascism, 46
industrialization, 60
Jair Bolsonaro, 61, 94
marginalization, 86
marginalization in revolutionary struggle, 93
military dictatorship, 30, 46, 52, 56, 81, 83, 84, 87, 92, 94
radio dramas, 52, 53
revolutionary literature, 81, 83, 84
soap operas, 52
social inequalities, 47
Surrealism, 231
Vargas, Getúlio, 46
Violão de rua, 301
war memoirs, 51
women, 11
Brazilian Modernism, 5
Breton, André, 68, 69, 70, 230, 234, 246, 251, 295
Bryce Echenique, Alfredo, 66

Cabrera Infante, Guillermo, 66
Cabrera, Lydia, 9, 23, 211, 212, 215, 216, 217, 218, 219, 221, 222, 223, 256
Callado, Antônio, 4, 46–60
A Assunção de Salviano, 54
and anti-fascist propaganda, 46
BBC Latin American Service, 52, 53
compared with Jorge Amado, 60
O Fígado de Prometeu, 54
politics and intellectual work, 54
Quarup, 47, 54, 58, 59, 60
radio dramas, 54, 57, 59, 60
response to military dictatorship, 46
socialist turn, 47

Campobello, Nellie, 11, 12, 151, 152, 153, 154, 155, 156, 161, 277, 278, 279, 281, 282, 283, 286, 288
Cartucho, 12, 151, 153, 154, 161, 277, 278, 281, 282, 283, 288
Cañedo, Diego, 122, 126
Cardenal, Ernesto, 8, 112, 301
and the Boom, 28
conversational poetry, 28
Cárdenas Acuña, Ignacio, 136
Caribbean, 3, 27, 30, 65, 70, 195, 230, 234, 251, 292, 303
Carpentier, Alejo, 1, 4, 5, 7, 11, 232, 245, 246, 247, 248, 249, 250, 251, 254, 255, 256, 259, 302
¡Écue-Yamba-Ó!, 71, 246, 250
and Spanish Civil War, 69
and the Boom, 25, 26, 74
anti-fascism, 69
biography, 68–70
El recurso del método, 72, 248, 256
El reino de este mundo, 1, 5, 65, 67, 70–71, 72, 77, 78, 231, 247, 252, 259
El siglo de las luces, 72, 254, 256, 258
Haiti, 70, 71, 247, 251
La música en Cuba, 70, 247
Los pasos perdidos, 72, 247, 251, 253, 259
Mexico, 70
perception of Cuba, 70
Spanish Civil War, 69
Surrealism, 70, 71
Casa de las Américas, 18, 20, 25, 26, 30, 149, 153, 260, 270, 271, 314
testimonio genre, 29
Castellanos, Rosario, 6, 7, 108, 110, 112, 149, 150, 151, 155, 160, 162, 182
"Memorial de Tlatelolco", 106–109
and state violence, 100
and Tlatelolco Massacre, 100, 105
Balún Canán, 28
Indigenous legacies, 100
Chávez, César, 7
Chile, 2, 3, 9, 198, 199, 200, 201, 243, 294, 298
Allende, Salvador, 19, 76
military dictatorship, 20, 30, 68
Nueva canción, 301
political theory, 275
Unidad Popular, 76
writers' conferences, 21
Cinema Novo, 57
Cold War, 1, 3, 4, 20, 21, 56, 57, 73, 103, 195, 262, 273
Brazil, 46
in Octavio Paz, 103

Index

colonialism, 8, 21, 30, 71, 183, 195, 269, 271, 272, 310
Cortázar, Julio, 1, 3, 6, 10, 12, 18, 23, 232, 239, 242, 265, 306, 307, 308, 309, 310, 311, 312, 313, 314, 315, 316, 317, 318, 319, 320, 321
  and the Boom, 26, 27, 65
  lector cómplice, 10
  literature and politics, 24, 25
  Rayuela, 6, 27, 74, 232, 239, 308, 311, 318
crime fiction, 6, 120–121, 122, 123, 125, 131, 132, 143
  and the noir genre, 131
  Buenos Aires, 132–136
  detective novel, 127, 139
  Havana, 132, 136–139
  Mexico City, 132, 139–143
  Santiago de Chile, 132
  women writers, 122
Cuba, 2, 3, 5, 7, 8, 9, 10, 183, 211, 212, 213, 214, 215, 216, 217, 218, 219, 220, 221, 222, 223, 231, 245, 246, 247, 248, 250, 251, 252, 254, 255, 257, 259, 260, 261, 262, 263, 264, 265, 266, 267, 268, 269, 270, 271, 272, 273, 277, 293, 300, 302, 310, 314
  Afro-Cuban, 9
  Batista, Fulgencio, 17, 254, 272
  Castro, Fidel, 17, 23, 76, 267
  Che Guevara, 20
  Cuban Revolution, 1, 3, 11, 17, 18, 19, 136
  Cultural Congress of Havana, 21
  cultural influence on Latin America, 23
  cultural production, 18
  Havana, 6, 17, 18, 69, 136–139, 212, 219, 220, 245, 246, 253, 255
  international interest, 17
  Latin American intellectuals, 17, 19, 24
  Literacy Campaign, 7, 266
  Nueva canción, 301
  Padilla Affair, 19, 66
Cuban Revolution, 3, 7, 22, 23, 57, 76, 247, 260, 261, 262, 266, 277, 300, 310, 314
  and Brazil, 81
  and the Boom, 66

Daniel, Herbert, 4, 5, 89, 91, 92, 93
  marginalization, 93
  Passagem para o próximo sonho, 84–88
Dávila, Ámparo, 127
de Andrade, Oswald, 48, 50, 243, 293, 296, 299, 300
  and anti-fascism, 49
de Beauvoir, Simone, 17
de Bittencourt, Silvia, 51
de Queiroz, Rachel, 47, 49, 51, 61
  Communist Party, 49
Debray, Regis, 23

decolonization, 18, 20
del Paso, Fernando, 66, 127
detective novel. *See* crime fiction
dictatorship, 4, 11, 54, 199, 246, 277, 310
Distinto amanecer, 116, 118, 119, 120, 122
do Amaral, Tarsila, 48, 293
Donoso, José, 4, 5, 18, 23, 202
  and the Boom, 76, 77
  biography, 76
  El jardin de al lado, 5, 67, 76, 77, 78
  El obsceno pájaro de la noche, 76
  homosexuality, 78
Drummond de Andrade, Carlos, 50, 296

Europe, 3, 4, 12, 22, 157, 199, 245, 247, 248, 250, 254, 265, 271, 285, 290, 291, 294
  classical ruins, 103
  Cold War, 21
  fascism, 71
  Latin American journals, 21

Fanon, Franz, 20
fascism, 11, 33, 56, 294
  Italian, 47, 48
feminism, 7, 8, 9, 11, 78, 152, 159, 199, 200, 203, 204, 231, 232, 242
  écriture feminine, 7
Fernández Retamar, Roberto, 25, 29, 30, 262, 270, 271, 274
Ferré, Rosario, 28
Frank, Waldo, 17
Fuentes, Carlos, 1, 5, 6, 7, 23, 124, 127, 155, 160, 232, 265, 278
  and the Boom, 26, 27, 65
  La muerte de Artemio Cruz, 27
  La región más transparente, 6

Gabeira, Fernando, 84
  Companheiro, 83
  Companheiro?, 87
  O que é isso, companheiro, 94
García Márquez, Gabriel, 1, 7, 8, 23, 213, 232, 265
  and the Boom, 27, 65
  Cien años de soledad, 1, 8, 17, 23, 27, 74, 265
  on Miguel Ángel Asturias, 74
Garro, Elena, 127, 151, 158
  Los recuerdos del porvenir, 28
Guatemala, 5, 7, 72, 74, 75, 76, 182, 187, 189, 190
  1917 earthquake, 73
  and Indigenous population, 75
  military dictatorship, 73
Guevara, Ernesto, 17, 19, 20, 23, 24, 76
  and Guatemala, 76
  Diario de Bolivia, 29

Index

325

Guillén, Nicolás, 2, 3, 7, 9, 10, 69, 201, 211, 219, 220, 221, 222, 223, 271, 293, 302
son, 2, 10, 156, 168, 177, 219, 220, 221, 223, 248, 257, 259, 267, 309
Guimarães Rosa, João, 25

Helú, Antonio, 121, 122, 126
heterogeneity, 7, 9, 167, 168, 171, 172, 174, 178, 262

imperialism, 3, 8, 18, 21, 159
indigenismo, 9, 155, 162, 166, 186, 190
intertextuality, 9

Latin American novel, 18, 27
foundational story, 28
Lezama Lima, José, 10, 259, 302, 303, 304
Lispector, Clarice, 7
Locas mujeres, 9
Los olvidados, 123

Macchu Picchu, 6
magical realism, 1, 10, 11, 27, 70, 76, 151, 260, 264, 266, 269, 273
Mariátegui, José Carlos, 23
Martí, José, 23
Martin, Gerald, 27, 65, 188, 195, 196
Martín-Barbero, Jesús, 116
marvelous real, 1, 70, 72, 232
Meirelles, Cecília, 50
Meneses Morales, Teodoro, 9, 164, 165, 166, 167, 168, 173, 174, 178, 179
Mexican miracle, 116–119, 122, 125
Mexico, 3, 5, 6, 8, 24, 149, 150, 151, 152, 153, 154, 155, 156, 157, 158, 159, 160, 161, 182, 185, 186, 199, 231, 239, 243, 246, 275, 279, 281, 289, 292, 294, 295, 301
1968 Olympics, 105, 109
and journalism, 120, 124
cosmopolitan culture, 124
Indigenous legacy, 109
Mexican Revolution, 12, 24, 105, 151, 153, 277, 278, 285
midcentury governance, 116
revolutionary nationalism, 117, 119
Tlatelolco Massacre, 3, 4, 7, 19, 100, 109–112, 158
World War II, 122
writers' conferences, 21
Mexico City, 5, 6, 105, 106, 107, 112, 113, 123, 295
and modernism, 117, 119
and Salvador Novo, 126
in film, 116
Mistral, Gabriela, 2, 7, 9, 10, 198, 199, 200, 201, 202, 203, 204, 206, 207, 208, 209, 298, 301
Locas mujeres, 9, 198, 202, 209

Monsiváis, Carlos, 121, 127, 162
Moura, Mariluce, 5, 50
marginalization, 93
Revolta das vísceras, 84, 88–93
Mundo Nuevo, 18, 21, 22

Négritude, 2
neocolonialism, 21
Neruda, Pablo, 1, 3, 6, 8, 10, 23, 69, 100, 112, 292, 294, 295, 298, 301
"Alturas de Macchu Picchu", 104, 108
and Macchu Picchu, 99
and the Boom, 28
anti-fascism, 68
Canto general, 100, 103
Odas elementales, 8
New Latin American Cinema, 8, 10
Nietzsche, Friedrich
and National Socialism, 34
Nixon, Rob
slow violence, 101, 111
Novo, Salvador, 6, 126, 127
"Nueva grandeza mexicana", 6, 126

Ocampo, Silvina, 7, 230, 242
Ocampo, Victoria, 2
Onetti, Juan Carlos, 23
and the Boom, 25, 26, 28, 66
Ortiz, Fernando, 9, 159, 183, 211, 212, 213, 214, 215, 216, 219, 221, 222, 223, 250

Pacheco, José Emilio, 6, 28, 107, 109–112
"Las voces de Tlatelolco", 109, 113
and Poniatowska, 108
and state violence, 100
and the Conquest, 100
and Tlatelolco Massacre, 100, 105
Paris, 3, 19, 186, 189, 232, 239, 246, 247, 248, 256, 258, 273, 293, 295, 306, 310, 314, 320
and Alejo Carpentier, 68
Surrealism, 68
Parra, Nicanor, 10, 297, 298, 299, 301, 304
and the Boom, 28
antipoesía, 28, 298, 301
Paz, Octavio, 1, 4, 5, 6, 10, 23, 100, 112, 239, 240, 295, 296, 297, 299, 300, 301, 304
and Mesoamerican ruins, 102–107
and Tenochtitlán, 99
critique of, 105
Piedra de sol, 100, 295, 297
Pérez, Armando Cristóbal, 6, 7, 137, 165
Cuban revolutionary crime fiction, 132
La ronda de los rubíes, 132, 137–139
Peri Rossi, Cristina, 67

326 Index

Peru, 2, 7, 9, 19, 164, 165, 167, 168, 169, 174, 182, 183, 185, 186, 190, 242, 243, 294, 295, 316
journal *Amaru*, 25
Piglia, Ricardo, 43
Pizarnik, Alejandra, 10, 233, 238, 239, 240, 241, 242, 296
polyphony, 9, 126
Poniatowska, Elena, 4, 29, 67, 127, 152, 153, 154, 158, 161
  La noche de Tlatelolco, 4, 29, 108, 158
Prague Spring, 19
Puig, Manuel, 66

Quechua language, 9, 164, 165, 166, 167, 169, 170, 171, 172, 173, 174, 175, 176, 177, 178, 179, 182, 186, 191, 192, 193

radio dramas, 46, 47, 61
Rama, Ángel, 26, 65, 118, 183, 193, 196, 197, 213, 225
  and the Boom, 26
  narrative transculturation, 65
Ramos, Graciliano, 47, 49, 60
  Memórias do Cárcere, 49
Reyes, Alfonso, 120, 123, 126
Roa Bastos, Augusto, 1, 182
Rodríguez Monegal, Emir, 18, 74
Rojas, Gonzalo, 21
Rulfo, Juan, 1, 11, 12, 23, 25, 160, 213, 278
  and the Boom, 25, 28
  El llano en llamas, 12, 278
  Pedro Páramo, 65

Sábato, Ernesto
  and the Boom, 26, 66
Salgado, Plínio, 47, 48, 49, 57
  and fascism, 48
  Integralismo, 47
  O Estrangeiro, 47
  São Paulo Art Week, 47
Sarmiento, Domingo Faustino, 20
Sartre, 17
Sartre, Jean-Paul, 20, 59
Seix Barral, 26
Sirkis, Alfredo, 84
  Os carbonários
    memórias da guerrilha perdida, 83
Somers, Armonía
  La mujer desnuda, 28
Sorensen, Diana, 77, 106
Spain, 3, 11, 52, 156, 184, 195, 247, 248, 258, 260, 285, 295, 302
  and the Boom, 66
  Chilean exiles, 77
  Civil War, 68

fascism, 71
  Spanish Civil War, 3, 5, 11, 69, 103, 156, 157, 294
Spengler, Oswald
  and National Socialism, 34
Spota, Luis, 124, 125, 126
Surrealism, 1, 7, 10, 11, 188, 190, 229, 230, 231, 232, 233, 234, 235, 236, 238, 239, 241, 242, 243, 251, 295, 297, 298
  Georges Ribemont-Dessaignes, 69
  surrealist, 236, 237, 238, 239, 240, 242, 243, 246, 294, 295, 296, 298
  "Un cadavre", 68

Taibo II, Paco Ignacio, 6, 139–143
  and crime fiction, 132
  Días de combate, 132
  Mexican *neopolicial*, 132
Tario, Francisco, 125, 126
Tenochtitlán, 6, 110, 112
testimonio
  and the 1960s, 29
Traba, Marta, 67

United States, 3, 4, 5, 7, 8, 159, 195, 199, 218, 283
  and Guatemala, 73
  and Mexico, 117
  and military dictatorships, 76
  CIA, 22, 138
  Cold War, 21
  cultural involvement in Latin America, 23
  mass media, 124
  The Times Literary Supplement, 23
  United Fruit Company, 73
  United States and Cuba, 17
Uruguay, 236, 237
  military dictatorship, 30
  Nueva canción, 301
  Surrealism, 231
  women, 11
Usigli, Rodolfo, 120, 121, 122

Valdéz, Luis, 7
  "El teatro campesino", 7
Vallejo, César, 2, 3, 10, 242, 292, 294, 295
  and the Boom, 28
Vanguard, 1, 10, 12, 20, 26
Vargas Llosa, Mario, 1, 19, 232
  and Cuban Revolution, 66
  and the Boom, 26, 27, 65
  and US interventionism, 73
  La ciudad y los perros, 27
  literature and politics, 24
  on Miguel Ángel Asturias, 74
  the total novel, 27

Index

327

Vicens, Josefina, 127
Villaurrutia, Xavier, 121, 294

Walsh, Rodolfo
  Operación Masacre, 29
Warsaw Pact, 19

World War II, 1, 4, 11, 202, 229, 234, 256
  and Borges, 32
  and Mexico, 122
  Brazil, 46, 53, 60
  Paris, 32
Wright Mills, C., 17

Printed in the United States
by Baker & Taylor Publisher Services